# Terrorism and Insurgency in Asia

The rise of Islamic State since 2014 has led to the re-emergence of terrorism as a serious security threat in Asia. Coupled with the ongoing terrorism and insurgency challenges from both radical religious extremists and also ethnonationalist insurgencies, it is clear that some parts of Asia remain mired in armed rebellion despite decades of nation-building. While the situation in Afghanistan and Pakistan has obviously deteriorated, there is also a growing terrorist challenge, on top of armed insurgencies, in other parts of Asia. A common theme in armed rebellions in the region has been the lack of legitimacy of the state and the presence of fundamental causes stemming from political, economic or social grievances. Addressing rebellion in the region thus requires a comprehensive approach involving transnational co-operation, addressing fundamental grievances, and also the use of more innovative approaches, such as religious rehabilitation and reconciliation programs.

**Benjamin Schreer** is Professor and Head of the Department of Security Studies and Criminology, Macquarie University, Sydney, Australia. Previous positions include senior analyst for defence strategy at the Australian Strategic Policy Institute (ASPI); senior lecturer at the Strategic and Defence Studies Centre (SDSC) at the Australian National University; and senior analyst at the German Institute for International and Security Studies (Stiftung Wissenschaft und Politik, SWP). He has published widely on international security and defence affairs, including East Asian strategic trends.

**Andrew T. H. Tan** is Associate Professor at the Department of Security Studies and Criminology, Macquarie University, Sydney, Australia. He was previously Associate Professor at the University of New South Wales and has also taught at Kings College London, UK. Andrew T. H. Tan has published 18 sole-authored, edited and co-edited books, and over 60 refereed journal and chapter articles. Some of his latest books include: *US–China Relations* (Cheltenham, UK and Northampton, MA: Edward Elgar Publishing, 2016), *Security and Conflict in East Asia* (London: Routledge, 2015), and *The Arms Race in Asia: Trends, Causes and Implications* (London: Routledge, 2014).

# Europa Regional Perspectives

Providing in-depth analysis with a global reach, this series from Europa examines a wide range of contemporary political, economic, developmental and social issues in regional perspective. Intended to complement the Europa Regional Surveys of the World series, Europa Regional Perspectives will be a valuable resource for academics, students, researchers, policymakers, business people and anyone with an interest in current world affairs with an emphasis on regional issues.

While the Europa World Year Book and its associated Regional Surveys inform on and analyse contemporary economic, political and social developments, the Editors considered the need for more in-depth volumes written and/or edited by specialists in their field, in order to delve into particular regional situations. Volumes in the series are not constrained by any particular template, but may explore recent political, economic, international relations, social, defence, or other issues in order to increase knowledge. Regions are thus not specifically defined, and volumes may focus on small or large group of countries, regions or blocs.

**Euro-Caribbean Societies in the 21st Century**
Offshore Europe on the Move
*Sébastien Chauvin, Peter Clegg and Bruno Cousin*

**Parliamentary Institutions in Regional and International Governance**
Functions and Powers
*Andrea Cofelice*

**Youth at the Margins**
Perspectives on Arab Mediterranean Youth
*Elena Sánchez-Montijano and José Sánchez García*

**Terrorism and Insurgency in Asia**
A contemporary examination of terrorist and separatist movements
*Edited by Benjamin Schreer and Andrew T. H. Tan*

For more information about this series, please visit: www.routledge.com/Europa-Regional-Perspectives/book-series/ERP

# Terrorism and Insurgency in Asia

A contemporary examination of terrorist and separatist movements

**Edited by
Benjamin Schreer and Andrew T. H. Tan**

LONDON AND NEW YORK

First published 2019
by Routledge
2 Park Square, Milton Park, Abingdon, Oxon OX14 4RN

and by Routledge
52 Vanderbilt Avenue, New York, NY 10017

*Routledge is an imprint of the Taylor & Francis Group, an informa business*

© 2019 Benjamin Schreer and Andrew T. H. Tan

The right of Benjamin Schreer and Andrew T. H. Tan to be identified as the authors of the editorial material, and of the authors for their individual chapters, has been asserted in accordance with sections 77 and 78 of the Copyright, Designs and Patents Act 1988.

All rights reserved. No part of this book may be reprinted or reproduced or utilised in any form or by any electronic, mechanical, or other means, now known or hereafter invented, including photocopying and recording, or in any information storage or retrieval system, without permission in writing from the publishers.

Trademark notice: Product or corporate names may be trademarks or registered trademarks, and are used only for identification and explanation without intent to infringe.

Europa Commissioning Editor: Cathy Hartley

Editorial Assistants: Eleanor Catchpole Simmons, Lucy Pritchard

*British Library Cataloguing in Publication Data*
A catalogue record for this book is available from the British Library

*Library of Congress Cataloging-in-Publication Data*
A catalog record has been requested for this book

ISBN: 978-1-85743-918-2 (hbk)
ISBN: 978-0-429-03103-8 (ebk)

Typeset in Times New Roman
by Taylor & Francis Books

# Contents

*List of figures* vii
*Acknowledgements* viii
*The editors and contributors* x

**PART 1**

    1

1 Introduction 3
ANDREW T. H. TAN AND BENJAMIN SCHREER

2 The causes of armed rebellion in Asia 14
ADAM LOCKYER

**PART 2**

    29

3 Social media and terrorism in the Asia Pacific 31
JULIAN DROOGAN AND LISE WALDEK

4 The long war: Afghanistan 45
LISE WALDEK

5 Strategy on autopilot: *Resolute support* and the continuing failure of Western strategy in Afghanistan 58
BENJAMIN SCHREER AND THOMAS WALDMAN

6 Pakistan's terrorist challenge 72
JULIAN DROOGAN

7 The internationalisation of the Central Asian terrorist threat 86
NODIRBEK SOLIEV

8 India's Maoist insurgencies 102
  DALBIR AHLAWAT AND SONIKA AHLAWAT

**PART 3**
  117

9 China's Uyghur problem: Terrorist acts and
  government responses 119
  CHIEN-PENG CHUNG

10 Anti-state armed groups in Myanmar: Origins, evolution
   and implications 133
   ARDETH MAUNG THAWNGHMUNG AND MIKE FURNARI

11 The chronic threat of insurgent groups in the Philippines 147
   RENATO CRUZ DE CASTRO

12 Thailand's restive south: Identity and neo-colonial resistance 161
   ZACHARY ABUZA

13 Terrorism in Indonesia, Malaysia and Singapore: Challenge
   and response 177
   ANDREW T. H. TAN

**PART 4**
  191

14 Terrorist rehabilitation and community engagement in
   Southeast Asia 193
   ROHAN GUNARATNA

15 Deradicalization of terrorist detainees and inmates: A soft
   approach to counter terrorism 214
   MALKANTHI HETTIARACHCHI

16 Counter-terrorism and counter-insurgency in Asia 231
   ANDREW T. H. TAN

*Index* 246

# Figures

| | | |
|---|---|---|
| 12.1 | IEDs and UXO (unexploded ordnance) January 2009 to December 2017 | 165 |
| 12.2 | Cumulative casualties, January 2009 to December 2017 | 166 |
| 12.3 | Total casualties by type, January 2009 to March 2018 | 166 |
| 12.4 | Thai military expenditure, 2004–2018, in Thai Baht (billions) | 170 |
| 12.5 | What a few coups can do for you: Royal Thai Armed Forces budget 2004–2018 in Baht billions | 171 |
| 15.1 | 6+1 Model | 220 |

# Acknowledgements

The contributors to this volume are an international team of recognized experts drawn from Macquarie University, Australia, as well as from around the world: a truly international, collaborative effort. The editors would like to thank them for their invaluable contribution to this work.

The editors would also like to thank the referees who assessed the proposal for this volume, as well as the referee who read and commented on the final manuscript, resulting in an improved final product.

The editors are grateful to the *Journal of Policing, Intelligence and Counter Terrorism* (*JPICT*, a Routledge journal), particularly its editor, Dr Julian Droogan, for the financial assistance which made possible the joint workshop between the Department of Security Studies and Criminology, Macquarie University, and the International Centre for Political Violence and Terrorism Research (ICPVTR), Rajaratnam School of International Studies, Nanyang Technological University. At this joint workshop in Singapore in January 2018, which was generously hosted by the Director of the ICPVTR, Professor Rohan Gunaratna, some of the draft chapters in this volume were presented.

Some of the papers have also, with the permission of Routledge, been published in a special edition of the *JPICT* (Volume 13, Number 2) in July 2018. Acknowledgement is therefore made of the following chapters which appeared in a longer form and with different titles in the *JPICT* special edition: Adam Lockyer, 'Civil War and Insurgency in Asia'; Andrew T. H. Tan, 'Evaluating Counter-Terrorism Strategies in Asia'; Julian Droogan, Lise Waldek and Ryan Blackhall, 'Innovation and Terror: An Analysis of the Use of Social Media by Terror-Related Groups in the Asia Pacific'; Chien-peng Chung, 'China's Uyghur Problem After the 2009 Urumqi Riot: Repression, Recompense, Readiness, Resistance'; Julian Droogan, 'The Perennial Problem of Terrorism and Political Violence in Pakistan'; Lise Waldek, 'Endemic Violence in Afghanistan: A Socio-Cultural Perspective'; Dalbir Ahlawat, 'Maoist Insurgency in India: Grievances, Security Threats and Counter-Strategies'; Malkanthi Hettiarachchi, 'Rehabilitation to Deradicalise Detainees and Inmates: A Counter-Terrorism Strategy'.

Last but not least, the editors are enormously grateful to the team at Routledge responsible for the production of this volume, particularly Cathy

Hartley for her support and encouragement, without which this important and timely work would not have been possible.

Benjamin Schreer and Andrew T. H. Tan
Department of Security Studies and Criminology
Macquarie University

# The Editors and Contributors

**Benjamin Schreer** is Professor and Head of the Department of Security Studies and Criminology, Macquarie University, Sydney, Australia. Previous positions include senior analyst for defence strategy at the Australian Strategic Policy Institute (ASPI); senior lecturer at the Strategic and Defence Studies Centre (SDSC) at the Australian National University; and senior analyst at the German Institute for International and Security Studies (Stiftung Wissenschaft und Politik, SWP). He has published widely on international security and defence affairs, including East Asian strategic trends.

**Andrew T. H. Tan** is Associate Professor at the Department of Security Studies and Criminology, Macquarie University, Sydney, Australia. He was previously Associate Professor at the University of New South Wales and has also taught at Kings College London, UK. Andrew T. H. Tan has published 18 sole-authored, edited and co-edited books, and over 60 refereed journal and chapter articles. Some of his latest books include: *US–China Relations* (Cheltenham, UK and Northampton, MA: Edward Elgar Publishing, 2016), *Security and Conflict in East Asia* (London: Routledge, 2015), *The Arms Race in Asia: Trends, Causes and Implications* (London: Routledge, 2014), *East and South-East Asia: International Relations and Security Perspectives* (London: Routledge, 2013), *Security Strategies in the Asia-Pacific* (London: Palgrave Macmillan, 2011) and *US Strategy Against Global Terrorism: How it Evolved, Why it Failed and Where it is Headed* (London: Palgrave Macmillan, 2009).

**Zachary Abuza** is a professor at the National War College where he specializes in Southeast Asian security and politics. He is the author of five books, including *Forging Peace in Southeast Asia: Insurgencies, Peace Processes, and Reconciliation* (Rowman Littlefield, 2016).

**Dalbir Ahlawat** (Ph.D.) is Senior Lecturer in the Department of Security Studies and Criminology, Macquarie University, Australia. He has over 15 years of experience in working with government agencies, academic institutions and conducting research both in Australia and overseas. He has published four books: *Australia–India Relations: Evolving Polycentric*

*World Order; Indo-Pacific: Emerging Powers, Evolving Regions and Challenges to Global Governance; State and Society in Latin America: Challenges of Globalization; Evolution and Role of the Communist Party in Cuba.* In addition, he has published 26 research papers in journals and edited books. His research interests include security and strategic affairs in the Indo-Pacific region with specific focus on India.

**Sonika Ahlawat** is a Doctoral scholar in the University School of Law and Legal Studies at Guru Gobind Singh Indraprastha University, New Delhi, India. Her field of study is to assess and analyse the legal challenges of inclusivity in India. With the economic liberalization in India, several legal challenges came to the forefront, including unequal economic development and the marginalization of rural strata of the society. This challenges the constitutional provisions such as the right to equality and fraternity. Sonia has presented papers at national and international conferences, and also works as a volunteer to advise people who migrate to urban areas, specifically women, about their rights.

**Chien-peng (C.P.) Chung** is a Professor in the Department of Political Science, Lingnan University, Hong Kong. His research interests include the politics and history of China, Chinese and Asian foreign and security relations, political change in Asia, and ethnic nationalism. Dr. Chung has written three books, *Contentious Integration: Post-Cold War Japan–China Relations in the Asia-Pacific*, published by Ashgate; *Domestic Politics, International Bargaining, and Territorial Disputes of China*; and *China's Multilateral Cooperation in Asia and the Pacific: Institutionalizing Beijing's 'Good Neighbour Policy'*, the last two published by Routledge. He has contributed chapters to edited books, and published articles in journals such as *Pacific Review, Asian Survey, Korean Journal of Defense Analysis, Problems of Post-Communism, China Report, China Quarterly, Pacific Affairs, Asian Affairs: An American Review, Issues & Studies, American Asian Review, Harvard International Review,* and *Foreign Affairs*. Dr. Chung received his doctorate and master's in political science at the University of Southern California.

**Renato Cruz De Castro** is a full professor in the International Studies Department, De La Salle University, Manila, and holds the Charles Lui Chi Keung Professorial Chair in China Studies. He was the National Institute of Defense Studies (NIDS) Visiting Fellow for 2018. In 2017, he was based in the Japan Institute for International Affairs (JIIA) as a research fellow. He was the US–ASEAN Fulbright Initiative Researcher from the Philippines and was based in the East-West Center in Washington from September to December 2016. He earned his Ph.D. from the Government and International Studies Department of the University of South Carolina as a Fulbright Scholar in 2001. A consultant in the National Security Council of the Philippines during the Aquino Administration,

Professor De Castro's research interests include Philippine–US security relations, Philippine defence and foreign policies, US defence and foreign policies in East Asia, and the international politics of East Asia. He has written over 90 scholarly articles on international relations and international security.

**Julian Droogan** is Senior Lecturer at the Department of Security Studies and Criminology, Macquarie University, where he is the editor of the *Journal of Policing, Intelligence and Counter Terrorism* (Routledge) and director of internationalization and outreach. Julian's academic background encompasses the anthropology and history of religions, violent extremism and countering violent extremism, and issues in contemporary terrorism studies. His research interests include countering violent extremism, religious radicalization, extremist narratives, and the history of terrorism and political violence in the Asia-Pacific. Julian currently leads a number of funded research projects including an ongoing partnership with the New South Wales (NSW) government looking at ways to install and evaluate counter terrorism and social resilience projects in NSW communities, and an Australian Research Council Discovery grant project examining the relationship between online extremist materials and real-world violent extremist action.

**Mike Furnari** is a graduate student at the Department of Peace and Conflict Studies at the University of Massachusetts Lowell. His research interests include conflict in Southeast Asia as well as the effects of the media on conflict. He will begin attending Hiroshima University in Japan in the Fall of 2018 to pursue a Ph.D.

**Rohan Gunaratna** is Professor of Security Studies and Head of the International Centre for Political Violence and Terrorism Research at the S. Rajaratnam School of International Studies, Nanyang Technological University, Singapore. He received his Masters from the University of Notre Dame, USA where he was Hesburgh Scholar and his doctorate from the University of St Andrews, UK where he was British Chevening Scholar. Gunaratna authored 16 books including *Inside al Qaeda: Global Network of Terror* (University of Columbia Press) and edits the Insurgency and Terrorism Series of the Imperial College Press, London.

**Malkanthi Hettiarachchi** is a Chartered Clinical Psychologist, and a counter terrorism researcher and instructor. She completed her Ph.D. in Policing Intelligence and Counter Terrorism at Macquarie University, Sydney, Australia, and has worked in Forensic (UK) and Terrorist Rehabilitation/Detention centers (Sri Lanka). Mal has conducted interviews and assessments with inmates in detention facilities in the Philippines, Indonesia, Maldives, Sri Lanka, Libya, and South America. She provides training and supervision for military, police, prison and rehabilitation staff on rehabilitation program design, prison management, deradicalization and psychosocial skills, as well as conducts psychometric testing, profiling and deradicalization with detainees/inmates. She has presented on terrorist rehabilitation at conferences and workshops in Spain, Italy, Malta, The Hague, Tajikistan, Montenegro, Tunisia, Algeria, Oman, Abu Dhabi, Kenya, Pakistan, Sri Lanka, Cambodia, Singapore, Thailand, Malaysia, Indonesia, the Philippines and Hawaii. Mal has published in the field of rehabilitation and reintegration; radicalization, deradicalization and re-radicalization; and on terrorist mindsets.

**Adam Lockyer** is a Senior Lecturer in Security Studies at Macquarie University. He held the 2015 Fulbright Scholarship in US–Australian Alliance Studies at Georgetown University. Before joining the Department of Security Studies and Criminology, Dr. Lockyer was a Research Fellow in Defence Studies at the University of New South Wales. He has also held positions at the United States Studies Centre at the University of Sydney, at the Center for Strategic and International Studies, in Washington, DC, and was the Lowy Institute's 2008 Thawley Scholarship in International Security winner.

**Nodirbek Soliev** is a Senior Analyst at the International Centre for Political Violence and Terrorism Research (ICPVTR), RSIS, Nanyang Technological University (NTU), Singapore. Nodirbek has authored 'The Endgame in Afghanistan Will Impact Central Asia' in Rohan Gunaratna and Douglas Woodall (eds.), *Afghanistan after the Western Drawdown* (Rowman and Littlefield Publishers, 2015), chapters on terrorism and extremism in Kazakhstan, Kyrgyzstan, Tajikistan, Turkmenistan, and Uzbekistan in Rohan Gunaratna and Stefanie Kam (eds.), *Handbook of Terrorism in the Asia-Pacific* (Imperial College Press, 2016), and 'Rehabilitation of Terrorists and Extremists: An Overview of Uzbekistan's Experience' in Rohan Gunaratna and Sabariah Hussin (eds.), *International Case Studies of Terrorist Rehabilitation* (Routledge, 2018).

**Ardeth Maung Thawnghmung** is Professor and Chair of Political Science at the University of Massachusetts Lowell. Before joining UMass Lowell, Ardeth taught at the University of Wisconsin, and University of Victoria, British Columbia, and was a visiting fellow at the Australian National University. Professor Thawnghmung's teaching interests are comparative politics, comparative political economy, transitional economies, peasant studies, political of collective identity, Southeast Asian politics, international relations, and politics of developing countries. Her research interests include Political Economy in Burma, Southeast Asia, Transitional Economies, Rural Development, Peasant Studies, and Ethnic Politics, and democratization.

**Lise Waldek** is a Lecturer in the Department of Security Studies and Criminology, Macquarie University, Sydney. She currently leads two funded research projects; an ARC Discovery grant examining youth engagement with online violent extremist content and a three-year evaluation of a state based CVE funded project focused on the Australian far-right. Lise has worked with a diverse range of government, private sector and academic institutions on security issues and the provision of socio-cultural analysis. Her work in the British Government included a number of Afghan focused projects. She is a member of the Executive Committee for the AVERT (Addressing Violent Extremism and Radicalisation to Terrorism) Research Network, Alfred Deakin Institute for Citizenship and Globalisation.

**Thomas Waldman** is a Lecturer in Security Studies at Macquarie University, Sydney. He has experience working in and on Afghanistan, having conducted research there in 2007, 2010, 2012, and 2014. His work currently focuses on American military strategy and contemporary warfare. He is author of two books: *Understanding Influence: The Use of Statebuilding Research in British Policy* (with Sultan Barakat and Andrea Varisco, Ashgate, 2014) and *War, Clausewitz and the Trinity* (Ashgate, 2013).

# Part 1

# 1 Introduction

*Andrew T. H. Tan and Benjamin Schreer[1]*

**Terrorism challenges and the rise of Islamic State**

In 2014, the surprising success and rise of Islamic State (IS) in Syria and Iraq attracted worldwide attention. It also galvanised radical Islamist elements throughout the world, attracting thousands of volunteer *mujahideen* fighters from an estimated 81 countries, including Europe, North America, Africa, Asia and the Middle East, to fight in the Levant, where IS initially succeeded in establishing a caliphate (Tarabay 2014). Even more seriously, the instability in the Levant spilled over to other parts of the world, as demonstrated by a string of IS-inspired terrorist attacks in Europe and Asia.

From around 2015, a string of spectacular IS-inspired terrorist attacks took place in Europe. In January 2015, an attack on the satirical weekly *Charlie Hebdo* in Paris, killed 12 people. Paris was again the target of coordinated attacks in November 2015, during which 130 people lost their lives. In March 2016, bombings in Brussels claimed the lives of 32 people. In July 2016, a truck drove into crowds celebrating Bastille Day in France, killing 86. In December, a similar truck attack at a Christmas market in Berlin killed 12 people. Another truck attack, this time in Stockholm, in April 2017, killed four people. In May, a major terrorist attack during a music concert in Manchester left 22 people dead. In August, a vehicle attack on pedestrians in Barcelona killed 14 people (Foster 2017).

In South and Southeast Asia, IS also galvanised militants to join the fight in the Middle East. In South Asia, the threat was particularly serious, with senior figures of banned extremist groups in Pakistan such as the Tehrik-e-Taliban (TTP) and the Lashkar-e-Jhangvi pledging allegiance to IS (Jamal 2016; Rana 2015). The Soufan Group also estimated that by January 2016 over 650 Pakistanis had joined IS in the Middle East (Barrett 2017: 13). Furthermore, IS activities added to the growing instability in Pakistan, a nuclear-armed state with serious political, economic and social problems. This was demonstrated by a series of major terrorist attacks within Pakistan, such as the deadly attack on an army school in Peshawar in 2014 that killed 154, including 135 school children (Jamal 2016). Indeed, with an estimated 80,000 casualties in terrorism-related violence between 2005 and 2013, Pakistan has been described as the "Ground Zero" in global terrorism (Gunaratna and Iqbal 2011).

IS has also operated in neighbouring India, though its impact has been more limited compared to Pakistan. By March 2017, around 75 fighters from India had joined IS in the Middle East (Barrett 2017: 12). More seriously, IS emerged in Afghanistan by around mid-2014, where it now has an estimated 3,000 fighters, adding to the growing insurgent threat (VOA News 2017). In early 2016, some Taliban commanders formally pledged allegiance to IS which announced its "Khorasan" theatre in Afghanistan (Comerford 2017).[2] After the formal end of the NATO-led International Security Assistance Force (ISAF) at the end of 2014 and the transition to the Resolute Support Mission (RSM) to train and assist Afghan security forces, the Taliban re-emerged and made significant gains against the central government. The Afghan National Army (ANA) proved largely ineffectual, requiring a continuation of the foreign military presence in the country. In view of the deteriorating security situation, the United States sent an additional 3,000 troops to the country in September 2017 to shore up the beleaguered Afghan government (BBC 2017). In June 2018, the RSM totalled about 16,000 troops (NATO 2018).

The situation in Southeast Asia has also remained challenging. While sustained counter-terrorism efforts by regional states since 9-11 have contained the threat from Al Qaeda, various other extremist groups and networks continue to operate across the region. Moreover, since 2014, the rapid rise in the influence of IS has become a major security challenge for some governments. This included the spread of IS ideology, its success in recruiting local extremists, and the threat posed to local governments. Indeed, IS managed to attract hundreds of volunteers from the region to fight in Syria and Iraq.

In July 2016, IS formed a Malay-speaking brigade in Syria, known as Katibah Nusantara, with around 1,000 fighters from Southeast Asia, predominantly from Indonesia and Malaysia (Sholeh 2016: 101). The Soufan Group estimated that by March 2017, 435 Indonesians had been intercepted in Turkey, the transit point for IS volunteers travelling to Syria. Around 384 Indonesians remained with IS, while 50 fighters had returned to Indonesia. By the end of 2016, an estimated 91 Malaysians had also joined IS in the Middle East (Barrett 2017: 12–13). By February 2017, Malaysian authorities had detained 234 people for being alleged IS sympathisers under preventive detention laws (*Malay Mail* 2017). In the Philippines, an insurgent group that had pledged allegiance to IS shocked the region when it occupied Marawi city in the southern Philippines, in May 2017. The "Marawi siege" lasted five months and drew in US and Australian forces to assist the Philippine army in intense urban combat. Combat operations ceased in October with the defeat of the militants, with over 1,100 people fatalities (ABC News 2017).

## On-going insurgencies in Asia

In addition to the growing threat posed by radical Islamist terrorism, a number of Asian nations also continued to experience armed rebellions by various groups, including ethno-nationalist separatist rebellions. While some of the separatist rebellions have taken on religious overtones, they remain focused on secession from the majority-dominated state, to either form independent states or to integrate with another neighbouring state with which the rebels share a similar ethnic and/or religious identity.

Since the end of World War Two, the process of decolonisation has meant the breakup of Western colonial empires and the emergence of many independent states. These newly formed states, however, often lacked legitimacy due to their artificial construction and the forced incorporation of many minorities who refused to accept the rule of the majority ethnic or religious group. The lack of legitimacy of the state often caused armed rebellions which have contested the authority of central governments. Minority groups have also been engaged in separatist rebellions due to political repression, poverty, socio-economic disparities, a sense of relative deprivation, discrimination and prejudice, as well as corruption and mismanagement by central governments. Underlying many of these rebellions has been a sense of alienation from the state, which has translated into a problem of states' legitimacy. Some states in Asia thus continued to suffer from fragility long after gaining independence from colonial powers and despite decades of efforts at nation-state building (Tan 2007: 14).

Several long-running separatist insurgencies attest to their longevity and persistence. The Moro Muslim separatist rebellion in the southern Philippines began in 1972 and persisted until recently. Although the main rebel movement, the Moro Islamic Liberation Front (MILF), signed a peace agreement with the Philippine government in 2014, violence in the south has continued due to the presence of other militant groups, such as the Abu Sayaff Group and IS. Separately, the Philippines continue to face a Maoist communist insurgency against the central government that is political and ideological in nature. In southern Thailand, the long-running Malay Muslim separatism, which can be traced to the signing of the Anglo-Siamese Treaty in 1909 that led to the former territory of the Pattani sultanate being incorporated into Siam (present-day Thailand), has continued to the present (Pongsudhirak 2007: 267).

In Myanmar, various ethnic minorities have been engaged in secessionist insurgencies against the central government since the country's independence in 1948. In 2017, despite the emergence of a civilian democratically elected government in Myanmar dominated by Nobel Prize-winning laureate Aung San Suu Kyi, tough counter-insurgency operations carried out by the armed forces against the minority Rohingya Muslims in Arakan State have led to hundreds of thousands fleeing across the border to neighbouring Bangladesh, leading to a major humanitarian crisis (Asrar 2017). The on-going Maoist insurgency in eastern India was described in 2006 by then Prime Minister Manmohan Singh, as the "single biggest internal security threat" to India. From a peak in violence in 2010, the number of casualties has declined but the Maoist insurgents remain a force in India due to enduring fundamental grievances over land rights for indigenous Indians (Roy 2017).

In China, Uighur separatists in Xinjiang province have carried out a number of recent attacks against civilians as well as the security forces. In 2014, several deadly attacks took place. In March, a knife-attack at Kunming's train station killed 29 people. In May, an attack on a market in Urumqi led to the deaths of 31 people. In July, a police station and government offices were attacked in Yarkant, leaving 96 dead. In September, a car crashed into tourists at Tiananmen Square in Beijing, killing five people (BBC 2014). China has responded with tough, repressive measures, which are certain to fuel the on-going insurgency (*The Economist* 2018).

Consequently, despite the recent emergence of IS in Asia, the terrorism and insurgency challenges in the region have had a much longer history as well as deeper historical, political, social and economic roots. These challenges are also multi-faceted, as they have involved various disaffected ethnic and religious groups, and have been the product of deep-seated alienation by such groups as a result of the presence of fundamental, long-standing socio-economic and political causes. This means that terrorism and insurgency in Asia have been, and will continue to be major challenges which deserve continued attention as to their causes, implications and counter-strategies.

## Objectives of the volume

Given the persistent threat of terrorism and insurgency in Asia, the objective of this volume is to examine the challenges arising from terrorist and insurgent groups in Asia and evaluate the responses to them. In doing so, the volume aims to make a scholarly and policy relevant contribution to our understanding of this serious security problem, one that could help policy makers and scholars alike to understand the nature of the challenge and how to better counter or manage it. This volume is a collaborative endeavour, given the need for expertise spanning the entire Asian region, a vast and diverse continent.

This volume also fills a gap in our contemporary understanding of the terrorist and insurgent problem in Asia, given the current attention to global terrorism, terrorism in Europe and the continuing war on terror in Iraq and Syria. Some of the best cited works on the problem of terrorism and insurgency in Asia, for instance, *A Handbook of Terrorism and Insurgency in Southeast Asia* (Edward Elgar, 2007), by Andrew Tan, and *Terrorism in Southeast Asia* (NOVA Science, 2008), by Bruce Vaughn and Emma Chanlett-Avery et. al., are now dated as a result of recent developments, such as the rise and the spread of Islamic State's radical extremist ideology, the political developments in Myanmar which may have a major impact on its long-running ethnic separatist insurgencies, and the continuing, and worsening situation in both Afghanistan and Pakistan.

This volume focuses on discrete security complexes where there are cross-border linkages (such as the Malay Archipelago states and the theatre consisting of Afghanistan and Pakistan), and those where their non-radical

Islamist nature provide a contrast (for instance, separatism in Myanmar, India's Maoist insurgencies, the communist Maoist insurgency in the Philippines, and also China's Uighur problem, despite some links with radical Islamism).

This volume is therefore timely and important, and fills a scholarly and policy gap on a long-standing security issue of continuing importance to Asia and the rest of the world.

## Organisation of the volume

This volume is organised into four parts and contains a total of 16 chapters. The first part has two chapters which include this introductory chapter. Chapter 2 by Adam Lockyer, which follows this chapter, is entitled "The causes of armed rebellion in Asia". This chapter provides the conceptual framework for the book, and examines the causes of armed rebellion including terrorism and insurgencies, such as poverty and the linkages between failed states and terrorism. The chapter surveys the literature, sums up key findings that shed light on the fundamental causes of political and religious violence, and assesses how they might throw new light on how terrorism and insurgencies could be countered.

Part 2 of this work examines the key conflict theatres in South and Central Asia, and has six chapters. Chapter 3, by Julian Droogan and Lise Waldek, is entitled "Social media and terrorism in the Asia Pacific". This chapter examines three violent extremist-related groups operating in the Asia Pacific: one "classic" terrorist, namely, Abu Sayyaf in the Philippines; one a dissident political party, namely, Jemaat-e-Islami in Bangladesh; and one a broad ethno-religious separatist movement, namely, the Uyghurs in China. Each case study explores how the proactive adoption of social media affords opportunities and risks on the ability of the group to maximise its reach, impact, and effect.

Chapter 4, by Lise Waldek, is entitled "The long war: Afghanistan" and provides an overview into the current conflict and endemic violence in Afghanistan. It argues that the current strategic approach that focuses almost exclusively on terrorist organisations, such as Al Qaeda and Islamic State, has pushed Afghanistan into the background where it has become a host, a carrier of the parasite for the unfolding violence and conflict. This approach has delivered primarily military focused solutions that deliver temporary fixes that dissipate almost as quickly as they are won. In her chapter, Waldek proposes a framework of analysis grounded in the historical, socio-cultural and geographical complexities of Afghanistan. Waldek identifies five different yet interconnected sources of instability. These are; power dynamics; identity politics; corruption; the fractured nature of the insurgency; and the broader geo-political context. Each section examines how these issues and relationships shape and generate the instability and violence found across Afghanistan. Waldek argues that developing a more nuanced understanding of the instability generates opportunities to identify and create longer-term solutions to a seemingly intractable violence.

Chapter 5, written by Benjamin Schreer and Tom Waldman, is entitled "Strategy on autopilot: Resolute support and the continuing failure of Western strategy in Afghanistan". According to the authors, Afghanistan has become the West's "forgotten war". Years of new strategies and initiatives have failed to generate strategic success. This chapter explores efforts by Western states to address the threat from terrorism and insurgency in Afghanistan since the commencement of NATO's Resolute Support Mission (RSM) in 2015. Despite repeated declarations of progress, Western strategy toward Afghanistan has essentially remained on autopilot. While NATO's efforts have had short-term positive impacts in terms of insurgent attrition, they still do little to address root causes of the conflict and might prove even counterproductive in the long-run by producing harmful effects and perverse incentives for domestic political players to continue the current conflict. The authors argue that the renewed focus on military efforts, without accompanying diplomatic and economic measures, threatens to further undermine progress toward a political settlement and risks to exacerbate cycles of violence and radicalization in the war-torn country.

Chapter 6, by Julian Droogan, is entitled "Pakistan's terrorist challenge". This chapter presents a survey of terrorism trends within Pakistan, particularly Baluchistan, and the neighbouring areas of Afghanistan and Kashmir. The Pakistani state remains highly vulnerable to the corrosive effects of violent extremism not least because of its ability to threaten Pakistan's relations with important partners and investors such as the USA and China. The Pakistani state's relationship with terrorism however, is complicated by three main drivers. First, there is a profound fear of Indian aggression among the military and intelligence communities that has led to the periodic support of violent groups in Kashmir and Afghanistan. Second, there is a growing affinity amongst civilian and military communities with extreme forms of Islam that sometimes support violence. Third, despite the success of some counter-terrorism operations, foreign powers and domestic politicians continue to occasionally support violent extremists in order to meet political objectives.

Chapter 7, by Nordibek Soliev, entitled "The internationalisation of the Central Asian terrorist threat", focuses on the interplay of three major factors which have played a crucial role in the recent evolution of Central Asian terrorism as an international threat. These factors are: the emergence of the Middle East as a new incubator for transnational jihad; increased economic migration and its associated vulnerabilities; and the advancement of digital media technologies and communications as a critical enabler of terrorism.

Finally, Chapter 8, written by Dalbir Ahlawat and Sonika Ahlawat, examines India's Maoist insurgencies. This paper traces the antecedents of the insurgency, the different phases of insurgency and the policy postures adopted by different governments to contain the Maoist insurgency. *Adivasi* insurgency, an offshoot of the colonial period, continued in independent India. Post-independence, government assurances to redress the forest and land rights remained mostly unimplemented. As an alternative, *adivasis* (i.e. the indigenous people of India) joined the Communist Party of India (Marxist Leninist, CPIML). However, after neutralization of the CPIML and failure to regain forest and land rights, *adivasis* joined the Communist Party of India (Maoist). The government, witnessing the expanding threat from the Maoist, adopted a dual strategy. One, it amended the Forest Act to woo the *adivasis*, and two, it placed the Maoists on the terrorist list. However, after not getting the expected results, the current Bharatiya Janata Party (BJP) government adopted an integrated and holistic approach by further amending the Forest Act, offering attractive surrender cum rehabilitation incentives and launching offensives against the Maoist leadership. However, though the insurgence has been contained, operational fault lines still remain.

Part 3 focuses on conflict theatres in East and Southeast Asia and has five chapters. Chapter 9 by Chien-peng Chung, is entitled "China's Uyghur problem: Terrorist acts and government responses". China's largely Turkic Muslim Xinjiang (Uyghur) Autonomous Region has been considered by the national leadership as the country's frontline in the fight against separatist terrorism since the 1990s. To forestall and punish acts of organized and premeditated violence, different administrations in Xinjiang have variably employed a "hard" repressive strategy, a "soft" reward-based strategy, or a "middling" surveillance/monitoring strategy, and sometimes a combination of all three. Chung concludes that many discontented Uyghurs see the government's approaches to dealing with ethnic unrests as means to achieve its integrationist/assimilationist ends, and this perception does not bode well for the state's endeavour to ensure a more peaceful, and stable society in Xinjiang.

This is followed by Chapter 10, which examines Burmese separatism. Written by Ardeth Maung Thawnghmung and Mike Furnari, this chapter offers a brief overview of the origins, evolution, and political implications of Myanmar's 50-year-old armed conflict. While the country's approximately 20 major non-state armed groups vary in size, objectives, and legitimacy, the majority of them represent minority ethnic or language groups which have fought for greater political, economic, and cultural autonomy since the country gained independence from Great Britain in 1948. Although these groups share common grievances generated by decades of excessive centralization and repression by the state and the military, which have been dominated by the country's majority ethnic group known as Bamar or Burman, they have failed to develop a unified front against the state. The authors conclude, pessimistically, that while civilian or semi-civilian governments have been more accommodating to anti-state armed groups than military governments, the authorities' desire to preserve and protect the central government's prerogatives, and the fragmentation of Myanmar's anti-state armed groups, have failed to address the roots of these conflicts, further deepened distrust, and created new grievances and perpetuated the cycle of violence.

Chapter 11, by Renato Cruz de Castro, is entitled "The Chronic Threat of Insurgent Groups in the Philippines". It examines how various insurgent groups in the Philippines have thwarted the Philippine government and the Armed Forces of the Philippines (AFP) from developing a credible territorial defense capability. Former President Benigno Aquino III shifted the AFP's focus from internal to territorial defense during his six-year term. President Rodrigo Duterte has continued his predecessor's modernization program that aimed to enhance the Philippine military's territorial defense and disaster response capabilities. The five-month battle for Marawi City, however, exposed a major structural problem for the AFP—the resilience of internal security threats has not only altered the country's security perceptions, but also imposed greater resource constraints as it seeks to improve its overall capabilities. Currently, there are five major insurgent groups defying the Philippine government—the New People's Army (NPA), the Moro Islamic Liberation Front (MILF), the Abu Sayaff Group (ASG), the Bangsamoro Islamic Freedom Fighters (BIFF), and the Maute Group. Castro argues that the most pressing security challenge the Philippine state faces is to effectively and decisively exercise its monopoly of the use of legitimate violence to overcome the armed challenges posed by several non-state actors in Philippine society.

This is followed by Chapter 12, which is written by Zachary Abuza and entitled "Thailand's Restive South: Identity and Neo-Colonial Resistance". This chapter focuses on the insurgency in southern Thailand, where an ethnic Malay insurgency in the southern three provinces of Thailand that erupted in 2004 has claimed the lives of over 7,000 people and wounded over 11,000. The low-level insurgency grew out of local madrassas, and is committed to winning a homeland for the Malay community, or at the very least greater autonomy. Though there are no ties to transnational actors, the insurgents routinely engage in mass casualty attacks against civilians. Violence has declined in recent years, and targeting has become more selective. Abuza argues that the Thai government's initial mishandling of the insurgency compounded the violence. Though there have been significant improvements in terms of military professionalism, government policy, exacerbated by two coups, has prevented any meaningful attempts to address core grievances. A peace process began in 2013 but to date has born little fruit, with the government unwilling to make any meaningful concessions.

Finally, Chapter 13, written by Andrew Tan, is entitled "Terrorism in Indonesia, Malaysia and Singapore – challenge and response". This chapter examines the threat of terrorism in the core areas of the Malay Archipelago, namely, Malaysia, Indonesia and Singapore. According to Tan, terrorism in the region has not been a new development, as there has been an enduring desire by some for an Islamic state in Indonesia, which in turn explains the persistence of terrorism in the Malay Archipelago. While the Al Qaeda-linked Jemaah Islamiah was progressively decimated by security forces after 9–11, the void it left has been filled by Islamic State. However, the historical persistence of a militant minority suggests an enduring alienation by some to the modern and independent post-colonial secular state. This implies that terrorism in the region will never really be defeated, and the realistic objective will therefore have to be containing it within acceptable boundaries. Tan thus argues that regional counter-terrorism remains a long-term endeavour as well as a work in progress, with continued room and urgency for improvement.

Part 4 of the volume is focused on rehabilitation and counter-terrorism, and has three chapters. Chapter 14, written by Rohan Gunaratna, is entitled "Terrorist rehabilitation and community engagement in Southeast Asia". Terrorist rehabilitation and community engagement are vital tools used in Southeast Asia for decades to manage ideological, ethno-political and politico-religious threats. However, the region faced an unprecedented threat with the rise of al Qaeda-centric and IS-centric threat groups in 2001 and 2014 respectively. The region was well placed to engage structured threat groups such as al Qaeda and their associated groups like Jemmah Islamiyah and Kumpulan Militan Malaysia as they had definitive ideological templates. With the disruption and destruction of structured groups, their followers and individuals with no group affiliation are turning to IS content on the Internet as their principal source of ideology. Rehabilitating IS terrorists and extremists who constitute their own ideology from propaganda on the Internet, however, is complex. Transforming IS followers involves bringing in a range of experts—clerics, teachers, social workers, artists, vocational instructors and others to engage the beneficiary and his or her family. With the expansion of IS into the region and likely future unity moves between IS and al Qaeda, the region's preventing exclusivism and countering extremism strategy should be to broaden existing rehabilitation and community engagement programs. More than ever before, governments will need to work with a range of partners—community organizations, civil society organizations and academia—to fight the current and emerging wave of terrorism, extremism, exclusivism both in the online and offline spaces. Gunaratna argues that although the intelligence driven countering the operational threat should continue, preventing exclusivism and countering extremism in Southeast Asia are the game changers in combating terrorism.

Chapter 15, by Melkanthi Hettiarachchi, is entitled "Deradicalization of terrorist detainees and inmates: A soft approach to counter terrorism". According to her, the "smart approach" to counter terrorism is a blend of both hard and soft approaches. Governments now adopt a whole of nation strategy to counter terrorist recruitment and deradicalise inmates and detainees. Rehabilitation is considered a global imperative, in the battle against terrorism. Rehabilitation programs must be designed to deradicalise inmates and detainees, a process that goes beyond disengagement. Hettiarachchi's analysis of Sri Lanka's rehabilitation program to reverse the process of radicalisation found six components targeted at bringing the beneficiary back to mainstream, plus one community component to ensure that treatment gains are sustained once reintegrated into community. Hettiarachchi also argues that rehabilitation is not a one-off intervention, and deradicalisation is not an all-or-none state. Civilians groomed into terrorism are vulnerable citizens, and upon reintegration, require ongoing engagement. However, the risks posed by weak governments that undermine security can damage the rehabilitation process and heighten the risk of re-radicalisation.

The volume concludes with Chapter 16, entitled "Counter-terrorism and counter-insurgency in Asia" written by Andrew Tan. Counter-terrorism responses in Asia have varied according to the scale of the terrorist/insurgent challenge. The diverse and complex nature of the terrorist challenge in Asia has meant that a variety of responses have been adopted by states in the region, including the criminal justice approach to counter-terrorism, the war model of counter-terrorism, and the waging of counterinsurgency operations. It is clear that the threat is most serious in South Asia, although Southeast Asia has also suffered from terrorism and insurgent threats. The chapter demonstrates that terrorism and insurgency in Asia have been persistent, enduring and in some cases, severe. Sustained counterterrorism and counterinsurgency have generally led to the problem being contained, in some cases, with difficulty. However, its very persistence suggests that political violence in the form of terrorism and insurgencies in Asia is an enduring, long-term challenge.

## Notes

1 The editors are grateful to the contributors for their abstracts, which form the latter part of this chapter.
2 Khorasan is a historical region which includes present-day northern Afghanistan, north-eastern Iran, and parts of Central Asia.

## References

ABC News (2017), "Marawi: Philippines Declares End of Siege as Troops Find 40 Suspected Gunmen Dead", 23 October, available at http://www.abc.net.au/news/2017-10-23/philippines-troops-find-dozens-dead-as-warawi-siege-ends/9077096 accessed 13 July 2018.

Asrar, Shakeeb (2017), "Rohingya Crisis Explained in Maps", *Aljazeera.com*, 28 October, available at http://www.aljazeera.com/indepth/interactive/2017/09/rohingya-crisis-explained-maps-170910140906580.html accessed 13 July 2018.

Barrett, Richard (2017), "Beyond the Caliphate: Foreign Fighters and the Threat of Returnees", The Soufan Center, October, available at http://www.satp.org/satporgtp/countries/India/document/papers/Beyond-the-Caliphate-Foreign-Fighters-and-the-Threat-of-Returnees-TSC-Report-October-2017.pdf accessed 13 December 2018.

BBC (2014), "Why is there Tension Between China and the Uighurs?" 26 September, available at http://www.bbc.com/news/world-asia-china-26414014 accessed 13 July 2018.

BBC (2017), "US Sends 3,000 More Troops to Afghanistan", 18 September, available at http://www.bbc.com/news/world-us-canada-41314428 accessed 13 July 2018.

Comerford, Milo (2017), "Islamic State's Khorasan Province, 2 Years on", *The Diplomat*, 26 January, available at https://thediplomat.com/2017/01/islamic-states-khorasan-province-2-years-on/ accessed 13 July 2018.

Foster, Alice (2017), "Terror Attacks Timeline: From Paris and Brussels Terror to Most Recent Attacks in Europe", *Express*, 18 August, available at https://www.express.co.uk/news/world/693421/Terror-attacks-timeline-France-Brussels-Europe-ISIS-killings-Germany-dates-terrorism accessed 13 July 2018.

Gunaratna, Rohan, and Khuram Iqbal (2011), *Terrorism in Pakistan*, London: Reaktion Books.

Jamal, Umair (2016), "Quetta Police College Attack Highlights Pakistan's Internal Divisions", 31 October, available at http://thediplomat.com/2016/10/quetta-police-college-attack-highlights-pakistans-internal-divisions/ accessed 13 July 2018.

*Malay Mail* (2017), "Home Ministry Says 234 Malaysians Detained on Suspicion of Islamic State Involvement", *Malay Mail*, 21 March, available at http://www.themalaymailonline.com/malaysia/article/home-ministry-says-234-malaysians-detained-on-suspicion-of-islamic-state-in accessed 13 July 2018.

NATO (2018), 'NATO and Afghanistan", 29 June, available at https://www.nato.int/cps/en/natohq/topics_8189.htm accessed 13 July 2018.

Pongsudhirak, Thitinan (2007), 'The Malay-Muslim Insurgency in Southern Thailand", in Andrew T. H. Tan, ed., *Handbook of Terrorism and Insurgency in Southeast Asia*, Cheltenham: Edward Elgar.

Rana, Muhammad Amir (2015), 'The Impact of the Islamic State on Pakistan", Norwegian Peacebuilding Resource Centre, January, available at https://www.files.ethz.ch/isn/186949/049ee274000481e510fd0414ba61d63b.pdf accessed 13 December 2018.

Roy, Siddharthya (2017), "Half a Century of India's Maoist Insurgency", *The Diplomat*, 21 September, available at https://thediplomat.com/2017/09/half-a-century-of-indias-maoist-insurgency/ accessed 13 July 2018.

Sholeh, Badrus (2016), "Daesh in Europe and Southeast Asia: An Indonesian Perspective", in *Countering Daesh Extremism: European and Asian Responses*, Singapore: Konrad-Adenauer-Stiftung.

Tan, Andrew T. H. (2007), "Terrorism and Insurgency in Southeast Asia", in Andrew T. H. Tan, ed., *Handbook of Terrorism and Insurgency in Southeast Asia*, Cheltenham: Edward Elgar.

Tarabay, Jamie (2014), "Why Islamic State Attracts Fighters from All Over the World", *Aljazeera.com*, available at http://america.aljazeera.com/articles/2014/9/10/the-worldwide-appealofjihad.html accessed 13 July 2018.

*The Economist* (2018), "China Has Turned Xinjiang into a Police State Like No Other", 31 May, available at https://www.economist.com/briefing/2018/05/31/china-has-turned-xinjiang-into-a-police-state-like-no-other accessed 17 July 2018.

VOA News (2017), "US Forces Vow to Defeat Islamic State in Afghanistan This Year", 22 March, available at http://www.voanews.com/a/us-forces-vow-defeat-islamic-state-afghanistan-this-year/3777755.html accessed 13 July 2018.

# 2 The causes of armed rebellion in Asia

*Adam Lockyer*

**Introduction**

From 1945 through to the start of the 21st century, Asia was one of the most civil war prone regions in the world.[1] Indeed, the Asian countries that have avoided experiencing, at least one armed rebellion, civil war or insurgency since 1945 are the exception rather than the rule. Over the past two decades, however, there has been a sharp decrease in the number of new armed rebellions beginning in Asia. What accounts for this initial high prevalence, then sharp decrease? This chapter assesses the factors that have contributed to Asia being particularly prone to internal conflict and the corresponding decrease in new civil wars over more recent decades. Although scholars are unlikely to ever be able to accurately "predict" the future onset of armed rebellions, the research on civil wars, rebellion and insurgency has advanced to a point where there is now a general scholarly consensus on the factors that place a country at risk of armed rebellion (Gates 2003; Lacina 2004). This chapter leverages this body of theoretical and empirical research to argue that, between 1945 and 2000, Asia represented a "perfect storm" where many of the contending risk factors for civil war onset were present, including state weakness, poverty, ideology and micro dynamics. This confluence of risks resulted in the region being particularly rebellious. Many of these factors have, however, since decreased in prevalence or severity which, in turn, suggests why new armed rebellions have decreased in frequency in the region.

Armed rebellions, civil wars and collective violence are some of the most researched phenomena in political science (Lockyer 2018b). Political scientists have been attracted to the topic for several reasons. First is the frequency of internal wars. Since 1945, internal wars have largely replaced international wars as the most common form of violent conflict in the world. According to the Correlates of War dataset (vol. 4), there were 187 intra-state wars between 1945 and 2007 compared to only 43 inter-state wars (Sarkees and Wayman 2010). The post-Cold War statistics are even more lopsided with only nine inter-state wars being recorded compared to 78 intra-state wars. Secondly, there are the human and economic impacts of civil wars. Since 1945, over 25 million people have been killed by civil wars with tens of millions more having become homeless or fleeing their countries as refugees (Saideman 2001). Civil wars also cast a long shadow over the nations that suffer through them. States that have experienced a civil war are more likely to endure ongoing poverty (Murdoch and Sandler 2002), poor public health (Ghobarah, Huth and Russett 2003) and child mortality (Black, Morris and Bryce 2003). The final reasons for the phenomena's popularity with scholars are the significant geopolitical and international consequences of civil wars and rebellions. As this chapter will discuss, civil wars tend to cluster, both geographically and temporally. A state that shares a border with a neighbour that is experiencing a civil war is at significantly higher risk of suffering a civil war itself. The civil wars in Vietnam, Laos and Cambodia, for instance, were not independent events. Each civil war affected the course of political and military events in its neighbours.

This chapter examines the risk factors for armed rebellion and discusses them within the contexts of Asian politics, economy and society. Despite every conflict possessing its own unique social and historical backgrounds, the literature on civil war onset suggests that there are certain indicators that make rebellion and political violence more likely. This chapter is divided into three sections. It first discusses state weakness. State weakness has been shown to considerably increase the risk of civil war. State weakness decreases the deterrent effect of government's coercive instruments and opens the political and military space for discontented groups to use violence towards achieving their goals. The second section examines the international dimensions of rebellion, insurgency, terrorism and civil war. It advances several explanations for why Asia was particularly prone to political violence over the second half of the 20th century. It argues that regional dynamics place states at either heightened or decreased risk of civil violence. Finally, the chapter concludes with a discussion of agent motivations. These might include poverty, political grievances and ideology.

## State weakness

The most common structural explanation for rebellions, insurgencies and civil wars is state weakness. State weakness has long been cited as an underlying cause of civil war, rebellion and insurgency. In her highly influential work, Theda Skocpol (1979) argues that social revolutions occur due to old regimes finding themselves in crisis. According to Skocpol, states that experience social revolutions collapse not because of revolutionary action, but because of state weakness. That is, state collapse precedes revolution rather than follows it. Skocpol's argument begins with the potential revolutionary state facing an international crisis – either military or fiscal. An old regime, confronted by a crisis and the need to reform, can make the necessary reforms to avert a crisis under two conditions: (1) the current ruling elite is sufficiently disconnected from politics to act in the national interest (rather than being captured by interest groups or guided by their own self-interest) and (2) the working class is productive enough to uphold the state while the reforms are undertaken. Skocpol maintains that this is how Japan was able to modernise from above in the 1860s while avoiding a social revolution. In contrast, China in the mid-20th century experienced a social revolution because the Chinese political elites were able to play a spoiler role in defence of their own narrow self-interests and the agricultural peasantry was not productive enough to maintain economic and social stability while the state attempted to reform. The result was the Chinese social revolution (Skocpol 1979: 48).

Since Skocpol's seminal work, state weakness has been nestled within a number of important ongoing research agendas on rebellion. Stathis Kalyvas and Laia Balcells (2010: 422) model "civil peace" as being a condition where either the state has "a superior level of state capacity (roughly corresponding to that of advanced industrial societies)" or low rebel capacity. Kalyvas and Balcells argue rebellions are only possible if the state's relative power to potential rebellious groups is sufficiently low enough to allow the rebels the opportunity to employ violent means. They use GDP per capita and total military personnel as a proxy of state strength. Kalyvas and Balcells find, indeed, that rebellion is substantially less likely in states where the government has a preponderance of military power. The conditions for "civil peace" were not present in many Asian states in the early post-colonial period. The retreating tide of European colonisation followed by the Second World War created new states across Asia that possessed relatively weak institutions, underdeveloped economies and military forces that had intentionally been kept undertrained and underequipped by the colonial governments. The internal structural weakness of many post-colonial Asian states significantly increased the likelihood that they would experience an armed rebellion.

A related literature, has examined how relative state power influences the type of violence that emerges within an armed rebellion. The balance of military power between the belligerents has been shown to influence the rebel's choice of strategy. The relative military power between the government and rebel forces has been shown to be the single greatest influence in the rebel forces' decision to either pursue a conventional, guerrilla, militia, or terrorist strategy (Lockyer 2010). Andrew Janos (1963: 645), for instance, maintains that if guerrilla is the strategy of the weak, then terrorism is the strategy of the very weak.[2] In contrast, for a rebel group to adopt a conventional strategy (such as in the American, Russian and Spanish civil wars) it will generally require many of the trappings of a state; including a territory, a significant population from which to recruit, a tax and revenue base, and ready access to heavy weapons either through the international arms market, an indigenous arms industry, or the mutiny of entire government military units. It has been telling that most cases of armed rebellion across Asia in the late 20th century were waged either through guerrilla (e.g. Sri Lanka and Malaya) or terrorist strategies (e.g. Southern Thailand). This suggests that although many Asian states were weak, the insurgent groups were weaker. Consequently, as Asia's economies and militaries grew their relative strength to potential challenges made future rebellions less likely.

Besides the effect of the government's "hard power" on making rebellions less likely, political stability has also been shown to play a role. A prominent research agenda has sought to reveal the relationship between a state's form of government and the likelihood that it would experience a civil war. Although the question is far from being permanently settled, the current evidence suggests that the relationship resembles an inverted fishing hook shape with transitional regimes being the most war prone, followed by autocracies, with consolidated democracies being the least prone to civil wars (transitional regimes > consolidated autocracies > consolidated democracies). Stable autocracies and democracies appear to be less war prone as they permit less opportunity for would-be insurgent groups to launch a rebellion (Hegre et al. 2001). On the other hand, while states are transitioning from one form governance to another, the relative political instability presents potential insurgents with more opportunity to pursue violence in order to achieve their objectives. Groups within society can change the state's monopoly over the legitimate means of coercion. Once again, these risk factors are reflective of many Asian states between 1945 and 2000 with many possessing either a transitional government or autocratic government. Since 2000, however, an increasing number of Asian states can be described as democratic with relatively open elections being held followed by the peaceful change of government.

## The international dimensions of internal conflict

A frequent observation within the scholarship on armed rebellions is that they tend to cluster – both geographically and temporally (Gleditsch 2007; Salehyan and Gleditsch 2006; Sambanis 2001). Like a dynamic heat map of the world, the number of armed rebellions across different regions of the world tends to intensify and expand before cooling and contracting. This observation has led scholars to reconsider internal armed rebellions as more than simply a domestic phenomenon and begin studying their international dimensions. They have collectively advanced several underlying reasons for why internal armed rebellions tend to cluster.

The most commonly cited international explanation for why internal conflicts tend to cluster is the idea of "contagion" (Midlarsky 1978; Most and Starr 1980; Salehyan and Gleditsch 2006; Kathman 2010). Myron Weiner (1996) coined the description of "bad neighbours" and "bad neighbourhoods" to capture the notion of cross border contagion and diffusion of political violence. The mechanisms through which rebellions spread across borders has received substantial attention. This literature can be grouped into four different broad explanations. The first explanation is that ongoing conflicts in neighbouring states produce a reservoir of elements that can create the conditions that make civil war more likely in their neighbours. For example, an armed rebellion in a neighbouring state may increase access to cheap arms, attract mercenaries searching for employers and create rebel sanctuaries inside one's own territory. The second is that conflicts can become transnational through ethnic ties (Forsberg 2008). For instance, the irredentist conflict in the Ogaden region of Ethiopia was directly connected to the rise of militant Somali nationalism across the border in Somalia and Somaliland (Lockyer 2018a). A third possibility is that opposition groups emulate the actions of those in neighbouring countries. Lake and Rothchild (1998) described how opposition groups update their beliefs on the chances of success or failure after observing how things unfold in other countries, particularly those countries that share many characteristics with their own. Insurgents learn from each other, and where rebel groups appear to be making progress, this may spur copycat insurgencies in neighbouring countries. Finally, it has been suggested that refugee flows can be a driver of civil war diffusion. Salehyan and Gleditsch (2006) examined how refugee flows and the emergence of large sprawling refugee camps can exacerbate resource competition and alter the ethnic composition of the receiving country and potentially destabilise the existing political balance. The political instability caused by large refugee flows can be magnified by the fact that some of those fleeing the war would be former soldiers and rebels and possess the knowledge and network on how to launch a fresh insurgency in their receiving country.

A second line of research on civil war clustering has examined the role of foreign intervention. Foreign powers frequently intervene in civil wars to promote their own interests (Lockyer 2011; Lockyer 2017). As states generally have greater interests at stake in the outcome of an armed rebellion in their neighbour's territory and, being close, are in a better position to project military power into the conflict, motive and opportunity combine to make neighbouring states the most likely external actors to intervene in civil wars. However, if a neighbouring state intervenes, then it increases the chances that it itself might be pulled into the conflict. As a consequence, civil wars and insurgencies can assume a multi-dimensional character where neighbours are simultaneously fighting against internal insurgents and cross border intrusions by agents of a foreign government. In these cases, the clear division between civil wars and international wars quickly begins to break down. Indeed, supporting insurgents in neighbouring states has become a more popular means of waging war against a neighbour than pursuing a conventional international war. In turn, this has had major consequences for the strength of the state in many parts of the world.

In a seminal work, Charles Tilly (1985) outlined the relationship between war, extraction, protection and state making. Tilly showed that the historical development of European states was tied to fighting external wars. The demands of external war and strategic rivalry with other emerging European states meant they needed to develop more efficient and effective ways to monitor their citizens and extract taxation and conscripts, which meant larger and more professional state bureaucracies and internal state policing and intelligence agencies. External war created a cycle of state making, where "war made the state, and the state made war" (Tilly 1975: 42). Anthony Giddens (1985: 112) concurred that, for early European states, "it was war and preparation for war, that provided the most potent energizing stimulus for the concentration of administrative resources and fiscal reorganization". Within the fierce competitive and violent strategic rivalry of European history, weaker states were consumed by more efficient war fighting states. The result of early modern European wars was that the state either prevailed and was more powerful as a result, or it perished and was consumed by its more proficient neighbour. Insurgencies, in contrast, weaken the state while not necessarily making it stronger. Weak governments can resist insurgencies for extended periods, while continuing to become weaker. Tilly's belief that "war made the state, and the state made war" does not necessarily hold for armed rebellions.

Post-colonial states have followed a very different development trajectory. In post-colonial states, particularly in Africa and Asia, it has been a more popular strategy of assisting insurgent groups in their rivals' territory than engaging in international war. Ann Hironaka (2005: 7) persuasively argues that:

> the population of states before 1945 was composed mostly of strong, battle-scarred states that had proven their capability to withstand both interstate and civil war. Since 1945, most colonies have achieved independence and sovereign statehood not through victory in war, but through the encouragement and support of the international system. Furthermore, international norms and laws increasingly discourage territorial reshuffling through wars of annexation or secession.

This post-1945 international system's norms and expectations have essentially locked the territorial boundaries of the sovereign member states. One of the most striking aspects of the international system over the past 80 years is how infrequently international borders have been redrawn. In the rare cases it has happened it has usually been the result of civil wars (e.g. the former-Yugoslavia, South Sudan) not international wars. The result of these norms has been twofold. First, it has meant that weak, or even failed states, have been able to survive in the post-1945 world, when a comparable state in earlier times would have been quickly annexed by a more efficient neighbour. These weak states are less capable of using conventional military power as "politics by other means". Instead, as Zeev Maoz and Belgin San-Akca (2012: 720) point out: "states that are dissatisfied with the status quo, but lack the capability required for a direct confrontation with their rivals, are likely to offer support to [non-state armed group] targeting their rivals. This strategy is used to substitute for direct confrontation with the rival." Second, even those states that do possess the military power to mount conventional operations are largely blocked from doing so by the post-1945 norm against international wars of annexation. Consequently, providing arms, training, finance, and even direct military assistance, to one side in a civil war has largely become the preferred means through which to apply force against a rival state. Indeed, as Hironaka (2005) points out, Patrick Regan's (2000) assumption that foreign interventions in civil war are always aimed at ending the conflict is mistaken. In many cases, foreign powers pump in sufficient amounts of military assistance to ensure that their preferred side is not defeated, but not enough to seize victory. The US Afghan policy during the 1980s has often been said to have been aimed at "bleeding" the Soviet Union; much in the same way that Soviet assistance to North Vietnam was sufficient to hurt the United States without defeating it outright (see, for example, Payne 1988: 62–62).

In Asia, the result of this post-1945 pattern of intervention has been longer, more frequent, and more deadly civil wars, insurgencies and rebellions. Over the course of Afghanistan's long crisis since 1978, at different times, foreign intervention has come from all four sides: Russia, Iran, Pakistan and China (Lockyer 2017: 142–192). Similarly, the internal conflicts in Cambodia, Vietnam and Loas during the 1960s and 1970s were not atomistic events, rather the course and nature of each armed rebellion influenced the course of conflicts in the neighbouring states.

Finally, there is a body of academic research that is more sceptical of the international dimensions of armed rebellion. These scholars emphasise the fact that many of the same risk factors of civil war onset – such as poverty, political stability, ethnic composition, population demographics and natural resources – also tend to cluster. In other words, if risk factors relating to country-level attributes tend to cluster, then it is not surprising that armed rebellions also cluster (Gleditsch 2002). Indeed, Håvard Hegre and colleagues (2001: 41) found little evidence of "bad neighbourhoods" and instead concluded that civil war clustering is wholly the result of domestic factors, such as GDP per capita and regime type.

## Poverty, greed and grievances

It has long been observed that rebellions and civil war are mostly a third-world problem (Collier 2003). Indeed, GDP per capita is one of the most significant and recurring risk factors for civil war onset. Explaining why poor countries are more at risk of rebellion and civil war has become a major research agenda within the civil wars literature. The two major competing explanations have come to dominate the debate. The shorthand of "greed" and "grievance" is often used to summarise these two competing explanations.

Broadly, greed explanations assume that potential recruits perform a cost–benefit calculation before joining the insurgency and if the economic benefit is predicted to be better fighting than not, then they will side with the rebels. Rational choice approaches to understanding civil war onset have been particularly popular since "the economic turn" in the study of civil wars during the late-1990s (Gutiérrez Sanín and Wood 2014: 213). The greed argument is most closely associated with Paul Collier and Anke Hoeffler (2002), who found that countries with low GDP per capita and natural resources that could be easily looted, such as diamonds and oil, were most at risk of civil war onset. Under these circumstances, Collier and Hoeffler argued that joining the rebellion is a rational choice. The personal economic rewards of being a rebel and sharing in the loot are greater than those of more traditional occupations.

"Grievance" is a shorthand term that captures the idea that rebellions are primarily caused by a religious, ethnic or class group's interests being infringed by another group. Ted Gurr (1970), for instance, advances a psychological explanation for revolutions, insurgencies, civil wars and terrorism. Gurr argues that individuals rebel due to "relative deprivation", which is a significant divergence between what people believe would be fair for them to receive from what they think they get. As Gurr (1970: 24) writes, the "potential for collective violence varies strongly with the intensity and scope of relative deprivation among members of a collectivity". Relative deprivation does not necessarily mean that people must be living in poverty. Gurr's theory accommodates instances where people might be living well below the poverty line and unable to acquire even the basics for survival and still not rebel. The cause of rebellion, according to Gurr, is not an absolute measurement, rather the intense frustration that grows from individual's belief they are being shortchanged.[3]

The greed and grievance debate gained particular traction during 1990s, when rebel groups were increasingly portrayed as being apolitical pseudo-criminal groups that exploited their government's weakness to seize the state's natural resources and pray upon the civilian population. This image of civil wars developed into the "new wars" narrative (Münkler 2004; Snow 1996).[4] Mary Kaldor (2001: 5) summarises:

> The new wars occur in situations in which state revenues decline because of the decline of the economy as well as the spread of criminality, corruption and inefficiency, violence is increasingly privatized both as a result of growing organized crime and the emergence of paramilitary groups, and political legitimacy is disappearing. Thus the distinction between external barbarity and domestic civility, between the combatant as the legitimate bearer of arms and the non-combatant, between the soldier or the policeman and the criminal, are breaking down.

In other words, as the state's monopoly over the means of coercion decreases, opportunistic elements within society who are already proficient in the use of violence (e.g. football hooligans and criminal gangs) morph into rebel and insurgent groups. Similarly, as corruption and the inefficient management of the state instruments grows, military and police forces can increasingly become predatory seeking rent from the civilian population or the exploitation of the country's natural resources. In other words, the line of distinction between government forces and rebels begins to break down. Robert Kaplan (1994) speculated that much of the violence in many post-Cold War civil wars were the actions of bandits, disaffected solders, drugged child-soldiers and teenage football hooligans that emerged in the political vacuum created by weak states. In Sierra Leone, these actors became known as "Sobels" (soldier/rebel), who were renegade soldiers who would moonlight as rebels looting and pilfering from civilians and the country's diamond mines (Zack-Williams 1999).

Within Asia, the "new war" thesis has been most commonly applied to the Afghan Civil War. The war economy in Afghanistan relies heavily on the cultivation and trafficking of opium and heroin (Rubin 1995: 117–119; Goodhand 2004). Afghanistan has become the largest opium producer in the world (Dorronsoro 2005: 143–146; Rashid 2001: 204–219). Opium has been cultivated in Afghanistan for hundreds of years, but it only become a major commercial crop towards the end of the Soviet occupation. As the rival Afghan commanders found their respective international sources of arms and finance withdrawing from the conflict they needed to explore alternative resourcing. Over the 1990s the cultivation of opium become increasingly popular and, despite a momentary drop in 2000 due to a Taliban government anti-drug initiative, it has steadily increased since the latest phrase of the war. As Monika Heupel and Bernhard Zangl (2010: 40) describe:

> The erstwhile dominant ideological (i.e. religious) motives were at first substituted by identity-based motives. Rivalries surfaced, especially between Pashtuns, Usbeks and Tajiks, and were exploited by the various warlords. Yet, against the background of the emerging drug-based war economy these motives too were gradually superseded by economic motives. The warlords increasingly regarded the war as part of the 'business', as it constituted the precondition for their extensive involvement in the drug trade and other illicit economic activities.

The argument that ideological motivations have been replaced by economic motives has increasingly come under criticism. It has become increasingly popular to assume that insurgent motives are often complex and are likely motivated by both greed and grievance (Keen 2008). Kalyvas (2003: 475) points to an instance in Afghanistan where 15 police officers were killed when their police station was attacked. Some witnesses claimed the assailants were Taliban, while other witnesses believed the attackers were bandits and looters seeking to control the local roads for revenue. This would appear to be a clear instance of greed or grievance in civil war; however, Kalyvas convincingly demonstrates that these two positions are not mutually exclusive and, indeed, it is quite possible for the attackers to simultaneously be motivated by both greed and grievance.

## Conclusion

Understanding the causes of rebellion remains important for policymakers as they directly inform counterinsurgency and counterterrorism strategies. The dominant approach to counterinsurgency, for instance, has not evolved much since Vietnam where the "hearts and minds" school of thought gained ascendency. It assumes that grievance is the main driver of insurgencies and rebellions. Under this approach, rebellions were violent elections where the side (either the government or the insurgents) that won the support of the population would eventually be victorious. The "hearts and minds" approach to counterinsurgency speculates that if the government can supply public works, such as clean water, schools and hospitals, and economic opportunities thaen the population would support the government against the insurgents. However, as the discussion above suggests, there are good reasons to suspect that the hearts and minds approach might not be effective (Lockyer 2012; Hazelton 2017). The chapters assembled in this volume will offer fresh approaches to countering terrorism, rebellion, insurgency and civil war.

Although Asia continues to experience many cases of insurgency, terrorism, rebellion and civil war, it has overall experienced a dramatic decrease in violence since its height in the late 20th century. Analysing the causes for the initial prevalence followed by the sharp decline can help policymakers arrive at better counterinsurgency and counterterrorism policies. This chapter has made a modest step towards this goal by presenting three of the leading explanations for civil war onset, namely state weakness, international intervention and poverty and grievance. This survey is, however, far from an exhaustive survey on the causes of rebellion, insurgency and civil war. There is an extensive literature, for example, that explore the organisational aspects of rebellion (Olson 1965; Weinstein 2005; Grossman 1991, 1999; Gates 2002), bargaining models of civil war onset (Azam 1995; Roemer 1985; Fearon 2005), there is also a literature that shows that the causes of rebellion are different from the reasons they continue. Nevertheless, it is hoped that outlining the main explanations will provide a useful launching pad for the discussions to come.

## Notes

1. This is a reprinted version of an earlier article (Lockyer 2018b). I would like to thank the journal for allowing its reprinting. Naturally, the exact number of civil wars varies depending on the coding rules. Fearon and Laitin (2003: 77) found that sub-Saharan Africa was the most civil war prone region (34) followed closely by Asia (33) before a large gap to the Middle East and Latin America. The rate of outbreak, however, has been highest in Asia at three civil wars per 100 country-years.
2. Similar statements are littered throughout the literature on guerrilla and terrorism; see, for instance, Crenshaw 1981; Merari 1993; Pape 2003.
3. Gurr's explanation for internal war is related to Power Transition Theory in international relations. PTT postulates that hegemonic wars occur when the distribution

of power is not reflected in the distribution of global benefits (Organski 1958; Organski and Kugler 1980; Kugler and Lemke 1996).
4 For a critique of this literature see, Kalyvas 2001 and Newman 2004.

## References

Rashid, Ahmed (2001), *Taliban: Militant Islam, Oil, and Fundamentalism in Central Asia*, New Haven, CT: Yale University Press

Azam, Jean-Paul (1995), "How to Pay for the Peace? A Theoretical Framework with References to African Countries", *Public Choice*, 83(1/2)

Black, R., S. Morris and J. Bryce (2003), "Where and Why are 10 Million Children Dying Every Year?" *Lancet*, 361(9376)

Collier, Paul and Anke Hoeffler (2002), *Greed and Grievance in Civil War*, Research Working Paper 2355, Washington, DC, The World Bank

Collier, Paul (2003), *Breaking the Conflict Trap: Civil War and Development Policy*, Washington, DC: The World Bank

Crenshaw, Martha (1981), "The Causes of Terrorism", *Comparative Politics*, 13(4)

Dorronsoro, Gilles (2005), *Revolution Unending: Afghanistan, 1979 to the Present*, New York, Columbia University Press

Fearon, James (2005), "Primary Commodities Exports and Civil War", *Journal of Conflict Resolution*, 49(4)

Fearon, James D. and David D. Laitin (2003), "Ethnicity, Insurgency and Civil War", *The American Political Science Review*, 97(1)

Forsberg, Erika (2008), "Polarization and Ethnic Conflict in a Widened Strategic Setting", *Journal of Peace Research*, 45(2)

Gates, Scott (2003), "Empirically Assessing the Causes of Civil War", paper presented at the Human Security Centre at the Liu Institute for Global Issues of the University of British Columbia conference on "Mapping and Explaining Civil War: What To Do About Contested Datasets and Findings?", Oslo, 18–19 August

Gates, Scott (2002), "Recruitment and Allegiance: The Microfoundations of Rebellion", *Journal of Conflict Resolution*, 46(1)

Ghobarah, H. A., P. K. Huth and B. Russett (2003), "Civil Wars Kill and Maim People—Long After the Shooting Stops", *American Political Science Review*, 97(2)

Giddens, Anthony (1985), *The Nation State and Violence*, Berkeley: University of California Press

Gleditsch, Kristian S. (2002), *All International Politics Is Local*, Ann Arbor, MI: University of Michigan Press

Gleditsch, Kristian S. (2007), "Transnational Dimensions of Civil War", *Journal of Peace Research*, 44(4)

Goodhand, Jonathan (2004), "Afghanistan in Central Asia", in Michael Pugh and Neil Cooper (eds.), *War Economies in a Regional Context: Challenges of Transformation*, Boulder, CO: Lynne Rienner Publishers

Grossman, Herschel I. (1991), "A General Equilibrium Model of Insurrections", *American Economic Review*, 81(4)

Grossman, Herschel I. (1999), "Kleptocracy and Revolution", *Oxford Economic Papers*, 51(2)

Gurr, Ted Robert (1970), *Why Men Rebel*, Princeton, NJ: Princeton University Press

Gutiérrez Sanín, Franciso and Elisabeth Jean Wood (2014), "Ideology in Civil War: Instrumental Adoption and Beyond", *Journal of Peace Research*, 51(2)

Hazelton, Jacqueline L. (2017), "The 'Hearts and Minds' Fallacy: Violence, Coercion and Success in Counterinsurgency Warfare", *International Security*, 42(1)

Hegre, Håvard, Tanja Ellingsen, Scott Gates and Nils Petter Gleditsch (2001), "Toward a Democratic Civil Peace? Democracy, Political Change, and Civil War, 1816–1992", *American Political Science Review*, 95(1)

Heupel, Monika and Bernhard Zangl (2010), "On the Transformation of Warfare: a Plausibility Probe of the New War Thesis", *Journal of International Relations and Development*, 13(1)

Hironaka, Ann (2005), *Neverending Wars: The International Community, Weak States, and the Perpetuation of Civil War*, Cambridge, MA: Harvard University Press

Janos, Andrew C. (1963), "Unconventional Warfare: Framework and Analysis", *World Politics*, 15(4)

Kaldor, Mary (2001), *New and Old Wars: Organized Violence in a Global Era*, Cambridge, Polity

Kalyvas, Stathis N. and Laia Balcells (2010), "International System and Technologies of Rebellion: How the End of the Cold War Shaped Internal Conflict", *The American Political Science Review*, 104(4)

Kalyvas, Stathis N. (2001), "'New' and 'Old' Civil Wars: A Valid Distinction?" *World Politics*, 54(1)

Kalyvas, Stathis N. (2003), "The Ontology of "Political Violence": Action and Identity in Civil Wars", *Perspectives on Politics*, 1(3)

Kaplan, Robert (1994), "The Coming Anarchy: How Scarcity, Crime, Overpopulation, and Disease are Rapidly Destroying the Social Fabric of our Planet", *Atlantic Monthly*, 44

Kathman, Jacob D. (2010), "Civil War Contagion and Neighboring Interventions", *International Studies Quarterly*, 54(1)

Keen, David (2008), *Complex Emergencies*, Cambridge, Polity

Kugler, Jacek, and Douglas Lemke (eds.) (1996), *Parity and War: Evaluations and Extensions of the War Ledger*, Ann Arbor, MI: University of Michigan Press

Lacina, Bethany (2004), "From Side Show to Centre Stage: Civil Conflict after the Cold War", *Security Dialogue*, 35(2)

Lake, David A., and Donald Rothchild (1998), "Spreading Fear: The Genesis of Transnational Ethnic Conflict", in David A. Lake, and Donald Rothchild (eds.), *The International Spread of Ethnic Conflict: Fear, Diffusion and Escalation*, Princeton, NJ: Princeton University Press

Lockyer, Adam (2010), "The Dynamics of Warfare in Civil War", *Civil Wars*, 12(1/2)

Lockyer, Adam (2011), "Foreign Intervention and Warfare in Civil Wars", *Review of International Studies*, 37(5)

Lockyer, Adam (2012), "Evaluating Civil Development in Counterinsurgency Operations: The Case for a Field Experiment in Afghanistan", *Australian Journal of International Affairs*, 66(1)

Lockyer, Adam (2017), *Foreign Intervention, Warfare and Civil Wars: External Assistance and Belligerents' Choice of Strategy*, London, Routledge

Lockyer, Adam (2018a), "Opposing Foreign Intervention's Impact on the Warfare in Civil Wars: The Case of the Ethiopian-Ogaden Civil War, 1976–1980", *African Security*, 11(2)

Lockyer, Adam, (2018b) "Civil War and Insurgency in Asia", *Journal of Policing, Intelligence and Counter Terrorism*, 13(2)

Maoz, Zeev, and Belgin San-Akca (2012), "Rivalry and State Support of Non-State Armed Groups (NAGs), 1946–2001", *International Studies Quarterly*, 56(4)

Merari, Ariel (1993), "Terrorism as a Strategy of Insurgency", *Terrorism and Political Violence*, 5(4)

Midlarsky, Manus I. (1978), "Analyzing Diffusion and Contagion Effects: The Urban Disorders of the 1960s", *American Political Science Review*, 72(3)

Most, James C., and Harvey Starr (1980), "Diffusion, Reinforcement, and Geopolitics and the Spread of War", *The American Political Science Review*, 74(4)

Münkler, Herfried (2004), *The New Wars*, Cambridge, Polity Press

Murdoch, J. C., and T. Sandler (2002), "Economic Growth, Civil Wars, and Spatial Spillovers", *Journal of Conflict Resolution*, 46(1)

Newman, Edward (2004), "The 'New Wars' Debate: A Historical Perspective is Needed", *Security Dialogue*, 35(2)

Olson, Mancur (1965), *The Logic of Collective Action: Public Goods and the Theory of Groups*, Cambridge, MA: Harvard University Press

Organski, A.F.K. (1958), *World Politics*, New York, Knopf

Organski, A.F.K., and Jacek Kugler (1980), *The War Ledger*, Chicago, IL: University of Chicago Press

Pape, Robert A. (2003), "The Strategic Logic of Suicide Terrorism", *American Political Science Review*, 97(3)

Payne, Richard J. (1988), *Opportunities and Dangers of Soviet-Cuban Expansion: Toward a Pragmatic U.S. Policy*, Albany, NY: State University of New York Press

Regan, Patrick M. (2000), *Civil Wars and Foreign Powers: Outside Intervention in Intrastate Conflict*, Ann Arbor, MI: University of Michigan Press

Roemer, John E. (1985), "Rationalizing Revolutionary Ideology", *Econometrica*, 53(1)

Rubin, Barnett R. (1995), *The Search for Peace in Afghanistan: From Buffer State to Failed State*, New Haven, CT: Yale University Press

Saideman, Stephen M. (2001), *The Ties That Divide: Ethnic Politics, Foreign Policy, and International Conflict*, New York, Columbia University Press

Salehyan, Idean and Kristian Skrede Gleditsch (2006), "Refugee Flows and the Spread of Civil War", *International Organization*, 60(2)

Salehyan, Idean and Kristian Gleditsch (2006), "Refugees and the Spread of Civil War", *International Organization*, 60(2)

Sambanis, Nicholas (2001), "Do Ethnic and Non-ethnic Civil Wars Have the Same Causes? A Theoretical and Empirical Inquiry (Part 1)", *Journal of Conflict Resolution*, 45(3)

Sarkees, Meredith Reid and Frank Wayman (2010), *Resort to War: 1816–2007*, Washington, DC: CQ Press

Skocpol, Theda (1979), *States and Social Revolutions: A Comparative Analysis of France, Russia, and China*, Cambridge, Cambridge University Press

Snow, Donald M. (1996), *Uncivil Wars: International Security and New Internal Conflicts*, Boulder, CO: Lynne Rienner

Tilly, Charles (1975), *The Formation of National States in Western Europe*, Princeton, NJ: Princeton University Press

Tilly, Charles (1985), "War Making and State Making as Organized Crime", in Peter Evans, Dietrich Rueschemeyer and Theda Skocpol (eds.), *Bringing the State Back In*, Cambridge, Cambridge University Press

Weiner, Myron (1996), "Bad Neighbors, Bad Neighborhoods: An Inquiry into the Causes of Refugee Flows", *International Security*, 21(2)

Weinstein, Jeremy M. (2005), "Resources and the Information Problem in Rebel Recruitment", *Journal of Conflict Resolution*, 49(4)

Zack-Williams, Alfred B. (1999), "Sierra Leone: The Political Economy of Civil War, 1991–1998", *Third World Quarterly*, 20(1)

# Part 2

# 3 Social media and terrorism in the Asia Pacific

*Julian Droogan and Lise Waldek*

## Introduction

The impact of social media[1] technology on classic terrorist groups, dissident political groups, and persecuted ethnic and religious minorities in the Asia Pacific has been profound. Classic terrorist groups, such as Al Qaeda (AQ), Islamic State (IS), the Abu Sayyaf Group (ASG), alongside dissident political groups and persecuted ethnic and religious minorities have seized the opportunities social networking platforms, such as Twitter and Facebook, and encrypted peer-to-peer messaging services such as WhatsApp and Telegram have generated (Bertram 2016; Conway 2017; Dean et al. 2012; West 2016). Opening up access to global communication networks, social media platforms create important new opportunities to engage with sympathetic audiences at home and abroad and create transnational communities for purposes of force multiplication, recruitment, and funding. The ramifications for terrorism in Asia Pacific are significant. During his 2012 trial Umar Patek, instigator of the 2002 Bali nightclub bombing, stated "For those who do not know how to commit jihad, they should understand that there are several ways", later adding "[t]his is not the Stone Age … this is the Internet era, there is Facebook, Twitter and others" (Weimann 2016). However, as this chapter will detail, these opportunities are not without risk for both terror-style groups and the governments seeking to counter them.

The creation of MySpace and Facebook in 2003–4 marks the emergence of social media. These technologies are representative of online channels and virtual networks that enable users to interact with audiences through user generated content and interaction, including many-to-many communication (Carr and Hayes 2015; Kaplan and Haenlein 2010). The availability of faster internet speeds that facilitate uploading, recording, and distribution occurred in parallel with the generation of cheap and easy to use hardware, particularly mobile phones. These characteristics of social media contributed to its attraction as a medium for terrorist actors. According to one recent study, 76% of UK terrorists used the internet to research and plan their actions (Gill et al. 2017), while 90% of online terrorist activity uses social networking platforms (Weimann 2016). Overcoming geographical limitations, online platforms offer numerous benefits; they are easy to access and use, cost-effective, grant instant access to vast audiences targeted via simple search functions, and to date their use has resulted in surprisingly few repercussions from law enforcement (Alarid 2016). Perhaps most crucially, the accessibility and openness of social media has meant that terrorist groups are no longer reliant on traditional mass media for spreading propaganda and fear.

The migration of terrorist groups online has facilitated structural and operational changes resulting in a globally dispersed management of terrorism, aiding its reach and resilience through the creation of a self-sustaining and decentralised mode of violence that can operate largely beyond formal organisational structures (Aistrope 2016). Yet the inherent openness and anonymity that has driven the uptake of social media among terror-style groups also creates vulnerabilities and risks. This chapter will examine the complexities inherent in the changes that social media has brought about for the Asia Pacific landscape. It commences with a review of the specific attributes and challenges created within the social media environment and then examines how these are shaping the evolution of terror-style groups in the Asia-Pacific using three case studies; the ASG in the Philippines, Jamaat-e-Islami (JEI) in Bangladesh, and the Uyghurs in China.

## The influence of social media on terrorist organisations

Social media platforms and the unprecedented access to audiences they provide, are now an essential tool for many terrorist organisations. Embedding terrorist groups in a 24-hour news cycle, groups are afforded opportunities to disseminate propaganda to targeted audiences through interactive and user-generated propaganda. Embracing a technology that encourages and facilitates freedom of speech and expression, social media has empowered groups across Asia Pacific, particularly marginalised segments of the population, such as youth, the impoverished, or ethnic and religious minorities, to engage in sophisticated brand development and exert pressure on national governments.

The ability to transmit information instantaneously across vast distances, and create and sustain virtual networks of like-minded individuals, has made social media platforms exceedingly attractive to political, ethno-nationalist and terrorist groups looking to influence or seek support from fellow ideologues or sympathetic diasporas. Peer-to-peer transmission of content, through multiple platforms, allows material to spread across jurisdictions and into multiple audiences. In this environment, small groups, or even individuals, can instigate a cascade or domino effect that can affect and shape attitudes and behaviours across the globe (Thompson 2011). The impracticalities involved in halting this transmission of information and its rapid dissemination through sharing, reblogs, retweets, and memes, makes social media particularly attractive to dissident groups facing repressive censorship at home. For instance, video footage of the July 2009 Urumqi riots, Xinjiang, Western

China, that left 156 dead and 1,000 injured, was dispersed widely across YouTube and other social media platforms. This content raises public awareness and concern about the alleged discriminations suffered by the local Uyghur minority group at the hands of the state, despite attempts by the Chinese government to prevent the release of footage of the event.

The internet and social media technologies are not only useful to terrorist organisations for purposes of propaganda and recruitment. Terrorist groups have begun to incorporate mobile phones and peer-to-peer networking sites for purposes of communication and coordination during attacks. Social media platforms offer opportunities for instantaneous and relatively secure communications. An early example was the use of mobile phones linked to handlers that allowed members of Lashkar-e-Taiba (LET) greater access to situational information and awareness during their four-day attack in Mumbai in November 2008 (Agrawal and Raqhav 2010). In addition, there has also been a rise in the use of the internet and social media for clandestine fundraising. Groups such as Abu Sayyaf in the Philippines have been particularly adept at advertising kidnaps for ransom online, to raise the stakes and price for release (see p. 00).

The ability to disseminate information across diverse audiences has empowered remote individuals to acquire information that has assisted in attack planning. Groups such as Al-Qaeda in the Arabian Peninsula (AQAP) and IS have used e-magazines such as *Inspire* and *Rumiyah*, distributed and spread as attachments through social media sites, to disseminate instructional information about terrorist tactics such as weapons production or attack planning (Droogan and Peattie 2016). Most recently, IS has used its *Rumiyah* publication to advocate the use of vehicle attacks on pedestrians as one available low-tech way to instigate mass gathering attacks. This modus operandi was prefigured in the October 2013 Tiananmen Square attack by members of the Uyghur separatist Turkistan Islamic Party (TIP) which killed five people when a car was driven into a group of massed pedestrians (Wan 2013).

Perhaps most significantly, social media has amplified the impact of terror attacks, imparting fear to wider audiences in an unprecedentedly immediate and dramatic manner. The ubiquitousness of social media in global societies has made it the perfect transmitter for the performance of 'propaganda of the deed', where the fear and response to the violent act far outweighs the importance of the act itself. The ability for relatively limited terror attacks to spark mass fear and even hysteria amongst exposed audiences is well documented (Payne 2009), and there is evidence to suggest that audiences often perceive themselves to be at far greater risk of terrorism than any sober risk analysis suggests (Nellis and Savage 2012). Drawing on these fears, groups have been quick to use social media to spread terror and engineer panic. For example, live-streaming attacks through social media platforms including Twitter and Instagram acts as a force multiplier, reinforcing and exacerbating societal fears of terrorism and terror attacks (Keene 2011). Government counter terrorism measures following attacks involving social media are frequently limited, blunt, and reactionary. For example, on December 1, 2017, three members of the Tehreek-e-Taliban (TeT) attacked the Agriculture Training Institute in Peshawar. A mobile phone tied to the jacket of one of the attackers' recorded the deaths of the nine victims and resulted in the suspension of cellular services across Pakistan (Ahmed, 2017).

## Social media and the 'social' aspect of terrorism

Social media and peer-to-peer networking has become an influential part of terrorists' strategies and tactics in part because its fundamentally social function resonates with many of the drivers contributing to processes of radicalisation to violent extremism. These include the appeal of belonging to an exclusive community, the construction of a subversive identity, or the desire for camaraderie and heroism among a group of peers. In many cases group identities and social ties have proven more important to radicalisation processes than commitments to abstract ideologies (Abrahms 2008). By establishing prominent platforms for content dissemination and communications, groups such as Hizb ut-Tahrir (HT), and Ansarulah Bangla Team (ABT) in Bangladesh have been able to sustain themselves as credible, authentic, and meaningful online movements attracting and radicalising alienated youth seeking out a cause and community (Bashar 2013).

The facilitation and creation of linkages between people and communities represent the foundational principles of many social media platforms. These characteristics facilitate the use of processes such as narrowcasting that afford terrorist organisations the ability to tailor the content of their propaganda to a particular audience (Soriano 2012; Weimann 2016). Likewise, mining data from sites such as Facebook and Twitter facilitates audience profiles used to design and shape targeted content. These types of techniques, drawn from the marketing world, have enabled the targeting of new or underrepresented groups such as women, as evidenced by the dramatic increase in the number of women traveling to join groups such as IS (Huey and Witmer 2016). Attempts to radicalise, recruit and train remote groups and individuals through social media have ranged from publishing regular motivational reports of the terror group's successes to using high quality images and online clips showing brutal violence and evocative imagery, accompanied by high production values and music (Aly et al. 2017; Gates and Podder 2015). This has granted some terrorist groups such as AQ and IS the ability to create radicalised transnational communities through shared narratives and images that evoke emotional responses such as feelings of sympathy, a desire to seek revenge or gain honour. In the Asia Pacific, IS recruitment has targeted large numbers of young, mostly male, participants to travel to Syria/Iraq to become part of jihadi society. This recruitment process has in part relied on the accessibility and hipness of social media content selling the narrative to impressionable youth. The use of social media to disseminate images and narratives of violent warfare is not without its own risks as evidenced by the confiscation of phones from IS recruits by senior officers to limit the sharing of uncensored or vetted battlefield videos and prevent intelligence leaks.

## Social media and counter terrorism

The innovation and dynamism associated with social media has generated unique challenges for counter terrorism, with fears that counter terrorism measures are failing to keep up with technological and social trends (McCoy and Knight 2015: Amble 2012). Significant limitations exist to how authorities can limit or hinder social media usage, including the lack until recently of effective control measures over platforms, content, and producers. Social media companies such as Facebook and Twitter are facing growing pressure from regulatory bodies to shut down terrorist content (LaFree 2017). In addition, there have recently been partially successful attempts by states such as Indonesia and the Philippines to gain backdoor entry into encrypted peer-to-peer messaging services, highlighting arguments about the reach and control of authorities over free communication.

Recently, many states have adopted more proactive strategies drawing on social media to counter all manner of anti-state narratives including terrorism. Counter terrorism strategies have drawn on social media platforms to disseminate content that promotes unity, peace-building and community resilience, and promote alternative narratives to those exposed to violent extremism (Burnap et al. 2014; Silverman et al. 2015). Smarter preventing violent extremism (PVE) and countering violent extremism (CVE) programs are themselves adapting terrorist social media tactics (Rothenberger 2012) through the creation of slick social media campaigns aimed at preventing youth from being attracted to terrorist propaganda. However, there are very few of these programs and many face significant challenges to their effectiveness and credibility, particularly given government credibility amongst potential violent extremists is relatively low. A recent development in the Asia Pacific is the ASEAN commitment encouraging member states to adopt proactive online counter terrorism strategies. The 2017 announcement indicated a shared lead between Japan, Malaysia, and Singapore, with a focus on the Philippines in order to "make full and effective use of social media to counter the spread of terrorist narratives online" (Chairman's Statement of the 24th ASEAN Regional Forum 2017).

## Case studies

The following section presents three case studies that illustrate some ways in which terror related groups across the Asia Pacific have used social media and how this is changing the way these organisations operate. Case studies are presented from a 'classic' terrorist organisation, the Filipino Abu Sayyaf Group (ASG), a dissident Islamist political party alleged to have promoted and been involved in terror activities, the Bangladeshi Jamaat-e-Islami (JEI), and an ethno-nationalist struggle by ethnic Uyghur minorities in Western China that is often – and controversially – labelled by China as a terrorist group.

## Abu Sayyaf (ASG), the Philippines

The Abu Sayyaf Group ('Sword of God') is a Salafi Jihadist terrorist organisation seeking the formation of a separate Islamic state in the Mindanao region of the southern Philippines. Since its formation in 1991 the group has been responsible for terror attacks, assassinations, kidnappings for ransom and the 2004 SuperFerry bombing that killed 116 people in the world's largest terror attack at sea. The group has engaged in numerous organised criminal activities such as extortion, human trafficking and the drugs trade (Fabe 2013). Over the decades, ASG's motives have shifted across a spectrum linking ideologically motivated terrorism with profit motivated criminal behaviour, illustrated by its policy of sometimes ransoming kidnapped victims and other times engaging in brutal decapitations. ASG has received funding and limited support from both AQ and Jemaah Islamiyah (JI), and maintains contact with other terrorist organisations in the Philippines, Indonesia and the Arab world. There are divisions in the group and currently two key factions have emerged. One led by Radulan Sharion, in Sulu, and the other based in Basilan proclaiming allegiance to IS.

Geographical and technological limitations, such as the group's location in rainforest terrain with limited facilities, have affected its capability to construct and maintain custom-made blogs and online communication platforms. The ASG relies primarily on mainstream social media platforms such as YouTube, Facebook, Twitter, and more recently Telegram for encrypted messages. The group use mobiles and cellular networks to access content, messaging services, and networks and as such has adopted a relatively simplistic social media strategy. However, the group's ability to easily and effectively brand themselves through social media posts, and claim affinity with much larger and more notorious terrorist organisations such as AQ and IS, has contributed to their reputation and reach. Perhaps the most appropriate description of ASG's use of social media is that of a marketing and branding tool. For example, since part of the group's affiliation with IS, social media content has been used to identify the group as rebels, militants, and IS mimics (Smith and Reyes 2015). Social media communications provide the group with a useful, quick, and effective way to rebrand and seize opportunities. Declarations of allegiance to AQ, 2011, and IS, 2014, can be interpreted as a form of strategic branding, as opposed to a substantive partnership. For instance, the allegiance with IS promoted a new form of legitimacy and symbolised a measure of global unity, strength and success that was largely superficial. The continued reporting by traditional media companies and outlets of these un-confirmed international terrorist links inflate public perceptions of Abu Sayyaf's reach and capabilities (Ugarte 2010). In particular the ASG has taken advantage of the recent support of IS globally by attempting to persuade sympathisers within the region to join their local struggle, framed as an extension of IS's caliphate building project.

The use of YouTube has afforded ASG opportunities to access new audiences through the process of automatic narrowcasting. Coding in YouTube allows the platform to 'suggest' materials for further viewing that are likely to be of interest, based on previous viewing trends and habits. Exposing new viewers to ASG kidnappings or other promotional videos widens the potential target audiences. For example, a much younger demographic, such as school children, inadvertently researching the Philippines as part of unrelated projects can now stumble across direct and unmediated ASG propaganda. Exposing youth in such a way is particularly concerning as it is young people who often seek to engage in risky or daring behaviour, and who thus might be vulnerable and receptive to these messages (Ramakrishna 2013).

The ASG has also used social media to illicit tactical advantages, promoting kidnappings to raise the value of the hostages. For example, in 2013, the ASG abducted Australian Warren Roddwell and held him for 472 days. The group used YouTube and Facebook to share ransom videos and to demonstrate proof of life. These videos served a dual purpose of celebrating and boasting about the group's prowess while directly targeting parties paying ransoms undercutting the government. The use of social media to establish direct lines of communication with the victim's families and communities enabled the ASG to undermine the Filipino government's law enforcement capabilities, thereby highlighting the fragility and potential illegitimacy of the government.

Although social media platforms have enabled the ASG to circumvent traditional media companies to advertise its cause and spread terror, traditional media is still important. For example, an analysis of 9,026 tweets related to the kidnapping of Victor Okonek noted that four out of five top tweeters were news organisations (Smith and Reyes 2015). The emerging symbiosis between terror groups, social media operations and traditional media companies acts to provide greater public exposure to terror activities and provides legitimacy to the ASG, while simultaneously driving traffic to news corporations' social media pages.

### *Jamaat-e-Islami (JEI), Bangladesh*

Jamaat-e-Islami ('Islamic Assembly') is a political Islamist turned extremist group with a long history in Bangladesh politics having rotated in and out of government as a legitimate political organisation since before independence in 1941 (Stern 2000). In 2013, the Bangladeshi Supreme Court ruled JEI was illegal. Since then the group has operated clandestinely. Reports indicate the group has been involved in or associated with the promotion of politically motivated murders, although it continues to deny these claims (Stern 2000; Qazi 2017).

Similar to ASG in the Philippines, social media has enabled JEI to control the delivery of its propaganda to a mass audience, even though its proscription has forced its operations underground. JEI uses a range of social media platforms to promote what it hopes will be the gradual Islamization of Bangladesh and enables the group to engage with the public, expose them to propaganda, and counter unaligned and opposing political and religious opinions (Willis and Fellow 2017). The group actively scans social media and online commentary to identify conflicting messages and unwanted commentary. JEI not only uses social media platforms to challenge opposing opinions, online operators also actively seek out ways to degrade the position of the commentator (South Asia Democratic Forum 2015). Allegedly, the group also actively tracks down and murders some of the most vocal anti-JEI secular bloggers and publishers (Shawon 2016). The group appears to prefer popular social media platforms for three reasons: they provide greater traffic for potential audiences, offer pre-constructed interfaces, and are cost efficient. This strategy is particularly effective in Bangladesh where 80 percent of the population use Facebook and where social media has supplanted older technologies such as TV as the preferred source for daily news (Willis and Fellow 2017).

However, the dynamism and ubiquity of social media make it difficult for terrorist groups to control and predict the reactions and messages that create online and offline traction amongst target audiences. In 2013, large segments of the Bangladeshi population engaged in protests against JEI in response to the perceived overly lenient sentencing of Abdul Quader Molla. Molls was a JEI politician accused of war crimes, in particular the beheading of a poet, rape of an 11 year old girl, and the murder of 344 people during the 1971 war of independence. The resulting mass 'shahbag protests' were incited by digitally prolific segments of the population through a range of blogs and social media sites, particularly Facebook, mobilised for online activism (Muni and Chadha 2013). Although incredibly useful for terrorist and extremist organisations, the medium of social media creates significant vulnerabilities for these same groups (Soriano 2012). As JEI experienced to their detriment, censorship of opposing content is a multi-way phenomenon in the online environment and no single group can completely block alternative views, unsympathetic public opinion and trolling by dissenting users. The presence of these grass-roots, user-generated counter narratives that can 'talk back' to terrorist organisations, can reduce the overall strength and impact of the extremist's message on the audience (Waldmann and Verga 2016).

## The Uyghurs, China

The Uyghurs are a Turkic speaking, predominantly Islamic, ethnic group located throughout Central Asia. The largest Uyghur population lives in China's vast and restive Xinjiang autonomous region where they make up almost 50% of the population. Culturally and religiously distinct from the

Han Chinese, and complaining of repressive and exclusionary policies imposed against them by the Chinese state, some Uyghurs have agitated for a fully autonomous or independent state akin to the Central Asian republics to their west, which detached during the collapse of the Soviet Union. Elements of the Uyghur community have sought to use social media to create an active social diaspora and politically mobilise at a transnational level (Clarke 2016; Potter 2013).

Most of the alleged Uyghur terrorist action appears to occur in a wider and more generalised atmosphere of social unrest and struggle for recognition. Conflicting propaganda from the Uyghur groups and the Chinese government creates confusion around the extent of civil disobedience among the Uyghur population, the existence of formal groups using terrorist tactics to achieve separation from the Chinese state, and connections, if any, with established global terrorist brands such as AQ and IS. The state has accused groups such as the East Turkestan Islamic Movement (ETIM) and the Turkish Islamic Party (TIP) of perpetrating several bombings and knife attacks in the region, including a 2013 car attack that killed five and injured 38 in Tiananmen Square.

The presence of the Internet and social media platforms has led to the development of a unique relationship between the Chinese government and the Uyghur people, with both competing to control internal and international perceptions of the Uyghur predicament. Uyghur groups inside China utilise blogs, personal websites, WeChat and other websites such as Misranim that contain an upload and chat function. In part, social media provides a platform to cultivate social solidarity and promote resistance to authoritarian structures. The diaspora community's active use of global platforms such as Facebook, Twitter and YouTube sustain a transnational movement built around Uyghur culture and grievance (Culpepper 2012; Zheng 2011). These communities disseminate a narrative highlighting Chinese suppression of Uyghur culture, the lack of social and economic opportunities for Uyghurs in Xinjiang and particularly, unemployment and poor health and education systems. In parallel, the Chinese state propagates a counter-argument that positions the Uyghur community as a non-state group striving for illegal independence from China by any means, effectively a terrorist organisation (Klimeš 2010). Outbreaks of violence, such as the 2009 riots, conflate these perceptions, with social media messaging depicting the Uyghur community actively assaulting Han Chinese and the Han Chinese actively targeting the Uyghur population in return.

The location of the Uyghurs in an authoritarian and heavily internet-censored country such as China has generated a unique operating environment in the Asia Pacific. The internet arrived in China over 23 years ago and estimates suggest there are over 583 million internet users in the country. However, the government has actively sought to control this online environment using three levels of censorship to ensure continual monitoring of online behaviours and expression. The first level of censorship – sometimes termed 'the great firewall of China' – is designed to block Chinese citizens' ability to view a large number of banned websites supposedly detrimental to public opinion towards the Chinese government. The second level consists of monitoring by the Chinese State Council and Information Office who filter over 1,041 prohibited words from public viewing (Clothey and Emmanuel 2016; MacKinnon 2012). The final level is the censorship by the Chinese Communist Propaganda Department, which employs over two million staff to police public opinion. Reporting suggests that the Chinese government also pays members of the public to comment and influence online discussions in favour of the government (Schichor 2005).

This layering of state control and censorship presents several challenges for the Uyghurs. Fear of police responses has limited political discussion and mobilization (Clothey and Emmanuel 2016; Olson 2014), particularly as the Xi Jinping government continues to increase monitoring of online communications. In early 2017, WhatsApp and WeChat were restricted from posting political images in China (Shih 2017), illustrating the increasing ability of the government to monitor platforms and block unwanted communications on a vast scale. Groups and individuals are not only heavily censored before their views and opinions are released, but state-generated counter narratives are swiftly provided and next to impossible to combat due to the ubiquitous nature of Chinese state propaganda and its control over the internet. Deletion rates of social media posts are higher amongst content originating from Xinjiang (25%) as opposed to that from Beijing (10%). The perceived role of social media and online activity in the 2009 riots and the 2006 online upload of a video 'Jihad in Eastern Turkistan' resulted in a ten-month internet blackout and the issuing of life imprisonment sentences to several key offending parties and website administrators (Zheng 2011). In response, some Uyghurs have turned to uncensored social media platforms outside of Chinese control (Klimeš 2010). Servers from the US, UK and Germany are accessed via virtual privacy networks (VPNs) and utilised to communicate an anti-Chinese narrative to the international community as well as access private and uncensored peer-to-peer encrypted messages services such as WhatsApp (Shih 2017).

The Uyghurs' response has also capitalised on the global dimensions of social media platforms and the broader global audience, particularly the creation and maintenance of an online diaspora and supportive community. Using highly visible platforms including Facebook, Twitter, Instagram and YouTube facilitate the targeting of Western audiences and opening up opportunities to expose them to content promoting Uyghur politics and culture. The ability to access and publish blogs gives voice to political opinions and helps shape a social movement in an anonymous and relatively safe manner (MacKinnon 2012). Censorship and the conflated facts coming out of China make it difficult to assess the effectiveness of the Uyghur social media campaigns. It is likely that the heavy Chinese restrictions on the online environment and the country's own extensive social media campaign greatly impede the Uyghur's operating space. Yet equally, the very presence of the

Uyghur-generated narratives in the online environment is a testimony to the power of social media as a tool for propagating alternative voices. The continued presence of communications demonstrates the ongoing dynamism of the online environment and how even in the face of significant state controls, it continues to provide opportunities for those seeking to distribute and engage with alternative, conflictual, and potentially subversive narratives.

## Conclusion

The advent of the internet and more specifically social media platforms have created an online environment that gives little credence to geographical, political, and national boundaries as well as traditional mechanisms of state-based authority (Weimann 2016). The decentralised nature of social media, the growth of affordable technology, the ability to disseminate and access content anonymously and the capacity to reach global and targeted audiences have afforded these groups and organisations opportunities including propaganda, recruitment, radicalisation, fundraising, and operational planning. These dynamics have contributed to the emergence of globally interconnected networks that, in superseding traditional forms of state control, have fundamentally changed the operating environment for terrorist groups, dissident political groups and persecuted ethnic and religious minorities, as well as for the nation states seeking to counter them.

The three case studies examined in this chapter highlight the complexities involved when engaging in this new environment. Given the centrality of the notion of 'propaganda of the deed' in the decisions by groups to adopt terror tactics, it is easy to see how the capacity of social media technology to generate communications to global audiences is inherently advantageous to terrorist organisations. The three case studies examined in this chapter, however, demonstrate the complexity of this engagement. The same technological specificities that cultivate these possibilities expose the groups to vulnerabilities and risks. The advent of social media has created an environment where understandings and perceptions of what qualifies as the 'truth' have become fluid. The inability to control content once it has left the producers' computer means that its navigation encompasses as many opportunities as it does risks. Managing these effectively, whilst keeping up with the rapid innovation found in the online space, will ensure that social media remains a highly challenging operating space for all those seeking engagement, whether they be nation states or terror-related groups.

## Note

1 Social media is defined by Boyd and Ellison (2007) as "web-based services that allow individuals to (1) construct a public or semi-public profile within a bounded system, (2) articulate a list of other users with whom they share a connection and (3) view and traverse their list of connections and those made by others within the system".

## References

Abrahms, M. (2008), "What Terrorists Really Want: Terrorist Motives and Counter-terrorism Strategy", *International Security*, 32(4)

Agrawal, H. and R. Raqhav (2010), "Information Control and Terrorism: Tracking the Mumbai Terrorist Attack through Twitter", *Information Systems Frontiers*, 13(1)

Ahmed, R. (2017), "Peshawar Attack: Terror Rampage 'Live Streamed'", *The Express Tribune*, 2 December, accessed on 4 January 2018 at https://tribune.com.pk/story/1574135/1-agriculture-training-institute-peshawar-closed-indefinite-period/

Aistrope, T. (2016), "Social Media and Counter Terrorism Strategy", *Australian Journal of International Affairs*, 70(2)

Alarid, M. (2016), "Recruitment and Radicalization: The Role of Social Media and New Technology", in M. Hughes and M. Miklaucic (eds.), *Impunity: Countering Illicit Power in War and Transition*, New York: Progressive Management.

Aly, A., S. Macdonald, S. Jarvis and T. Chen (2017), "Introduction to the Special Issue: Terrorist Online Propaganda and Radicalization", *Studies in Conflict & Terrorism*, 40(1)

Amble, J. (2012), "Combating Terrorism in the New Media Environment", *Studies in Conflict & Terrorism*, 35(5)

Bashar, I. (2013), "Violent Radicalisation in Bangladesh: A Second Wave?" *RSIS Commentary*, 187, accessed 12 January 2018 at www.rsis.edu.sg/rsis-publication/rsis/2075-violent-radicalisation-in-bang/#.WmPu6ZP1VsM

Bertram, L. (2016), "Terrorism, the Internet and the Social Media Advantage: Exploring how Terrorist Organizations Exploit Aspects of the Internet, Social Media and how these Same Platforms could be used to Counter Violent Extremism", *Journal for Deradicalization*, 23(7)

Boyd, D. and N. Ellison (2007), "Social Network Sites: Definition, History, and Scholarship", *Journal of Computer-Mediated Communication*, 13

Burnap, P., M. Williams and L. Sloan (2014), "Tweeting the Terror: Modelling the Social Media Reaction to the Woolwich Terrorist Attack", *Social Network Analysis and Mining*, 4

Carr, C. and R. Hayes (2015), "Social Media: Defining, Developing, and Diving", *Atlantic Journal of Communication*, 23(1)

Chairman's Statement of the 24th ASEAN Regional Forum (2017), ASEAN 50, Philippines, 7 August, accessed 12 February 2018 at http://asean.org/storage/2017/08/Chairmans-Statement-of-the-24th-ARF-FINAL.pdf

Clarke, M (2016), "Xinjiang From The 'Outside-In' and the 'Inside-Out': Exploring the Imagined Geopolitics of a Contested Region", in Clarke, M. E. and A. M. Hayes (eds.), *Inside Xinjiang: Analysing Space, Place and Power in China's North-West*, New York and Oxford: Routledge

Clothey, R. and F. Emmanuel (2016), "Oppositional Consciousness, Cultural Preservation, and Everyday Resistance on the Uyghur Internet", *Asian Ethnicity*, 18(3)

Conway, M. (2017), "Determining the Role of the Internet in Violent Extremism and Terrorism: Six Suggestions for Progressing Research", *Studies in Conflict & Terrorism*, 40(1)

Culpepper, R (2012), "Nationalist Competition on the Internet: Uyghur Diaspora Versus the Chinese State Media", *Asian Ethnicity*, 13(2)

Dean, G., P. Bell and J. Newman (2012), "The Dark Side of Social Media: Review of Online Terrorism", *Pakistan Journal of Criminology*, 3(3)

Droogan, J. and S. Peattie (2016), "Reading Jihad: Mapping the Shifting Themes of Inspire Magazine", *Terrorism and Political Violence*, doi:10.1080/09546553.2016.1211527

Fabe, A. (2013), "The Cost of Terrorism: Bombings by the Abu Sayyaf Group in the Philippines", *Philippine Sociological Review*, 61(1)

Gates, S. and S. Podder (2015), "Social Media, Recruitment, Allegiance and the Islamic State", *Perspectives on Terrorism*, 9(4)

Gill, P., M. Conway, A. Thornton and M. Bloom (2017), "Terrorist Use of the Internet by the Numbers: Quantifying Behaviors, Patterns, and Processes", *Criminology & Public Policy*, 16(1).

Huey, L. and E. Witmer (2016), "#IS_Fangirl: Exploring a New Role for Women in Terrorism", *Journal of Terrorism Research*, 7(1)

Kaplan, A. and M. Haenlein (2010), "Users of the World, Unite! The Challenges and Opportunities of Social Media", *Business Horizons*, 53(1)

Keene, S. (2011), "Terrorism and the Internet: A Double-edged Sword," *Journal of Money Laundering Control*, 14(4)

Klimeš, O. (2012), "The Uyghurs – Strangers in Their Own Land", *Asian Ethnicity Journal*, 13(2)

LaFree, G. (2017), "Terrorist Use of the Internet", *Criminology & Public Policy*, 16(1)

MacKinnon, R. (2012), "The Netizen", *Development*, 55(2)

McCoy, J. and A. Knight (2015), "Homegrown Terrorism in Canada: Local Patterns, Global Trends", *Studies in Conflict & Terrorism*, 38(4)

Muni, S. and V. Chadha (2013), *Asian Strategic Review*, Langley, VA: Pentagon Press.

Nellis, A. and J. Savage (2012), "Does Watching the News Affect Fear of Terrorism? The Importance of Media Exposure on Terrorism Fear", *Crime & Delinquency*, 58(5)

Olson, J. (2014), "Rethinking the Unreasonable Act", *Theory & Event*, 17(2)

Payne, K. (2009), "Winning the Battle of Idea: Propaganda, Ideology and Terror", *Studies in Conflict & Terrorism*, 32(2)

Potter, B. (2013), "Terrorism in China: Growing Threats with Global Implications", *Strategic Studies Quarterly*, 7(4)

Qazi, L. (2017), "How to Islamize an Islamic Republic: Jamaat-e-islami in its Own Words", Brookings, 25 April, accessed 14 February 2018 at https://www.brookings.edu/research/how-to-islamize-an-islamic-republic-jamaat-e-islami-in-its-own-words/

Ramakrishna, K. (2013), "From Global to Micro Jihad: Three Trends of Grassroots Terrorism", RSIS Publications, 7 May, accessed 6 February 2018 at www.rsis.edu.sg/rsis-publication/cens/1978-from-global-to-micro-jihad-th/#.WrG67JNubVo

Rothenberger, L. (2012), "Terrorist Groups: Using Internet and Social Media for Disseminating Ideas. New Tools for Promoting Political Change", *Romanian Journal of Communication and Public Relations*, 14(3)

Schichor, Y. (2005), "Decision-making in Triplicate: China and the Three Iraqi Wars", in A. Scobell and L. M. Wortzel (eds.), *Chinese National Security: Decision-making Under Stress*, Carlisle: Strategic Studies Institute

Shawon, A. (2016), "Bangladesh", *ArtAsiaPacific Almanac*, 11

Shih, G. (2017), "China Users Report WhatsApp Disruption amid Censorship Fears", *VOA News*, 18 July, accessed 4 January 2018 at www.voanews.com/a/china-users-report-whatsapp-disruption-amid-censorship-fears/3948669.html

Silverman, T., C. Stewart, A. Zahed and J. Birdwell (2015), *The Impact of Counter-Narratives*, London: Institute for Strategic Dialogue.

Smith, T. and J. Reyes (2015), "Analysing Labels, Associations, and Sentiments in Twitter on the Abu Sayyaf Kidnapping of Viktor Okonek", *Terrorism and Political Violence*, 29(6)

Soriano, M. (2012), "The Vulnerabilities of Online Terrorism", *Studies in Conflict & Terrorism*, 35

South Asia Democratic Forum (SADF) (2015), "Democracy Stalemate in Bangladesh. What Role for the International Community?" *SADF Policy Brief No.1*, Brussels: South Asia Democratic Forum.

Stern, J. (2000), "Pakistan's Jihad Culture", *Foreign Affairs*, 79(6)

Thompson, R. (2011), "Radicalization and the Use of Social Media", *Journal of Strategic Security*, 4

Ugarte, E. (2010), "In a Wilderness of Mirrors: The Use and Abuse of the 'Abu Sayyaf' Label in the Phillipines", *South East Asian Research*, 18(3)

Waldmann, S. and S. Verga (2016), "Countering Violent Extremism on Social Media: An Overview of Recent Literature and Government of Canada Projects with Guidance for Practitioners, Policy-makers, and Researchers", Centre for Security Science Defence Research and Development Canada Scientific Report, accessed 14 January 2018 at http://cradpdf.drdc-rddc.gc.ca/PDFS/unc262/p805091_A1b.pdf

Wan, W. (2013), "Chinese Police Say Tiananmen Square Crash was 'Premeditated, Violent, Terrorist Attack'", *The Washington Post*, 20 October, accessed 6 January 2018 at www.washingtonpost.com/world/asia_pacific/chinese-police-say-tiananmen-square-crash-was-premeditated-violent-terrorist-attack/2013/10/30/459e3e7e-4152-11e3-8b74-d89d714ca4dd_story.html?utm_term=.b50925407bfe

Weimann, G. (2016), "Why Do Terrorists Migrate to Social Media?" in A. Aly, S. Macdonald, L. Jarvis and T. Chen, *Violent Extremism Online: New Perspectives on Terrorism and the Internet*, Abingdon: Routledge.

West, L. (2016), "#Jihad: Understanding Social Media as a Weapon", *Security Challenges*, 12(2)

Willis, J. and A. Fellow (2017), *Tweeting to Freedom: An Encyclopedia of Citizen Protests and Uprisings around the World*, Santa Barbara, CA: ABC-CLIO.

Zheng, L. (2011), *Media and Minkaohan Uyghurs: Representation, Reaction and Resistance*, Doctoral Thesis, University of Colorado.

# 4 The long war
## Afghanistan

*Lise Waldek*

### Introduction

Since the 2014 drawdown of international security forces, Afghanistan has faced rising levels of violence and a dramatic increase in terror-style attacks. The turbulent and unstable environment creates numerous opportunities for militant and terrorist organisations to exploit rivalries, grievances, and the continual power vacuums that exist at local, regional, and national levels. The Taliban, Haqqani network, and other insurgent groups operate successfully across large parts of the country, with shelter, provided when necessary, by Pakistan. In 2017, the *Long War Journal* estimated that out of 398 districts, the Taliban were in control of 41 and heavily contesting the control of 117 districts (https://www.longwarjournal.org/mapping-taliban-control-in-afghanistan). Reporting from international organisations highlights a worrying trend in the increased numbers of civilian deaths and near endemic levels of violence across the country (United Nations Assistance Mission in Afghanistan 2017). With the 2019 Presidential elections looming, questions are being raised over the viability of the government, and indeed any government, to counter the insurgency and provide long-term stability to a population exhausted by years of destruction and violence.

Arguably, it is not the endemic violence and instability facing the domestic Afghani population that has returned the country to the international limelight. The current conflict emerged from the events of 9/11 and the decision by the United States (US) and its allies to wage "war on terror". It remains a tired point, but because terror is a strategy taken up by groups rather than a physical entity, a war on terror is not possible. Therefore, the US went to war with the leadership of Al Qaeda (AQ) and the Taliban who were providing them with sanctuary in Afghanistan. In 2001, the US launched Operation Enduring Freedom, invaded Afghanistan, and in doing so brought about the collapse of the Taliban and the commencement of a cycle of violence that remains unresolved 17 long years later. It is the threat emanating from terrorist organisations located in Afghanistan that shaped the original intervention by the US and continues to motivate international interest in the country. The current renewal of interest in the ongoing conflict has been influenced by the growing number of terror-style attacks, often attributed to Islamic State (IS), and the potential opportunities for IS fighters to seek sanctuary and/or recruit among populations frustrated with the Government of Afghanistan (GoA), international players, and the insurgents. In March 2017, the then US Secretary of State Rex Tillerson noted how "Daesh [Islamic State (IS)] is stepping up its recruitment of young people from Pakistan, Afghanistan … in order to send a message that they are still standing and they want those young people to fight in its ranks" (Tillerson 2017, cited in Basit 2017: 29). With the memories of the opportunities afforded to AQ through its sanctuary in Afghanistan during the 1990s still fresh in the minds of international players, terrorism and terrorist groups continue to provide the default framework and language that politicians, strategists, military operators, and the media return to, when seeking to understand and counter the instability raging across Afghanistan. Indeed, the Trump administration's new Afghan strategy, delivered in August 2017, promises a return to the original terrorism focused mandate and a return to a military focused solution. Trump states how this strategy will ensure that "The killers…know they have nowhere to hide, that no place is beyond the reach of American might and American arms" (Trump 2017).

The decisions of groups to adopt terrorist strategies and tactics are diverse and draw on numerous political, social, and cultural aspects of their environment and landscapes (Crenshaw 1981). Afghanistan presents an example of the importance of grappling with the intimate and dynamic relationship between environment and terrorism. Years of conflict have created a radical milieu open to exploitation by multiple local, national, regional, and international players (Malthaner and Waldmann 2014). This chapter therefore proposes a re-framing of the problem. It argues that in focusing on the perpetrators of violence and instability, Afghanistan has become a mere backdrop to the conflict. A physical landscape whose complex political, social, and cultural milieu has been deemed largely irrelevant to those seeking to counter a threat (Cowper-Coles 2011). Pushed into the shadows, its agency has been reduced to simple geography, a pawn in the hands of outside influences both State and Non-State (Barfield 2010). The consequences of the absence and misunderstanding of the political, social, and cultural dynamics that shape the conflict have been dire. The International Security Assistance Force (ISAF) and Afghan Security Forces (ASF) have found themselves trapped in bubbles of security that repeatedly fail to translate into medium or long-term solutions. In this context, it is imperative that Afghanistan returns from the shadows.

The remainder of this chapter identifies and examines five key sources of instability that continue to drive and shape the instability and violence in Afghanistan. Firstly the issue of power is explored, particularly its fragility and fluidity and the consequences this has on the formation of allegiances and the construction of enemies. The chapter then examines the issues of identity politics, corruption, and the fractured nature of the insurgency before returning to the country's broader geo-political context. Although conceptualised in the singular, it is likely that any emerging solutions to this complex conflict will have to engage in the shades of grey generated by the ongoing interconnections of these issues. However, returning Afghanistan to centre stage provides a useful vantage point to examine its seemingly intractable conflict.

## Sources of instability

There is a tendency to lose sight of the fact that the logic of terrorism has its roots in strategic decision making at the group and individual level (Crenshaw 1981). If solutions to the conflict in Afghanistan are to be found, the answer does not lie with those that focus solely on the violence itself (Gunaratna 2002). Instead, attention needs to be paid to Afghanistan and the complex dynamics feeding the endemic violence. Della Porta describes the interrelationships of these dynamics as "micro-mobilisation contexts" (Della Porta 1995). Examining these affords a more nuanced reading of the conflict that continues to enmesh the Afghan population and intervening global players in an endless cycle of violence. The most significant of these contexts is the formation of power. This dynamic interweaves with four other central dynamics that will be considered in this chapter; identity politics, corruption and governance, a fractured and ever fracturing insurgency, and the diverse geo-political agendas of the numerous regional and international stakeholders involved directly and indirectly in the conflict (Felbab-Brown 2017). Engaging with these micro-mobilisation contexts faces the time old problem that arises from attempts to generalise about social groups and behaviours. It is inevitable that for each statement made an example will be raised that demands the application of a qualifying sentence. Yet even within this complex milieu, general tendencies have been observed and warrant deeper examination (Ruane and Todd 1996). For perhaps it is in these, often highly emotive debates, that potential ways forward focused on the long-term stability of Afghanistan will emerge.

## The power dynamic

The social phenomenon of power is frequently found at the heart of conflicts. As the British historian, Lord Acton memorably noted in a letter to Bishop Mandell Creighton in 1887, "power tends to corrupt, and absolute power corrupts absolutely" (Dalberg-Acton, cited in Figgis and Laurence 1907: 504). This adage certainly rings true in Afghanistan where reckless behaviour in pursuit of power by politicians, warlords, insurgents, regional and international stakeholders alike has continued to push the country further towards all out civil war. Indeed, many would argue it is these "rapacious, predatory, and self-centred political schemes and predilections" (Felbab-Brown 2016: 3) that represent the greatest threat facing Afghanistan. Examining the evolution of the absolute corruption of power and its underpinning role in all aspects of the current conflict requires an appreciation of the specific socio-cultural and political attributes that shape this central phenomenon (Azoy 2011).

Hobbesian tradition emphasises the inherent struggle within the phenomenon of power for acquisition, noting that power is conceived in relation to the power others hold. In the West, however, this acute sense of relativity has diminished replaced by associations of finality and rigidity that are reinforced through institutional structures and conventions. In contrast, power in Afghanistan has retained a far greater sense of temporality with its acquisition closely connected to an individual's ability to deliver security, physical and economic (Barfield 2010). Demonstrations of power are particularly important in the generation of political legitimacy. Here reputation and performances of power are intimately connected, with any perceived deficiencies undermining reputation, access to resources and ultimately power. As Azoy notes

> loyalty seems problematic beyond the extended family. And without loyalty, there can be few lasting institutions of authority...For all practical purposes, the Afghan form of authority resides neither in permanent corporations nor in formal statuses, but rather in individual men who relate to each other in transient patterns of cooperation and competition...Fragile groups combine and collapse under the weight of changing circumstances.
>
> (Azoy 2011: 25)

Power is therefore inherently fragile, dependent on a continued ability to deliver security (Barfield, 2009). The symbiotic relationships between power and the remaining four sources of instability examined in this chapter are critical, particularly given the criticism that has at times been justifiably wielded at attempts to insert "culture" into the military strategies of intervention and defeat (Wimpelmann 2013).

## Identity politics

Although identity construction is part of a dynamic process, the narratives used to elicit membership are often rooted in ideas of timelessness. Like power, it too is relational, defined against those deemed to be "outsiders" or "strangers" (Centlivres and Centlivres-Demont 2000), for "without outsiders there are no insiders" (Hobsbawm 1996: 40). In Afghanistan, narratives of identity coalesce around a mosaic of tribal, ethnic, and religious affiliation drawing on the diverse ethnic groups found across the country that include Pashtun, Tajik, Hazara, and Uzbek. Each of these groups assumes a common ancestry, homeland and mythology and a degree of ethnic solidarity (Kareem 2015), creating sectarian divisions that criss-cross group boundaries. Understanding how these webs of relationships intersect with the relentless quest to acquire power provides a useful starting point from which to navigate through the current conflict (Tomsen 2011). Failing to comprehend the interplay of these fluid identity-based power relationships has repeatedly seen security operations drawn into power plays between different tribal, ethnic, and militant interlocutors. In addition, the short-term nature of many of the resources, particularly those linked to ISAF and US military operations or external aid donors, has magnified the inherent temporality of power further embedding corruption into the country.

The GoA has repeatedly failed to balance these complex and competing identities. This failure is not representative of an inherent incompetence in state invested leaders or suggestive of an absence of Afghan national consciousness. Rather, it is demonstrative of the complexity involved in the processes of identity formation (Centlivres and Centlivres-Demont 2000). However, this failure has significant consequences on the ability of the GoA to govern effectively. A telling example is the recent crisis that has emerged over the issuing of national identity cards, known as e-Tazkira. Presented as a remedy to the repeated accusations of electoral fraud in prior elections, the National Unity Government (NUG) has been unable to move forward on the issue. The problem centres on the use of the term "Afghan" as a catchall identity descriptor. The use of this term in the past to describe the Pashtun ethnic group has created serious tensions amongst other ethnic groups, particularly the Tajiks who perceive its use as a reference to the dominance of Pashtuns in the political system. The decision to rollout the card in February 2018 brought the tense relationship between President Ghani and Chief Executive Abdullah Abdullah into sharp relief, with the latter refusing to attend and calling for the process to be delayed (Salahuddin and Constable 2018). This political crisis is indicative of the growing problems within the NUG and the inability of its leaders to balance the complex myriad of identities.

Navigating through this fractured tribal landscape has been particularly problematic for the international players involved in the conflict. Attempts to deliver "culturally-sensitive" security solutions have at times exacerbated tensions between power brokers at local, regional, and national levels, impeding the GoA's already tenuous grasp on power. The 2010 decision by the US to fund the creation of the Afghan Local Police (ALP) is a useful example of the complexities involved in cultural appropriation for purposes of security. The ALP drew on the notion of *arbaki*, loosely conceptualised as a form of tribal policing that engages local power brokers to enforce judicial rulings (often through violent means) (Hakimi 2014). It was envisioned as a short-term solution to the inability of ISAF and the GoA to deliver local security (Goodhand and Hakimi 2014). When appropriately funded and resourced, and where recruitment has been sensitive to local power balances, there is evidence to suggest that the ALP has been an effective deterrent to insurgents (Farrell and Semple 2015). However, there have also been significant allegations of abuse with the ALP used as a resource by elites at the national and provisional level, to consolidate power and as a force multiplier to secure control over infrastructure assets (Goodhand and Hakimi 2014). For example, the ALP in Kandahar was formed under the leadership of Abdul Razzik, previously the commander of the notoriously corrupt Afghan Border Police (ABP). Razzik used the ALP to assert his control away from his usual base exacerbating tensions with other power brokers and ultimately leading to the outbreak of violence (Belcher 2018). Although it is possible to disarm ALP units that repeatedly engage in corrupt and violent behaviours, this is in reality difficult to enforce, particularly given the GoA's already limited control over these locales. The inability of the GoA to constrain these abuses and control the ALP erode its ability to project authority, legitimacy, and ultimately power across Afghanistan.

## Corruption

State building has become a major policy priority for the US and its allies, with the relatively peaceful transfer of power in 2014 from President Karzai to the NUG held up as a measure of success. However, the political landscape remains deeply divided, eroded by pervasive levels of corruption, fundamentally a political problem intimately linked to the complex processes of power acquisition between competing elites (Sullivan and Forsberg 2013). Corruption has become endemic in all aspects of life. The failure of the GoA to address the issues of corruption and deliver effective governance fuels the Taliban's narrative that depicts their shadow government as the sole purveyors of legitimate and effective governance. Reporting by long-standing war correspondent Dexter Filkins is particularly telling; he notes that while "ordinary Afghans don't like the Taliban…they dislike the Afghan Government even more" (Filkins 2017, cited in Kolenda 2017: 41).

Since its conception in the Bonn Agreement of 2001, the political landscape and structure of government in Afghanistan have been dominated by the competition, negotiations, and conflicts between different networks of political power that cross ethnic and tribal affiliations. These fault lines have been exacerbated by the flood of resources into a country with limited absorptive capacity (Kilcullen 2014). As Sharan and Bose note:

> Within this milieu of interdependency and power asymmetry, each individual network competes, negotiates and bargains over the distribution of political and financial resources in an attempt to expand and extend its influence…The availability of numerous patrons and the clients' ability to defect (exit) provides the client considerable leverage within the political network.
>
> (Sharan and Bose 2016: 617)

Within this context it is perhaps unsurprising that the decision to place the investiture of plenary power to nominate national and regional political and security positions within the Presidency, has become a tool that has embedded corruption within the heart of government. In 2015–16, reporting indicated that a position as a Provincial chief could be brought for around 3 million US dollars (Kolenda 2017). Acquiring these positions opens up a range of resources to the individual, both legal and illegal, that in turn reinforce the individual's acquisition of power. For instance, the emergence of President Karzai's brother Ahmed Wali Karzai as the dominant powerbroker in Kandahar was facilitated by his access to and ability to influence commercial dealings in the region (Hussain 2012). The presence of these strongmen and the reliance of the GoA on their networks of allegiance undermine its ability to engage in political, economic, and social reform and therefore ultimately its legitimacy.

The non-violent departure of President Karzai was viewed as an opportunity to move away from these embedded networks and the corrupting plays for resources, dominance, and power. However, the NUG has been undermined by the vagueness of the power sharing agreement between Ghani and Abdullah, with the latter believing authority would be split equally between the Presidential and Chief Executive, particularly in relation to the selection of government appointees (Sharan and Bose 2016). With both leaders dependent on different networks of allegiance, tensions have arisen over the appointment of positions that in turn, have remained wedded to tribal and ethnic affiliation rather than ability and competence. These tensions have also hindered the ability of the NUG to begin enacting the systemic political reforms required to bring coherency and efficiency to the political landscape (Sharan and Bose 2016). For example, despite electoral promises much of the country suffers from an absence of state controlled rule of law, with judicial institutions remaining chronically weak. Reporting indicates that many courts and judges demand extortionate bribes that prevent the average family from accessing justice. In contrast, the Taliban routinely provide mediation in tribal, criminal, and personal disputes that, while arbitrary and harsh in nature, rarely incur financial cost (Weigand 2017). There is reporting of a high degree of satisfaction among domestic audiences with non-state judicial services (Felbab-Brown 2017), further eroding the authority of the NUG and empowering the Taliban and other groups.

## An insurgency fractured

Scholarship on terrorism has undergone a transformation over the past decades, moving away from a reliance on singular tropes such as evil and insanity towards a growing recognition of the complex web of relationships involved in decisions to engage in violent extremism (Crenshaw 2011; Sageman 2011). One of the greatest problems facing Afghanistan however, has been the inability to translate these more nuanced readings of "terrorism" into policy. Instead, politicians and military operators have often aggregated insurgents and terrorist organisations under a single strategy of engagement

(Davis 2017). The aggregation of the different groups operating across Afghanistan has contributed to a misreading of the ground situation and the military and political failures that have reverberated across the country (Barfield 2010). Competing parties would re-frame local rivalries as "Taliban" in order to leverage resources from external military operators, thus shifting the balance of power in their favour (Tomsen 2011). The retreat of these resources exacerbated the fragility of these new balances of power leading commentators to note how rival parties simply had to wait for military operators to depart before reasserting their claims to power. Understanding who, when, and what constituted the enemy has been a perennial problem in the conflict.

The Taliban have always been equally entangled in the mesh of tribal alliances and patronage demands, with most of its key positions held by individuals from the eastern Pashtun tribes in the Ghilzai confederation (Gunaratna and Kam 2016). The death of Mullah Omar has exacerbated the internal fracturing, with the current leader, Maulawi Haibtullah Akhundzada, unable to negotiate and effectively manage competing power bases (Kolenda 2017). For instance, the leadership's reliance on the Mansour network has drawn the Quetta based leadership into the long-standing rivalry between the Mansour founder, Malawi Nasrulah Mansur and the leader of Hezb-i-Islami Gulbuddin (HiG), Gulbuddin Hekmatayr, reducing opportunities to operate in HiG controlled lands (Gunaratna and Kam 2016). Likewise, while the Haqqani network is often described as part of the Taliban, it maintains its own command and control and lines of operation under Siraj Haqqani, son of the famous anti-Soviet fighter Jalauddin Haqqani (Dressler 2010). The reputation of the Haqqani network for well-planned and deadly attacks (Wolf 2016) make it a valued asset, yet its relationship with Pakistan and particularly the Inter-Services Intelligence (ISI) creates tensions with the current Taliban leadership, keen to demonstrate distance from Pakistan influence and control (Giustozzi 2010).

The Taliban has recently engaged in a strategy to expand its reach of influence outside its traditional Pashtun power base. Using narratives that emphasise its "nationalistic" agenda that seeks to counter the corruption of the GoA, it has developed a policy of "localised" leadership appointments, facilitating its spread into non-Pashtun areas such as the predominately Tajik province of Badakhshan (Ali 2017). Although this expansion increases its operational capabilities and power base, it also adds another layer of complexity to the already fractured leadership, leading some commanders to suggest that the armed struggle has lost direction and purpose (Farrell and Semple 2017). This sense of disillusionment along with the power vacuums within the leadership have facilitated opportunities for other players to enter into the arena.

The scale of IS presence in Afghanistan is highly contested. However, a few insurgent commanders have pledged allegiance and carried out, or facilitated, some of the higher profile terror attacks that occurred in 2017 and 2018. The IS presence is reportedly drawn from three groups; former Tehrik-i-Taliban Pakistan (TTP) members, former disgruntled Taliban, and former IS fighters from Syria/Iraq. The role of disgruntled Taliban leaders is a reoccurring theme in the reporting on IS in Afghanistan, and highlights the pervasive spread of power politics across the insurgency. For instance, one of the first commanders to pledge allegiance to IS was Rauf Khadem. His decision was motivated in part, by long-standing frustrations with the Taliban leadership that he believed had been prioritising rival Ishaqzai leaders over his Alizai tribe (Osman 2015). Associating with IS offers leaders such as Khadem opportunities to access alternative resources to shore up their power.

The perceived presence of IS and the opportunities for expansion have contributed to the re-focus on Afghanistan by a range of players including Russia and Iran, both of whom have been reported as providing resources to the Taliban as a counter-balance to concerns around the spread of IS into their own lands. However, the ability of IS to operate successfully in Afghanistan remains questionable. They are entering an already crowded theatre of operation where internationally focused ideologies are likely to bring them into conflict with domestic insurgent groups and strongmen, including the Taliban. It remains to be seen how the group navigates the shifting sands of power politics and its associated alliances that have a tendency to fracture control and power.

## Geo-politics: Rivalries and resources

Long-term political stability in Afghanistan will no doubt require an "Afghan path"; an internally constructed negotiated solution that reaches out to groups and individuals who are currently out of favour with the GoA (Farrell 2017). Notwithstanding the importance of ground-up solutions to violence, the current instability is also the product of Afghanistan's geographical location; one that places it in what David Kilcullen has politely described as a "tough neighbourhood" (Kilcullen 2014: 9). Its geographical position at the crossroads of Central and South Asia and the Middle East has seen Afghanistan repeatedly cast as a buffer zone between dominant regional powers. Pakistan, India, China, Iran, Russia, and Western states, are all actively involved in the internal affairs of the country. It is not that all of this influence is explicitly nefarious. For instance, Chinese investment in Afghanistan has continued to grow steadily, influenced by its own domestic security concerns after the 2009 and 2014 riots in Xinjiang, and the development of the China-Pakistan Economic Corridor (CPEC) (Hanif 2010). The influence of external powers is never simple. Russian engagement, for instance, has largely been centred on supporting the GoA through the Northern Distribution Network that provided a vital alternative supply route when Pakistan closed its own route in 2011. However, Russian concerns with the Islamic Movement of Uzbekistan (IMU) and IS, both present in Afghanistan, have led to reports of the channelling of funds to the Taliban. This type of influence irremovably shifts the balances of power across the country (Theros and Kaldor 2018), particularly when it involves the support of insurgent groups.

Afghanistan's geographical location has provided the Taliban with opportunities to access resources and sanctuary from a range of regional and transnational players. These have been pivotal to the Taliban's resilience in the face of enduring military campaigns. Its relationship with Pakistan is particularly influential and complex. Despite Pakistan's position as a key ally in the global war on terror and its ongoing relationship with the US, insurgent groups including the Taliban and Haqqani network have benefited from provision of sanctuary in Baluchistan, The Federally Administrated Tribal Areas (FATA) and Waziristan; all areas with a significant Pashtun population. The presence of a large Pashtun population in Pakistan has also generated a high degree of domestic sympathy for the Afghan Taliban, making it harder for Pakistan to act decisively against the group (Kolenda 2017). At the same time, Pakistani proxy support to the insurgency is driven by its tense and dominating regional rivalry with India. The instability in Afghanistan has been viewed as a buffer against Indian regional expansion. These fears are exacerbated by the influence of pro-Indian Tajik elites in the GoA, the uneasy relationship between the Pashtun and Pakistan leadership, and the increasing presence of Indian economic development in Afghanistan (Chaudhuri and Farrell 2011). Pakistan continues to position itself as a key interlocutor for any negotiated political settlement with the Taliban, yet its own interests in sustaining the insurgency impede its neutrality and reputation among other external players.

## Ways forward and conclusion

The latest US strategy once again reimagines the problem through its own security concerns with terrorist organisations. Its primary motivation remains fixated on the destruction of available operating spaces for these groups, as opposed to the regeneration of a stable Afghanistan. Military strategies are, however, unlikely to provide any more than a temporary balm. As Senator Rand Paul noted in his address to the US War Committee, if the deployment of 100,000 troops under the Obama Administration failed to deliver lasting security, the engagement of 15,000 US soldiers will do little to stem the violence and resulting threat to America (Landay 2018). What is needed then?

Long-term solutions must be cemented in an Afghan-led and Afghan-generated process. In 2001, the then UN Special Representative to Afghanistan, Lakhar Brahimi, described the decision to exclude the Taliban from the Bonn Agreement negotiations as "our original sin" (cited in Farrell 2017: 67). The absence of the voice of the enemy from the proposed "solution" is representative of the oft-repeated strategic error that frames Afghanistan as a passive target of foreign intervention and foreign concerns, rather than as a dynamic and complex actor in its own right (Hussain 2012). In 2018 the Kabul Process sought to generate commitment towards a more Afghan-centric peace process that would incorporate direct talks between the GoA and the Taliban. Yet the Taliban of 2018 is very different to the organisation excluded from the Bonn Agreement. Its fractured leadership has created power vacuums that have been exploited by various networks including dissident Taliban that have pledged allegiance to IS. These wider networks of power brokers need to be acknowledged if future negotiations are to have the opportunity to take root and move towards non-violence (Farrell and Semple 2017).

Solutions will also need to include the broader cacophony of voices that has evolved during this conflict. It is impossible to imagine the 2018 Kabul Process succeeding if the US is not brought into the process or a parallel process, particularly given the growing involvement of Russia and China. Previous attempts to negotiate with the Taliban have been derailed by its demand for the immediate withdrawal of international and US forces prior to the commencement of discussions. Navigating the stormy waters necessitates direct talks with a US that is open to and able to comprehend alternative solutions. Equally, internal players will have to find ways to manage the seemingly irresistible pull of resources from external interlocutors, whilst generating and sustaining narratives that move beyond those of invasion and exploitation. All of these competing players will ultimately, have to acknowledge the elephant in the room – the fragility of power acquisition – and its influence on the key factors of instability, identity formation, corruption, a fractured insurgency, and the geo-political ambitions of regional and international interlocutors. In doing so, Afghanistan will be brought back into the frame and back into the limelight facilitating pathways that may help establish social, political, and economic equilibrium between the competing networks embedded in this long war.

## References

Ali, O. (2017), "The Non-Pashtun Taleban of The North (1): A Case Study from Badakhshan", 3 January, *Afghanistan Analysts Network*, accessed 30 April 2018 at https://www.afghanistan-analysts.org/the-non-pashtun-taleban-of-the-north-a-case-study-from-badakhshan/

Azoy, G. W. (2011), *Buzkashi: Game and Power in Afghanistan*, Long Grove, IL, Waveland Press

Barfield, T. (2010), *Afghanistan, A Cultural and Political History*, Princeton and Oxford, Princeton University Press

Basit, A. (2017), "IS Penetration in Afghanistan–Pakistan: Assessment, Impact, and Implications", *Perspectives on Terrorism*, 11(3)

Centilvres, P., and M. Centilvres-Demont (2000), "State, National Awareness and Levels of Identity in Afghanistan from Monarchy to Islamic State", *Central Asian Survey*, 19(3)

Chaudhuri, R., and T. Farrell (2011), "Campaign Disconnect: Operational Progress and Strategic Obstacles in Afghanistan, 2009–2011", *International Affairs*, 87(2)

Cowper-Coles, S. (2011), *Cables from Kabul: The Inside Story of The West's Afghanistan Campaign*, Glasgow, Harper Press

Crenshaw, M. (1981), "The Causes of Terrorism", *Comparative Politics*, 13(4)

Crenshaw, M. (2011), *Explaining Terrorism: Causes, Processes, and Consequences*, London, Routledge

Davis, T. (2017), "The Haqqani Network: International Friends, Local Enemies", *Small Wars Journal*, accessed 30 April 2018 at http://smallwarsjournal.com/jrnl/art/haqqani-network-international-friends-local-enemies

Della Porta, D. (1995), *Social Movements, Political Violence and the State: A Comparative Analysis of Italy and Germany*, Cambridge, Cambridge University Press

Dressler, J. (2012), *The Haqqani Network: A Strategic Threat*, Washington: Institute for the Study of War

Farrell, T. (2017), *Unwinnable: Britain's War in Afghanistan 2001–20014*, London, Penguin

Farrell, T., and M. Semple (2015), "Making Peace with the Taliban", *Survival*, 57(6)

Farrell, T., and M. Semple (2017), "Ready for Peace? The Afghan Taliban after a Decade of War", *RUSI Briefing Paper*, 31 January, accessed 30 April 2018 at https://rusi.org/sites/default/files/201701_bp_ready_for_peace.pdf

FDD's Long War Journal Mapping Taliban in Afghanistan (2017), accessed 12 January 2017 at https://www.longwarjournal.org/mapping-taliban-control-in-afghanistan

Felbab-Brown, V. (2016), "Blood and Faith in Afghanistan: A June 2016 Update", Brookings Institute, June

Felbab-Brown, V. (2017), "Afghanistan's Terrorism Resurgence: AQ, ISIS and Beyond", Brookings Institute, April 27

Figgis, J. N., and R. V. Laurence (eds., 1907), *Historical Essays and Studies by John Emerich Edward Dalberg-Acton*, London, Macmillan

Giustozzi, A. (2010), *Negotiating with the Taliban: Issues and Prospects*, New York, The Century Foundation

*Global Terrorism Index 2017: Measuring and Understanding the Impact of Terrorism*, Institute for Economics & Peace (IEP) accessed 30 April 2018 at http://visionofhumanity.org/app/uploads/2017/11/Global-Terrorism-Index-2017.pdf

Goodhand, J., and A. Hakimi (2014), *Counterinsurgency, Local Militias, and Statebuilding in Afghanistan*, Washington, DC: United States Institute of Peace

Gunaratna, R. (2002), *Inside Al Qaeda Global Network of Terror*, London: Hurst

Gunaratna, R., and S. Kam (2016), *Handbook of Terrorism in Asia-Pacific*, London: Imperial College Press

Gregory, D. (2004), *The Colonial Present: Afghanistan, Palestine, Iraq*, Malden, MA: Wiley-Blackwell

Hakimi, A. (2014), "Fetishizing "Culture": Local Militias and Counterinsurgency in Afghanistan", OpenDemocracy.net accessed 30 April 2018 at https://www.opendemocracy.net/aziz-hakimi/fetishizing-%E2%80%9Cculture%E2%80%9D-local-militias-and-counterinsurgency-in-afghanistan

Hanif, M. (2010), "Indian Involvement in Afghanistan in the Context of the South Asian Security System", *Journal of Strategic Security*, 3(2)

Hobsbawm, E. (1996), "Identity Politics and the Left", *New Left Review*, 217

Hussain, S. (2012), "Looking for 'Tribals' Without Politics, 'Warlords' Without History: The Drug Economy, Development and Political Power in Afghanistan", *Identities*, 19(3)

Kareem, K. (2015), "Understanding Taliban Resurgence: Ethno-Symbolism and Revolutionary Mobilization", *Studies in Ethnicity and Nationalism*, 15(1)

Kilcullen, D. (2014), "Afghanistan in 2024: Muddling Through?" *Stability: International Journal of Security Studies & Development*, 3(37)

Kolenda, C. D. (2017), "America's Generals Are Out of Ideas for Afghanistan", *Survival, Global Politics and Strategy*, 59(5)

Landay, J. (2018), "U.S. Senators Concerned Trump's Afghanistan Strategy Will Not Succeed", Reuters, 7 February, https://www.reuters.com/article/us-usa-afghanistan/u-s-senators-concerned-trumps-afghanistan-strategy-will-not-succeed-idUSKBN1FQ30Y

Malthaner, S., and P. Waldmann (2014), "The Radical Milieu: Conceptualizing the Supportive Social Environment of Terrorist Groups", *Studies in Conflict & Terrorism*, 37(12)

Osman, B. (2015), "The Shadows of Islamic State in Afghanistan: What Threat Does it Hold?" Afghan Analysts Network, 12 February, accessed 8 January 2019 at https://www.afghanistan-analysts.org/the-shadows-of-islamic-state-in-afghanistan-what-threat-does-it-hold/

Ruane, J., and J. Todd, (1996), *The Dynamics of Conflict in Northern Ireland: Power, Conflict and Emancipation*, Cambridge, Cambridge University Press

Sageman, M. (2011), *Leaderless Jihad: Terror Networks in the Twenty-First Century*, Philadelphia, University of Pennsylvania Press

Salahuddin, S., and P. Constable (2018), "New Afghan ID Cards. Aimed at Unifying the Country, Are Doing the Opposite", *Washington Post*, 10 March, accessed 30 April 2018 at https://www.washingtonpost.com/world/asia_pacific/new-afghan-id-cards-aimed-at-unifying-the-country-are-doing-the-opposite/2018/03/10/cab05128-1c9b-11e8-98f5-ceecfa8741b6_story.html?noredirect=on&utm_term=.98b4b050c21b

Sharan, T., and S. Bose (2016), "Political Networks and the 2014 Afghan Presidential Election: Power Restructuring, Ethnicity and State Stability", *Conflict, Security & Development*, 16(6)

Sullivan, T., and C. Forsberg (2013), "Confronting the Threat of Corruption and Organized Crime in Afghanistan: Implications for Future Armed Conflict", *Prism: a Journal of the Center for Complex Operations*, 4(4)

Theros, M., and M. Kaldor (2018), "The Logics of Public Authority: Understanding Power, Politics and Security in Afghanistan, 2002–2014", *Stability: International Journal of Security and Development*, 7(1)

Tomsen, P. (2011), *The Wars of Afghanistan: Messianic Terrorism, Tribal Conflicts, and the Failures of Great Powers*, New York, Public Affairs

Trump, D. (2017), "Full Transcript: Donald Trump Announces His Afghanistan Policy", *The Atlantic*, 21 August, accessed 8 January 2019 at https://www.theatlantic.com/politics/archive/2017/08/full-transcript-donald-trump-announces-his-afghanistan-policy/537552/

United Nations Assistance Mission in Afghanistan (2017), *Annual Report on the Protection of Civilians in Afghanistan*, accessed 10 February 2018 at http://unama.unmissions.org/protection-of-civilians-reports

Weigand, F. (2017), "Afghanistan's Taliban – Legitimate Jihadists or Coercive Extremists?" *Journal of Intervention and Statebuilding*, 11(3)

Wimpelmann, T. (2013), "Nexuses of Knowledge and Power in Afghanistan: The Rise and Fall of the Informal Justice Assemblage", *Central Asian Survey*, 32(3)

Wolf, S. O. (2016), "The Fallacy of State Rhetoric: Pakistan, Haqqani Network and Terror in Afghanistan", *SADF Focus*, No. 13, South Asia Democratic Forum (SADF).

# 5 Strategy on autopilot

*Resolute support* and the continuing failure of Western strategy in Afghanistan

*Benjamin Schreer and Thomas Waldman*

## Introduction

This chapter analyses recent efforts by Western states to address the threat from terrorism and insurgency in Afghanistan since the end of the long-running International Security Assistance Force (ISAF) and commencement of the new Resolute Support Mission (RSM) in 2015. Although the RSM era has seen responsibility for security increasingly transferred to the Afghan government, Western states remain heavily engaged in the country. The North Atlantic Treaty Organization (NATO) and partner countries have deployed some 14,000 troops in support of the RSM 'train, advise and assist' (TAA) mission (Special Inspector General for Afghanistan Reconstruction (SIGAR) 2018). For the US, Afghanistan remains its largest overseas military operation involving the deployment of thousands of civilian and military advisors as well as special operations forces as part of a separate counter-terror mission: *Operation Freedom's Sentinel*. Indeed, America continues to dominate the Western coalition's Afghanistan strategy, with European partners generally following its lead.

However, contrary to rhetoric of progress and declarations outlining new approaches, Western strategy toward Afghanistan has essentially been on autopilot since 2015. Indeed, this chapter argues that the strategic logic behind RSM is flawed, fails to address the root causes of conflict and extremism in Afghanistan, and has remained largely unchanged despite superficial alterations at the tactical and operational levels. Some policy alterations were implemented under the final years of the Obama administration, including a more aggressive targeting policy largely in response to the mounting threat from Islamic State (IS). These steps presaged President Trump's more far-reaching expansion and intensification of the military dimensions of the Western commitment. Nevertheless, not only were such military shifts of gear largely irrelevant from a strategic perspective but they may actually prove counterproductive in the long run through generating harmful effects and perverse incentives. In short, Western strategy in Afghanistan continues to fail and an achievable end state is not in sight.

The chapter is divided into three main sections. The first section outlines the context within which RSM has evolved since 2015. It surveys the internal political and security situation in Afghanistan and examines prominent developments in Western policy toward Afghanistan with a focus on the US and especially the Trump administration's much anticipated articulation of a new strategy in August 2017. The second section details the flaws in strategy underpinning Western engagement in the RSM era. The final section pulls these threads together, reflects on prospects for Afghanistan's security, and considers possible ways forward.

## Strategic context

RSM officially commenced on 1 January 2015, replacing the ISAF mission. Post-ISAF Western strategy initially focused on strengthening the capacity of Afghan forces to contain and eventually defeat the insurgent threat, while simultaneously containing the fallout from the disputed 2015 Afghan presidential elections to ensure the political survival of the new government. Positive momentum on both fronts was deemed vital in allowing the West to gradually extricate itself from the long-running Afghanistan commitment. However, progress was slow and faltering. In fact, NATO forces found themselves being drawn back into more active combat roles as key population centres fell to the Taliban and paralysis continued to hobble the Afghan government. RSM was geared around a TAA mission which would see specialised teams located in both central institutions and at five other locations around the country – the so-called 'hub and spoke' arrangement. The NATO-led mission, involving contributions from over 30 countries, was primarily focused on the provision of technical, administrative, and logistical support at command and ministerial levels. Advisory personnel assisted Afghan counterparts in making high-level decisions or reforming processes in key institutions, while Afghan forces were responsible for planning, overseeing and conducting major combat operations in the field.

This arrangement was subsequently derailed by high profile events such as the Taliban take-over of Kunduz city in September 2015, when Western forces had to be deployed in combat roles alongside Afghan commandos to retake the city in two weeks of hard fighting (*Economist*, 2015). Subsequently, Western involvement was stepped up through increased levels of air support, special forces activity, and strikes against IS positions. Obama's decision to loosen the rules of engagement and slow the drawdown of troops in 2016 was indicative of the deteriorating security situation. While he had originally planned to reduce troop levels to 5,500 by the end of the year, he decided to keep them at 8,400 after consultations with his military leadership (Landler 2016).

During 2016, the Taliban insurgency intensified and its survival of the surge of international forces between 2010–2012 was testament to the organisation's resilience and tenacity. Heavy fighting raged across more than a dozen provinces and the Taliban made gains in restive provinces such as Helmand, Kandahar, Kunduz, Badakhshan, Faryab, Ghazni, Uruzgan, Baghlan and Farah. Over half of the 21,000 security incidents recorded by the United Nations in 2017 were armed clashes and the security situation across the country was 'highly volatile' (United Nations 2017, 1). The potency of the insurgency was further underscored by a series of high profile, deadly attacks throughout 2017, culminating in a series of bombings in Kabul in December which killed hundreds of civilians. These bombings were also a reminder that Islamic State had been able to maintain a significant foothold in Afghanistan, particularly in the north and east, despite suffering major casualties in 2016–2017 (Osman 2017).

Nevertheless, NATO official statements maintained that the majority of the Afghan population lived in government-controlled territory and that most provincial and district centres were also 'secured'. However, this omitted the fact that Afghan insurgents threatened population centres and maintained significant influence over the population through parallel governance structures. Indeed, a US military study in late 2017 stated that the Taliban controlled 40 per cent of Afghan territory and one third of the population (US Department of Defense 2017). Moreover, the Special Inspector General for Afghanistan Reconstruction (SIGAR) claimed that less than 60 per cent of the country was under government control and this was part of a pattern of ongoing decline (SIGAR 2017b, 88–89). Furthermore, in 2017 only one third of Afghans believed the country was moving in the right direction (Asia Foundation 2017, 6). Since 2009 civilian deaths had risen to over 28,000 (UNAMA 2018, 1) and roughly 1.2 million Afghans had been internally displaced by fighting and general insecurity (Rasmussen 2016). Afghanistan ranked close to the bottom on almost all Human Development Index (HDI) indicators, including the world's second highest maternal mortality rate and unemployment over 40 per cent (United Nations Development Programme 2018). Despite years of massive investment of foreign assistance, the social and economic situation in Afghanistan remained dire. Consequently, the commander of US forces in Afghanistan General John Nicholson described the situation in early 2017 as a 'stalemate' (US Senate Armed Services Committee 2017). While some analysts pointed out that this did not automatically mean the Taliban were 'winning' (Jones 2018), the situation equally signalled ongoing problems with NATO's strategy.

All eyes thus turned to new US President Donald Trump and his approach to Afghanistan. While he campaigned on a platform of disengagement, he nevertheless ordered a "review" of America's Afghan strategy, apparently swayed by senior military leaders such as Secretary of Defense James Mattis and then-National Security Advisor H.R. McMaster. Ultimately, Trump announced a cautious escalation of the war effort in August 2017 (*New York Times* 2017). The centerpiece of the new plan was a 'mini-surge' through the deployment of 3,900 additional troops, mostly advisors. Additionally, US forces would be permitted to again embed with Afghan forces at combat level and authorised to call in significantly expanded and more flexible air power in support of Afghan National Defence and Security Force (ANDSF) operations. Moreover, US involvement would no longer be based on arbitrary timelines but now followed a 'conditions-based approach'. Simultaneously, the strategy called for increased pressure on Pakistan to deny the Taliban sanctuary and to force them to the negotiating table.

## The structural flaws of RSM

Trump's 'new strategy' met with approval by senior retired US military leaders such as former ISAF Commander General Stanley McChrystal (Sadat and McChrystal 2017), European allies, and partners such as Australia. Still, the new approach also failed to address the deeper structural problems driving conflict, insurgency and terrorism in Afghanistan. These include the legacy of the ISAF era; structural deficiencies in building ANDSF capabilities and effectiveness; ongoing promotion of harmful militia programs; militarisation of the conflict; and deficits in terms of political and diplomatic efforts.

## The ghosts of ISAF

When it commenced in early 2015, RSM inherited major strategic problems from the previous ISAF mission. Ever since the US-led intervention in Afghanistan began in December 2001 ISAF strategy had been hampered by inconsistencies, unrealistic political objectives, inappropriate resources, and, over time, dwindling domestic support in many Western countries. As the Afghan insurgency gained momentum during the 2000s, NATO's mission displayed increasing difficulties to conduct effective counter-insurgency operations; some scholars have even argued that its strategy was doomed to fail from the start (Farrell 2017). Toward the end of the 2000s it was clear that without a change in strategy, NATO's ISAF mission would go nowhere (Noetzel and Schreer 2009). By then, the list of problems was rather long: exclusion of the Taliban in the post-invasion political settlement; the 'light footprint' approach and shift of attention and resources to Iraq; ineffective and counterproductive responses to the mounting insurgency; operational deficiencies such as rapid troop rotations, lack of contextual understanding, and excessively 'kinetic' military approaches; agencies and coalition members pulling in different directions due to the lack of a unified and coherent strategy; and an overall mismatch between ambition and available resources.

In response, the US administration of Barack Obama announced a 'surge' at the end of 2009 which authorised a major temporary US troop increase from a little over 30,000 to more than 100,000 troops at the peak in 2011. Yet, eager to get out of Afghanistan he also conditioned the troop presence, announcing that by 2016 the US would only have an embassy presence in the country. This, however, provided the insurgency with a comfortable timeline to wait Western troops out. Indeed, Obama continued to draw down US forces in Afghanistan just when ISAF operations showed signs of success in consolidating gains in many provinces. By 2014, only 30,000 troops remained in the country – too few to prevent the insurgents from regaining momentum. Yet, until he left office in early 2017 it was clear that the preconditions for lasting peace in Afghanistan had not been met, despite the political symbolism of transitioning from ISAF to RSM.

RSM has struggled to turn ISAF's legacy around. At the time of writing in early 2018, roughly 13,000 NATO troops cannot seize and hold sufficient territory outside Kabul. It remains a truism of counter-insurgency operations that a small military footprint delivers a 'small payoff' (Biddle, Macdonald and Baker 2018). Little progress has also been made in addressing the high levels of corruption in Afghanistan which continue to erode government legitimacy, especially regarding the judiciary and security forces. Indeed, Western presence and large-scale infusions of often unaccountable assistance have fuelled a culture of dependency in many parts of the government. Afghan officials are not incentivised to accept responsibility and accountability, and pressure has remained low to maximise efficiency in bureaucratic processes. Afghanistan remains one of the most corrupt countries in the world (Transparency International 2018). There have also been few achievements in reducing the power of regional strongmen who have undermined central government authority and control across Afghanistan. Indeed, a major political crisis in Kabul in late 2017 paralysing the current government of President Ashraf Ghani was the direct result of regional powerbrokers amassing sufficient power to defy the central government authority. Finally, RSM was also handed confusion over NATO strategy – oscillating between peacebuilding, counter-insurgency and counter-terrorism – and a lack of willingness or ability of Western coalition powers to learn from past mistakes and to deliver a more concerted approach to address problematic practices and deeper organisational deficiencies.

## The enduring challenge of building Afghan security forces

One of those problems is the key assumption that Afghanistan's security forces will become capable of securing the country independent of Western support. This approach is understandable since it is a central precondition for long-term stability. Admittedly, some progress has been made in recent years. On paper, there are now over 370,000 ANDSF troops and police in the field as well as around 17,000 highly capable special forces. In addition, Afghan forces have demonstrated a capability of holding the line against insurgents despite minimal Western combat assistance, defending most major population centres, and even pushing Taliban forces back in some instances. The Ghani government's 2017 'ANDSF Road Map' process aims to build on these achievements and the president replaced several senior officers, instituted changes to the force structure, approved the procurement of new equipment and weapons platforms (especially for the Air Force), and vowed to renew the battle against corruption. As well, America's new strategy will likely provide a temporary boost to morale and confidence amongst Afghan troops.

Nevertheless, Afghan security forces continue to suffer from pervasive problems even after years of Western training and advisory efforts (Jalili 2016).

Foremost among those are deep-seated corruption (Bezhan 2017; Grant 2017; Walid 2017); factionalism and lack of cohesion (Wood 2012); operational deficits, especially in areas such as intelligence, logistics, and medical evacuation; and poor inter-service coordination, especially between the ANP and ANA, which obstructs a coherent and unified approach towards the insurgency (Giustozzi 2016, 12). The ANDSF also continued to experience high attrition from rates from desertion, low re-enlistment and 'shockingly high' casualties (SIGAR 2017b). Moreover, the special forces' capability suffers from an unsustainable tempo of operations and strain on personnel; their expansion also hollows out the conventional forces.

Western efforts to build-up the ANDSF are also still not sufficiently tailored to the Afghan context (SIGAR 2017a). Consequently, force structures are hampered by centralised processes as well as overly sophisticated and complex operational methodologies for Afghan institutions to handle. Narrow technocratic approaches to these reform efforts have also failed to address fundamental political-economy issues and deep-seated institutional pathologies within the security establishment, such as rent-seeking, clientelism and factionalism (Munch 2015, 4–7). For instance, an unintended effect of introducing expensive high-tech administrative systems and equipment has been to create new opportunities for corruption (SIGAR 2017a). It is thus questionable whether the new advisory teams will adopt different approaches (Giustozzi 2016). Indeed, early reports suggest that SFA brigades being deployed are understaffed, undertrained and inadequate for the task (Gibbons-Neff 2018).

Reintroducing large advisory functions at all levels could also compound the 'dependency syndrome' amongst Afghan leaders and preclude the evolution of a genuine sense of ownership and indigenously crafted counter-insurgency strategy (Giustozzi 2016, 5). The ANDSF massive reliance on foreign funding and support undermines its legitimacy as a truly Afghan institution. Long-term, the Afghan government needs to assume full responsibility for controlling the security administration of the country which appears unlikely as long as it remains 'fractured and fragile' (David Sedney quoted in McLeary and De Luce 2017). In sum, there is little to suggest that RSM has been able to address the structural problems of Afghan security reform. It remains unclear how the Trump administration's approval of a few thousand more advisers can achieve lasting change allowing the Afghan forces to stand alone. Meanwhile, the parallel reliance of Western strategy on irregular or semi-regular forces and militias not only undermines ANDSF morale but also contributes to a host of corrosive effects on Afghan security.

## The risk of militias

RSM has been unable to address the serious risk posed by Afghan militias. Since the mid-2000s, some Western strategists approved the support for local irregular militias as a means of extending government control into the countryside in the absence of sufficient numbers of international or national regular forces. One key rationale has been that they represent cheap and effective 'force multipliers' and that they possess inherent legitimacy insofar as they build on historical Afghan templates of community self-defence, most notably the tribal *arbakai* model (Jones and Munoz 2010). Following a number of iterations up until 2010, US special forces set up and nurtured the Afghan Local Police (ALP) as the preferred model, despite frequent talk of imminent closure and integration into the regular force structure. The ALP is now under the nominal control of the Ministry of Interior and funded solely by the US. Indeed, the ALP has been expanded in recent years with current force levels at around 30,000 personnel, and there are reported plans for the creation of a similar semi-regular Territorial Force (Mashal 2017). Beyond the ALP, other irregular armed groups often operate as private armies of regional powerbrokers (Mashal 2015; Mashal et al. 2015) or as part of so-called 'Popular Uprising' militias (Marty 2016).

To be sure, militia groups have on occasions effectively provided local security or prevented insurgent take-overs at local levels. However, such cases are highly specific and the enabling conditions do not apply across large swathes of the country – if anything, the opposite is true (Schmeidl and Miszak 2017). Overwhelmingly, the reliance on militias has proven counter-productive and potentially damaging. For many Afghans, the presence of multiple militia groups is a reminder of earlier turbulent periods, especially during the 1990s, when the 'rule of the gun' was the norm. Numerous reports have detailed how militias have engaged in unlawful activities such as killing, beatings, robberies, extortion, looting, rape and harassment (Felbab-Brown 2016). The fact that these groups are centrally sanctioned works to undermine trust in the government and the legitimacy of the state. Militias also often enjoy significant levels of immunity due to political connections in central government and there is a distinct lack of oversight.

The proliferation of unaccountable, self-interested armed groups with questionable loyalty to the government has evolved as a major problem for the country's stability. Rather than providing local security, many militias have focused their efforts on pursuing personal vendettas and rivalries. Such infighting and competition between local power mafia has led to a deterioration in local stability and opened fissures which can be manipulated by insurgents, in particular in areas of ethnic, religious or tribal rivalries. Moreover, ordinary villagers have been forced to turn to Taliban for protection against abusive local armed groups. Indeed, these dynamics have been identified as a major reason behind Taliban gains in the north of the country in recent years (Haymon and Kugelman 2017). In fact, the fall of Kunduz in September 2015 can largely be seen as a consequence of the security vacuum created by inter-militia battles.

Reliance on militias has also undermined state-building narratives even if, and arguably because, ALP militias are nominally under Interior Ministry control. The existence of predatory, abusive and corrupt armed groups has eroded the government's monopoly on legitimate violence and its perceived legitimacy amongst Afghans more generally; it has sustained the norm of disparate locally provided security and has empowered regional and local powerbrokers and warlords who may threaten the state in the future, or who may hold negotiations with insurgents hostage by threatening violence (Bearak 2017). The sobering lesson for Western strategy in Afghanistan is that such militias once established are very difficult to control, there is little guarantee they remain committed to their original task, and they may even turn against their sponsor (Ghazi and Mashal 2018). The continued reliance of RSM on these groups has been indicative of wishful thinking and a narrow focus on short-term security at the expense of deeper, longer-term consolidation of state authority.

## Creeping militarisation

The problem of building effective Afghan forces points to a much larger challenge for RSM to make effective strategy to defeat the insurgency. While RSM's mission was originally conceived principally to 'train, advise and assist' the ANSDF and other institutions, the increased trend towards kinetic operations displays a renewed effort aimed at finding a military solution for a complex political and societal problem (Rashid 2017a). Nevertheless, already under President Obama, targeting restrictions for US forces were eased and the drone campaign expanded. Trump's strategy appears to focus even more on kinetic operations against insurgents and terrorists, the destruction of narcotics facilities, and otherwise employing military force against enemy targets. Alongside increased use of airpower and special operations forces, major weapons systems such as F-16 and A-10 combat aircraft, high mobility artillery rockets systems (HIMARS) and Blackhawk attack helicopters were re-deployed into theatre. Between 2016 and 2017, US air strikes more than tripled. Indeed, with up to 4,000 strikes in late 2017 they reached their highest level since 2012 (Schmitt 2017). Reportedly, the Central Intelligence Agency (CIA) also requested permission to conduct drone strikes in Afghanistan for the first time (Schmitt and Rosenberg 2017), raising the risk of lower vetting over targets and diminished accountability for civilian deaths (Rashid 2017c).

To be sure, stepping up the kinetic campaign can deliver tactical effect and put pressure on insurgent groups. However, it is doubtful whether these measures are part of a realistic strategy to achieve a politically sustainable 'victory' in Afghanistan. It appears that 'population-centric' counterinsurgency has been replaced by a more narrow counter-terrorism campaign. The underlying assumption seems to be that the insurgents can be 'bombed' to the negotiating table in order to find a lasting political solution to the conflict. Yet if history is any guide there are reasons for scepticism. First, special forces raids have a long record of causing resentment amongst Afghans, as they often contribute to further radicalising segments of the population and to fuelling resentment of Western presence. Indeed, in the past ISAF's drone strike campaign directly contributed to patterns of increased radicalisation and recruitment into insurgent groups (Kilcullen 2009). Moreover, stepping up the air campaign continued to cause civilian casualties. Between January and September 2017, the UN recorded 466 civilian casualties (including 205 deaths) from aerial attacks, 70 percent of them women and children (United Nations, 2017, 7). Perhaps most worryingly, Afghan forces have adopted this predilection for kinetic military force as the default approach while simultaneously developing an unhealthy addiction to air support (Giustozzi, 2016, 7).

Large-scale military strikes can also prove politically damaging. The highly publicised use of the largest conventional munition in the US inventory – the 12,000-pound GBU-43/B, or 'Mother Of All Bombs' (MOAB) – to attack Islamic State positions in Nangahar on 13 April 2017 – has widely been viewed as a Taliban propaganda coup as the group was able to present the bombing as a disproportionate 'show of strength' aimed at regional audiences such as North Korea or Russia. It could claim that the US was using Afghanistan as a weapons test-range. The bombing also undermined the Ghani government: opponents, including former President Karzai, criticised the president for a failure to stop its employment (Rashid 2017a). The use of MOAB demonstrated a distinct lack of understanding among commanders about the long-term strategic effect on the overall campaign.

With its narrow focus on operational military issues, Trump's 'new' approach essentially pushed responsibility for the Afghanistan operation to the military leadership. Greater use of military force might be necessary to contain the immediate threats facing parts of the country. Nevertheless, there has been no indication that the creeping militarisation of RSM has been nested in a broader political strategy designed to end the conflict. 'More of the same' is unlikely to yield a different result this time.

## Small changes for political settlement

RSM has cemented the strategic stalemate between Western powers and the insurgent groups: both are too weak to win, yet too strong to be defeated. According to official Western statements, the purpose of military efforts is to bring the Taliban back to the negotiating table. Indeed, as analysts have long argued, the only long-term solution in Afghanistan is through a negotiated political settlement (Waldman 2014). But hopes that bombing the Taliban into accepting peace on Western terms will likely be disappointed (Farrell and Semple 2015–2016; Singh 2018). Critically, a political settlement requires a comprehensive diplomatic strategy and the use of force calibrated to clear political goals.

In the past, Western policymakers and commanders displayed a distinct lack of attention to managing vital political dynamics which fuel the continuing insurgency and prevent progress toward peace talks (Farrell and Semple 2015–2016). There are no indicators that this has changed significantly. Indeed, notably absent from Trump's 'strategy' for Afghanistan has been an emphasis on diplomatic, non-military solutions – aside from threatening to cut Pakistan's military aid should it continue to support insurgent movements. The administration's decision to marginalise the Department of State means that the US lacks a serious strategy and expertise for dealing not only with the Afghan government and insurgent leaders, but also for engaging effectively with critical neighbours such as Pakistan and China (Ahrari 2018).

This diplomatic deficit is painfully evident in America's policy toward Pakistan. It is common knowledge that elements within Pakistan's powerful military Inter-services Intelligence Service (ISI), have provided important material, moral and political support to elements of the Taliban as well as allowing them sanctuary within Pakistan. This is primarily driven by a motivation to establish a friendly Islamic regime in Kabul as a bulwark against Indian influence, its arch rival. Any long-term diplomatic solution in Afghanistan requires Pakistan to change its behaviour or at least apply pressure on the Taliban movement to enter into talks (Dostyar 2017; Maley 2016). It must also be noted that RSM remains critically dependent on Pakistan for sustaining supplies and the country remains too important a strategic asset for the US to be able to exert serious leverage over its foreign policy (Fair 2018). Previous attempts of US administrations to withhold military aid to Pakistan to stop its support for insurgents were ineffectual for these same reasons and it is unlikely that Trump's January 2018 announcement to suspend US$225 million in military assistance will enjoy greater success. Pakistan's strategic calculus will not be shifted by such moves, also since it has fostered a closer relationship with China in recent years.

Moreover, the Trump administration also has an uneasy relationship with China, Russia and Iran, powers crucial for forging a sustainable peace. Paradoxically, continued Western presence and backing of the Afghan central government reduces the pressure on regional powers to assume greater responsibility for Afghanistan's stability, despite their interest in preventing a rise in extremist Islamist activity, an Afghan civil war, or a further growth of the narcotics trade. Western strategy has to yet to find ways to better utilise shared interests with these countries. This problem is also not helped by the fact that some of those countries have made alliances of convenience with the Taliban to exert pressure on the US as part of a wider geostrategic rivalry. For instance, Russia's support for the Taliban is more a means of frustrating US strategy and to gain leverage on other agendas, than a serious meeting of minds between Moscow and Taliban leaders. Similar dynamics apply to Iranian support for the Taliban (Gall 2017).

In addition to regional consensus, a political settlement requires a stable and legitimate central Afghan government. It also necessitates political incentives for insurgent groups to lay down arms beyond mere punishment in military terms. However, the prospects of serious peace talks appeared bleak during the first half of 2018. Far from pushing parties to the table, the escalation of violence in 2017 and 2018 arguably solidified rejectionist positions. In response to a string of deadly insurgent attacks in December 2017 and

January 2018, the US president publicly rejected the idea of talks, in contradiction of the stated aim of his strategy. In contrast, the Afghan government in February 2018 made a sudden offer of talks (BBC News 2018) which was, however, reportedly dismissed by the Taliban (ABC News 2018). Unless there is a politically acceptable solution for insurgent groups, military pressure alone will not compel the Taliban to settle for lasting peace.

During the summer of 2018, there were tentative signs of diplomatic progress. This included, amongst other things, the opening of dialogue between the US and Taliban representatives in Doha, the highly publicised nationwide Eid ceasefire, and further generous peace offers made by President Ghani. Meanwhile, the US government maintained its narrative of how the new strategy was putting pressure on the Taliban to come to the negotiation table. However, the Taliban continued to make gains across the country and conducted a string of deadly attacks culminating in the bold offensive against the strategic town of Ghazni in August 2018, which resulted in hundreds of casualties. If anything, the Taliban were engaging in exploratory dialogue from a position of strength rather than weakness. At the time of writing, there was little sign that they were willing to abandon their long-held position rejecting direct talks with the Afghan government or their precondition of total withdrawal of US forces from the country.

In short, there was little reason to believe peace was around the corner, and certainly not a peace that would secure Western interests in any meaningful fashion.

## Conclusion

Afghanistan has become the West's 'forgotten war', despite having turned into NATO's longest and most expensive deployment, with billions of dollars added each year. More than 2,400 Western troops have lost their lives, as have many more Afghan soldiers, civilians and insurgent fighters. Countless strategies and initiatives have yet to deliver lasting progress towards long-term stability and security in the country. RSM has struggled with many of the same problems as the ISAF mission, and it is not clear that Western strategy has a better recipe for success.

In reality, few good options remain, posing a genuine dilemma for policy-makers. RSM and Trump's new strategy will almost certainly enable short-term impacts concerning metrics of territory controlled or numbers of insurgents killed. However, progress is likely to remain limited in relation to deeper political-economy issues, regional diplomacy, and the fundamental drivers and causes of conflict in the country. The militarisation of RSM strategy limits political flexibility, has counterproductive operational consequences, and undermines movement toward negotiations. Indeed, the focus on the military campaign has arguably led to a disproportionate lack of attention on and failure to address the acute domestic political crisis facing the embattled Ghani administration (Rashid 2017b). Furthermore, continuing to shoulder the burden for maintaining a minimum measure of stability acts as a disincentive for regional states to take responsibility and help fashion a sustainable solution to the conflict. It is therefore hard to disagree with Stephen Walt's conclusion that Western strategy in Afghanistan amounts to an 'endless, costly and unrealistic effort with no clearly discernible endpoint and little hope of success' (Walt 2017).

## Bibliography

ABC News (2018), 'Taliban Pours Cold Water on Afghanistan President's Peace Talk Invitation', 1 March.
Ahrari, E. M. (2018), 'US Strategy in Afghanistan Requires Diplomacy and Military Power', *YaleGlobal Online*, available at https://yaleglobal.yale.edu/content/us-strategy-afghanistan-requires-diplomacy-and-military-power accessed 29 March 2018.
Asia Foundation (2017), *Afghanistan in 2017: A Survey of the Afghan People*, San Francisco.
BBC News (2018), 'Taliban Offer: Afghan President Ashraf Ghani Seeks Talks', 28 February, available at http://www.bbc.com/news/world-asia-43227860 accessed 29 March 2018.
Bearak, M, (2017), 'These Ex-Warlords are Promising Afghanistan's "Salvation"', *Washington Post*, 6 August.
Bezhan, F. (2017), 'Away From The Fighting, Kabul Takes On Another Enemy: Corruption', *Radio Free Europe*, 11 June.
Biddle, S., J. Macdonald and R. Baker (2018), 'Small Footprint, Small Payoff: The Military Effectiveness of Security Force Assistance', *Journal of Strategic Studies*, 41(1–2).
Dostyar, A. (2017), 'The Challenges and Opportunities of a Negotiated Settlement in Afghanistan', *Strategic Analysis*, 41(1).
*Economist* (2015), 'Unhappy Anniversary', 3 October.
Fair, C. C. (2018), 'Pakistan Has All the Leverage Over Trump', *Foreign Policy*, 3 January.
Farrell, T. (2017), *Unwinnable: Britain's War in Afghanistan 2001–2014*, London, Vintage.
Farrell, T. and M. Semple (2015–2016), 'Making Peace with the Taliban', *Survival*, 57(6).
Felbab-Brown, V. (2016), 'Hurray for Militias? Not So Fast: Lessons from the Afghan Local Police Experience', *Small Wars and Insurgencies*, 27(2).
Gall, C. (2017), 'In Afghanistan, U.S. Exits, and Iran Comes In', *New York Times*, 5 August.
Ghazi, Z. and M. Mashal (2018), 'U.S. Bombs Afghan Militia Behind Insider Attack, Officials Say', *New York Times*, 11 January.
Gibbons-Neff, T. (2018), 'Training Quick and Staffing Unfinished, Army Units Brace for Surging Taliban', *New York Times*, 26 January.
Giustozzi, A. (2016), 'The Afghan National Army after ISAF', *Afghanistan Research and Evaluation Unit*, March.
Grant, S. (2017), 'The Toll Corruption Takes on Afghan Security Force Capacity', *The Global Anti-Corruption Blog*, 5 June, available at https://globalanticorruptionblog.com/2017/06/05/the-toll-corruption-takes-on-afghan-security-force-capacity/ accessed 29 March 2018.

Haymon, B. S. and M. Kugelman (2017), 'What's Behind the Taliban's Major Gains in Northern Afghanistan?' *The Diplomat*, 18 May.

Jalili, A. A. (2016), 'Afghanistan's National Defense and Security Forces: Missions, Challenges and Sustainability', United States Institute of Peace.

Jones, S. (2018), 'Why the Taliban Isn't Winning in Afghanistan: Too Weak for Victory, Too Strong for Defeat', *Foreign Affairs*, 3 January, available at https://www.foreignaffairs.com/articles/afghanistan/2018-01-03/why-taliban-isnt-winning-afghanistan accessed 29 March 2018.

Jones, S. and A. Munoz (2010), *Afghanistan's Local War: Building Local Defense Forces*, Santa Monica, CA: RAND.

Kilcullen, D. and A. Exum (2009), 'Death from Above, Outrage Down Below', *New York Times*, 16 May.

Landler, M. (2016), 'Obama Says He Will Keep More Troops in Afghanistan Than Planned', *New York Times*, 6 July.

Maley, W. (2016), 'Afghanistan on a Knife-Edge', *Global Affairs*, 2(1).

Marty, F. J. (2016), 'Afghanistan's Anti-Taliban Vigilantes: Blessing or Curse?' *The Diplomat*, 15 September.

Mashal, M. (2015), 'Afghan Vice President Raises Concerns by Turning to Militias in Taliban Fight', *New York Times*, 18 August.

Mashal, M. (2017), 'U.S. Plan for New Afghan Force Revives Fears of Militia Abuses', *New York Times*, 15 September.

Mashal, M., J. Goldstein and J. Sukhanyar (2015), 'Afghans Form Militias and Call on Warlords to Battle Taliban', *New York Times*, 24 May.

McLeary, P. and D. De Luce (2017), 'In Break From Obama, Trump Embedding More U.S. Forces With Afghan Combat Units', *Foreign Policy*, 10 November.

Munch, P. (2015), 'Resolute Support Light: NATO's New Mission Versus the Political Economy of the Afghan National Security Forces', *Afghan Analysts Network*, January.

*New York Times* (2017), 'Full Transcript and Video: Trump's Speech on Afghanistan', 21 August.

Noetzel, T. and B. Schreer (2009), 'NATO's Vietnam? Afghanistan and the Future of the Atlantic Alliance', *Contemporary Security Policy*, 30(3).

Osman, B. (2017), 'Another ISKP Leader "Dead": Where is The Group Headed after Losing so Many Amirs?' *Afghanistan Analysts Network*, 23 July.

Rashid, A. (2017a), 'Afghanistan: Making It Worse', *New York Review of Books*.

Rashid, A. (2017b), 'Afghanistan: It's Too Late', *New York Review of Books*.

Rashid, A. (2017c), 'What Troops Can't Fix', *New York Review of Books*.

Rasmussen, S. E. (2016), 'Number of Internally Displaced Tops 1.2 Million, Says Report', *Guardian*, 31 May, available at https://www.theguardian.com/global-development/2016/may/31/number-of-internally-displaced-afghans-tops-1-million accessed 8 January 2019.

Sadat, K. and S. McChrystal (2017), 'Staying the Course in Afghanistan: How to Fight the Longest War', *Foreign Affairs*, 96(6).

Schmeidl, S. and N. Miszak (2017), 'The Afghan Local Police: Unpacking a Hybrid Security Arrangement', *Third World Thematics: A TWQ Journal*, 1–19.

Schmitt, E. (2017), 'Hunting Taliban and Islamic State Fighters, From 20,000 Feet', *New York Times*, 11 December.

Schmitt, E. and M. Rosenberg (2017), 'C.I.A. Wants Autonomy to Conduct Drone Strikes in Afghanistan for the First Time', *New York Times*, 15 September.

Singh, V. J. (2018), 'Why Peace Talks Are Washington's Best Bet in Afghanistan', *Foreign Affairs*, 21 March, available at https://www.foreignaffairs.com/articles/afghanistan/2018-03-21/why-peace-talks-are-washingtons-best-bet-afghanistan accessed 29 March 2018.

Special Inspector General for Afghanistan Reconstruction (2017a), *Reconstructing the Afghan National Defense and Security Forces: Lessons from the U.S. Experience in Afghanistan*.

Special Inspector General for Afghanistan Reconstruction (2017b), *Quarterly Report to the United States Congress*, 30 October.

Special Inspector General for Afghanistan Reconstruction (2018), *Quarterly Report to the United States Congress*, 30 April.

Transparency International (2018), 'Policy, SDGs and Fighting Corruption for the People: A Civil Society Report on Afghanistan's Sustainable Development Goals', 8 March.

UNAMA (2018), *Afghanistan Protection of Civilians in Armed Conflict: Annual Report 2017*.

United Nations (2017), 'The Situation in Afghanistan and its Implications for International Peace and Security', 15 December, A/72/651-S/2017/1056.

United Nations Development Programme (2018), 'Afghanistan', available at http://hdr.undp.org/en/countries/profiles/AFG accessed 29 March 2018.

US Department of Defense (2017), *Enhancing Security and Stability in Afghanistan*.

US Senate Armed Services Committee (2017), 'The Situation in Afghanistan', 9 February, available at https://www.armed-services.senate.gov/imo/media/doc/Nicholson_02-09-17.pdf accessed 29 March 2018.

Waldman, T. (2014), 'Reconciliation and Research in Afghanistan: An Analytical Narrative', *International Affairs*, 90(5).

Walid, S. (2017), 'Afghan Generals Face Charges in Crackdown on Military Corruption', *Washington Post*, 29 March.

Walt, S. (2017), 'Mission Accomplished' Will Never Come in Afghanistan', *Foreign Policy*, 28 March.

Wood, J. (2012), 'The Importance of Cohesion in the Afghan National Army to Post-Transition Afghanistan', *RUSI Journal*, 157(4).

# 6 Pakistan's terrorist challenge

*Julian Droogan*

**Introduction**

Since its independence from British rule in 1947 Pakistan has suffered from, and been implicated in, rising levels of terrorism and sectarian violence that have impacted both it and its region. At over 200 million people, Pakistan is the world's fifth most populous country and the only Muslim majority state to have a nuclear weapons capability. Since the 1947 division of the Indian Subcontinent into the two culturally related but antagonistic states of Pakistan and India, Pakistan's domestic security and foreign relations have been dominated by complex and hostile relations with its larger neighbour, as well as the actions of outside powers such as Russia, the United States, China, and Saudi Arabia looking to use Pakistan as a staging board for influence in South Asia and beyond. Pakistan and India have fought three wars over the contested region of Kashmir plus a series of border skirmishes. While maintaining a conventional militarised line of control (LOC) through the disputed mountainous region, each has also accused the other of at times employing non-state proxies and terror groups to wage unconventional warfare within one another's borders, and to gain leverage in Kashmir and neighbouring Afghanistan.

Pakistan exists in a highly contested and complex strategic location at the crossroads of South Asia, Central Asia, the Middle East and the Indian Ocean. The country faces enormous pressures due to domestic factors such as massive population growth, a pronounced youth bulge, growing ethnic and religious sectarianism, poverty, endemic corruption, weak governance, and an entrenched civil–military divide. At the same time, because of its strategic location at the intersection of prominent geographic and cultural regions, Pakistan has had to balance and confront the sometimes clandestine actions of external powers jockeying for influence and operating inside its borders.

The country can be roughly divided into two spheres: a relatively stable and populous core region centred on the Indus River and the agrarian states of the Punjab and Sindh, and a less populous belt of harsh mountainous and desert lands stretching from the Karakoram and Hindu Kush mountains in the north, through the weakly governed Federally Administered Tribal Areas

(FATA) and Baluchistan regions adjacent to Afghanistan and Iran to the west and south. These sometimes remote and difficult to access borderlands are populated by tribal groups such as the Pashtun and Baluch. These groups often adhere to customary militant tribal traditions, are often animated by a host of sectarian and secessionist grievances, engaged in internecine local political power struggles that often involve militant non-state actors, and are at best loosely attached to or antagonistic towards Islamabad whose control beyond major towns and highways can at times be limited.

These volatile conditions have contributed to Pakistan becoming a victim of political violence, terrorist militancy, ethnic separatism, the use of proxies by foreign powers, and worsening ultra-conservatism and extremism throughout its society. This contested and complex human and geographical terrain has contributed to significant terrorist activities around much of the country's periphery. To its east, the conflict with India over Kashmir has resulted in a decade's long armed standoff with India as well the state's periodic support and use of militant terror groups such as Lashkar-e-Taiba (LeT) and Jaish-e-Muhammad (JeM) across the border in Indian Kashmir and beyond. To its north and west, Pakistan has repeatedly been drawn into the conflicts of its unfortunate neighbour Afghanistan. Islamabad has at times adopted a policy of utilising militant groups in Afghanistan in order to maintain influence in the region. This includes the US and Saudi-backed support of Mujahideen forces against the 1979 Soviet invasion, and the more recent use of non-state proxies such as the Afghan Taliban and Haqqani Network to promote Pakistani influence vis-à-vis India and other regional powers following the 2001 US-led invasion. To its southwest, Pakistan shares the volatile Baluchistan tribal region with Shiite majority Iran, a relationship that has been complicated by Shiite and Baluch minorities on both sides of the border, as well as mutual accusations by Iran and Pakistan about the use of militant and sectarian terror groups in order to destabilise the other.

The southern border fronting the Indian Ocean opens the country to the Arab Gulf states and the wider Middle East, where countries such as Saudi Arabia have been heavily involved in Pakistani politics and the alleged support of extremist and militant actors as part of a regional policy of confronting and containing Iran. The Indian Ocean also encourages Pakistan to act as a transit route for both licit and illicit goods from inner Asia. This makes Pakistan a desirable transhipment route for regional powers such as the US into Afghanistan, and China into its landlocked western province of Xinjiang, as well as opium smuggling and organised crime.

To add to this volatility, over the past three decades extremist ideologies, jihadi culture, and terrorist violence have spilled over from these border regions into the rest of the country and inflicted terrible domestic casualties. This has occurred in parallel with a broader social transformation that has seen the country influenced by a growth of Sunni–Shiite sectarianism, the spread of ultra-conservative and militant Islam, systemic violence, and the partial breakdown of central rule and the provision of basic human security in some regions. Financial support from conservative Arab states such as Wahhabist Saudi Arabia has contributed to a dramatic rise of ultra-conservative Islam within Pakistan's urban and rural populations. The growth of supremacist and extreme Islamic movements such as the Deobandi school at the expense of older more pluralistic South Asian Islamic traditions such as the Barevli and Sufi forms of Islam have made Pakistani society more conservative, extreme, and at risk of sectarian violence.

All this has combined to make Pakistan particularly vulnerable to numerous types of terrorist violence. Since the war against the Soviets in Afghanistan in the 1980s, and accelerating after the US-led invasion of Afghanistan following the 9/11 attacks, Pakistan has suffered from worsening violent extremism, to the point that it has come to threaten the stability and security of the country. Undoubtedly, Pakistanis have been affected and impacted by terrorism in horrendous numbers, and the Pakistani state has robustly confronted many terrorist groups such as the Tehrik-e-Taliban Pakistan (TTP) through the use of arrests, bans, and hard military and policing counter terrorism operations, including assistance from the international community, most prominently the US and its drone operations. Foreign policy and counter terrorism have been largely abrogated by the Parliament and civilian ruling government, however, and are controlled instead by the 'deep state' military and intelligence organisations.

The world of Pakistani terrorism is both murky and complex, with extremist, militant, and terrorist groups taking part in domestic and geopolitical conflicts along Pakistan's borders, where violence in Afghanistan, Baluchistan, Kashmir, and the rise of domestic sectarian conflict at home are all interconnected. Within this violent and extremist milieu the boundaries between militant groups are often fluid, with the names of organisations changing as they are banned or rebranded to suit new opportunities, for instance through adopting the transnational branding of well-known global terrorist groups such as Al Qaeda (AQ) or the so-called Islamic State (IS). What makes terrorism in Pakistan most difficult and challenging to understand or confront, however, are the links that exist at times between some terrorist groups and elements of government, police, military, and intelligence. Indeed, some militant non-state groups have been supported or tacitly encouraged by elements of the state, usually the Inter-services Intelligence (ISI) Directorate, in order to wage proxy asymmetric warfare across Pakistan's borders, but also to engage in domestic politics at home, to intimidate political opponents or critics, and to counter ethno-nationalist separatist movements.

The Pakistani state has done much to counter some militant and separatist groups, but never in a comprehensive or equitable way. Balancing the occasional and selective use of non-state groups in order to meet strategic goals with the threat of domestic terrorism blowback at home and a need to be seen to be working with allies such as the US as a reliable partner and responsible member of the international community have created contradictions and areas of opaqueness within Islamabad's counter terrorism policies. Pakistan's selective and occasional support of militant terrorist groups has created a difficult counter terrorism environment in which Islamabad has at different times pursued opposing policies in order to appease separate stakeholders. For instance, Pakistan needs to be seen to be taking action against internationally recognised terrorist groups, particularly as it wishes to attract aid and investment from the US and China, but at the same time some militant groups have proved useful in order to reach domestic and foreign policy goals.

## India and Kashmir

Pakistan's complex relationship with non-state terror groups waging unconventional warfare against India in Kashmir began in 1947 at the commencement of the nation's independence. The dispute between India and Pakistan over the inclusion of the predominantly Muslim, but Hindu ruled, princely state of Jammu and Kashmir into their respective nations during the partition of the Subcontinent led to Pakistan's infiltration of the region with a loose collection of tribal jihadi militias (*jihadi lashkar*). Following the informal 1948 partition of Kashmir into two parts administered by Pakistan and India, Pakistan has at times relied on a covert strategy of using various non-state jihadi groups to wage asymmetric warfare in an attempt to liberate the remainder of Kashmir from Indian rule, and enhance Pakistan's ability to inflict harm on its much larger and better equipped neighbour (Blom 2009). This support and subsequent withdrawal of state assistance to militant proxies following the 9/11 attacks in 2001 served to drive some terror groups underground, cultivate jihadi culture and violence throughout the northern and western parts of the country, and turn a generation of jihadi ideologues against the Pakistani state.

Following the successful use of jihadi Mujahideen proxies against the Soviets in Afghanistan in the 1980s, it was perhaps logical that Pakistan would decide to adopt a similar strategy against India in Kashmir. Covertly supporting non-state groups through financing, training, and recruitment presented a relatively cheap way of balancing against India's greater numerical strength and armed forces. The preexistence of a popular mood of discontentment with Indian rule among large segments of the Kashmiri population in the late 1980s, accompanied by mass demonstrations by pro-Pakistan Kashmiri youth, allowed Pakistani intelligence to infiltrate Indian Kashmir with a large number of proxy jihadi groups (Chalk 2001). By the late-1990s and early 2000s, Pakistan was supporting four main jihadi organisations in Kashmir through the operation of almost a hundred training camps inside its territory: Jaish-e-Muhammad (JeM), Lashakr-e-Taiba (LeT), Hakat-ul-Mujahideen (HuM), and Hizbul Mujahideen (HM). Of these, JeM and LeT are currently still active, although they no longer enjoy assistance from the Pakistani state.

After the 2001 9/11 attacks, Pakistan was induced to support the US-led Operation Enduring Freedom in Afghanistan and join its wider global coalition against terrorism, putting enormous pressure on Pakistan's covert support of terrorist proxies in Kashmir. Pakistan's then president General Pervez Musharraf withdrew state assistance from the Kashmiri jihadi groups following two attempts on his life in which Kashmiri militants were implicated. This sudden withdrawal of state support and subsequent crackdown served the purpose of alienating some groups and sending them underground. Some turned their attention instead to anti-US and anti-Pakistan operations in Afghanistan and the FATA regions.

Founded by former Afghanistan jihadi Maulana Masood Azhar in 2000, Jaish-e-Muhammad ('Muhammad's Army') emerged from a rebranding of the older group Harkatul Mujahideen. It follows a Salafi jihadi ideology focussed on the reunification of Kashmir and subsequent conquest of greater India and incorporation of it into an Islamic state. Although the group has been involved in some attacks against religious minorities and Westerners inside Pakistan, it mainly focusses its violence against the people of predominantly Hindu India. JeM was responsible for the daring attack on the Indian parliament in New Delhi in 2001, which led to an armed standoff between India and Pakistan lasting almost one year. As well as being briefly supported by Pakistani intelligence after its creation, JeM reportedly also had close links with, and received financial support from, Al Qaeda. The group lost Pakistani state support and was banned in 2002 following its designation as a terrorist organisation by the US State Department the previous year. It has subsequently rebranded and changed its name numerous times, most recently posing as a charity (Al-Rehmat Trust). Masood Azar, the group's founder and prominent Deobandi scholar, has seemingly continued to enjoy the protection of Pakistani state. In 2017, for instance, Pakistan convinced China to prevent the United Nations Security Council from listing Mr. Masood Azhar as a globally designated terrorist; a decision that raised eyebrows amongst the international community (Aneja 2017).

Lashkar-e Taiba ('The Army of the Pure') was founded in 1987 as the military wing of Markaz Dawa al Irshad, an ultraconservative Muslim proselytising organisation. LeT's goal is the establishment of an independent Islamic Kashmir, as well as the wider liberation of Indian Muslims from what it perceives as repressive Indian Hindu rule. The group was designated a terrorist organisation by the US in 2001, and it was similarly designated and banned by Pakistan the following year. Subsequently, the group has renamed (Pasban-e-Ahle Hadith), and later divided into the ostensibly political Jamaat-ud-Dawa (JuD) and militant LeT. Both the JuD and LeT were designated as terrorist groups by the Pakistani state in late 2008 following LeT's week long devastating siege of a series of prominent locations in Mumbai in which 168 people were killed.

Although banned and apparently no longer receiving Pakistan state support, LeT remains operational and commands a network of branches and cells across the country. The group is now believed to be led by Zakiur Rehman Lakhvi. It has been accused of receiving funding through donations from religious organisations throughout Pakistan and the Arab Gulf states. Although never formally aligned with Al Qaeda, links between the groups' leaders do exist and LeT operatives have apparently been sent to international sites of jihadi conflict in the Balkans, Caucuses, and Southeast Asia (Rana 2010).

Mr. Hafez Mohammad Saeed, an internationally designated terrorist and former head of the LeT, has remained protected by the Pakistani state. Saeed, who is often accused of masterminding the 2008 Mumbai attack and has had a US$10 million bounty placed on him by the US, has at times been put under house arrest, but never imprisoned. His organisation Jamaat-ud-Dawah has been able to continue to operate and fundraise within Pakistan under various names. In early 2018, Mr. Saeed received the backing of the Pakistani military to move into politics in order to challenge former Prime Minister Nawaz Sharif (Shahid 2018), possibly as part of an attempt to bring the group into the mainstream and away from militancy.

## Afghanistan and Central Asia

The 1979 Soviet invasion of Afghanistan created the conditions in which Pakistani intelligence supported and directed a new generation of jihadi groups throughout the Federally Administered Tribal Areas and across its border in Afghanistan. This policy of covertly sponsoring Mujahideen fighters as anti-Soviet proxies in an Afghan Jihad was actively encouraged, led and financed by both the US and Saudi Arabia. Within the context of Cold War rivalry, a covert US-led coalition of nations created and drew on an international network of ideologues and recruiters to radicalise Muslim youth against the Soviet threat and bring them to Pakistan's North-West Frontier Provence (renamed Khyber Pakhtunkhawa in 2010). This US-led coalition provided Pakistan with the funding and responsibility for the creation of an extensive infrastructure of over 1,000 madrassas and training camps in its territory that would train and educate guerrilla fighters in extremist and militant jihadi ideology (Rana 2010).

Ultimately there were seven state-sponsored jihadi groups operating within Afghanistan and being supplied and directed from inside Pakistan. Although drawing on some international recruits from the Arab world and beyond, most of the militants who were trained and equipped were Pashtuns from the Afghan-Pakistan (Af-Pak) tribal belt, some of whom would go on to form the core of the later Afghan Taliban or join or support terror groups such as Tehrik-e-Taliban Pakistan.

This explosion of state sponsored jihadism and militancy throughout the northwest of Pakistan resulted in the spread and entrenchment of violence and extremist culture within Pakistani society, as well as the empowerment of an ultraconservative and Saudi influenced Islamic clergy who have since remained a powerful force in Pakistani politics. Indigenous expressions of Islam, which were until then usually influenced by either a traditional South

Asian relaxed and pluralistic approach to religion or tribal attitudes where Islam was secondary to local culture, were challenged by a new conservative and universalist approach to Islamic faith. Popular Sufi and Barelvi Islamic cultures, as well as traditional *Pashtunwali* codes among the Pashtun, were challenged and in some cases replaced by this new militant, supremacist and ultraconservative approach to religion, leading to a rise of sectarian hostility and violence in the country (Haider 2011).

International sponsorship of militant jihadism in northwest Pakistan and Afghanistan came to an abrupt stop when the Soviets withdrew from the country in 1989. Although the funds supporting the Afghan jihadis and their Pakistani masters dried up overnight, there was no effort by Pakistan or the wider international community to address the worsening jihadism growing through the region until after the 2001 9/11 attacks and subsequent US-led invasion of Afghanistan in pursuit of Al Qaeda and their Taliban protectors. In 2004, Pakistan deployed its armed forces into FATA – the first time since British rule that the state had sent troops into the region. The aim of the campaign was to find and destroy Al Qaeda forces taking refuge in the Waziristan region. Resistance by AQ fighters and their Central Asian allies such as the Islamic Movement of Uzbekistan (IMU), as well as local Taliban, resulted in the creation of a host of new militant terrorist organisations whose primary enemy was the Pakistani state. By 2008, AQ and IMU militants had banded together with a loose collection of other foreign fighter jihadis as well as local Pashtun communities who resented the presence of NATO forces in Afghanistan and Pakistani troops in FATA to form an umbrella Taliban organisation the Tehrik-e-Taliban Pakistan (TTP).

Tehrik-e-Taliban Pakistan ('Taliban Movement of Pakistan') was formed in December 2007 when a dozen or so militant groups and organisations coalesced in opposition to coalition forces in Afghanistan and the Pakistani presence in FATA. They did so under the charismatic leadership of Baitullah Mehsud, who was later killed in a US drone strike in 2009. The group initially served two strategic functions: to liberate Afghanistan from foreign occupation and establish an Islamist Taliban state in South Asia, and to create a collective of militant organisations who could effectively defeat the Pakistani armed forces and monopolise the licit and illicit economy of the Af-Pak borderlands. The group was not adverse to violently opposing and exterminating other militant organisations who either refused to join them or were unwilling to attack Pakistani targets (Gunaratna and Iqbal 2010).

The TTP operates through a *shura* council representing the major groups and affiliates operating under its umbrella. Unlike the Afghan Taliban who are solely concerned with the establishment of a Taliban state in Afghanistan, the TTP follow a global Salafi Jihadist agenda in which the establishment of an Islamic state across South Asia will be a precursor to wider global conquest. The group is linked with AQ through its ideology, membership, and finances, and gains further revenue through a host of organised crime and smuggling operations throughout Pakistan and beyond. The TTP is currently led by Hakimullah Mehsud, and is probably the most active, networked, and well-organised terrorist group operating within Pakistan. It is well known and feared for its attacks against Pakistani security forces within FATA, civilian communities who refuse to support it, and its indiscriminate use of suicide bombing terror tactics.

TTP's presence in the Af-Pak borderlands has complicated Pakistan's strategy of sometimes supporting the Afghan Taliban and Haqqani Network in order to wield leverage in Afghanistan and to counter India's ambitions in the reconstruction of the nation. This has led to the informal use of terminology in the past such as the 'good' and 'bad' Taliban in Pakistan, with the 'good' being those who operate uniquely within Afghanistan and the 'bad' being the TTP who wage unconventional warfare against the Pakistani state and populous. This has created tensions in Pakistan's relationship with the international community, especially the US, which have accused the country of adopting a double standard in its relationship to Afghan terror groups.

Indeed, in early 2018 Pakistan and the US appeared to be rethinking and possibly ending their close post-9/11 alliance over concerns on both sides about the effects of the other's counter terrorism operations within Afghanistan and Pakistan. President Trump bluntly tweeted his resentment on New Year's Day 2018, stating that the US had 'foolishly' spent over $33 billion in aid in Pakistan in the last 15 years and had received only 'lies & deceit' in return (Gannon 2018). Trump signaled his wish to end almost all security aid to the country until such time as Pakistan demonstrated its commitment to fight all terrorist groups operating in the region (Iqbal 2018). More widely, and perhaps in the long-term more worryingly for Pakistan, in September 2017 the BRICS countries (China, Russia, India, Brazil and South Africa) singled out Pakistani-backed militant groups such as the Afghan Taliban, the Haqqani network, and LeT as regional security threats in a joint statement at the close of the Ninth BRICS summit in Xiamen, China (Xinhua 2017). Pakistan's Defence Minister subsequently fiercely rejected this statement.

### Baluchistan and Iran

Baluchistan occupies a strategically important and resource rich region in Pakistan's southwest roughly the size of Turkey and bordering Iran and Afghanistan. The province is largely desert and is sparsely populated by ethnic Baluch or Pashtun peoples who make up nearly 80% of the population. Baluch society is traditionally organised along tribal lines and based on a feudal agricultural economy. Some of the ethnic insurgent groups such as the Lashkar-e-Baluchistan (LeB) operate as enforcement for the leaders (*sardars*) of powerful tribes in the perennial jostling for advantage in local politics and tribal competition for resources. Baluch ethnic identity and culture is shared between the Pakistani province and the large Baluch population across the border in the Iranian state of Sistan and Baluchistan, as well as in parts of Afghanistan.

Baluchistan is a restive and remote region that provides strategic depth and shelter for the Afghan Taliban as well as opportunities for cross-border drug smuggling between Afghanistan, Pakistan, Iran, and the Indian Ocean. As well as being a politically important region bordering Iran and Afghanistan, the region has recently taken on heightened economic and strategic importance for China. Since 2016, Pakistan's relations with China have massively expanded, with the creation of the $50 Billion China–Pakistan Economic Corridor (CPEC) through the mountainous Karakoram–Xinjiang region. Baluchistan is rapidly becoming a vital node that sustains China's Belt and Road initiative through the newly constructed port of Gwadar linking western China with the Indian Ocean and Persian Gulf.

Militant groups in Baluchistan can be divided between nationalist separatists and Islamist jihadists, with Pakistani intelligence at times allegedly supporting Islamic groups against the nationalists in order to drive a wedge between the Baluch factions (Dorsey 2018). Prominent ethno-nationalist groups include the Baluch Republican Army (BRA) and Baluch Liberation Army (BLA), both of whom agitate for Baluch self-determination or at least greater representation in Islamabad. Both draw advantage from operating in part out of neighbouring Afghan territory. Other groups such as the Baluchistan Liberation United Front (BULF), and the Baluchistan Liberation Front (BLF), are smaller and promote separatist aspirations.

Baluchistan's nationalist groups have a reputation for conducting irregular and *ad hoc* acts of violence against Pakistani military cadets, lawyers and the judiciary in the state capital Quetta, non-Baluch living and working in the state, tourists, foreign companies, and – most recently – Chinese nationals involved in the rapidly growing Chinese investment projects that traverse the province.

It has been argued that militant groups in the region have been engaged by third parties such as the US and Saudi Arabia to participate in proxy conflicts in Iran (Dorsey 2018). Pakistan has claimed that India covertly supports some Baluch militants and separatists as a way of countering Pakistan's promotion of jihadist militants in Kashmir. Islamabad used the capturing of an Indian Naval commander and alleged spy, Kulbhushan Jadhav, in Baluchistan in 2016 as evidence that Indian intelligence (Research and Analysis Wing—RAW) has been covertly supporting separatist terrorism in the state by Baluch and TeT forces, possibly through the intermediary of Afghan intelligence (Chandran 2018).

China in particular seeks stability in Baluchistan in order to ensure its significant investment and strategic interest in the transshipment corridor between the warm-water port and its landlocked Central Asian provinces. Recently, however, this stability has been undermined, with Baluch militants targeting Chinese businesses, professionals, and non-Baluch workers on Chinese investment and infrastructure programs. Although Pakistan has created a special 15,000 strong military unit designed to protect the thousands of Chinese currently working in the country, this has not prevented kidnappings and acts of sabotage and violence. In mid-2017, for example, gunmen from the militant BLA fired on non-Baluch construction workers at Gwadar port. The attack raised concerns regarding growing resentment among Baluch tribesmen regarding access to the economic benefits of China's investment (Shah 2017).

Baluchi nationalist groups have stated their intention to thwart Chinese investment in the state, with BLA spokesman Jeander Baloch recently stating: 'This conspiratorial plan [CPEC] is not acceptable to the Baloch people under any circumstances. Baloch independence movements have made it clear several times that they will not abandon their people's future in the name of development projects or even democracy' (*News Pakistan* 2017). In December 2017 in response to these threats, China released an unprecedented warning for its nationals to be alert in the face of 'imminent' terrorist attacks on Chinese targets in Baluchistan and the rest of Pakistan (Reuters 2017).

Sipah-i-Sahaba Pakistan (SeS – 'Guardians of the Prophet's Companions') is an anti-Shiite and anti-Iranian group, and sometime political party, which operates inside Baluchistan and throughout wider Pakistan. It is neither ethnically Baluch nor involved in ethno-nationalist separatism, but is instead focussed on a Deobandi anti-Shiite and anti-Iranian agenda. SeS is one of Pakistan's most longstanding groups, having been founded in 1985 in part in response to the fear of a nationalist Shiite uprising among Pakistan's significant Shiite minority (20% of the population) following the 1979 Iranian revolution and attempt to export Shiite militancy abroad. SeS was banned in Pakistan in 2002 and again in 2012 as a terrorist organisation, and has now rebranded as Ahl-e-Sunnat Wal Jamaat.

In the past SeS has allegedly at times been backed by Pakistan intelligence and foreign powers as part of an anti-Shiite and anti-Iranian strategy. It, and subsidiary groups such as Lashkar-e-Jhangvi (LeJ), have also been alleged to enjoy local government and police protection (Dorsey 2017b). SeS offshoots and cells Lashkar-e-Jhangvi ('The Army of Jhangvi'), Jundallah ('Soldiers of God'), and Jaish al-Adl ('Army of Justice') have engaged in numerous terrorist campaigns in Baluchistan along the Iranian border as well as inside Iran. Groups such as Lashkar-e-Jhangvi also apparently cooperated with elements of the Islamic State (IS) to conduct a series of attacks against civilian, police, and Sufi religious targets in 2016.

In 2005, Jundallah executed a failed assassination attempt against Iranian President Mahmoud Ahmadinejad, and bombed an Iranian Royal Guard bus. Police and army patrols, border posts, conveys, and Shiite mosques and religious shrines have all been attacked. SeS also operates religious seminaries in Baluchistan in which its strict *Deobandi* philosophy is taught and – possibly – militants are trained (Dorsey 2017b). Iran has engaged in robust counter terrorism operations against militants adjacent to the Pakistani border whose actions lead to periodic tensions between the two countries. In May 2017, the leader of Iran's defence forces delivered a warning to Pakistan stating that Iran would target terrorist instillations inside Pakistan if Islamabad did not do more to confront and control militant groups (*Dawn* 2017).

## Sectarianism and terrorism

The jihadism, militancy, and non-state violence that has been cultivated along Pakistan's borders has affected the social, religious, and political fabric of the country, exacerbating a series of simmering sectarian religious conflicts that are in part perpetuated by terror groups such as LeT, SeS, and Lashkar-e-Jhangvi (LeJ). One result of the conflicts in Kashmir, Afghanistan, and Baluchistan has been the establishment of networks of ultra-conservative madrassas that have flourished across Pakistan, filling in a gap left by an inadequate state education system. While diverse, many of these madrassas offer a harsh and austere interpretation of Islam that provides an avenue for everyday Pakistanis to reconcile Islam with the pressures of modernity, and perhaps console them for a loss of confidence in weak and uneven economic development, venal politics, and corrupt secular leadership.

Pakistan occupies a challenging human terrain. Although the country is Muslim majority (with about a 10% Hindu minority, as well as smaller communities of Christians), it is divided along Sunni/Shiite lines. It has the world's largest Shiite minority who make up a little less than a quarter of the country's population and attract suspicion in some quarters of being potential proxies for Shiite Iran next door. Non-Shiite Islam is divided between traditional tolerant and pluralistic expressions such as the Barelvi and wider Sufi traditions that condone the visiting of shrines that are often the graves of holy figures, and participating in religious dance and music – particularly Sufi devotional songs that induce religious trance and ecstasy – and the much more conservative Deobandi sect. Deobandism is an anti-Shiite and anti-Western movement that was developed in north India in the late 19th century as a response to the dislocation that European dominion over the subcontinent caused, and today forms the ideological basis of many of the jihadist groups operating in the country.

Although conservative and sectarian forms of Islam such as Salafism, Wahabbism, and Deobandism do not always or necessarily explicitly support or condone active and violent jihadism, many expressions do so, while others turn a blind eye. Recently, this environment of ultraconservative religious militancy has attracted an affinity with the similar and related ideology of the so-called Islamic State, for instance in proclaiming Shiites to be non-Muslims and thus liable to be killed in jihad. In early 2017, for example, TeT and IS allied to attack a Sufi shrine in southern Punjab that killed 83 devotional worshippers, as well as targeted military and police stations and the Punjabi state parliament building. Many attacks on Sufi or Shiite religious places and communities have been orchestrated by alliances between the LeJ, TTP, SeS and either AQ or, more recently, IS.

The steady rise of religious conservatism and jihadism drawn from Deobandi and Arab Wahabbist influences is distrustful of civil society, Shiite or other religious minorities, festivals, music, and dancing. Its spread over the 20 years since the end of the state supported jihad in Afghanistan (and later

Kashmir) has coincided with a rise of sectarian violence and intolerant laws such as harsh blasphemy laws in which allegedly irreligious individuals are sometimes put to death by religiously or politically motivated mobs – but that have also been used to silence dissident voices (Waseem 2017). In general, parts of Pakistan, outside the elite sophisticated and cosmopolitan social bubbles found in Islamabad and Lahore, remain a violent society. In some places, local tribal councils (*jirgas*) retain significant authority and preside over a retributive justice system that at times still draws on honour killings, feuds, and gang rapes. It is worth noting and remembering in any account of the dangers of Pakistani terrorism that almost certainly many more Pakistani women are murdered at the hands of their families during honour killings or because they are accused of 'immoral' behaviour than Pakistanis are killed by terrorism.

Complicating this rise of sectarianism and violence is Pakistan's role as a major arena in predominantly Sunni Saudi Arabia and predominantly Shiite Iran's decades-long proxy conflict, which has partly been played out along Sunni/Shiite sectarian lines. Saudi Arabia has spent billions of dollars promoting ultra-conservative organisations in Pakistan that, while not sharing the official Wahabbism of the Saudi kingdom, are equally intolerant, puritanical, and supremacist. Whether this massive investment in Saudi exported cultural diplomacy continues in the context of the current crown prince Muhammad bin Salman's apparent determination to overhaul Saudi Arabia's close relationship with extremist Wahabbism and move towards a moderate religious identity remains to be seen. Certainly, it has been argued that, in the past, Pakistani military and intelligence have cooperated with Saudi Arabia to promote and facilitate militant sectarian organisations who target non-Sunni minorities such as Sufis, Shiites, Ahmadis, Christians, and Hindus (Dorsey 2017a). In return, Shiite terror groups have operated in Pakistan, for instance the Sipah-e-Muhammad ('Army of Muhammad') is widely believed to have been covertly sponsored by Iran.

A desire to support Saudi Arabia and use ultra-conservative militant organisations domestically to control the political aspirations of the Shiite minority, has been balanced by a concern by Pakistan not to be seen as being too closely aligned with its ultra-conservative ally for fear of setting off much wider sectarian religious violence at home. Pakistan, for instance, surprised Saudi Arabia by initially declining to join its war against Shiite rebels in Yemen in 2015. It also showed concern in 2017 about appointing its former top general, Raheel Sharif, as head of a Saudi-led 'Islamic Military Alliance to Fight Terrorism', consisting of over 40 states, and considered by some as being primarily aimed at containing Shiite Iran (*Al Arabiya English* 2017).

## Conclusion

A profound obsession with and fear of Indian aggression and encirclement among the military and intelligence communities has led to the periodic support of violent groups and actors in neighbouring Kashmir and Afghanistan.

While Pakistan has made concerted efforts at rooting out analogous groups operating within its territory, particularly through its military interventions in FATA, the state still provides protection to some key violent extremist figures.

The growing affinity amongst civilian and military communities with extreme, conservative, and exclusivist forms of Islam that sometimes tacitly support violence is an issue that drives violent extremist activity throughout the country. Extremist forms of Islam do not necessarily support or condone violence, or create terrorist actors. However, exclusivist religious groups that follow a supremacist worldview and accept the legitimacy of externalised violence have created an environment in which sectarianism and religious violence have grown.

Finally, despite successful counter terrorism operations by the Pakistani state against groups such as Tehrik-e-Taliban Pakistan, some extremist organisations operating within the country allegedly continue to be supported by both international and domestic actors. In places, the boundary between violent non-state groups and local political actors remains hazy. Overall, this means that the Pakistani state remains highly vulnerable to the corrosive effects of violent extremism, not least its ability to threaten Pakistan's relations with important allies and investors such as the US and China.

## References

*Al Aribya English* (2017), 'Pakistan Opposition Fury over Ex-army Chief role in Saudi-led Military Alliance', *Al Aribya English*, 27 March, available at https://english.alarabiya.net/en/News/gulf/2017/03/27/Pakistan-to-draw-opposition-s-fury-over-Sharif-s-new-role-in-Saudi-led-military-alliance-.html accessed 12 January 2018.

Aneja, A. (2017), 'China to Block UN Ban on Masood Azhar, Yet Again', *The Hindu*, 30 October, available at www.thehindu.com/news/international/china-to-block-un-ban-on-masood-azhar/article19949628.ece accessed 12 January 2018.

Blom, A. (2009), 'A Patron-Client Perspective on Militia-State Relations: The Case of the Hizb-ul-Mujahiden of Pakistan', in L. Gayer and C. Jafferlot, *Armed Militias of South Asia: Fundamentalists, Maoists and Separatists*, London: C. Hurst and Co.

Chalk, P. (2001), 'Pakistan's Role in the Kashmir Insurgency', *The Rand Blog*, available at www.rand.org/blog/2001/09/pakistans-role-in-the-kashmir-insurgency.html accessed 15 January 2018.

Chandran, S. (2018), 'Will Indo-Pak Relations Improve in 2018?' *Pakistan Reader*, 9 January, available at www.pakistanreader.org/ accessed 9 January 2018.

*Dawn* (2017), 'Iran Warns Will Hit "Militant Safe Havens" Inside Pakistan', *Dawn*, 8 May, available at https://www.dawn.com/news/1331829 accessed 12 January 2018.

Dorsey, J. (2017a), 'Whither the Muslim World's NATO?' *The Turbulent World of Middle East Soccer*, 21 February, available at https://mideastsoccer.blogspot.com.au/2018/01/pakistani-politics-risk-aggravating.html accessed 10 January 2018.

Dorsey, J. (2017b), 'Pakistan Caught in the Middle as China's OBOR Becomes Saudi-Iranian-Indian Battleground', *The Turbulent World of Middle East Soccer*, 5 May, available at https://mideastsoccer.blogspot.com.au/2017/05/pakistan-caught-in-middle-as-chinas.html accessed 12 January 2018.

Dorsey, J. (2018), 'Pakistani Politics Risk Aggravating Problems and Heightening Regional Tension', *The Turbulent World of Middle East Soccer*, 9 January, available at https://mideastsoccer.blogspot.com.au/2017/02/whither-muslim-worlds-nato.html accessed 10 January 2018.

Gannon, K. (2018), 'Pakistan Fires Back After "Incomprehensible" Trump Tweet', *The Washington Post*, 2 January, available at www.washingtonpost.com/world/the_americas/pakistan-summons-us-envoy-to-protest-trump-tweet/2018/01/02/ accessed 5 January 2018.

Gunaratna, R. and Iqbal, K. (2010), *Pakistan: Terrorism Ground Zero*, London: Reaktion Books.

Haider, Z. (2011), 'Ideologically Adrift', in M. Lodhi (ed.), *Pakistan: Beyond the Crisis State*, Karachi: Oxford University Press, 113–130.

Iqbal, A. (2018), 'America Suspends Entire Security Aid to Pakistan', *Dawn*, 5 January, available at https://epaper.dawn.com/DetailImage.php?StoryImage=05_01_2018_001_005 accessed 8 January 2018.

*News Pakistan* (2017), 'Gunmen Kill 10 Labourers in Balochistan's Gwadar', *News Pakistan*, 13 May, available at https://www.aljazeera.com/news/2017/05/gunmen-kill-10-labourers-balochistan-gwadar-170513111330168.html accessed 20 January 2018.

Rana, M. (2010), 'Evolution of Militant Groups in FATA and Adjacent Areas', in M. Rana, S. Sial, and A. Basit (eds.), *Dynamics of Taliban Insurgency in FATA*, Islamabad: Pak Institute for Peace Studies, 37–58.

*Reuters* (2017), 'CPEC's Chinese Workers in Pakistan may be Targeted by Terrorists, Chinese Embassy Warns', *Zee News*, 8 December, available at http://zeenews.india.com/world/cpecs-chinese-in-pakistan-could-be-targeted-in-terror-strikes-china-embassy-warns-2064237.html accessed 20 January 2018.

Shah, S. (2017), '10 Labourers Killed in Gwadar as Unidentified Assailants Open Fire at Construction Site', *Dawn*, 13 May, available at www.dawn.com/news/1332896 accessed 12 January 2018.

Shahid, K. (2018), 'Terror Chief Saeed Plans to Run against Nawaz Sharif in Election', *Asia Times*, 4 January, available at www.atimes.com/article/terror-chief-saeed-plans-run-nawaz-sharif-poll/ accessed 5 January 2018.

Waseem, M. (2017), 'Who Killed Mashal Khan?' *The News: International*, 30 April, available at www.thenews.com.pk/print/201590-Who-killed-Mashal-Khan accessed 9 January 2018.

Xinhua (2017), 'Full Text of Xiamen Declaration of BRICS Leaders', *China Daily*, 5 September, available at www.chinadailyasia.com/articles/44/150/109/1504582539856.html accessed 9 January 2018.

# 7 The internationalisation of the Central Asian terrorist threat

*Nodirbek Soliev*

## Introduction

The coordinated suicide attacks carried out by a Chechen-led terrorist cell of the self-styled Islamic State (IS) at Istanbul's Ataturk International Airport in June 2016 marked a major turning point in the evolution of Central Asia's terrorism as an international threat. This act of violence, with 45 deaths and 230 injuries, was the first time that individuals from Central Asia, specifically the citizens of Kyrgyzstan and Tajikistan, were implicated in an attack on Western soil (Podolskaya 2016). Subsequently, there has been an unprecedented surge in terrorist attacks committed by Central Asians across big cities in Eurasia and North America, including Bishkek, Istanbul, Stockholm, Saint Petersburg and New York. Prior to these attacks, the threat from Central Asian militants was largely regional and no attack had been carried out by them beyond Central and South Asia, as they had been fighting for survival in neighbouring Afghanistan and Pakistan for the past two decades.

An interaction of a range of internal and external factors has contributed to the emergence and persistence of terrorism in Central Asia since the 1990s. Internal factors have included a surge in Islamic revivalism that took place against the backdrop of the ideological and security vacuum left by the collapse of the Soviet Union and its totalitarian communist ideology in 1991; a struggle for power between the secular mainstream majority and Islamist fundamentalist elements; post-independence hardships such as a rapid economic downturn and high unemployment, among others. The external factors consist of the protracted war in Afghanistan and its cross-border implications on Central Asia; the rise of the Taliban and Al Qaeda in the Afghan armed conflict and the subsequent transnational expansion of terrorist networks and extremist ideologies; and geopolitical rivalry among regional and major powers involving Russia, the US, Turkey, Pakistan, Saudi Arabia and Iran.

However, none of the factors in this incomplete list would offer a full and adequate understanding of the recent international expansion of terrorist activities related to Central Asian individuals. As it has been observed, even though the perpetrators were Central Asians, none of the attacks listed above were planned, prepared or executed from Central Asia directly. On the contrary, it appears that the attackers had left their homelands several years prior to the attacks and had mostly been radicalised, recruited and militarised elsewhere. For instance, the suspected perpetrators behind the April 2017 Saint Petersburg metro bombing were naturalised Russian citizens born in Kyrgyzstan. The October 2017 vehicular attack in New York was carried out by a legal permanent resident who immigrated to the US from Uzbekistan on a diversity visa in 2010. However, they did not show any obvious signs of extremism in their countries of origin. It also should be noted that militant groups presently have no visible foothold in much of Central Asia, and the threat of terrorism has been considerably reduced in the region since the mid-2000s.

This chapter argues that an interplay of three major factors has played a crucial role in the internationalisation of the Central Asian terrorist threat. First and foremost has been the emergence of the Middle East as a new incubator for transnational jihadism. Empirical evidence suggests that, like many other regions of the world, the current evolution of Central Asian terrorism is consistent with the IS and Al Qaeda phenomenon. Indeed, the perpetrators of the attacks, except for the self-radicalised individual who become inspired by IS ideology to carry out the New York vehicular attack, were operating under the direct order and guidance of either IS or Al Qaeda senior operatives based in the Middle East.

The second factor is increased economic migration and its associated vulnerabilities. The recent attacks have been a reflection of increasing cases of radicalisation amongst the Central Asian diaspora and migrant communities abroad. For instance, more than 80 percent of nearly 1,300 Tajik nationals who travelled to the Middle East to fight were radicalised and recruited while working in Russia as foreign labourers (Burskaya 2016).

The third factor is the advancement of digital media technologies and communications as a critical enabler of terrorism. Almost all of the attacks listed above involved the use of encrypted messaging applications particularly Telegram as a safe platform in the communication and coordination between the masterminds, mediators and perpetrators.

In an effort to bring a wider perspective and contribute to long-term solutions, this chapter seeks to examine the process of the internationalisation of Central Asian terrorism within the changing context of global terrorism. The chapter provides a summary of six attacks and, through comparative analysis of empirical data, identifies key nuances and common patterns in the processes of radicalisation, recruitment and operational preparation and execution of the attacks.

After briefly discussing the contemporary dynamics of terrorist threats inside Central Asia, it maps out Central Asian militant groups in the Middle East and evaluates their linkages to and role in the IS and Al Qaeda transnational networks. By conducting content analysis of relevant propaganda statements and extremist materials in Uzbek and Russian, the chapter further examines strategic objectives and propaganda tactics of IS, Al Qaeda and their Central Asian affiliates. It then explains the impact of the evolution of social media and encrypted communication platforms on the nature of radicalisation and the terrorist threat that has been linked to Central Asians at home and abroad. Finally, the chapter concludes by presenting an assessment of future trajectories.

## Mobilisation of Central Asians for terrorism at home and abroad

Since 2016, there were at least six instances of international attacks attributed to individuals of Central Asian origin. These attacks included the coordinated suicide attacks at Ataturk International Airport in Istanbul (Turkey) in June 2016, the suicide car bomb attack at the Chinese embassy in Bishkek (Kyrgyzstan) in August 2016, the Reina nightclub shooting in Istanbul (Turkey) in January 2017, the truck-ramming attack in Stockholm (Sweden) in April 2017, the suicide bombing at metro station in Saint Petersburg (Russia) in April 2017 and the vehicular attack in New York in October 2017. This section offers brief profiles of each of the six attacks in order to lay the foundation for understanding the dynamics that shape the current terrorist threat that is linked to Central Asia.

## The attacks

### *Istanbul airport attack*

On 28 June 2016, a semi-autonomous clandestine IS cell that comprised of Russian, Kyrgyz and Tajik nationals attacked the Ataturk international airport of Istanbul (Podolskaya 2016). The coordinated suicide assaults, with at least 44 deaths and 238 injuries, heralded the beginning of a new era in the terrorist threat linked to Central Asia, as it was the first time that Central Asian individuals were mobilised by the international terrorist group to carry out an attack on Western soil, as the airport is located on the European side of the city (Soliev 2017a, 27). The cell was operating under the command and coordination of Akhmed Chataev, a Russian citizen of Chechen origin, who was alleged to be a key IS figure in Turkey. However, neither the media nor authorities in Turkey and Central Asia has provided further details about the Kyrgyz and Tajik attackers. Thus, possible motives of these individuals and their path to terrorism remain largely unclear. In spite of the Turkish government's accusations, IS did not claim responsibility for the attack.

### *Chinese Embassy bombing in Bishkek*

On 30 August 2016, a suicide bomber driving a minivan loaded with 100 kilograms of TNT attacked the Chinese embassy in the Kyrgyz capital of Bishkek, killing himself and wounding six others. Kyrgyz security authorities revealed that the attack was a joint operation between the Turkistan Islamic Party (TIP) and Kateeba Tawhid wal Jihad (KTJ) operatives coming from

Kyrgyzstan, Turkey, Syria, and allegedly Tajikistan (Putz 2017). The perpetrators arrived in Bishkek from Turkey with fake passports not long before the attack and managed to flee undetected. It was also believed that al Nusra Front (now Hayat Tahrir Al-Sham), Al Qaeda's former affiliate in Syria, authorised and financed the attack (Interfax 2016). However, there has been no claim of responsibility for the bombing by any of these terrorist groups.

## Istanbul nightclub massacre

On 1 January 2017, a lone gunman launched a massive shootout in Istanbul's famous Reina nightclub and killed 39 revellers as well as injured 70 others who were celebrating the New Year. The attacker was identified as an IS militant named Abdulqodir Masharipov (also known by his nom de guerre, Abu Mohammed Khorasani) from Uzbekistan who migrated to Afghanistan to join the Islamic Movement of Uzbekistan (IMU), a former Al Qaeda-linked terrorist group, in 2011. At the time of the attack, Masharipov was wanted by the national police in Uzbekistan. However, it is unclear when exactly and under which circumstances he became radical. During the investigations, the Turkish police established that in 2015, Masharipov had moved from Afghanistan to Iran where he joined IS. At some later point, he was detained by Iranian authorities for carrying a fake passport but released after a month (*Sözcü Gazetesi* 2017). The Reina nightclub shooting was the first time that IS publicly acknowledged its involvement in a mass-casualty terrorist attack in Turkey.

## Stockholm truck attack

On 7 April 2017, a hijacked beer delivery truck was rammed into a crowd of people in a pedestrian shopping street in Stockholm, the capital of Sweden, killing four people and injuring 15 others (Ringstrom and Hellstrom 2017). Soon after, the Swedish police captured the perpetrator, a 39-year-old Uzbek named Rakhmat Akilov. There was a suitcase filled with unexploded homemade explosives in the truck. Swedish authorities revealed that Akilov had resided in Sweden in 2014 and applied for permanent residency but the request was denied as his applications were found to be a 'hoax' (Glaser 2018: 22). In December 2016, Sweden's Migration Agency gave him four weeks to leave the country. However, Akilov disregarded a deportation order and went into hiding to avoid the deportation. In February 2017, Swedish police had put him on a wanted list for failing to comply with a deportation order. But they seemed to have considered him not to be a potential security threat (BBC 2017).

According to an unnamed law enforcement official in Uzbekistan, Akilov came under the ideological influence of the IS Tajik cell operating in Syria while he was living in Sweden. In 2015, he was captured at the Turkish–Syrian border on his way to Syria to join IS and immediately deported back to Sweden (Interfax 2017). Although Akilov acknowledged that he was acting on the behalf of IS, the jihadist group never claimed responsibility for the attack. Analysts believe that the IS leadership chose to stay silent on attacks, if perpetrators were captured alive, as was the case in Stockholm, otherwise the militant group would rush to claim responsibility (Chan 2017).

### *Saint Petersburg metro bombing*

On 25 April 2017, a suicide attacker supported and directed by a cell led by Akram Azimov and his younger brother Abror Azimov detonated a bomb at a subway system in Russia's Saint Petersburg. The Azimov brothers are ethnic Uzbeks from southern Kyrgyzstan who obtained Russian citizenship several years ago. Soon after the bombing, a previously unknown militant group which called itself Kateeba al-Imam Shamil (The Imam Shamil Battalion) claimed responsibility for the attack that killed at least 17 people and injured 50 others. The militant group claimed that its 'heroic soldier' had carried out the attack 'on the orders' of Al Qaeda's leader Ayman al Zawahiri in 'revenge for Russia's interference' in Syria. The Saint Petersburg metro bombing represented the first time that a militant group had conducted an attack in Russia based on Al Qaeda's direct order. Previously, it had been more common for Chechen and Dagestani militants from the restive North Caucasus to take responsibility for such attacks. It is also significant that foreign-born individuals from Central Asia were the perpetrators of this bombing (Soliev 2018).

### *New York City truck attack*

On 31 October 2017, a 29-year old Uzbek national named Sayfullo Saipov drove a rented pickup truck into a crowded bike path in Lower Manhattan, New York City. The attacker killed eight cyclists and runners and injured 11 others before being shot and captured by police. Saipov reportedly came to the US in 2010 under the diversity lottery program and settled in Florida, before moving to New Jersey. Saipov left a note at the scene of the attack indicating his allegiance to the IS leader, Abu Bakr al-Baghdadi.

## Misconceptions and the dimensions of the threat

The above attacks have kindled heated debates in the media and amongst counter-terrorism experts about the possible drivers pushing Central Asians to engage in violence in foreign countries. Some analysts came to assume that these attacks were the direct consequence of the growing radicalisation inside Central Asia, by portraying the region as a 'terrorist breeding ground' (Dalton, 2017), a 'ripe recruiting territory' (Hille 2017), or an area with 'significant militant Salafism' (Sonmez 2017: 15–17). However, attempts to explain the issue by solely focusing on the origin of the attackers and labelling it to be a Central Asian problem oversimplifies a complex situation.

The analysis of the above attacks indicates that the current Central Asian terrorism is developing in two distinct dimensions. The first dimension includes attacks carried out by full-time operatives of IS and Al Qaeda affiliates fighting in Syria and Iraq. The incidents in Turkey and Kyrgyzstan exemplified such attacks. While some of these individuals became indoctrinated and recruited by a terrorist group during their stay in foreign countries, there have been cases where Central Asians travelled to the conflict zones directly from their home countries, as was the case in the Reina nightclub attack.

The other dimension comprises of attacks carried out by individuals belonging to Central Asian foreign diaspora and migrant communities who underwent the process of radicalisation in the destination countries. For instance, the perpetrators of the Stockholm, Saint Petersburg and New York attacks had emigrated from their home countries several years ago and were exposed to radical ideologies elsewhere.

Regardless of which of the two categories they belong to, all relevant attacks had connections to either Al Qaeda or IS in the Middle East in one way or another. Looking at the phenomenon only through the prism of Central Asian linkages would contrast with the reality that terrorism has long been in decline inside Central Asia. Such a description would also omit the domestic context in the host societies outside of Central Asia in evaluating what might have fostered the radicalisation of foreign diaspora communities.

## Terrorism in decline inside Central Asia

Central Asia is one of the two Sunni Muslim areas – the other is Pakistan – that share a long common border with war-torn Afghanistan. For decades, the countries of the region, namely Kazakhstan, Kyrgyzstan, Tajikistan, Turkmenistan, and Uzbekistan, have been affected by the protracted Afghan conflict. Islamist militancy in Central Asia evolved and reached its peak during the Tajik civil war (1992–1997) and the reign of the Taliban in neighbouring Afghanistan (1996–2001). Militant incursions of the IMU from Afghanistan into Tajikistan and Kyrgyzstan in 1999 and 2000 were the most serious security challenge that the region experienced from Islamist militants so far. Aside from that, a handful of Central Asians, together with Uyghur fighters from China, took part in the Chechen insurgency against the Kremlin rule in Russia's Northern Caucasus in 1990s.

It is worth noting that there have also been cases in the past where individuals linked to Central Asian terrorist groups were arrested in Germany and the United States. Notably, in September 2007, the German police successfully thwarted a series of bomb attacks by a terrorist cell affiliated to the Islamic Jihad Union (IJU), an Al Qaeda-linked Central Asian jihadist organisation, against American targets in the country. German authorities viewed the plotters, which have since become known as 'Sauerland cell', as a 'homegrown jihadist threat' as they all were German and Turkish citizens who became radicalised inside Germany (Eijkman 2014). However, no Central Asian individuals were found to have been involved in this plot.

The U.S. counterterrorism mission in Afghanistan has been successful in restricting the ërganisatiënal and ëperatiënal capabilities of Al Qaeda, Taliban and their Central Asian allies such as IMU, IJU, Jund al-Khilafah (JK), Jamaat Ansarullah (JA) and Jaishul Makhdi (JM). The sustained counterterrorism operations destroyed these militant groups' operational bases and networks of support inside Afghanistan and also killed a number of key terrorist leaders such as Juma Namangani and Takhir Yuldashev. Over the last one and a half decades, terrorist attacks in Central Asia have taken place less frequently and on a small-scale, as these militants have focused their energies on fighting for survival in Afghanistan and Pakistan.

Indeed, militant groups currently have no visible foothold in Central Asia. Over the years, the Central Asian republics designated countering terrorism and extremism as one of their top security priorities and adopted a 'zero-tolerance approach' in their military, security, and law-enforcement responses against terrorism. These efforts have resulted in the creation of a hostile environment for radicalisation and have curbed the terrorist threat domestically.

The governments have outlawed dozens of violent groups and blocked extremist websites. It is common in every republic that foreign religious organisations cannot operate legally without registering with state authorities. Thus, the people of Central Asia have limited access to radical and Salafi-jihadist preachers, extremist websites or publications in both the virtual and physical domains. However, the usage of encrypted and secure messaging by terrorists as a dissemination and communication platform in recent years has presented a new challenge in countering the virtual dimension of extremist activities.

After the civil war started in Syria in 2011, jihadist groups worldwide shifted the main focus of their activity away from neighboring Afghanistan to the Middle East. This has been another major factor for the reduction of terrorist activities inside Central Asia.

## The war in Syria and Iraq – a game changer

Armed conflicts have always been a powerful catalyst for the expansion of transnational violence (Nesser 2006: 323–324). The ongoing turmoil in the Middle East has profoundly transformed the nature and trajectory of the jihadist threat across the globe, with Central Asia being no exception. Since the outbreak of the civil war in Syria in 2011, jihadist forces led by Al Qaeda and IS have called on Sunni Muslims around the world to travel to the Middle East to support their fighting against the Syrian government, against what they often label as an 'infidel regime' (Bin Ali 2014).

In the past, Central Asian militants had largely confined their operations to Central and South Asia. However, strong sympathy toward their Sunni Muslim co-religionists and images of suffering Syrians have inspired a few thousand individuals from the region to volunteer to participate in the jihadist insurgency in the Middle East.

According to estimates from the region, more than 3,500 Central Asians, including 1,100 to 1,300 nationals of Tajikistan (ASIA-Plus 2017), 860 of Kyrgyzstan (Shamsiev 2016), 500–600 of Kazakhstan (Sidorov 2017), 500 of Uzbekistan (Sputnik-news.uz 2016) and 360 of Turkmenistan (*Sputnik-news. uz* 2016) left their homelands for Syria and Iraq.

## Central Asian fighters split between IS and Al Qaeda

In recent years, Central Asian militants in Syria and Iraq have established and organised themselves into a number of independent combat units known as *kateebat* (battalion) or *jamaat* (group) on the basis of ethnicity, kinship or language. The militant unit comprising Kazakh fighters is known as 'Kazakh Jamaat', and it was fighting alongside IS. The majority of Tajik jihadists have come together under IS as 'Tajik Jamaat'. Ethnic Uzbeks on the other hand have established Kateebat Imam Al-Bukhari (KIB)/'Imam Al-Bukhari Battalion' and Kateebat at Tawhid wal Jihad (KTJ)/'Battalion for Monotheism and Jihad'. KIB and KTJ have operated under Al Qaeda's former affiliate in Syria, al Nusra Front (now Hayat Tahrir Al-Sham) (Soliev 2016: 75).

Al Qaeda, IS and their affiliates have been key in grooming, protecting and guiding a new generation of Central Asian fighters in the Middle East. In spite of their independent status, Central Asian units have mostly depended on the support, protection and guidance of IS and al Nusra Front. Without this, these units would not be able to survive in the Middle Eastern battlefield as they have been fighting in an unfamiliar environment.

## IS' and Al Qaeda's approaches to international attacks

Decoding the broader strategy of IS and Al Qaeda and their possible vision designed specifically for Central Asia is crucial to understanding the recent rise in attacks committed by Central Asians internationally. Because the attacks appear to have more to do with the priorities of these two groups than any radical tendencies emerging from Central Asia itself, Central Asians' involvement in international terrorist activities has taken place along the lines of their operational and ideological linkages to either IS or al Nusra Front.

The analysis of recent attacks and online propaganda statements of terrorists suggests that, in spite of similarities in their ideological orientation and strategic goals, the two groups have pursued two different visions for Central Asia and their militant associates from this region. Until recently, IS and Al Qaeda separately were in pursuit of a similar goal – the recruitment and mobilisation of radical sympathisers across the world to replenish their fighting contingents in the Middle East. However, in terms of operational strategy towards Central Asia, these groups seemed to position themselves differently.

In their propaganda statements, both IS and al Nusra Front have denounced Central Asian republics among many other regions and countries including Europe, the US, Russia, Iran, and China. In reality, despite propaganda to the contrary, IS has restrained from getting involved in direct operations in Central Asia as the group's leadership has pointed out that attacking this region was not the highest priority. Unlike IS, however, al Nusra Front has placed a stronger emphasis on attacking Central Asia and Russia, but it has been reluctant to run an active terrorist campaign in other parts of the world.

The dearth of immediate interest on the side of IS in expanding its operational activities into Central Asia was apparent in a video released by Tajik fighters in January 2015. In the video, a Tajik fighter under the nom de guerre, Abu Umariyon, claimed that a group of Tajiks passed on a message to the IS leader Abu Bakr al-Baghdadi asking permission to return to Tajikistan to wage 'jihad against infidels' together with Jamaat Ansarullah (JA), a Tajik militant group fighting in Afghanistan. However, Baghdadi refused permission, telling them to wait (Ahmadi 2015).

There could be two possible explanations for this. Firstly, although all Central Asian countries have outlawed IS and cracked down on its activities, they have not participated in any international military interventions against the group in the Middle East. This might have kept Central Asia out of the direct focus of IS operations. The second reason might be related to the group's main strategic interest – to survive and maximise its share of power while fighting an active guerrilla warfare against multiple coalition forces on the ground in the Middle East. It should be noted that Baghdadi's discouragement came when IS became more focused on building the caliphate after announcing the establishment of an Islamic state in June 2014. For this to happen, the IS needed to continuously replenish and increase the number of its foot soldiers in Syria and Iraq instead of sending its fighters back to their home countries to fight.

At the time of writing in 2018, IS and IS-linked local groups have not conducted any direct operations inside Central Asia. However, the region has not fully been immune from the IS threat. For instance, Kazakhstan has been the first and only Central Asian country that saw home-grown attacks inspired by IS. The incident took place in June 2016 when a group of 27 gunmen attacked two commercial gun stores and attempted to storm a military base in the western Kazakh city of Aktobe. The attackers were inspired by the speeches of IS spokesperson and top strategist Abu Mohammad al-Adnani (deceased). 25 people, including 18 attackers, were killed and 38 others injured. The authorities established that the perpetrators were aiming to obtain heavier weapons from the military base before proceeding to target local government buildings. No group has claimed responsibility for the attack (Soliev 2017b, 61).

Unlike many other regions where IS grew rapidly, the ground realities in Central Asia are largely different. In the context of Central Asia, the threat from Al Qaeda remains more serious than the threat posed by IS. The vast majority of Central Asians who travelled to the Middle East have aligned themselves with Al Qaeda-linked militant units, mostly with al Nusra Front. These militants might have thought that it would be safer for them to align with al Nusra Front, instead of IS, as unlike IS, al Nusra Front operations have remained focused on battlefield operations in Syria and Iraq, as the group did not consider attacks outside the Middle East a top priority.

In an interview with *Al Jazeera* in May 2015, Abu Mohammad al-Julani, the top commander of al Nusra Front, stated that his group's main goal was to invade Damascus and overthrow the Bashar al-Assad regime in Syria. He claimed that the group had no intention to mount attacks in the West 'unless provoked'. 'We are only here...to fight the regime and its agents on the ground...al Nusra Front doesn't have any plans or directives to target the West. We received clear orders not to use Syria as a launching pad to attack the U.S. or Europe in order to not sabotage the true mission against the regime...' he said (*Al Jazeera* 2015).

Al Nusra Front and its Central Asian allies have so far been known to carry out two attacks outside the Middle East: the suicide car bombing at the Chinese embassy in Bishkek in 2016 and the metro bombing in Saint Petersburg in April 2017. According to the Kyrgyz police, the Bishkek bombing was a joint operation between KTJ and TIP that took place on the 'order and financial support' of al Nusra Front. However, none of these groups has claimed responsibility for the attack (Interfax 2016). In the case of the Saint Petersburg bombing, a previously unknown militant group which called itself Kateeba al-Imam Shamil ('The Imam Shamil Battalion') announced its responsibility for the attack by claiming that the attack was authorised by Al Qaeda's leader Ayman al Zawahiri in 'revenge for Russia's interference' in Syria. The separate investigations conducted by Kyrgyz and Russian security agencies revealed that the mastermind of both attacks was KTJ's leader named Abu Saloh (real name – Sirojidin Mukhtarov), an ethnic Uyghur from the southern Kyrgyz province of Osh (Solopov et al. 2017). The group pledged allegiance to al Nusra Front in September 2015, by stating that the purpose was to 'win' in what it calls a 'global battle against Islam waged by the US and Russia' (Weiss 2015).

The attacks targeting the Chinese embassy in Bishkek and public transport system in Saint Petersburg might indicate the heightened interest within al Nusra Front and its Central Asian and Uyghur allies in attacking China and Russia. This is due to Beijing's diplomatic support for the Assad regime and Russia's military involvement in the Syrian conflict. For instance, Abu Mohammad al-Julani called for reprisal attacks in Russia as a response to what he said was the 'indiscriminate killing of Sunni Muslims' (Soliev 2018). However, with attempts not to heavily engage in terrorist campaigns outside the Middle East, and by not claiming responsibility for the above attacks, the al Nusra Front militant network might have sought to project itself as an insurgent movement and not a terrorist one. In doing so, these groups were possibly hoping to avoid the full attention of the international coalition forces and thus survive longer.

## Encrypted jihad and terrorist's exploration of migrant vulnerabilities

In many respects, the benefits of the advancement of digital technologies has been immense. However, the potential risk that they have spawned cannot be dismissed. With the advent of new jihadist hotspots in the Middle East and the development of encrypted digital communication platforms, combined with the heightened interest and propaganda capabilities among terrorist groups in exploiting migrant vulnerabilities, there has been a shift in the ideological dimension of radicalisation.

The recent wave of attacks was the reflection of radicalisation within a tiny minority of Central Asian diaspora and migrant communities abroad. Radicalisation is a complex process that combines structural (socio-economic, cultural), individual (psychological) and situational/triggering factors. Engagement in violent behaviour is the end product of the radicalisation process. While radicalisation of belief does not necessarily lead to violence, radicalisation of action is always preceded by radicalisation of views (Litmanovitz et al. 2016). The drivers of radicalisation leading to acts of terrorism vary in context and time. To establish specific reasons, each case of radicalisation needs to be thoroughly studied. However, there is one reason that appears common – the ideological factor has been a very powerful driving force behind radicalisation.

The popularity of propaganda disseminated by Al Qaeda-linked Central Asian groups overshadows that of IS. Al Nusra Front-affiliated Central Asian groups, such as KIB and KTJ, have tailored whole sets of online extremist materials toward ethnic Uzbeks from Central Asia.. Since 2014, the two groups have produced more than 50 online video and audio propaganda materials in the Uzbek language. In comparison, IS has produced only a few extremist materials, mostly in Tajik.

Experts have generally refuted the assumptions proposing that the perpetrators of the recent attacks were radicalised in their host countries and that they brought the radicalisation threat from Central Asia to their countries of destination (Lemon and Heathershaw 2017). The Stockholm, Saint Petersburg and New York attackers did not show any visible signs of radicalisation in their homelands before migrating to foreign countries. On the contrary, there has been sufficient evidence to suggest that these individuals became influenced by extremist ideologies in their countries of destination (Cornell 2017).

The Internet and encrypted networking tools have provided modern terrorists with the unprecedented ability to have ubiquitous access and real-time communication with their target audiences in any part of the world. Thanks to online platforms, jihadist ideologies have easily gained traction in many contemporary Muslim societies. Likewise, some vulnerable segments within

Central Asian foreign communities living abroad could not stay fully immune from the influence of such extremist indoctrination.

Terrorist groups understand the importance of diaspora communities as important factors in producing and sustaining terrorist activities. The mobilisation of representatives of Central Asian for its international operations seemed to be a deliberate attempt by IS to recruit more volunteers by alienated Muslim diaspora communities. In this process, encrypted communication platforms have become a key facilitator on the pathway to radicalisation and in operational planning and execution of attacks.

Media reports revealed that Rakhmat Akilov was operating under the influence and guidance of the IS Tajik cell based in Syria. He used encrypted messaging applications such as Telegram and Zello to communicate with IS commanders to plan and perform the 'martyr operation'. After the attack, Uzbekistan's Foreign Minister Abdulaziz Kamilov stated that Akilov was recruited by IS after he had left Uzbekistan in 2014 and settled in Sweden (Radio Free Europe/Radio Liberty 2018). Akilov was an active Facebook user. His Facebook page carried at least two IS propaganda videos, one even showing the aftermath of the Boston marathon bombing. The evolution of the cyber dimension of extremism has greatly changed the nature of radicalisation and terrorism. The Stockholm attack was part of a larger trend. Several vehicular attacks have been carried out in Europe and the US after the rise of IS. Indeed, these attacks took place just a few months after IS called on its supporters to use vehicles to ram into pedestrians.

According to estimates that came in 2017, there were nearly 5 million Central Asians living in Russia – 2.6 million Kazakhs, 1.1 million Uzbeks, 590,000 Kyrgyz, 470,000 Tajiks and 190,000 Turkmen (Pew Research Center 2018a). Most Central Asians have become exposed to extremist ideologies in foreign countries, particularly in Russia. Studies suggest that between 80 and 90 percent of the Kyrgyz, Tajik and Uzbek nationals who went to the Middle East to fight were influenced by extremism and recruited while working as foreign labourers in Russia. This reality led a Russian news outlet *Novaya Gazeta* to describe Moscow as a 'road' to IS (Cornell 2018: 76).

In June 2017, Russian security services revealed that the cell that attacked the Saint Petersburg metro station used Telegram and WhatsApp as a platform to facilitate communication and to plot the bombing. Authorities had received 'reliable information about the use of the Telegram messenger by a suicide bomber, his accomplices and foreign curator to conceal his criminal intentions at all stages of organising and preparing a terrorist act' (Crime Russia 2017). In previous years, Russian security agencies have thwarted several terrorist plots by self-radicalised Central Asian migrants. These individuals were reportedly radicalised mostly through the Internet. In one of the latest cases, Russian security agencies arrested eight Central Asian individuals in the westernmost region of Kaliningrad for their alleged links to KTJ (TASS 2018).

The New York vehicular attack mirrored similar radicalisation and recruitment patterns common to other terrorist attacks in the West.

Reportedly, Saipov's path into radicalisation began after he moved to the US in 2010. New York Governor Andrew Cuomo emphasized that Saipov was 'radicalised domestically' (Yan and Andone 2017). It appears Saipov acted alone, having no support from any accomplices. The lone actor terrorists, as was the case with Saipov, are mostly driven by online extremist ideology. The attacks took place against a backdrop of the wide dissemination of online extremist propaganda in Uzbek that is accessible to wider Central Asian diaspora communities abroad.

Police discovered that Saipov downloaded and stored about 90 terrorist propaganda videos on his phone. These propaganda instructions appeared to have inspired him to engage in the violence. These groups are exploiting the grievances to recruit Central Asians to support global terrorist agendas. It is worth noting that in 2017, the number of Central Asian immigrants in the US was nearly 120,000, most of whom reside in New York City (Pew Research Center 2018b). Indeed, there have been multiple arrests in the US of Central Asian individuals, including Uzbek and Kazakh citizens, on terrorism charges, particularly for attempting to provide material support to terrorist groups such as the IS and IMU.

The Reina nightclub attack was carried out by a cell supported by a large network on the ground. IS reportedly mobilised more than 50 individuals and allocated US$ 500,000 to plot and carry out the attack. The network members coordinated their activities mainly via Telegram. Masharipov's path to terrorism remains largely unclear. What is known is he graduated from a university in the Uzbek town of Ferghana, at some point became radicalised, and went to Afghanistan to join IMU in 2011 (Yayla 2017).

## Looking ahead

The future trajectory of the Central Asian terrorist threat will be determined by two main factors: the ongoing armed conflicts in the Middle East and Afghanistan and the future of IS and Al Qaeda. Given the fact that the Central Asian international diaspora is expanding, radicalisation involving individuals who had come from the region remains a security concern both at home and abroad. To effectively contain the threat, it is important to establish concerted efforts within the region and with other interested countries hosting Central Asian diaspora and migrant communities.

The shift by terrorist groups from open-end to encrypted messaging tools has made their detection challenging. Governments should cooperate with the tech giants and social media providers in creating regulations that would allow the timely detection and blocking of extremist content in the cyber domain, though this will have to be done without violating the fundamental rights to information and privacy. Social media companies such as YouTube and Facebook would need to hire more staff with knowledge of Central Asian languages, as they could help filter and block terrorist content in those languages.

The attacks in Istanbul and Stockholm have shown that there is a need for coherent intelligence-sharing arrangements and closer cooperation between both state and international non-governmental organisations, such as Interpol, in charge of countering terrorism. The absence of effective intelligence-sharing resulted in the Stockholm attack taking place. Swedish authorities admitted they had received intelligence in 2016 regarding Akilov's possible radicalisation from their Uzbek counterparts, but they did not view him as a potential security threat.

## References

Ahmadi, Mumin (2015), 'Boeviki "Islamskogo Gosudarstva" Ugrojayut Tadjikistanu "Djihadom"' ['Islamic State' Fighters Threaten Tajikistan with 'Jihad"], Radio Ozodi – RFE/RL's Tajik Service, 4 January [in Russian], available at http://rus.ozodi.org/content/article/26775997.html accessed 31 July 2018.

Al Jazeera (2015), 'Nusra Leader: Our Mission is to Defeat Syrian Regime', *Al Jazeera*, 28 May, available at https://www.aljazeera.com/news/2015/05/nusra-front-golani-assad-syria-hezbollah-isil-150528044857528.html accessed 31 July 2018.

ASIA-Plus (2017), 'V Afghanistane Na Granice S Turkmenistanom Vyhodtsy Iz Tadjikistana, Uzbekistana I Kavkaza Voyuyut Na Storone IG' ('People from Tajikistan, Uzbekistan and the Caucasus are Fighting on the Side of the IS in Afghanistan, on the Border with Turkmenistan'), 11 December, available at: https://news.tj/ru/news/centralasia/20171211/v-afganistane-na-granitse-s-turkmenistanom-vihodtsi-iz-tadzhikistana-uzbekistana-i-kavkaza-voyuyut-na-storone-ig accessed 31 July 2018.

BBC (2017), 'Stockholm Truck Attack: Who is Rakhmat Akilov?', 7 June, available at https://www.bbc.com/news/world-europe-39552691 accessed 31 July 2018.

Bin Ali, Mohamed (2014), '"Jihad" in Syria: Fallacies of ISIS' End-Time Prophecies', *RSIS Commentary*, available at https://www.rsis.edu.sg/wp-content/uploads/2014/07/CO14149.pdf accessed 31 July 2018.

Burskaya, Zinaida (2016), 'The Road to IGIL Passed Through Moscow' ('Doroga v IGIL Prolegla Cherez Moskvu') [in Russian], *Novaya Gazeta*, 18 January, available at https://www.novayagazeta.ru/articles/2016/01/18/67080-doroga-v-igil-prolegla-cherez-moskvu accessed 31 July 2018.

Chan, Sewell (2017), 'Suspect in Stockholm Attack Was an ISIS Recruit, Uzbek Official Says', *The New York Times*, 14 April, available at https://www.nytimes.com/2017/04/14/world/europe/stockholm-attack-isis-rakhmat-akilov.html accessed 31 July 2018.

Cornell, Svante (2017), 'Central Asia Is Not a Breeding Ground for Radicalization', *The Diplomat*, 15 November, available at https://thediplomat.com/2017/11/central-asia-is-not-a-breeding-ground-for-radicalization/ accessed 31 July 2018.

Cornell, Svante E. (2018), 'Central Asia: Where Did Islamic Radicalization Go?', *Religion, Conflict, and Stability in the Former Soviet Union*, RAND Corporation, 76, available at https://www.rand.org/content/dam/rand/pubs/research_reports/RR2100/RR2195/RAND_RR2195.pdf accessed 31 July 2018.

Crime Russia (2017), 'Court Fined Telegram for Refusing to Provide FSB with Access to Accounts of Alleged Organizers of St. Petersburg Terrorist Act', 31 March, available at https://en.crimerussia.com/gromkie-dela/court-fined-telegram-for-refusing-to-provide-fsb-with-access-to-accounts-of-alleged-organizers-of-st/ accessed 31 July 2018.

Dalton, Ben (2017), 'NYC Attack: Is Central Asia a "Hotbed for Extremism"?' *Al Jazeera*, 6 November, available at https://www.aljazeera.com/news/2017/11/nyc-attack-central-asia-hotbed-extremism-171105115954669.html accessed 31 July 2018.

Eijkman, Quirine (2014), 'The German Sauerland Cell Reconsidered', *Perspectives on Terrorism*, 8(4), available at http://www.terrorismanalysts.com/pt/index.php/pot/article/view/363/html accessed 31 July 2018.

Glaser, Matilda Svensson (2018), 'Ideology or Psychology? A Comparison of the News Media Framing of the Crimes of Anton Lundin Pettersson and Rakhmat Akilov', p. 22, available at http://www.diva-portal.org/smash/get/diva2:1217438/FULLTEXT02.pdf accessed 31 July 2018.

Hille, Peter (2017), 'New York Attack: Is Central Asia a Terrorism Breeding Ground?' *Deutsche Welle*, 2 November, available at http://www.dw.com/en/new-york-attack-is-central-asia-a-terrorism-breeding-ground/a-41207424 accessed 31 July 2018.

Interfax (2016), 'Kyrgyzstan Was Named the Culprit of the Terrorist Attack near the Chinese Embassy in Bishkek' ('V Kirgizii nazvali vinovnika terakta u posolstva KNR v Bishkeke') [in Russian], 6 September, available at http://www.interfax.ru/world/526964 accessed 31 July 2018.

Interfax (2017), 'Obvinyaemiy V Terakte V Stokgolme Malo Smislil V Islame I Prinimal Narkotiki" ('The Suspect in Stockholm Terrorist Attack Had Little Understanding In Islam And Took *Drugs*') [in Russian], 12 April, available at http://www.interfax.ru/world/558117 accessed 31 July 2018.

Lemon, Edward, and John Heathershaw (2017), 'How Can We Explain Radicalisation Among Central Asia's Migrants?', *openDemocracy*, 2 May, available at https://www.opendemocracy.net/od-russia/edward-lemon-john-heathershaw/can-we-explain-radicalisation-among-central-asia-s-migrants accessed 31 July 2018.

Litmanovitz, Yael, David Weisburd, Badi Hasisi, and Michael Wolfowicz (2016), 'What are the Social, Economic, Psychological and Environmental Risk Factors that Lead to Radicalization and Recruitment to Terrorism?', *The Campbell Collaboration*, available at https://campbellcollaboration.org/media/k2/attachments/CCJG_Litmanovitz_Title.pdf accessed 31 July 2018.

Nesser, Petter (2006), 'Jihadism in Western Europe aAfter the Invasion of Iraq: Tracing Motivational Influences from the Iraq War on Jihadist Terrorism in Western Europe', *Studies in Conflict & Terrorism*, 29(4): 323–324.

Pew Research Center. (2018a), 'Origins and Destinations of the World's Migrants, 1990–2017', 28 February, available at http://www.pewglobal.org/2018/02/28/global-migrant-stocks/?country=RU&date=2017 accessed 1 September 2018.

Pew Research Center (2018b), 'Origins and Destinations of the World's Migrants, 1990–2017', 28 February, available at http://www.pewglobal.org/2018/02/28/global-migrant-stocks/?country=US&date=2017 accessed 31 July 2018.

Podolskaya, Darya (2016), 'Turkish President Says that there is Citizen of Kyrgyzstan among Involved in Terrorist Attack at Istanbul Airport', *24.kg News Agency*, 6 July, available at https://24.kg/archive/en/community/181083-news24.html/ accessed 31 July 2018.

Putz, Catherine (2017), '3 Convicted for Chinese Embassy Attack in Bishkek', *The Diplomat*, 30 June, available at https://thediplomat.com/2017/06/3-convicted-for-chinese-embassy-attack-in-bishkek/ accessed 31 July 2018.

*Radio Free Europe/Radio Liberty* (2018), 'Stockholm Attacker Linked to Tajik IS Militants, RFE/RL Investigation Finds', 9 February, available at https://www.rferl.org/a/sweden-attacker-islamic-state-links/29031330.html accessed 31 July 2018.

Ringstrom, Anna, and Johannes Hellstrom (2017), 'Suspect in Stockholm Truck Attack Admits Terrorist Crime', *Reuters*, 11 April, available at https://www.Reuters.com/article/us-sweden-attack-suspect-detention/suspect-in-stockholm-truck-attack-admits-terrorist-crime-idUSKBN17D0UD accessed 31 July 2018.

Shamsiev, Suyunbek (2016), 'V Ryadah IGIL Voyuyut 860 Kyrgyzstancev' ('860 Kyrgyz People Are Fighting in the Ranks of ISIS'), *24kg*, 22 December, available at https://24.kg/obschestvo/42148_v_ryadah_igil_voyuyut_860_kyirgyizstantsev_/ accessed 31 July 2018.

Sidorov, Oleg (2017), 'Pochemu Idut v IGIL?' ('Why do people join ISIL?'), *365info.kz*, 9 August, available at https://365info.kz/2017/08/pochemu-idut-v-igil/ accessed 31 July 2018.

Soliev, Nodirbek (2016), 'An Annual Threat Assessment on Central Asia', *Counter Terrorist Trends and Analysis*, 8(1), available at http://www.rsis.edu.sg/wp-content/uploads/2016/01/CTTA-January-2016.pdf accessed 31 July 2018.

Soliev, Nodirbek (2017a), 'The Terrorist Threat in Turkey: A Dangerous New Phase', *Counter Terrorist Trends and Analysis*, 9(4), available at http://www.rsis.edu.sg/wp-content/uploads/2017/04/CTTA-April-2017.pdf accessed 31 July 2018.

Soliev, Nodirbek (2017b), 'An Annual Threat Assessment on Central Asia', *Counter Terrorist Trends and Analysis*, 9(1), available at http://www.rsis.edu.sg/wp-content/uploads/2017/04/CTTA-April-2017.pdf accessed 31 July 2018.

Soliev, Nodirbek (2018), 'Understanding the Terror Threat to the 2018 World Cup in Russia', *TODAYonline*, 14 June, available at https://www.todayonline.com/commentary/understanding-terror-threat-2018-world-cup-russia accessed 31 July 2018.

Solopov, Maksim, German Petelin, and Amaliya Zatari (2017), 'Oshskiy Djikhad Prishel Iz Sirii' ('The Osh Jihad came from Syria') [in Russian], *Gazeta.ru*, 25 April, available at https://www.gazeta.ru/army/2017/04/24/10641767.shtml accessed 31 July 2018.

Sonmez, Goktug (2017), 'Violent Extremism Among Central Asians: The Istanbul, St. Petersburg, Stockholm, and New York City Attacks', *CTC Sentinel – Combating Terrorism Center at West Point*, 10(11), available at https://ctc.usma.edu/app/uploads/2017/12/CTC-Sentinel_Vol10Iss11-18.pdf accessed 31 July 2018.

*Sözcü Gazetesi* (2017), 'Reina Saldırganının İfadesi Ortaya Çıktı' ('The Reina attacker's statement has been revealed') [in Turkish], 19 January, available at https://www.sozcu.com.tr/2017/gundem/reina-saldirganinin-ifadesi-ortaya-cikti-1630563/ accessed 31 July 2018.

*Sputnik-news.uz* (2016), 'IG i Novie Ugrozy Bezopasnosti Postsovetskikh Gosudarst' ('IS and new security threats to the post-Soviet countries') [in Russian], 9 March, available at https://ru.sputniknews-uz.com/analytics/20160309/1965841.html accessed 31 July 2018.

TASS (2018), 'Eight Suspects Detained in Kaliningrad for Helping Terrorists', 23 May, available at http://tass.com/world/1005836 accessed 31 July 2018.

Weiss, Caleb (2015), 'Uzbek Group Pledges Allegiance to Al Nusrah Front', *The Long War Journal*, 30 September, available at https://www.longwarjournal.org/archives/2015/09/uzbek-group-pledges-allegiance-to-al-nusrah-front.php accessed 31 July 2018.

Yan, Holly and Andone, Dakin (2017), 'Who is New York Terror Suspect Sayfullo Saipov?', *CNN*, 2 November, available at: https://edition.cnn.com/2017/11/01/us/sayfullo-saipov-new-york-attack/index.html accessed 31 July 2018.

Yayla, Ahmet S. (2017), 'The Reina Nightclub Attack and the Islamic State Threat to Turkey', *CTC Sentinel – Combating Terrorism Center at West Point*, March 2017, 10(3), available at https://ctc.usma.edu/the-reina-nightclub-attack-and-the-islamic-state-threat-to-turkey/ accessed 31 July 2018.

# 8 India's Maoist insurgencies

*Dalbir Ahlawat and Sonika Ahlawat*

## Introduction

Since its independence in 1947, India has faced several insurgencies but among them the Maoist insurgency stands out as it is one of the longest and poses the biggest internal security threat. This insurgency has been steered by the Communist Party of India (Maoist) (CPIM) since 2004 but its genesis goes back several centuries. The people living in the forests (*adivasis*) over the centuries became marginalised, cut off from the mainstream and developed a self-sustained, self-governed order. They also established their dependency on the forests and developed their own customs, traditions and governance structure. Economically, *adivasis* relied on agriculture, hunting and gathering, and enjoyed extensive control and unrestricted access to their lands and forests with minimal interference from outside (Morrison 2017: 263).

After colonising India, the British added a new dynamic to the existing order by transferring the proprietary rights over the forests to the government (Guha 1983: 1940–47). For the collection of revenue, they allocated (the *adivasi*) land to the feudal lords (*zamindars*). As a result, the *adivasis* not only lost control over their own properties but were also subjected to work in subordination of the non-*adivasis*/outsiders. This drastically changed the existing social and economic order. Furthermore, to dilute the *adivasi* majority, *zamindars* imported labour from other states and deprived them of the "forests and resources they traditionally depended on and sometimes coerced [them] to pay taxes" (Mhaiske, Patil and Narkhede 2016: 6). Further, to subdue the *adivasis*, the British enacted the Indian Forest Act of 1878. Under its provisions, "hundreds and thousands of acres of forest lands that *adivasis* had used unfettered for centuries were suddenly kept in reserve" (Verghese 2016: 1623). After reservation of the forest areas, the *adivasis* lost all claims to the land and forests. This marginalisation and change in political, social and economic status gave rise to insurgencies in the late 19th and early 20th centuries against the British. Although these insurgencies were brutally crushed, in order to preserve their identity and territories, the *adivasis* not only continued to maintain their fervor for their autonomy but also contributed to the momentum towards the independence of India (Khan 1986: 23).

## Genesis of the insurgency

After the independence of India in 1947, the government assured the *adivasis* that it would give necessary consideration to their grievances such as land and forest rights. However, the "transition from colonial to independent status, forest resource management changed little: [the] exclusionary processes accelerated ... to consolidate state authority over forest resources" (Haeuber 1993: 49–50). Thus, the *adivasis*, resorted to a mix of violent and punitive actions in their struggle to regain their land rights, control over forests and autonomy until 1967.

### *Ideological framing of the grievances (1967–71)*

The year 1967 proved a turning point, when landlords killed a landless worker in Naxalbari village in Bengal for ploughing a patch of land. This sparked the consolidation of the on-going grievances of the *adivasis* and proved instrumental in bringing them onto a single platform. A radical group from Naxalbari and the *adivasis* came in contact with the Communist Party of India (Marxist Leninist) (CPIML). The CPIML identified all the basic tenets of the communist ideology in the *adivasi* movement, blended the existing situation into their ideological fold and advocated an armed revolution. This resulted in a conglomeration of the *adivasis*, Naxals and communists. This movement, spearheaded by a local leader, Charu Mazumdar, based on his Historic Eight Documents, formed the ideological precept for the uprising at Naxalbari. Between 1967 and 1971, it became a force to be reckoned with. However, considering its intensity, nature, and challenge, the government managed to crush the movement within 45 days.

The movement headed by the CPIML waned because of its imported ideology, failure to assuage grievances of the *adivasis* and lack of cognisance of the ground realities in India. Moreover, citations such as "China's chairman (Mao) is our chairman" failed to develop an *Adivasi*-centric movement to redress their grievances (Mazumdar 1969).

### *Traversing grievances sans ideology (1972–2004)*

The next eight years (1972–1980) witnessed decline and splinter in the communist movement (Ramana 2011: 29–30). The *adivasis* were left to fend for themselves. Because of regional disparities, the *adivasis* lacked unity and a comprehensive action plan. At the same time, assurances by the government raised hopes for the redressal of their grievances. Notwithstanding assurances, by 2004, the *adivasis* lost hope as the welfare projects initiated by the government failed to yield promised development goals.

### Redressing grievances through protracted war (2004–2018)

Marginalised, exploited, and leaderless, the *adivasis* perceived the government to be full of phony assurances and disparaging policies. Against this backdrop and in the context of the rollout of India's liberalisation of the economy, the continued marginalisation of the *adivasis* and exploitation of forest resources by the private sector; the People's War Group, Maoist Communist Centre of India and CPIML, after concerted efforts and several deliberations, merged on 21 September 2004 to form the CPIM. Subsequently, this new conglomeration inspired by Chinese leader Mao Zedong's philosophy, released a strategic document, *Strategy and Tactics of the Indian Revolution* (STIR), a blueprint for its political, organisational and military actions. The STIR placed emphasis on "seizure of political power through protracted armed struggle … by taking into account the specific characteristics … of the Indian situation" (*Strategy and Tactics of the Indian Revolution* 2004). It underlined three strategic stages: Strategic Defensive, Strategic Stalemate and Strategic Offensive.

To implement the first stage of the STIR, the Maoists attacked infrastructure, ambushed government officials, stole weapons from police stations and attacked prisons to release their cadres. These attacks increased year after year and reached an extreme in 2006, when the insurgents conducted several high-impact attacks and inflicted severe causalities. Given the CPIM's increasing sphere of influence that engulfed 194 districts in 18 states as well as the intensity of the attacks on security forces, Prime Minister Manmohan Singh labelled it "the single biggest internal security challenge ever faced" by India (Government of India Press Information Bureau 2006).

In addition to the operational gains, Maoists also strengthened their legitimacy through speaking *adivasi* languages, adapting their culture and establishing social bonds. Also, to mitigate local issues and to counter the state's presence, the CPIM initiated a multi-prong strategy that included targeting government officials, helping the needy, redistributing the land, enforcing minimum wages, providing justice through people's courts, and destroying the government-built infrastructure such as bridges, roads, schools and hospitals. In a way, the CPIM's actions reflected solidarity with the *adivasis* and their aspirations for full autonomy (Sood 2011: 161–2).

Thus, the failures of the government led to gains for the Maoists and facilitated the establishment of their legitimacy by becoming savours of the *adivasis* against the exploitative government machinery. This enabled the expansion of the Maoist's stronghold in nine states: Chhattisgarh, West Bengal, Jharkhand, Bihar, Madhya Pradesh, Maharashtra, Karnataka, Andhra Pradesh and Odisha, that is, one-third of India, with a 40,000-strong militia and over a million sympathisers. Maoists, taking note of the liberalisation of the economy, shifted their focus from *zamindars* to business organisations, and from agricultural enterprises to mineral rich mines. This shift facilitated revenue generation through extortion, taxes, blackmailing and kidnapping. It is estimated that between 2004 and 2011, they inflicted around

700 causalities and generated around US$18.4 million revenue annually (Lynch III 2016: 13).

## Countering the insurgency

### *Abstruse approach (1947–71)*

After independence, the Indian government faced an ethical dilemma of whether to bring the marginalised communities into the national mainstream or give them autonomy to preserve their identities, cultures and ways of life. After considering popular opinion, its own financial limitations, and the limitation of the governance infrastructure, the government opted for the latter. However, regional autonomy, failed to assuage the *adivasis'* grievances, such as issues of identity, land and forest rights. *Adivasis* living in the forests and remote areas throughout the country continued to be classified together as Schedule Tribes under Schedules Five and Six of the Constitution, with few rights. The government also failed to introduce major changes to the Forest Law that had been framed by the British.

Furthermore, the government branded around 40 socio-politico-economic organisations formed by the *adivasis* to press for their rights as a "'Maoist' conspiracy...though not a single one of the resistances...have been led by the Maoists or even assisted by their guerrilla forces" (*Sanhati* 2010). Additionally, the leadership of such organisations was either co-opted, harassed, discredited or even neutralised. Some of the incidents such as the arrest of Pravir Chandra in Baster in 1966 resulted in *adivasi* protests, the killing of 13 protesters and later Pravir Chandra by the police (Sundar 1997: 218–9). Since this incident, 25 March is celebrated as a day of sacrifice by the *adivasis* in Bastar. Many such instances proved counterproductive for the government in establishing its legitimacy.

Similarly, instead of acknowledging the root causes of the discontentment that triggered the rebellion in 1967 at Naxalbari, the government attributed an ideological motive to the insurgency (i.e. Maoism), with the possibility of a foreign hand. Facing a looming threat, it neutralised the insurgency within 45 days (1 July to 15 August 1971) through Operation Steeplechase that was jointly conducted by the Indian Army, Central Reserve Police Force (CRPF) and the state police.

### *Non-kinetic approach (1972–90)*

The ruthless crushing of the insurgency proved instrumental in segregating the *adivasis* from the communists. To garner support and establish legitimacy, the government announced several developmental schemes. This initiative infused some hope among the *adivasis* but as the policies unfolded, they became mired by mismanagement, exploitation and the imposition of the national culture and values on the *adivasis*. In addition, "corrupt local officials, were able to privately reserve forest and village lands, and buy forest produce at below-market prices" (Verghese 2016: 1637).

Most of these initiatives proved not only counter-productive but wherever new development projects, such as building dams and constructing canals were initiated, the *adivasis* were forcefully displaced, while the exploitation of the forests continued unhindered without the *adivasis* having any share or say. Moreover, the national political parties appeared to follow a well-calculated policy of keeping the *adivasis* leaderless by co-opting their leaders, discrediting or even physically removing them (Mukherjee 2006). In the process, "these non-kinetic approaches ... created their own problems with corrupt security forces, increased criminal activity, and a litany of human rights complaints and investigations" (Lynch III 2016: 6). During this phase the plight of the *adivasis* largely remained hostage to local vote bank politics.

## People-centric approach (1991–2008)

A new policy orientation took place in the early 1990s when India transited from its semi-socialist economic structure to liberalisation of its economy. During this period, the government emphasised a people-centric approach, in an attempt to win the hearts and minds of the *adivasis*, and responding only when insurgent attacks took place. To counter the CPIM's agenda of an exploitative capitalist economy, the government initiated several welfare schemes. However, these overlapping schemes lacked accountability. Instead of enriching the *adivasis*, these "simply vanished into the bottomless pit benefiting corrupt politicians, bureaucrats, contractors and even the insurgents" (Routray 2017: 58). No major people-oriented infrastructure development programme was initiated, such as electricity, communication, roads and transportation, health and education facilities. Rather, the granting of licenses to private firms for mining, construction and infrastructure development, increased pressure on the *adivasis* to give space to this sector.

Against these developments, the *adivasis* continued their sympathy for the CPIM, and the CPIM's taking arms against the state, Prime Minister Manmohan Singh, perturbed by the increasing support and clout of the CPIM, declared the Maoists in 2006 as "the single biggest internal security challenge ever faced by our country" (Government of India Press Information Bureau, 2006).

However, the *adivasi* movements did not really pose a serious threat to the state until 2006; it was only when these movements and Maoists halted development projects and posed a threat to some 40 new MOUs signed between the state and industrial developers that the *adivasis* who opposed the MOUs (Memoranda of Understanding) were branded as supporters of Maoists (Malreddy 2014: 598). The state governments in Andhra Pradesh, Karnataka and Jharkhand attempted to counterbalance the Maoist upsurge by forming local organisations with *advasis* who had disassociated themselves from the Maoists. One such organisation, *Salwa Judum* (People's Resistance Movement) launched in 2006 to unite *adivasis* against the Maoists, initially proved effective; but its members became involved in violence, forced displacement of *adivasis* and criminal acts. After Salwa Judum emerged as a front organisation for the security forces, a Supreme Court decision criticised the government, stating that: "It is a question of law and order. You cannot give arms to somebody (a civilian) and allow him to kill. You will be an abettor of the offence" (*The Indian Express* 2008).

In the new environment, with the government's disinvestment spree, the active role played by the private sector as well as the creation of local organisations to fight the Maoists, the *adivasis* faced multiple challenges. The government initiated mega infrastructure projects without engaging the *adivasis* as partners in the process, subjected them to displacement and offered low wages. In addition, there was also competition from inter-state labour. The private sector also targeted mining in the forest areas by often flouting forest laws.

By 2006, the government began to acknowledge that the situation had become critical. The government then attempted to address the root cause of the insurgency by enacting the Scheduled Tribes and Other Traditional Forest Dwellers (Recognition of Forest Rights) Act in 2006, which granted legal recognition to the rights of traditional forest dwelling communities (Ministry of Tribal Affairs 2006). It entitled individuals, families and communities a right over their own land. Though innovative, it took the government around seven decades to address the root cause. However, the new initiative still had several operational fault lines, as the onus was on the *adivasis* to prove their claims. The Home Secretary, G.K. Pillai, admitting this precarious situation in 2009 stated "the government and its policies were largely to blame for the rise of Naxalism" (*The Times of India* 2010).

A major reason for this has been that law and order is a state issue. Several states governed by the opposition parties followed different counterinsurgency (COIN) strategies instead of a comprehensive and coordinated national approach. Some states, "did not want to alienate the vote banks ... who sympathized with the Naxalite view of economic injustice" (Lynch III 2016: 19). This was evident in the 2009 Jharkhand election, when *Jharkhand Mukti Morcha* achieved an unprecedented victory, thanks to Maoist support.

Nevertheless, the government continued to hold elections at regular intervals, expanded welfare schemes, and resisted the urge to use military force against the Maoists. However, the government's soft power measures to empower *adivasis* against the Maoists proved counterproductive. The expected insurgency fatigue, splits in the insurgency leadership, diminution in legitimacy in the long term and possibility of the Maoists indulging in criminal activities, did not materialise. Rather the Maoists appeared more calculated and strategic in their approach (Ahlawat 2018: 258).

## *Enemy-centric approach (2009–14)*

As a result of the increasing geographical area under the Maoist fold, the central government included the CPIM in the Schedule of Terrorist

Organisations in June 2009, along with all its formations and front organisations under the existing Unlawful Activities (Prevention) Act, 1967. (National Investigation Agency 2016). Section 3 of the Prevention of Terrorism Act, 2002 (POTA) defined a terrorist act as "intended" to "threaten the unity, integrity, security and sovereignty of India" or "strike terror in the people or any section of the people", or "any other unlawful act with the said intent" (Kalhan 2006: 155).

To deter the ongoing attacks on the government officials and security forces, the government changed its strategy from people centric (winning hearts and minds) to enemy centric. This meant a 'force first approach' to weaken the Maoists first and then from a position of strength offer a political solution. To enforce this strategy, with the backup of POTA, the central government initiated targeted actions against the rising tide of Maoists, through Operation Green Hunt in November 2009, aimed at "all-out offensive" with over 50,000 troops (Sethi 2013). This included deploying the army for advice and training, the CRPF battalions to strengthen operations launched by the Indo-Tibetan Border Police, Border Security Forces, *Shashastra Seema Bal* and the state police. This operation made significant inroads in the previously Maoist-held no-go zones but also exposed the government's operational shortcoming when the Maoists ambushed and killed 76 security personnel in April 2010 (Chopra 2010). These actions further forced Prime Minister Singh to repeat in 2010 that the Maoist insurgency posed the "biggest internal security challenge" India has ever faced (*The Hindu* 2010).

The killing of ten police personnel in May 2011 proved critical, leading the government to adopt a kinetic approach and launch several operations aimed at the core of the Maoists. For example, Operation Anaconda in June 2011 was to flush out Naxals from their fortified den in Saranda forest, while Operation Monsoon in July 2011 aimed to destroy the CPIM training camps. Operation Green Hunt resulted in the killing of a senior Maoist leader, Koteswara Rao, in November 2011 and the capturing or killing of several senior leaders by the end of 2012. In addition, substantial progress was made with the surrender of 440 cadres and the arrest of 1,800 affiliates (Lynch III 2016: 16).

Considering the insurgency was at its ebb, the government allotted mining leases to 19 private businesses in the Maoist dominated region (Ismi 2013). Although the backbone of the insurgency was broken, the Maoists ambushed and killed 24 political leaders to demonstrate their continued presence. In response, the CRPF and the police jointly launched an offensive COIN operation in December 2013 and discovered a weapons making factory in Munger, Bihar. This proved a turning point. Faced with the lack of weapons supply and on the run from the security forces, several senior Maoist leaders surrendered (Verma 2014: 309–10). Prominent among them were G.V.K. Prasad Rao, spokesperson of the CPIM, a key member of the organisation for 25 years, and Commander Ade Prabhu, member of the organisation for 30 years as well as his wife Talandi Kantha, a member for 23 years. Others included Jageshwar Komra, a key leader and commander, and Chambala

Ravinder, along with his wife Wetti Adime, who had both been involved in several incidents (Pradhan 2014). These concerted COIN successes proved to be a big blow to the Maoist leadership and the morale of its cadres.

## Integrated and holistic approach (2014–18)

The Bharatiya Janata Party (BJP) government, after coming into power in May 2014, adopted an "integrated and holistic approach ... by simultaneously addressing the areas of security, development and good governance" (Ministry of Home Affairs 2016–17: 22). To achieve this, the government launched a National Policy and Action Plan that emphasised a "multi-pronged strategy".

In the context of low morale and a high casualty rate suffered by the security forces, the government pursued a kinetic approach that was more proactive and aggressive, as opposed to the previous reactive approach. In addition, it enhanced inter-state coordination and the role of the National Investigation Agency (NIA) in collecting intelligence across the states.

To deter attacks on police forces, the government constructed 400 fortified police stations and 1,299 mobile towers to keep track of the Maoist communications and movements. New Delhi also approved the use of advanced technology such as drones, unmanned aerial vehicles and helicopters for operational requirements, supplies and reinforcement. This new strategy proved effective in disrupting the communication and supply of the Maoists. Though this hard-line approach came under scrutiny, the government justified that a people-centric approach would unnecessarily protract the insurgency.

Apart from the use of kinetic force, the government also adopted a bottom-up approach by broadcasting the local cultural and social programs in the national media, and named projects such as bridges, airports, new infrastructure after the local people. The revised guidelines for the Surrender-cum-Rehabilitation Scheme also proved successful in wooing the insurgents. The Scheme offered an immediate grant of US$3,000–5,000, depending on the rank, with the condition that this amount would be deposited in their bank accounts and would be accessible only after three years subject to good behaviour. In the meanwhile, they were offered vocational training with a monthly stipend of US$75 for three years. To further encourage surrender, the government initiated an open jail facility. Under these provisions, compared to 2013, there was an increase of 411% in surrenders in 2016–17 (Ministry of Home Affairs 2016–17: 4).

The Central Armed Police Forces also worked on several Civic Action Programmes to build trust and project the humane face of the security forces. While strengthening legitimacy, the NIA also played a vital role in stopping the flow of finance and money laundering. Further, through the demonetisation of 500 and 1,000 currency notes by the government in 2016, the Maoists were starved of cash funding (Chauhan 2016).

Another stride was the amendment of the Scheduled Tribes and Other Traditional Dwellers (Recognition of Forest Rights) Act, 2006 in August

2014. This was "to recognize and vest the forest rights and occupation of forest land in forest dwelling Scheduled Tribes and other traditional forest dwellers, who have been residing in such forests for generations, but whose rights could not be recorded" (Ministry of Tribal Affairs 2014). This amendment widened the scope for the *adivasis* to claim their rights on the agriculture and forest lands that the Maoists had exploited for so long. Notwithstanding this amendment, and criticising his own ministry, Union Tribal Minister Jual Oram admitted: "Losing of land and livelihood because of 'poor' implementation of the Forest Rights Act is one of the prime reasons for the surge of Maoist insurgency". To rectify it, he emphasised the need to sincerely implement forest rights (*The Indian Express* 2016).

Despite these achievements, the government was shocked by the killing of 11 paramilitary commandos and 25 CRPF personnel in early 2017. Home Minister Rajnath Singh responded that "we have taken the attack as a challenge" (First Post 2017). To stop the re-emergence of the Maoists, Singh declared a new doctrine called SAMADHAN, a coordinated technology and intelligence based strategy (Sandhu 2017). The success of this strategy was witnessed in April 2018, when based on an intelligence tip-off, police intercepted the movement of high profile inter-state Maoist leaders who were heading for a secret meeting to chalk out future strategy, killing 37 without any police casualties. Since then no major attack or incident has been perpetrated by the Maoists (Jadhav 2018).

## Disconnect between professed ideology and actions

It is beyond doubt that the Maoists had at one time successfully reigned over one-third of India, wooed *adivasis* into their fold and emerged as the biggest internal security threat. However, the goals set in the STIR have not yet been achieved, and Maoist ideology is facing a challenge to remain relevant in the fast changing political and economic milieu in India.

Chapter 5 of the STIR states that the "struggle for people's democracy is … against the counter-revolutionary, semi-colonial, semi-feudal politics, economics and culture" (*Strategy and Tactics of the Indian Revolution* 2004). This delineation does not reflect the ground reality of the Indian democracy. Maoists have been unable to make inroads in urban areas and unable to justify the doctrinal concepts like 'semi-feudal' and 'semi-colonial' with the realities of the 21st century, and appear to be outdated in their analysis.

Chapter 6 states that the "path followed by the Chinese revolution is also applicable in semi-colonial, semi-feudal India". It is quite pertinent that even China has moved from what it was. Indian history, culture, politics and the current level of development is much different to Mao's China. Chapter 6 further states that "the 'protracted people's war' will pass through three strategic stages: Strategic Defensive; Strategic Stalemate; and Strategic Offensive". It appears this open-ended war is still in the first stage. When it indicated symptoms of strategic stalemate, the government initiated an all-out operation and pushed the insurgency back onto the defensive.

Finding it difficult to reinforce the STIR agenda, the CPIM shifted its focus to anti-liberalisation and anti-globalisation to foment a New Democratic Revolution. However, the trend indicates that the younger generation is more prone to availing itself of the opportunities offered by the government. Moreover, whenever the security forces increased pressure, the Maoist left the *adivasis* behind and themselves disappeared in deep forests to return only when it was safe for them (Mukherji 2012: 22–3). After returning, they targeted the *adivasis* as police informers and even killed and tortured them. Thus, the CPIM-led insurgency is losing appeal and legitimacy among the youth.

The CPIM mobilised the *adivasis* against the liberalisation and privatisation process, and even boycotted and destroyed the development projects, "seeing the potential dissipation of local grievance as a challenge to their movement" (Eynde et al. 2015). However, over a period of time, Maoists have themselves become involved in generating revenue through the private sector, for instance, through the collection of protection money from businesses like any other mafia, as well as supporting illegal mining to generate additional revenue. As the *adivasis* consider resource extraction as an assault on their land and forest rights, this in turn has affected the CPIM's legitimacy and support base. Considering the amount of revenue generated, even cadres have splintered and started operating on their own. This has given rise to gang wars, kidnappings and ransoms (Noronha 2017). Yet another factor that bedevils the CPIM's legitimacy is the shift in its stance from seizing power through the barrel of the gun to protecting its interests by influencing the electoral process, supporting opposition party candidates and the candidates who support its cause (Lea-Henry 2018: 22).

However, pragmatic and updated the STIR may be, it appears to be outpaced by the changing national and international economic, political, ideological and security environment. If the Forest Act reforms are implemented in earnest, Maoists will struggle for their survival. As Lea-Henry (2018: 31) observed, the Maoists have "become the same embodiment of intolerance, corruption, and uncaring authoritarianism, against which they once claimed to be fighting; an unscrupulous and predatory movement".

Even the early success of the Maoist insurgency can be credited to the government's idealist counter-insurgency approach underlined by India's first Prime Minister Jawaharlal Nehru: "The measure of the success of a COIN effort is not the number of militants killed or captured or the amount of territory cleared of insurgent influence. The overriding objective is political reconciliation…reintegrating insurgents" (Fidler and Ganguly 2012: 306). However, Home Secretary Pillai has also admitted that "there were many districts where the government had not existed for decades" (*The Times of India* 2010). This reflected the government's failure to prepare an appropriate COIN response.

In sum, the insurgency has declined since 2014. The government achieved this while not using the army, air force or heavy weapons and avoided any large-scale collateral damage. Even though of late, disproportionate force has been used and pro-active actions taken, these were mainly aimed at pressurising the insurgents to bring them to the negotiation table. At the same time, the government maintained the channels of communication open for a political solution and held local, state and national elections regularly within the purview of the Constitution of India. Notwithstanding the government's own limitations faced in a representative democracy, the CPIM is on its downward trajectory.

## Conclusion

Since 2014 the Maoist insurgency has been down but not out. The basic causes that existed in 1947 are still present, though some efforts have been made to amend the Forest Law and empower the *adivasis* through development plans. However, the question is how these will be operationalised.

The Maoists, even with their outdated ideology, became the saviours of the *adivasis* by attacking corrupt government officials, destroying the infrastructure used to exploit the *adivasis* and even leading the people out of the exploitative system. Whatever, the Maoists have done, they have certainly demonstrated what the government could not do despite the government having launched several development and welfare programmes. The Maoists were able to unite the *adivasis*, make them conscious of their rights and educate them to understand economic and political systems.

The government has adopted various strategies ranging from soft power to hard power, people-centric to enemy-centric, but is yet to reach a comfortable solution. It appears the Maoists have done the groundwork by bringing the *adivasis* to this level of consciousness of their rights. In addition, the process of economic liberalisation will place more pressure for natural resources, exploitation of forests and mines, and this will pose a challenge to the government.

It is quite pertinent that around 100 million *adivasis* are neither communist nor Maoist but have genuine historical grievances of identity, forest and land rights. The government can further isolate the Maoists by wooing their mass base and strengthening legitimacy by providing land rights and recognising the identity of the *adivasis*. The government should focus more on developing the capacity of the *adivasis* rather than increasing their dependency on welfare schemes. While Maoist ideology is heading to its natural demise, the government also faces a trust deficit. In such a scenario, the local elders and village panchayats (councils) could act as a firewall between the *adivasis*, Maoists and the government. Moreover, the government needs to implement the Indian Forest Act and grant rights to the *adivasis* relating to the land and minor forest produce, in order to demonstrate that its policies are people-oriented in a true sense. At the same time, it could use an integrated set of strategies that include the use of soft power, electoral participation, economic development, rights over land and forests, skill development, as well as the use of hard power to deal with the violence perpetrated by the Maoists. Nonetheless, caution must be taken that the use of force over a sustained period of time does not undermine democracy.

## References

Ahlawat, Dalbir (2018), "Maoist Insurgency in India: Grievances, Security Threats and Counter-Strategies", *Journal of Policing, Intelligence and Counter Terrorism*, 13(2).

Chauhan, N. (2016), "Demonetisation Leads to Highest Ever Surrender of Maoists in a Month", *The Times of India*, 29 November, available at http://timesofindia.indiatimes.com/india/Demonetisation-leads-to-largest-Maoist-surrenders/articleshow/55675983.cms accessed on 13 January 2018.

Chopra, Anuj (2010), "India's Failing Counterinsurgency Campaign", *Foreign Policy*, 14 May, available at http://foreignpolicy.com/2010/05/14/indias-failing-counterinsurgency-campaign/ accessed on 13 January 2018.

Eynde, Oliver Vanden, Jamie Hansen-Lewis, Austin L. Wright and Jacob Shapiro (2015), *Connecting the Red Corridor: Infrastructure Development in Conflict Zones*, London: International Growth Centre, 19 June, available at https://www.theigc.org/publication/connecting-the-red-corridor-infrastructure-development-in-conflict-zones/ accessed on 13 January 2018.

Fidler, David P., and Sumit Ganguly (2012), "Counterinsurgency in India", in Paul B. Rich and Isabella Duyvesteyn, eds., *The Routledge Handbook of Insurgency and Counterinsurgency*, London: Routledge.

*First Post* (2017), "Sukma Attack: Narendra Modi Calls Maoist Killing of 26 CRPF Jawans 'Cowardly and Deplorable'", 24 April, available at http://www.firstpost.com/india/sukma-attack-narendra-modi-calls-maoist-killing-of-26-crpf-jawans-cowardly-and-deplorable-3401880.html accessed on 13 January 2018.

Government of India Press Information Bureau (2006), *Prime Minister's Speech to the 2nd Meeting of the Standing Committee of the Chief Ministers on Naxalism*, 13 April.

Guha, Ramachandra (1983), "Forestry in British and Post-British India: A Historical Analysis", *Economic and Political Weekly*, 18(45/46).

Haeuber, R (1993), "Indian Forest Policy in Two Eras: Continuity or Change?", *Environmental History Review*, 17(1).

Ismi, Asad (2013), "Maoist Insurgency Spreads to Over 40% of India. Mass Poverty and Delhi's Embrace of Corporate Neoliberalism Fuels Social Uprising", *Global Research*, 20 December, available at https://www.globalresearch.ca/maoist-insurgency-spreads-to-over-40-of-india-mass-poverty-and-delhis-embrace-of-corporate-neoliberalism-fuels-social-uprising/5362276 accessed on 13 January 2018.

Jadhav, Rajendra (2018), "Police Kill at Least 37 Maoist Militants in Central India", *Reuters*, 24 April, available at https://www.Reuters.com/article/us-india-militants-maoists/police-kill-at-least-37-maoist-militants-in-central-india-idUSKBN1HV0NV accessed on 28 August 2018.

Kalhan, Anil (2006), "Colonial Continuities: Human Rights, Terrorism, and Security Laws in India", *Columbia Journal of Asian Law*, 20(1).

Khan, Ismail (1986), *Indian Tribes through the Ages*, New Delhi: Vikas Publishing House.

Lea-Henry, Jed (2018), *Imagined Wounds: The False Grievance behind India's Maoist Movement*, New Delhi: Institute of Peace and Conflict Studies, January.

LynchIII, Thomas F. (2016), *India's Naxalite Insurgency: History, Trajectory, and Implications for U.S.-India Security Cooperation on Domestic Counterinsurgency*, Washington, DC: National Defense University Press, October.

Malreddy, Pawan Kumar (2014), "Domesticating the "New Terrorism": The Case of the Maoist Insurgency in India", *The European Legacy*, 19(5).

Mazumdar, Charu (1969), *Liberation*, 3(1), 1 November, available at http://www.bannedthought.net/India/CPI(ML)-Orig/Mazumdar/ChinaChairmanOurChairman-CM-691106.pdf accessed on 13 January 2018.

Mhaiske, Vinod M., Vinayak K. Patil, and S.S. Narkhede (2016), *Forest Tribology and Anthropology*, New Delhi: Scientific Publishers.

Ministry of Home Affairs (2016–17), *Annual Report*, available at http://mha.nic.in/sites/upload_files/mha/files/EnglAnnualReport2016-17_17042017.pdf accessed on 13 January 2018.

Ministry of Tribal Affairs (2006), *Forest Rights Act, 2006: Act, Rules and Guidelines*, 29 December, available at https://tribal.nic.in/FRA/data/FRARulesBook.pdf accessed on 13 January 2018.

Ministry of Tribal Affairs (2014), *Scheduled Tribes and Other Traditional Forest Dwellers (Recognition of Forest Rights) Act, 2006: Rights of Tribals and Forest Dwellers*, 7 August, available at http://pib.nic.in/newsite/PrintRelease.aspx?relid=108222 accessed on 13 January 2018.

Morrison, Kathleen D. (2017), "Losing Primeval Forests: Degradation Narratives in South Asia", in Ursula K. Heise, Jon Christensen and Michelle Niemann, eds., *The Routledge Companion to the Environmental Humanities*, London: Routledge.

Mukherjee, Anit (2006), "Lessons from Another Insurgency", *New York Times*, 4 May, available at http://www.nytimes.com/2006/03/04/opinion/lessons-from-another-insurgency.html accessed on 13 January 2018.

Mukherji, N. (2012), *The Maoists in India: Tribals Under Siege*, New Delhi: Amaryllis Publishing.

National Investigation Agency (2016), available at http://www.nia.gov.in/banned-terrorist-organisations.htm accessed on 13 January 2018.

Noronha, R. (2017), "Chhattisgarh: Canadian National Detained by Maoists Released', *India Today*, 29 March, available at http://indiatoday.intoday.in/story/chattisgarh-canadian-nationalmaoists/1/916002.html accessed on 13 January 2018.

Pradhan, Fakir Mohan (2014), "Maoists: Cracks at the Base?", *South Asia Intelligence Review*, 13(13), 29 September, available at http://www.satp.org/satporgtp/sair/Archives/sair13/13_13.htm#assessment2 accessed on 13 January 2018.

Ramana, P.V. (2011), "India's Maoist Insurgency: Evolution, Current Trends, and Responses", in Michael Kugelman, ed., *India's Contemporary Security Challenges*, Washington, DC: Woodrow Wilson International Center for Scholars.

Routray, Bibhu Prasad (2017), "India: Fleeting Attachment to the Counterinsurgency Grand Strategy", *Small Wars & Insurgencies*, 28(1).

Sandhu, Kamaljit Kaur (2017), "12 Takeaways From Centre's New Strategy to Deal With Naxals", *India Today*, 8 May, available at http://indiatoday.intoday.in/story/naxals-mha-rajnath-singh-narendra-modi-government-strategy/1/949072.html accessed on 13 January 2018.

Sanhati (2010), "Adivasis, Mining and Monopoly Capital", 4 May, available at http://sanhati.com/literature/2318 accessed on 13 January 2018.

Sethi, Aman (2013), "Green Hunt: The Anatomy of an Operation", *The Hindu*, 6 February.
Sood, K.S. (2011), "The Naxal Insurgency: Challenges for the Para Military Forces", in V.R. Raghavan, ed., *The Naxal Threat: Causes, State Response and Consequences*, Chennai: Centre for Security Analysis.
*Strategy and Tactics of the Indian Revolution* (2004), available at https://redstarover indiadotcom.files.wordpress.com/2016/03/strategy-tactics-of-the-indian-revolution2. pdf accessed on 13 January 2018.
Sundar, N. (1997), *Subalterns and Sovereigns: An Anthropological History of Bastar*, Oxford: Oxford University Press.
*The Hindu* (2010), "Naxalism Biggest Threat to Internal Security: Manmohan", 24 May, available at http://www.thehindu.com/news/national/Naxalism-biggest-threat-to-internal-security-Manmohan/article16302952.ece accessed on 13 January 2018.
*The Indian Express* (2008), "Hearing Plea against Salwa Judum, SC Says State Cannot Arm Civilians to Kill", 1 April, available at http://archive.indianexpress.com/news/hearing-plea-against-salwa-judum-sc-says-state-cannot-arm-civilians-to-kill/290932/ accessed on 13 January 2018.
*The Indian Express* (2016), "Tribal Ministry to Focus on Forest Rights Law Implementation in 2017", 28 December, available at http://indianexpress.com/article/india/tribal-ministry-to-focus-on-forest-rights-law-implementation-in-2017-4448500/ accessed on 13 January 2018.
*The Times of India* (2010), "Maoists Looking at Armed Overthrow of State by 2050", 6 March, available at http://timesofindia.indiatimes.com/india/Maoists-looking-at-armed-overthrow-of-state-by-2050/articleshow/5648742.cms accessed on 13 January 2018.
Verghese, Ajay (2016), "British Rule and Tribal Revolts in India: The Curios Case of Baster", *Modern Asian Studies*, 50(5).
Verma, Arvind (2014), "The Police and India's Maoist Insurgency", in C. Christine Fair and Sumit Ganguly, eds., *Policing Insurgencies: Cops as Counterinsurgents*, London: Oxford University Press.

# Part 3

# 9 China's Uyghur problem
## Terrorist acts and government responses

*Chien-peng Chung*

### China's persistent Uyghur problem

Xinjiang (Uyghur) Autonomous Region is the largest provincial-level unit in the People's Republic of China (PRC). Xinjiang covers an area of 1.66 million square kilometres, and contained 22.98 million people at the end of 2014, about 60% of whom are from ethnic groups other than the Han-Chinese, or Han, the dominant ethnic group of China. Parts of Xinjiang are home to Uyghurs, a Turkic-speaking people who mostly practice Sunni Islam and are the largest ethnic group in the autonomous region (An 2017). About 45% of Xinjiang's population is constituted by Uyghurs, 10% by Turkic Muslim Kazaks, and 40% by Han. Language and religion are salient markers of Uyghur identity.

For top officials in Xinjiang, the biggest challenge has been to prevent terrorist activities, especially by alleged Uyghur separatists, as the region has been considered by the national leadership as China's frontline in the fight against terrorism since the 1990s. As Chinese Communist Party (CCP) Secretary of Xinjiang, the region's most powerful position, from 1994 to 2010, Wang Lequan adopted a hard-handed approach that led to several days of rioting in July 2009 in Urumqi, the capital of Xinjiang, which involved at least 1,000 Uyghurs and resulted in 197 deaths, most of them Han (Battaglia 2017). Wang was then replaced by Zhang Chunxian in 2010, when the region was still recovering from the riots, who on assuming his position, developed a softer people-oriented approach based on security alertness as well as economic development.

In response to the deadly rioting in Urumqi, a Xinjiang Work Forum (*Xinjiang gongzuo zuotanhui*) was conducted in May 2010, for the first time in the history of Xinjiang under the PRC. As poverty and material inequality have always been seen by the CCP leadership as the root causes of discontent in Xinjiang and elsewhere in China, the First Xinjiang Work Forum (IXWF), in setting the promotion of "leapfrog development to ensure lasting political stability" (*kuayueshi fazhan he changzhijiu'an*) as its prime objective, basically reemphasized economic development as a panacea to resolve violent ethnic separatism in Xinjiang (Chaudhuri 2014: 2). However, the steady escalation of tensions and increasing frequency of incidents of violence in the region and elsewhere in China perpetrated by Uyghurs led to the perception that a greater dose of economic development was an inadequate solution to the problem.

The Second Xinjiang Work Forum (2XWF), attended by the entire CCP Politburo and over 300 top Party officials in Beijing from 28–29 May 2014, and occurring only a mere four years after the first such gathering, indicates how much of a pressing concern Xinjiang is to the leadership (Leibold 2014). The Chinese leadership undertook a major shift in both focus and strategy at the 2XWF, moving from the growth-oriented "leapfrog development" strategy to a renewed stress on ensuring security and stability, and promoting a new policy of "ethnic intermingling". The 2XWF asserted that "Xinjiang's most sustained problem is the problem of ethnic unity", which requires "strengthening interethnic contact, exchange and mingling" (*jiaqiang minzu jiaowang jiaoliu jiaorong*), with CCP Secretary-General and PRC State Chairman Xi Jinping urging "all ethnic groups to show mutual understanding, respect, tolerance and appreciation, and to learn from and help each other, so as to bind them tightly together like the seeds of a pomegranate" (Leibold 2014). The leadership seems to have recognized that the lack of ethnic minority identification with the predominantly Han-Chinese state could be the root of violence and disaffection in Xinjiang.

Zhang Chunxian was subsequently replaced as Xinjiang's Party secretary, rumored to be due to his ineffectiveness in curbing the rise of ethnic unrest and separatist violence in the region. Zhang's removal could be read as a signal that the central government considered his approach as being too lenient and wanted to show an iron fist in the region. As Xinjiang is a hub in China's "One Belt, One Road" development initiative that seeks to revive the ancient Silk Road by linking Central Asian and Eurasian economies into a China-centered trading network, the region is integral to the geopolitical ambitions and legacy of Xi Jinping. This makes stability in Xinjiang a strategic imperative. Chen Quanguo, Zhang's successor who assumed his position in August 2016, went back to Wang Lequan's hard-knuckled security-first approach, and has tried to project an even more uncompromising image. It has been speculated that Chen not only wanted to look tough on terror in the eyes of the Han and Uyghur populations of Xinjiang, but was also using his hardline stance on terrorism to successfully angle for a Politburo seat at the 19th CCP Congress, which took place in the fall of 2017 (Wong 2017).

Although different administrations in Xinjiang might have emphasized different strategies – "hard" coercive, "soft" reward-based, or "middling" surveillance/monitoring – and their degrees of effectiveness may be debatable, the objectives of the CCP-PRC party-state have always been clear: to forestall and punish acts of organized and premeditated violence in the region, while integrating it politically, militarily, economically, demographically, and socioculturally into China.

## The "hard" strategy of repression

PRC's legislature, the National People's Congress, passed the country's first comprehensive "Counter-terrorism Law" at the end of 2015, which took effect on 1 January 2016 (*Xinhuanet*). Salient aspects of the law merit pointing out (Zhou 2016):

1. The definition of terrorism reads: "Any advocacy or activity that, by means of violence, sabotage, or threat, aims to create social panic, undermine public safety, infringe on personal and property rights, or coerce a state organ or an international organization, in order to achieve political, ideological, or other objectives." The term "advocacy" (*zhuzhang*), punishable by fine, incarceration or execution, is vague enough to be interpreted as "speech," "writing" or "drawing".
2. The law requires telecommunications operators and Internet service providers to furnish the government with technical support, including backdoor access and decryption, for the prevention and investigation of terrorist activities.
3. To prevent copycat acts, the law allows no one to disseminate details of terrorist incidents, publish identifying information on response personnel or hostages, nor on anti-terror responses, without the permission of the relevant authorities.
4. Implementing a "people's war" strategy that highlights the participation of civilians is a top principle of the counter-terrorism law (Article 5), which specifically says that the authorities should establish joint coordination mechanisms to mobilize grassroots organizations (Article 8), set up formal forces or volunteer groups in communities (Article 74), and encourage civilians to work as informants to promote intelligence gathering (Article 44).
5. The law may apply restrictions on individuals suspected of being involved in terrorist activities, which includes bans on traveling outside the suspect's area of residence or the country, taking public transportation, or entering specified venues without police approval, as well as confiscation of identity card and passport.
6. The law allows the People's Liberation Army (PLA) to seek approval from the CCP's Central Military Commission for engaging in counter-terrorism abroad.

Under this tough strategy, quick and determined responses to terrorist attacks by the authorities are deemed necessary to demonstrate a forceful will to preempt or deter future acts of violence, and reprise against past ones. Around every anniversary of the July 2009 Urumqi riot, the security presence in the cities and major towns of Xinjiang has thus been visibly heightened. Twenty-four-hour patrols are conducted by the People's Armed Police (PAP), a paramilitary riot police force responsible for domestic security.

On 31 December 2016, authorities in Xinjiang staged a massive show of military force with an anti-terror exercise attended by the region's Communist Party chief, Chen Quanguo, senior party and government officials, and security forces. The drill involved parading armored vehicles, rescuing hostages, and demonstrating how police booths which dot the streets of Xinjiang can defend themselves if they come under attack (Li 2017).

After three knife-wielding assailants killed five people in a residential compound on 14 February 2017 in Xinjiang's Pishan County, Hotan Prefecture, tensions were much heightened in the county where most Uyghur villages cannot understand Putonghua, and detachments of the PAP in bulletproof vests could be seen patrolling every 10 to 20 meters on Pishan's streets (Chen 2017). In the aftermath of the killings, thousands of armed soldiers held mass rallies and columns of armored vehicles were deployed on the streets of Urumqi and other major cities in Xinjiang, with Chen Quanguo urging these forces to "bury the corpses of terrorists in the vast sea of a people's war (Gracie 2017)."

On Saturday 18 February 2017, about 10,000 police officers and members of the PAP attended a rally in a central square in Urumqi, after similar rallies had taken place in Hotan on Thursday and in Kashgar on Friday, both oasis towns in southern Xinjiang with predominantly Uighur populations (Wong 2017). A similar counter-terrorism exercise involving more than 10,000 PAP personnel was conducted over three-and-a half days in September 2017 simultaneously in all the major cities of Xinjiang (*Xinhua* 2017).

Convinced that fervent religiosity is a major motivation for engaging in terrorism, Xinjiang has since September 2016 established religious and residential committees to which local residents have to report their religious activities, including circumcisions, weddings and funerals (Zhao 2016). People organizing unauthorized religious travels abroad could face fines of up to 200,000 Yuan (US$30,000), and Muslims making unauthorized Hajj pilgrimages to Mecca may be jailed (Rife 2017). In line with cracking down on underground Muslim religious schools, or *madrassas*, in Xinjiang in recent years, new education rules promulgated by the authorities for Xinjiang on 1 November 2016 banned all forms of religious activities in schools, for while China officially guarantees freedom of religion, minors (below age 18) are forbidden to engage in religious activity, including fasting. The rules also decreed that parents or guardians cannot "organize, lure or force minors into attending religious activities," on pain of arrest by the police (Reuters 2017).

In March 2017, lawmakers in the Xinjiang People's Congress' standing committee passed the first region-wide legislation to combat "religious extremism". The laws, which took effect from 1 April 2017, banned behavior such as sporting an "abnormally long" beard (no standard measurement given), wearing face-covering veils in public places, refusing to watch state television, and marrying using religious rather than civil procedures (Shepherd and Blanchard 2017). To enforce the regulation, special task forces would be set up by regional, prefectural and county governments, civil servants would be required to report violators to the police, and local leaders would be evaluated annually for their localities' adherence to the legislation (Gan 2017).

Under the CCP's "Naming Rules for Ethnic Minorities", which went into effect in April 2017, dozens of baby names used by Muslims throughout the world were also banned in Xinjiang. These names are considered "overly religious", and "any babies registered with such names would be barred from the *hukou*, or household registration system, that gives access to health care and education", according to an Urumqi police station employee (Xin 2017). Names such as "Jihad", "Islam", "Imam", "Hajj", "Wahhab", "Saddam", "Arafat", "Quran", "Mecca", "Medina", and "Cairo" are on the proscribed list (Xin 2017).

The government has also set up "political education centers" throughout Xinjiang, in which targets for thought reform, especially those deemed by the authorities to have demonstrated ultra-religious behavior, and which has already affected over 2,000 people in Hotan Prefecture alone, may be detained indefinitely and required by party cadres to learn Chinese, recite relevant laws and policies, watch pro-government videos, shout pro-government slogans, and clarify or rectify their political stance (Human Rights Watch 2017a). According to US senators Marco Rubio and Chris Smith, as many as 500,000 to a million ethnic minority people in Xinjiang are being or have been detained since these education facilities began operation in April 2017 (*Radio Free Asia* 2018).

Mandatory anti-terror drills for civilians are conducted under police supervision in towns and cities throughout Xinjiang, in which shopkeepers rush out of their stores swinging government-issued wooden clubs to fight off imaginary knife-wielding assailants. Aside from taking part in drills, shopkeepers must, at their own expense, install password-activated security doors, "panic buttons" and cameras that film not just the street outside but also inside their stores (Wen 2017).

### The "soft" strategy of recompense

This strategy relies on the authorities taking measures to change behavior by aiming at the pockets and minds of targets. These measures include the following.

*Rewards for terror tip-offs*: The public security authority of Altay prefecture, which borders Kazakhstan, Russia and Mongolia, has announced in 2017 that it is offering up to 5 million yuan (US$725,000) for information on terrorist attack plans that target government buildings, public venues or important events; up to 4 million yuan to whistle-blowers who report explosives- or gun-making activities; and 3 million yuan for tip-offs on terrorists entering or leaving China (Huang 2017).

*Payments for intermarriages*: The promotion of Han-Uyghur marriages is one of the policies to emerge from the 2XWF. Since then, officials in Cherchen County, known as Qiemo in Putonghua, which has a population of

10,000, of whom 73% are Uyghur and 27% are Han, has begun offering payments of 10,000 yuan (almost $1,600) a year for five years to newly married couples in which one member is Han and the other is from one of China's officially recognized 55 ethnic minorities (Wong 2014). The couples will also get priority consideration for housing and government jobs, as well as substantial subsidies for their own medical bills and education expenses for their children (Meyer 2014).

*Compensation for birth control*: Authorities in southern Xinjiang's rural Hotan prefecture, which is poor and heavily dominated by Uyghurs, have been encouraging residents to "have fewer children and get rich quick", with a 3,000 yuan payout for those who forgo having the third child allowed to rural ethnic minority couples under China's family planning rules (AFP 2015).

*Winning hearts and minds*: Since 2014, some 200,000 officials in Xinjiang have been sent to live in rural areas, particularly southern Xinjiang, which is strongly rooted in Islamic traditionalism, under a program aimed at winning the hearts and minds of the local people, particularly Uyghurs, by helping villagers with farm work, clearing land, and planting trees (Silk and Chen 2014). Han cadres were also required to visit ethnic minority families regularly and interact closely with them to gain a better understanding of non-Han local culture in Xinjiang (Gan 2016).

*Ethnic mingling*: At a CCP Politburo meeting on Xinjiang on 23–24 September 2013, Yu Zhengsheng, Chairman of the National Committee of the Chinese People's Political Consultative Conference, called for more inland elites to work in the region, for the purposes of "fostering local talent with professional quality and managerial capabilities", and providing "talent support", for the sake of the region's stability and development (Uyghur American Association 2013). It is in this spirit that Beijing hopes to trigger a new influx of immigrants into the region with the most liberal residency rules in China.

*Job creation and work placements*: Competition for jobs with local and migrant Han-Chinese for jobs has been mitigated in the public sector through affirmative action policies in the form of hiring quotas for Uyghurs. However, this has been undermined by the shrinking size of the state sector, and as shown in a 2012 study, Uyghur workers in non-state occupations earn on average 52% less than Han workers (Grieger 2014). Nonetheless, under a "national assistance pairing program", with central ministries and economically developed provinces and municipalities supporting Xinjiang in building new infrastructure and boosting local development, 5,161 assistance projects were launched in the region with a combined investment of over 58 billion yuan ($8.63 billion) between 2011 and 2015, of which 74% went to livelihood improvement programs such as housing upgrade, school construction, and job creation (Yuan 2017).

At the 2XWF, Xi expressed his wish that more Uyghurs should be moved to Han-dominated parts of China for education and employment, and the

Forum's concluding statement called for "orderly expanding the number of Xinjiang minorities who receive education, find employment and live in the interior" (Leibold 2014). Provincial governments were "encouraged" to offer young Uyghurs work and educational opportunities "to enhance mutual understanding", and as one of China's wealthiest provinces, Guangdong committed itself to take 5,000 of these individuals up to the end of 2016 (Meyer 2014).

## Between "hard" and "soft" – a "middling" strategy of (combat)-readiness

This security strategy to guard against the threat of terrorism by monitoring and regulating the lives of Xinjiang residents, through the use of both the latest technology as well as old-fashioned neighborhood-watch schemes, has gained currency with the authorities in recent years. Unlike both the intimidating ("hard") and incentivizing ("soft") strategies discussed, which are obviously aimed at recalcitrant non-Han ethnic minorities, this strategy is supposedly targeted at no particular ethnic group.

In 2005, the administration of former CCP Secretary-General cum PRC State Chairman Hu Jintao began constructing "Skynet" ("*Tianwang*"), China's nationwide surveillance system to "improve social management", a euphemism for tightening security monitoring, the pace of which quickened with the riots in Tibetan-populated areas and Urumqi in 2008 and 2009 respectively (Langfitt 2013). By July 2010, Xinjiang authorities had installed high-definition video surveillance cameras on public buses and at bus stops; on roads and in alleys; in markets and shopping centers; and in schools and mosques (Famularo 2015).

In 2015, the PRC Ministry of State Security initiated the development of a comprehensive face recognition system that, when fully implemented, should be able to identify every single one of the 1.3 billion citizens of the country within three seconds by matching his or her facial features against a national database (Gesellschaft für bedrohte Volke 2017). One of the Ministry of Public Security's most ambitious big-data projects is the Police Cloud (*jingwuyun*) System, which aggregates and analyses information from people's medical history, to their supermarket membership, to home delivery records, much of which is linked to people's unique national identification numbers (Human Rights Watch 2017b). This system allows the police to track where the individuals have been, who they are with, and what they have been doing, as well as make predictions about their future activities. Furthermore, since July 2017, authorities in Urumqi have ordered local residents to install an app on their smartphones that would "automatically pinpoint the location of video or audio containing terrorist content or illegal religious content, images, e-books or documents, and delete them automatically" (Qiao and Wang 2017).

In October 2016, residents in many parts of Xinjiang, both Muslim Uyghurs and Han, were told to hand over their passports to the local police for review and safekeeping, and those wishing to travel abroad had to first seek permission from the authorities before reclaiming their passports (Gan 2016). The reason for these orders became clear the following month, when the Public Security Bureau in Xinjiang required all passport applicants in the region henceforth to supply DNA samples as part of their application. Police in Xinjiang's north-western Yili (Ili) prefecture have since June 2017 been asking residents to supply not only a blood sample for DNA identification, but also fingerprints and a voice recording when applying for travel documents (BBC 2017).

To strengthen everyday policing, a sprawling net of several thousand "convenience police stations" located normally 400–600 meters apart and at street intersections are being built across cities, towns and rural areas of Xinjiang. These compact one- or two-storied concrete structures, typically measuring about 40 square meters to 120 square meters, are stocked with wheelchairs, first-aid kits, repair tools, umbrellas and even phone chargers for public use, but they also come equipped with surveillance cameras and guards on 24-hour patrols (Gan 2016).

Beginning in 2017, authorities in western Xinjiang's Bayingolin prefecture have ordered all vehicles registered there to be installed with satellite tracking devices, using the homegrown Chinese *Beidou* GPS system, which would enable the authorities to pinpoint the position of vehicles at all times (Wong and Sing 2017). Authorities in Urumqi have since August 2017 also required all ethnic Uyghur and Kazak individuals to undergo stringent background checks before registering a vehicle in the city (Niyaz 2017).

## Violence involving Uyghurs

There has been a string of recent terrorist incidents involving Uyghurs. On 28 October 2013, a four-wheel drive vehicle ploughed through a group of pedestrians near Tiananmen Square in central Beijing, crashed into a stone bridge and caught fire, killing the three Uyghur vehicle occupants and two pedestrians, and injuring dozens. While the Turkistan Islamic Party (TIP) has claimed responsibility for the Tiananmen Square attack, Chinese authorities blamed it on the shadowy Xinjiang-based East Turkestan Islamic Movement (ETIM).

On 1 March 2014, a group of Uyghur men armed with long knives and machetes killed 31 people and injured 141 at the main railway station in Kunming, Yunnan province (Newton 2015). Four of the assailants were shot dead at the scene and the fifth, a pregnant woman, was captured alive and later sentenced to life in prison on the charges of joining a terror group and committing murder (AP 2015). On 18 September 2015, on the eve of celebrations to mark the 60th anniversary of the establishment of the Xinjiang (Uyghur) Autonomous Region, knife-wielding separatists killed some 50 miners and security guards at a coalmine in Baicheng county of Aksu prefecture before fleeing into the mountains (*Radio Free Asia* 2015).

Overseas, increasing numbers of Uyghur fleeing or migrating from Xinjiang through Southeast Asia have led to a number of detentions in 2013 and 2014 by the authorities in Malaysia, Indonesia, and Thailand, who claimed that the detainees had been travelling on forged Turkish passports or citizenship papers. This issue achieved prominence in the aftermath of the bombing of the Erawan Shrine in Bangkok on 18 August 2015, which some speculated was perpetrated by Uyghurs in retaliation for the deportation to China of 109 Uyghurs discovered by Thai authorities in a people-smuggling run camp in Muslim southern Thailand (Clarke 2017: 18–19). At the request of Chinese authorities, Egypt has deported dozens of Uyghur students back home to China and detained hundreds of others for repatriation in 2017 (Kashgary 2017).

## Scant evidence of foreign involvement

Comparing the speeches given by Hu at the 1XWF and Xi at the 2XWF, the focus of Hu was on promoting Uyghur employment through economic growth, while that of Xi was on actively suppressing terrorism. However, notwithstanding the difference in emphasis, the logic driving Xinjiang policy throughout both the Hu and Xi administrations are basically the same, namely: a) the CCP's policies toward Xinjiang are correct; and b) the causes of the occurrences of crises are inherently external and brought in from outside Xinjiang's international borders (Suzuki 2014). As such, dealing with the infiltration of foreign religious extremists and Uyghurs under their influence would justify the use of any strategy by the authorities.

Beijing has long claimed a connection between Xinjiang violence and global Islamic terrorism, accusing what it says are separatist groups based abroad such as ETIM/TIP of being behind attacks in Xinjiang, and maintaining that the so-called Islamic State (IS) has been recruiting Uyghurs from China. Beijing has contended that ETIM was responsible for a suicidal car bomb attack through the east gate of the Chinese embassy at Bishkek, Kyrgyzstan, in August 2017 (Putz 2017). It seems that, despite Beijing's best efforts to cut off transit routes via Central and Southeast Asia, more than 100 Uyghurs have made their way to join IS in Iraq and Syria (Gracie 2017). More recently, on 1 March 2017, IS released a video, which appeared to threaten China by showing Uyghur fighters training, and threatening to "shed rivers of blood and avenge the oppressed" in China (Battaglia 2017).

Notwithstanding the video threat, there has been no significant terrorist attack outside Xinjiang in the rest of China since 2014, and reported attacks within the region have been sporadic and small-scale, with no claims that they have been designed or executed by foreign agents or masterminds. Rather than Uyghurs being driven by the IS agenda, it is very possible that IS had made use of them to boast of its own reach and militancy.

While foreign instigators or agents may well be present, they do not appear to be the direct causes or major perpetrators of violence in Xinjiang. More likely, both external and internal dimensions of the security threat have been talked up by powerful vested interests in China whose objectives are advanced by securitization, such as politicians angling for promotion and thus wanting to appear tough before the CCP Congress in the autumn of 2017, security services wanting to expand their bureaucratic empires, and businesses that produce surveillance equipment and software wanting to make more money. What needs to be addressed are questions such as: By highlighting violent activities, and devising ever new strategies to deal with them, would the authorities inadvertently play up and fuel the resentment of ethnic minorities in Xinjiang? Does the Chinese party-state need more violence and problems to deal with, which the country already has aplenty? Would "securitizing" terrorist violence in Xinjiang into an existential threat that justifies the taking of extreme and unusual measures against it, end up discouraging hydrocarbon pipeline and infrastructure investments in the region, thus affecting "One-Belt-One-Road?"

## A continuous vicious cycle of Uyghur resistance and official reaction

The ultimate aim of all power strategies employed by the central and local authorities of the PRC is to exercise effective rule over the Uyghurs and other ethnic minorities in Xinjiang and eradicate the threat of terrorism from the region. As Chinese citizens typically have high expectations that the government should keep them safe, and political careers oftentimes depend on keeping the peace in one's precinct, China's leaders are generally intolerant of failure to prevent or contain outbreaks of organized violence, no matter how minimal or localized, hence their militaristic actions and tough talking.

However, Xinjiang has concentrations of urbanized high-density populations whose local ethnic minority population is only grudgingly loyal to the authorities. Many Uyghurs see the large and continuous influx of Han-Chinese into Xinjiang, keen competition with these immigrants for jobs, restrictions by the authorities on indigenous customs and religious practices, and pressure to learn the Chinese language even to get by in Xinjiang as official attempts to marginalize or even eradicate Uyghur ethnic and cultural identities. They also perceive the government's strategies to deal with ethnic unrests – whether "hard", "soft" or somewhere in between – as just means to achieve its integrationist ends. This perception does not bode well for the party-state's endeavor to ensure a more socially cohesive, inter-mingled, peaceful, and stable society in Xinjiang, or the rest of China.

The absence of any dialogue with the Uyghur population underscores the top-down approach in addressing the region's most pressing problems. The ethnic Uyghur population of Xinjiang has no discernible political voice, let alone has it reflected in the formulation of official policies, and in the midst of a "people's war on terror", called for by the 2XWF, it is dangerous for them to speak up, unless to echo the government's message. In 2014, making the case for an honest appraisal of the dangers of repression earned China's most illustrious Uyghur academic, Ilham Tohti, a life sentence in prison. The risk of demonizing such mild dissent may only be to leave China's Uyghurs with the voice of the separatist, religious fundamentalist, or "terrorist".

Aside from their very different languages, religions and cultural traditions, "Uighurs, in the eyes of most Han, are dangerous criminals and thieves to be avoided; the Han, for most Uighurs, are dirty and infidel invaders who cannot be trusted" (Leibold 2014). Despite the improvements in the livelihood of many locals in Xinjiang due to China's economic and investment policies, separatist sentiments, resentment towards government policies and ill-feeling against the Han immigrants in Xinjiang will remain, and to vent these emotions, a section of the Uyghur population will occasionally seek to use violence indiscriminately. This will only lead to more repressive actions on the part of the authorities, thus resulting in a continuous cycle of resistance and suppression.

## References

AFP (2015), "China's Drive to Settle New Wave of Migrants in Restive Xinjiang", *South China Morning Post*, 8 May, available at http://www.scmp.com/news/china/society/article/1789160/chinas-drive-settle-new-wave-migrants-restive-xinjiang#comments accessed 5 February 2017.

An Baijie (2017), "Cherish Ethnic Unity, President Tells Xinjiang", *China Daily*, 11 March, available at http://www.chinadaily.com.cn/china/2017twosession/2017-03/11/content_28515253.htm accessed 5 February 2017.

AP (2015), "Three Men Executed in China over Railway Station Knife Attack that Left 31 Dead", *South China Morning Post*, 25 March, available at http://www.scmp.com/news/china/article/1746165/three-men-executed-over-kunming-railway-station-knife-attack accessed 5 February 2017.

Battaglia, Gabriele (2017), "What Do Islamic State and Tibet Have to Do with China's Crackdown in Xinjiang?" *South China Morning Post* (Hong Kong), 19 March, available at http://www.scmp.com/week-asia/geopolitics/article/2079542/what-do-islamic-state-and-tibet-have-do-chinas-crackdown accessed 5 February 2017.

BBC (2017), "Chinese Police Require DNA for Passports in Xinjiang", 7 June, available at http://www.bbc.com/news/world-asia-china-36472103 accessed 5 February 2017.

Chaudhuri, Debasish (2014), "Second Xinjiang Work Forum: Old Policies in New Language", *ICS (Institute of Chinese Studies) Analysis*, August 2014.

Chen, Stephen (2017), "Chinese Police Out in Full Force after Xinjiang Terror Attack", *Star* (Malaysia), 15 February, available at http://www.thestar.com.my/news/regional/2017/02/15/chinese-police-out-in-full-force-after-xinjiang-terror-attack/ accessed 5 February 2017.

Clarke, Michael (2017), "Xinjiang and the Trans-nationalization of Uyghur Terrorism: Cracks in the 'New Silk Road'?" 10 February, *The Asian Forum*, 5(3).

Famularo, Julia (2015), "How Xinjiang Has Transformed China's Counterterrorism Policies", *National Interest* (Washington DC), 25 August, available at http://nationalinterest.org/feature/how-xinjiang-has-transformed-china%E2%80%99s-counterterrorism-13699?page=2 accessed 5 February 2017.

Gan, Nectar (2016), "Passports Taken, More Police ... New Party Boss Chen Quanguo Acts to Tame Xinjiang with Methods Used in Tibet", *South China Morning Post*, 12 December, available at http://www.scmp.com/news/china/policies-politics/article/2053739/party-high-flier-uses-his-tibet-model-bid-tame-xinjiang accessed 5 February 2017.

Gan, Nectar (2017), "Ban on Beards and Veils – China's Xinjiang Passes Law to Curb 'Religious Extremism'", *South China Morning Post*, 30 March, available at http://www.scmp.com/news/china/policies-politics/article/2083479/ban-beards-and-veils-chinas-xinjiang-passes-regulation accessed 5 February 2017.

Gesellschaft für bedrohte Volke (2017), "Police State China: People's Republic Relies on Total Control", 13 October, available at https://www.gfbv.de/en/news/police-state-china-peoples-republic-relies-on-total-control-8845/ accessed 5 February 2017.

Gracie, Carrie (2017), "All-out Offensive in Xinjiang Risks Worsening Grievances", *British Broadcasting Corporation*, 2 March, available at http://www.bbc.com/news/world-asia-china-39137420 accessed 5 February 2017.

Grieger, Gisela (2014), "China: Assimilating or Radicalizing Uighurs?" European Parliamentary Research Service, 19 November, available at http://epthinktank.eu/2014/11/19/china-assimilating-or-radicalising-uighurs/ accessed 5 February 2017.

Huang, Kristin (2017), "Big Payouts in Xinjiang for Terror Tip-Offs", *South China Morning Post*, 14 April.

Human Rights Watch (2017a), "China: Free Xinjiang 'Political Education' Detainees", 10 September, available at https://www.hrw.org/news/2017/09/10/china-free-xinjiang-political-education-detainees accessed 5 February 2017.

Human Rights Watch (2017b), "China: Police 'Big Data' Systems Violate Privacy, Target Dissent", 19 November, available at https://www.hrw.org/news/2017/11/19/china-police-big-data-systems-violate-privacy-target-dissent accessed 5 February 2017.

Kashgary, Jilil (2017), "Uyghur Student in Cairo Narrowly Avoids Arrest by Chinese, Egyptian Agents", *Radio Free Asia*, 25 July, available at http://www.rfa.org/english/news/uyghur/student-07252017162120.html accessed 5 February 2017.

Langfitt, Frank (2013), "In China, Beware: A Camera May Be Watching You", *National Public Radio* (USA), 29 January, 3:30 AM ET, available at http://www.npr.org/2013/01/29/170469038/in-china-beware-a-camera-may-be-watching-you accessed 5 February 2017.

Leibold, James (2014), "Xinjiang Work Forum Marks New Policy of 'Ethnic Mingling'", *China Brief*, 14(12), Jamestown Foundation, 19 June, available at https://jamestown.org/program/xinjiang-work-forum-marks-new-policy-of-ethnic-mingling/ accessed 5 February 2017.

Li, Eva (2017), "Show of Force in Xinjiang Sends Hardline Message", *South China Morning Post*, 3 January, available at https://uyghuramerican.org/article/show-force-xinjiang-sends-hardline-message.html accessed 5 February 2017.

Meyer, Eric (2014), "China Offers Work Placements and Mixed Marriage Incentives as Solutions for its Xinjiang Problems", *Forbes*, 13 November, available at https://www.forbes.com/sites/ericrmeyer/2014/11/13/chinas-newest-recipes-for-solving-its-xinjiang-problem-work-placements-and-mixed-marriage-incentives/#46c1423a5098 accessed 5 February 2017.

Newton, Jennifer (2015), "Three Chinese Separatists Executed for Role in Train Station Attack that Killed 31 People Last Year", *Daily Mail* (UK), 24 March, available at http://www.dailymail.co.uk/news/article-3008996/China-executes-three-men-convicted-mass-stabbing-train-station.html accessed 5 February 2017.

Niyaz, Kurban (2017), "Urumqi Officials Confirm Security Checks for Uyghur, Kazakh Vehicle Registrants", *Radio Free Asia*, 28 August, available at http://www.rfa.org/english/news/uyghur/checks-08292017154534.html accessed 5 February 2017.

Putz, Catherine (2017), "3 Convicted for Chinese Embassy Attack in Bishkek", *The Diplomat*, 30 June, available at https://thediplomat.com/2017/06/3-convicted-for-chinese-embassy-attack-in-bishkek/ accessed 5 February 2017.

Qiao Long and Xi Wang (2017), "China Orders Xinjiang's Android Users to Install App that Deletes 'Terrorist' Content", *Radio Free Asia*, 14 July, available at http://www.rfa.org/english/news/china/china-orders-xinjiangs-android-users-to-install-app-that-deletes-terrorist-content-07142017102032.html accessed 5 February 2017.

*Radio Free Asia* (2015), "At Least 50 Reported to Have Died in Attack on Coalmine in Xinjiang in September", *Guardian* (London), 1 October, available at https://www.theGuardian.com/world/2015/oct/01/at-least-50-reported-dead-in-september-attack-as-china-celebrates-xinjiang accessed 5 February 2017.

*Radio Free Asia* (2018), "Survey: Three Million, Mostly Uyghurs, in Some Form of Political "Re-Education' in Xinjiang", 3 August, available at https://www.rfa.org/english/news/uyghur/millions-08032018142025.html/ accessed 21 August 2018

Reuters (2017), "China's New Rules for Xinjiang Ban Parents from Encouraging or Forcing Children into Religion", *South China Morning Post*, 6 January, available at http://www.scmp.com/news/china/policies-politics/article/2027342/chinas-new-rules-xinjiang-ban-parents-encouraging-or accessed 5 February 2017.

Rife, Roseann (2017), "Why China Must Scrap New Laws that Tighten the Authorities' Grip on Religious Practice", *Amnesty International*, 31 August, available at https://www.amnesty.org/en/latest/news/2017/08/china-must-scrap-new-laws-tighten-authorities-grip-on-religious-practice/ accessed 5 February 2017.

Shepherd, Christian and Ben Blanchard (2017), "China Sets Rules on Beards, Veils to Combat Extremism in Xinjiang", *Reuters*, 30 March, available at http://www.Reuters.com/article/china-xinjiang-int-idUSKBN1710DD accessed 5 February 2017.

Silk, Richard, and Te-Ping Chen (2014), "Chinese Officials Head to Countryside to Try to Win Over Locals", *Reuters*, 15 May, available at https://blogs.wsj.com/chinarealtime/2014/05/15/chinese-officials-head-to-countryside-to-try-to-win-over-locals/ accessed 5 February 2017.

Suzuki, Takashi (2014), "Uighur Question and Why Beijing's Policies in Xinjiang are Not Working", *Asahi Shimbun*, 10 September, available at http://ajw.asahi.com/article/forum/politics_and_economy/east_asia/AJ201409100060 accessed 5 February 2017.

Uyghur American Association (2013), "Same Mistakes, No Real Solutions from Beijing's Misguided 2013 Xinjiang Work Forum", 24 September, available at http://uyghuramerican.org/article/same-mistakes-no-real-solutions-beijing-s-misguided-2013-xinjiang-work-forum.html accessed 5 February 2017.

Wen, Phillip (2017), "Terror Threats Transform China's Uighur Heartland into Security State", *Reuters*, 31 March, available at http://uk.*Reuters*.com/article/uk-china-xinjiang-security-insight-idUKKBN1713AY accessed 5 February 2017.

Wong, Edward (2017), "Chinese Security Forces Rally in Xinjiang in a Show of Power", *New York Times*, 20 February, available at https://www.nytimes.com/2017/02/20/world/asia/xinjiang-china-police-rallies.html?mcubz=2 accessed 5 February 2017.

Wong Siusan- and SingMan (2017) "Vehicles to Get Compulsory GPS Tracking in Xinjiang", *Radio Free Asia*, 20 February, available at http://www.rfa.org/english/news/uyghur/xinjiang-gps-02202017145155.html accessed 5 February 2017.

Xin Lin (2017), "China Bans 'Extreme' Islamic Baby Names among Xinjiang's Uyghurs", *Radio Free Asia*, 20 April, available at http://www.rfa.org/english/news/uyghur/names-04202017093324.html accessed 5 February 2017.

*Xinhua* (2017), "China's Armed Police Hold Anti-Terror Exercise in Xinjiang", 12 September, available at http://news.xinhuanet.com/english/2017-09/12/c_136604065.htm accessed 5 February 2017.

*Xinhuanet* (n.d.), "Zhonghua Renmin Gongheguo fan kongbu zhuyi fa", (People's Republic of China Counter-terrorism Law), available at http://news.xinhuanet.com/politics/2015-12/27/c_128571798.htm accessed 5 February 2017.

Yuan Yuan (2017), "Go West", *Beijing Review*, No. 31, 3 August, available at http://www.bjreview.com/Nation/201707/t20170728_800101243.html accessed on 5 February 2017.

Zhao Yusha (2016), "Xinjiang Sets up Local Committees to Better Serve Religious Activities", *Global Times*, 22 November, available at http://www.globaltimes.cn/content/1019614.shtml accessed 5 February 2017.

Zhou Zunyou (2016), "China's Comprehensive Counter-Terrorism Law", *The Diplomat*, 23 January, available at http://thediplomat.com/2016/01/chinas-comprehensive-counter-terrorism-law/ accessed 5 February 2017.

# 10 Anti-state armed groups in Myanmar
## Origins, evolution and implications

*Ardeth Maung Thawnghmung and Mike Furnari*

## Origins

Since Myanmar gained independence from Great Britain in 1948, a motley array of groups have taken up arms against the government. A majority of them are ethnicity-based organizations which have fought for greater autonomy and independence against governments dominated by the country's majority group known as Bamar or Burman, which constitutes 68% of the population. Many of these groups represent minority ethnicities (such as Shan, Kayin (Karen), Rakhine, Mon, Kachin, Chin and Kayah, which are, respectively, estimated to represent 8.5, 6.2, 4.5, 2.4, 1.4, 2.2, and 0.4% of the total population) and live in Myanmar's resource-rich peripheral regions and in the border areas with China, Thailand, India, and Bangladesh (Silverstein 1997: 169). They share the common goal of establishing a federal system of governance as well as grievances generated by decades of rule by highly centralized and militarized governments which have suppressed the cultural and political rights of the country's minorities and extracted their resources without sharing the profits with local communities.

Some of these groups are ideologically motivated, such as the communist parties which were formed in the 1940s and which immediately after independence took up arms against civilian governments which they considered to be based on Western capitalist principles (Lintner 1990).

Other organizations – such as the All Burman Students' Democratic Front (ABSDF), led by prominent Bamar student leaders or those who had fled military retaliation against the student-led nationwide anti-government protests in 1988; or the National Coalition Government of the Union of Burma (NCGUB), formed in 1990 and led by exiled leaders who were elected members of political parties – have advocated for regime change, for the withdrawal of the military from politics, and for the implementation of democratic government. A handful of organizations, such as those representing the self-described Rohingya, have fought for citizenship and human rights, but have received little sympathy within Myanmar as the result of decades-long hostility to the descendants of immigrants from South Asia and anti-Islamic sentiment.

## The evolving nature of the conflicts

Over the 70 years since Myanmar gained independence in 1948, at least 40 non-state armed groups have taken up arms against the government (Smith 1991). These actors vary in size, objectives, and legitimacy, and have evolved in response to changes in government policy and in the larger geopolitical and economic environment. While civilian or semi-civilian governments (1948–1962 and 2010 to present) have been more accommodating to anti-state armed groups than military governments (1962–2010), official responses to armed groups have consistently failed to address the roots of these conflicts (Silverstein 1997: 169). They have largely been temporary, ad-hoc reactions, which have not only failed to address long-held resentments against the central government and the military, but have rather deepened and perpetuated existing grievances, and created new ones.

The military coup d'état of 1962 was led by senior officers who considered that too many concessions were being offered to ethnic minority armed groups. The successive military regimes in power between 1962 and 2010 responded to unrest with harsh military campaigns against armed resistance groups and civilians suspected of supporting them. They also used 'divide and rule' policies to pre-empt a united insurgent front forming to oppose the government by offering some groups bilateral ceasefire agreements, or creating militias as proxy forces with the aim of defeating the armed groups and wresting territory away from them (Buchanan 2017).

These tactics succeeded in pushing many anti-state armed groups operating in the country's core areas, such as the Irrawaddy Delta and Pegu Yoma, back to the border areas by the late 1980s. However, these groups continued to thrive given the vast extent of Myanmar's contested territories, their topography of remote hills and forests, and the lucrative economic opportunities generated by a vigorous border trade and abundant natural resources.

Myanmar's neighbors have also played a role in influencing the nature, intensity, and direction of anti-state armed resistance. Neighboring countries, particularly Thailand, China, and (to some extent) India have provided a range of economic opportunities, as well as protection and military support to non-state armed groups (Myoe 2002; Steinberg and Fan 2012). For example, until the early 1980s the Chinese government supported the Communist Party of Burma (CPB), which controlled large swathes of territory along the Chinese border east of the Salween River, while Thailand supported various anti-communist groups along its northern border.

These insurgent groups have also utilized long-standing cross-border trade routes and the opium economy to finance their activities. The state's isolationist policies and mismanagement of the national economy in the 1970s and 1980s further boosted the insurgent-controlled border trade which in turn fueled a black-market economy that provided basic foodstuffs and the ability to access consumer goods to a majority of the population.

However, in the late 1980s and early 1990s the dynamics of the country's armed conflicts were transformed by a number of developments. Following the military's brutal crackdown on the nationwide protests that erupted in 1988, the army came under a new military administration known as the State Law and Order Council (SLORC) and abandoned its isolationist, quasi-socialist policies by partially opening the economy to foreign and local investors.

In 1988 the cash-strapped government legalized the thriving cross-border trade by installing government-controlled checkpoints along its borders with China, Thailand, India, and Bangladesh. It oversaw the implementation of large-scale cross-border logging, mining, and dam-building, the construction of oil and gas pipelines, and granted commercial concessions to foreign and local companies in agriculture, fisheries and gemstone mining (Buchanan, Kramer and Woods 2013). Both China and Thailand reduced their support to armed groups along the borders and strengthened their ties with Myanmar's central government in an attempt to secure further access to natural resources and expand cross-border trade. Western economic sanctions against the country's military regime only strengthened the government's dependence on China, which soon became Myanmar's major investor and the leading supplier of arms to the military regime.

The break-up of the Communist Party of Burma (made up of various ethnic armed groups) in 1989 also offered the SLORC the opportunity to reduce the security threat by reaching ceasefire deals with the four main splinter groups within the former CPB. By 2009, 40 non-state armed groups either disarmed, or were transformed into people's militias, or made ceasefire arrangements with the government (Oo and Min 2007; Oo 2014: 13). These ceasefire agreements, which lasted until 2009, allowed armed groups to retain their weapons in their designated territories and conduct economic activity. They also enabled the government to intensify resource extraction and cross-border trade, to secure greater control over territory previously controlled by insurgent groups, and to reduce the possibility of renewed insurgencies while delaying talks aimed at concluding political settlements (Woods 2011).

Ceasefire arrangements also allowed the military to intensify its campaigns against non-ceasefire groups, particularly the Karen National Union (KNU) in the 1990s. This resulted in a significant erosion of the territories controlled by the KNU, displaced increasing numbers of Karen civilians and added to the refugee population along the Thailand–Burma border (Thawnghmung 2008). In addition, although many ethnic armed groups also profited from the ceasefire agreements, the adverse environmental and social consequences of large-scale extractive and infrastructural projects on local populations, and the Tatmadaw's efforts to take territory and revenue-generating enterprises away from the armed groups, did nothing to extinguish long-held resentments against the central government. These factors undermined the army's efforts to disarm and demobilize ethnic armed groups, which were eager to retain their weapons to back up their bargaining power in negotiations.

Following the military's refusal to hand over power to the National League for Democracy (NLD) following its landslide victory in the 1990 elections, 16 ceasefire groups were invited to attend the National Convention (NC) which was established to draft Myanmar's new constitution and which ran from 1992 to 2007 (Smith 2006: 63–66). Some groups, including the NLD and ethnic political parties which form alliance with the NLD, left the NC in protest against its heavy-handed and highly centralized decision-making practices. For example, the constitution emphasizes the continuing role of the military in politics, including the reservation of 25% of the legislative seats for the military, which makes it difficult to pass constitutional amendments that require the support of more than 75% of national legislature members. In 2008, the military staged a popular referendum on the constitution which had an alleged 92.4% approval rate (BBC 2008). In 2010 the government held elections for the national and local legislative assemblies, which were won by the Union Solidarity and Development Party (USDP), an organization created by the military and led by ex-army officials. By the time the new government came to power in 2011, 35 out of 40 groups that took part in the ceasefire process were either disarmed or transformed into pro-government's forces. Five groups insisted on retaining arms and remaining autonomous, and 11 additional groups (including splinters from ceasefire groups) were engaged in fighting against the Myanmar army (Oo 2014: 15).

The USDP government (2011–2015) nevertheless surprised the world by implementing a series of political and economic reforms. It also managed to renew bilateral ceasefire agreements with 13 armed groups by mid-2012 (Oo 2014: 17); to conclude a ceasefire with one of Myanmar's oldest and largest anti-state groups, the Karen Nation Union; and to negotiate and sign a set of multilateral agreements, known as the Nationwide Ceasefire Agreement (NCA), in 2015.

The NCA was negotiated between 16 non-state armed organizations and the government in 2013, and is unique in several ways (Thawnghmung 2017). First, unlike previous ceasefire arrangements that were bilateral, informal, and unwritten, the NCA is a formal, written, and multi-lateral agreement that is intended to include almost all armed opposition groups. Second, while in the past the military had pressured the armed groups to give up their arms and had refused to discuss political issues such as federalism, NCA signatories were allowed keep their weapons, recognized as legal organizations, and given the right to participate in a series of nationwide peace conferences aimed at reforming Myanmar's future political structures based on the principles of democracy and federalism, as 'equal partners' with the government. These developments have helped remove some of the roadblocks to negotiation, given that many non-state armed organizations trace the origins of their resistance to the excessive control and monopoly of power exercised by a Bamar-dominated government. Third, the parties to the NCA have agreed to continue their negotiations over issues that remain unresolved in future peace talks. These issues include the role of ethnic armed groups in a future federal state and power-sharing between central and state governments. Questions about redress for victims of violence or the establishment of a truth commission, which could potentially threaten the legitimacy of both sides to the talks, have so far been excluded.

Although the NCA was negotiated and agreed to by the government and 16 opposition groups, some of the most influential organizations refused to sign after the Myanmar Army blocked six groups from signing the text (Thawnghmung 2017). The achievement of a national agreement, even a partial one, is nevertheless a remarkable outcome. Key factors such as Myanmar's increasing democratization combined with some unilateral concessions by the state go a long way to explaining the October 2015 agreement. The new democratic institutions (albeit partial) provided space for increased levels of public scrutiny and accountability by both the government and armed groups, as well as strong incentives on the part of the state to make concessions to the armed groups in order to enhance the ruling regime's chances of electoral success (Bertrand, Pelletier and Thawnghmung 2018).

## Armed groups in Myanmar

The country's many non-state armed groups vary in size, legitimacy, and objectives. Some groups, such as the United Wa State Army (UWSA), Karen Nation Union (KNU), Kachin Independence Organization (KIO), Shan State Army-Restoration Council of Shan State (SSA-RCSS), have large military forces, operate like sovereign states by imposing taxes, and enjoy legitimacy among their constituents. The KNU, KIA, and New Mon State Party (MNSP) have wider nationalist aspirations, explicit political agendas, and provide education and healthcare services within the areas under their control. Others are small groups chiefly concerned with self-advancement and operating business ventures, including illicit operations such as drug production and trafficking. In 2015, there are approximately 21 ethnic armed organizations in the country ("Myanmar National Ceasefire," 2015). The largest group, the United Wa State Army, has 30,000 armed personnel, while many of the smaller organizations can field only 100–400 combatants and a few either have no armed members or are no longer militarily active.

Over the past 60 years since Myanmar's independence, some armed groups have disappeared or collapsed as a result of military defeat, or of arrangements that granted them amnesty or transformed them into militias or border guard forces. Many have modified their objectives from full independence to becoming part of a federal system. Some groups maintained ceasefire agreements which lasted for more than a decade before renewing hostilities. Other groups are in a state of limbo – neither at peace nor war with the government.

Myanmar's armed groups often fight among themselves as bitterly as they oppose the government. Internal disagreements and defections are commonplace, with splinter groups joining government forces as militias, or morphing into new resistance groups. Some groups (such as the KNU and the KIO) were formed during the early independence period while others, such as Taang National Liberation Army and the Arakan Army, are relative newcomers.

Although attempts have been made at forming a united front against successive governments, they were undermined by the sheer number and diversity of the groups involved, the military's divide-and-rule tactics, and communication problems across a large and diverse country. Anti-state alliances were split along ideological, geographical, and ethnic lines and often led by the more politically and military powerful groups. They were then typically joined by smaller groups based on geographic proximity or the benefits (support and resources) anticipated from such alliances (Bertrand, Pelletier and Thawnghmung 2018). Disagreements within anti-state alliances have occurred along a number of axes: pro- versus anti-communist agendas (1970s and 1980s); democracy versus federalism; or support for versus opposition to Bamar-led coalition movements (Smith 1991).

As a result of these tensions, in the 1990s ceasefire arrangements weakened the Democratic Alliance of Burma and triggered the gradual disintegration of the National Democratic Front (NDF). The KNU felt betrayed as a number of large armed groups which had initially committed to collective bargaining defected in pursuit of their own interests. In like manner, the United Nationalities Federal Council (UNFC), an alliance formed in 2011 to represent all ethnic armed groups during negotiations with the government, was fatally weakened as two of the largest groups, the Karen National Union and the Restoration Council of Shan State (RCSS), defected. The KNU broke off first and signed its own ceasefire agreement in January 2012, and later joined up to the NCA. Karen armed splinter groups from within the Karen state, and weak organizations such as the Chin National Front (CNF), the Arakan Liberation Party (ALP), the Pa-O National Liberation Organization (PNLO), and the National Socialist Council of Nagaland-Khaplang (NSC-NK) signed the NCA to seize the opportunity to make at least some gains (Bertrand, Pelletier and Thawnghmung 2018).

The KNU, the largest and oldest ethnic armed organization in the country, took up arms against the government in 1949, and initially controlled a large swathe of territory and population. Over the years, however, its reach has shrunk due to relentless government military campaigns and the defection of splinter groups. More than six decades of war have resulted in hundreds of thousands of deaths, at least one million refugees and internally displaced people, and widespread poverty and under-development in Karen-populated areas. This situation has fostered a high degree of distrust of the government and the Myanmar Army, as well as the Bamar population, who are closely associated with the forces of state oppression. Attempts to conclude bilateral ceasefire deals between the KNU and the government repeatedly failed under the various military regimes in power between 1962 and 2010. However, the KNU responded positively to the conciliatory gestures made by the USDP administration and signed a bilateral ceasefire agreement in 2012. Since then it has played a major role in crafting and implementing the NCA.

The signing of a bilateral ceasefire agreement, followed by the NCA, brought an end to armed conflict between government and KNU forces and enhanced security and freedom of movement in KNU-controlled territory, allowing civilians to pursue their livelihoods. Signing the NCA has also promoted communication and cooperation among Karen communities across different regions and socio-economic groupings. In particular, the peace process has provided both a venue and financial support for a dialogue that allows Karen from different areas to voice their concerns and work together to draft Myanmar's future political and economic structures. In addition, the policy positions developed by the KNU do not focus narrowly on the benefits that might accrue to a handful of small armed groups, but rest broadly on a restructuring of the political landscape based on the concept of federalism, with the aim of expanding the rights and autonomy of ethnic minorities and regional governments (Thawnghmung 2017).

These positive developments, however, have increasingly been undermined by the state's failure to implement the agreement and to adhere to agreed procedures, and also by ongoing hostilities between the military and four of the country's ethnic armed groups.

## The NLD and ongoing challenges for the peace process

In November 2015, Myanmar witnessed a historic watershed with the landslide victory of the National League for Democracy (NLD), which had served as the main opposition party against the military dictatorship since 1988 and is led by the charismatic Nobel peace prize winner, Aung San Suu Kyi, who had spent most of her life under house arrest. However, the initial elation and optimism that surged across the country following the NLD's electoral victory has gradually turned to pessimism following the party's failure to make significant progress in Myanmar's ongoing ethnic and religious conflicts.

When the NLD assumed power on March 30, 2016, 14 out of 21 armed groups had signed bilateral ceasefire agreements and eight had signed multilateral pacts (ISDP 2015: 2). Four groups, known as the Northern Alliance, were still at war with the military. Nine additional groups were either considering signing the NCA or, like the UWSA, joining the peace talks through alternative avenues.

The NLD government faced three major challenges in achieving reconciliation with the various armed groups: (1) finding ways to stop the fighting with the four armed groups still engaged in hostilities in northern Myanmar; (2) convincing those non-NCA signatories not engaged in fighting to sign the agreement; and (3) working with NCA signatories to consolidate the peace-building process through the implementation of the pact. To compound these challenges, the NLD has been increasingly criticized by Western governments, international organizations, and human rights activists for its poor performance in addressing human rights violations by the military against

Rohingya Muslims and its failure to address communal tensions between Buddhists and Muslims in northern Rakhine state.

Very little progress has been made in any of these areas in the year since the NLD came to power. The government has failed to stop the war in the north or to convince many non-signatories to sign the NCA. There are various reasons why the hostilities in the north of the country have continued. Although the bilateral ceasefire agreement between the government and the KIO lasted for 17 years (1994 to 2011), operations against the KIO (one of the strongest non-state armed groups) and Myanmar National Democratic Alliance Army (MNDAA) resumed under the USDP government in 2011 after both organizations rejected the military's 2009 plan to bring all armed groups under the control of the Tatmadaw as a border guard force. Although the USDP government later agreed to involve the KIA in the drafting of the NCA, this was too little, too late. A military campaign that has killed thousands and displaced over 100,000 civilians has hardened Kachin sentiment against the Bamar-dominated army and government, and Kachins now refuse to settle for anything short of complete autonomy.

Renewed military conflicts with the MNDAA, the Ta'ang National Liberation Army (TNLA) in northern Shan state, and the Arakan Army (AA) in Kachin state (all located along the Chinese border) were fueled mainly by the military's refusal to allow these groups to sign the NCA unless they first surrendered their arms. The reasons for the military's stand were various: it considered them either too new or too small or, in the case of the AA and TNLA, to have been supported by the KIO, and in the case of the MNDAA, to enjoy the backing of the Chinese government and therefore to constitute a threat to Myanmar's sovereignty. Many minority groups have been particularly dismayed by Suu Kyi's silence on the ongoing military campaigns against these groups and on the plight of civilians displaced by war and the death and destruction that the ongoing conflicts have brought to their areas.

The NLD's record on convincing additional groups to sign up to and implement the NCA has been equally poor. As of April 2018, only two additional ceasefire groups (the New Mon State Party and Lahu Democratic Union) have signed the NCA. As far as the existing signatories are concerned, the situation has deteriorated as a result of the government's failure to adhere to the agreed processes set out in the agreement and renewed hostilities between the army and some NCA signatories.

While the signatories now have the opportunity to make the NCA process more inclusive and participatory by mobilizing and involving grassroots communities, the actual decision-making process remains top-down. The military, and to some extent the government, exert disproportionate power in shaping and influencing the peace process in the joint committees, restrict the freedom of NCA signatories to consult local communities, and have failed to adhere to the agreed process for political dialogue. Specifically, the military has asserted effective control over the matters that are discussed, as well as the venues and timing of the various dialogues. The fact that any agreements from the Peace Conference will also have to be adopted by the national parliament, which the signatory armed groups have no control over, underlines anxieties that any emergent federal union will differ from the ideals envisioned by the country's minority ethnic groups.

The lack of progress in implementing the NCA in ceasefire areas has confirmed skeptics in their belief that neither the government nor the military are fully committed to the peace process. Steps desired include the establishment of joint mechanisms to facilitate the return of internally displaced populations, provide humanitarian assistance, and clear landmines, as well as interim arrangements allowing ethnic armed groups to deliver health, education, and socio-economic services in their areas. Local residents in ceasefire areas lack effective mechanisms that would protect them against land confiscation by large-scale business and infrastructure development activities and their adverse social and environmental consequences. Further undermining signatories' autonomy is the expansion of government education and health services to populations that were previously under the control of anti-state armed groups (Jolliffe 2016).

The mechanisms put in place to monitor violations of ceasefire agreements, both in respect to the building or strengthening of military bases by the Myanmar Army and expanding its domain into areas previously controlled by the signatories, have been very weak. These deficiencies resulted, for instance, in armed conflict between the Restoration Council of Shan State (RCSS) and the military in March and April 2017 and with the KNU's 5th Brigade in March 2018.

The NCA has also been undermined by the fact that only four out of ten organizations have troops in the range of 1,500–8,000 (constituting approximately 25% of the total armed forces controlled by non-state armed groups) that signed the NCA have credible armed components. Agreeing to the NCA process has meant that armed groups have accepted the restrictions imposed by the pact and changed their focus from the battlefield to the negotiating table. This shift requires a different skill set, which ranges from becoming acquainted with the varieties of federalism that have been practiced elsewhere, and the highly complex and technical expertise involved in resource-sharing schemes, to research, negotiation, persuasion, and presentation skills. However, many of these groups are not equipped with the knowledge, skills, and technical expertise required for the dialogues and meetings that lie ahead.

Although the NLD government has invited seven further ethnic armed groups as well as the KIO to sign the NCA, many of these groups are debating whether they will seek alternative ways of participating in the peace process. Notable among them is the UWSA, which, with 30,000 soldiers, is the largest non-state armed group in Myanmar and operates as a de facto state within northern Shan State. The UWSA leadership considers anything short of complete autonomy to be unacceptable, and has recently taken a lead among the non-signatories by proposing that armed groups enter a political dialogue with the government on genuine autonomy without signing the

NCA. These alternative proposals pose a direct challenge to the credibility of the NCA.

## Accounting for the lack of progress under the NLD government

Although the civilian government enjoys a higher level of legitimacy and popular support to lead the NCA processes than its predecessors, there has been a marked lack of progress in national reconciliation since the NLD came to power. This failure can be explained by a number of factors. First, because the USDP government was composed of former high-ranking military officers who still enjoyed considerable influence over their peers in the army, the military was able to work with it more easily. A long history of hostility and ideological conflict between the army and the NLD also hindered them in developing common strategies. Electoral considerations may also have played a role in the army's unwillingness to cooperate with the NLD, since success in peace-building might well enhance the NLD's popularity at the expense of the USDP at the polls. Second, Aung San Suu Kyi's apparent desire to micromanage the entire peace process, her lack of willingness to delegate power, and the lack of skilled and experienced negotiators with a comprehensive understanding of ethnic issues have all slowed its momentum. Her actions have also been emboldened by the knowledge that the NLD enjoys higher levels of legitimacy and popular support than the previous government (Thawnghmung 2017).

## The Rohingya issue

The rise of the NLD administration has coincided with the emergence of the Arakan Rohingya Salvation Army (ARSA), an armed organization that claims to be fighting for the rights of the self-described Rohingya people of northern Rakhine province and that gained international attention after launching attacks against government military posts in October 2016 and later in 2017. The attacks, which killed 24 (nine soldiers in 2016, and 14 soldiers and one government official in 2017) government personnel, resulted in a brutal retaliatory campaign that razed villages, killed thousands, and forced hundreds of thousands to flee to border areas in Bangladesh (ICG 2016). As of February 2018, it is estimated that at least 6,700 Rohingya have been killed and over 650,000 displaced in Bangladesh as a result of the violence (Albert 2018).

The emergence of ARSA is part of a long history of simmering tensions and outbreaks of violence between Rohingya and Buddhists in Northern Rakhine state and the development of an armed resistance movement among the Rohingya since Myanmar gained independence. With an estimated population of over 1 million, the Rohingya are a Muslim people living in a predominantly Buddhist country, mostly descendants of Bangladeshi immigrants who arrived in Burma during the British colonial period. Animosity between Buddhists and Muslims emerged as these immigrants gradually took over land previously occupied by Buddhist residents and culminated in outbreaks of communal violence during the Japanese occupation of Myanmar during World War II (Christie 2000: 165). Many Rakhine Muslims were given citizenship under the civilian government (1948–1962), which also recognized the name Rohingya and promised them a level of territorial and cultural autonomy. However, successive military governments have pursued harsh policies towards Rohingya and revoked their citizenship rights (Thawnghmung 2016: 523–547; Thawnghmung 2014). They saw them as illegal immigrants from Bangladesh and deported large numbers to Bangladesh in 1978 and again in 1991, when 200,000 and 250,000 Rohingya were displaced, respectively. Under the terms of a UN-brokered settlement, a majority were returned home, but continued to live in extreme poverty and subject to various forms of discrimination (Human Rights Watch 2000).

The USDP government presided over a resurgence of communal violence between Buddhists and Muslims in Rakhine state in 2012 which quickly spread across the rest of the country and fueled anti-Islamic sentiment, resulting in the passage of 'laws for the protection of race and religion' which placed restrictions on religious conversion (mainly from Buddhism), interfaith marriage, birth control, and polygamy (Rahman and Zeldin 2015). In August 2012, President Thein Sein established a commission to investigate communal violence in Rakhine State; its comprehensive report shed light on the root causes of the conflict and provided recommendations for considering eligibility for citizenship (Advisory Commission on Rakhine State 2017).

The NLD has adopted neutral language to refer to Rohingya as 'Muslims from Rakhine state', rather than the traditional derogatory term of 'Bengalis' — which reinforces the belief held by most Bamar Buddhists that they are interlopers from Bangladesh – and formed a nine-member advisory commission, including three foreign members (including former United Nations Secretary General Kofi Annan who chairs the commission), to provide 'rigorously impartial' assessments and recommendations to the government for dealing with the state's problems (Thawnghmung and Robinson 2017: 248). However, this approach failed to appease either the international community, which believes that the NLD has not done enough to address human rights violations and repatriate displaced Rohingya, or Rakhine Buddhists (representing Myanmar's majority population) who continue to see them as illegal immigrants. An attack by the ARSA on 30 military and police compounds in Rakhine took place just hours after the advisory commission released its final report and Kofi Annan presented its recommendations to preserve peace (Amnesty International 2018; Edroos 2017).

ARSA is not the first group to defend the rights of Rohingya. The first Rohingya uprising was carried out by the Mujahid in 1948 who were advocating for the establishment of an autonomous Muslim territory between the west bank of the Kaladan River and the east bank of the Naaf River. They also sought recognition of Muslims in Arakan (Rakhine) as an official nationality; of the Mujahid Party as a legal political organization; and of Urdu as the 'national' language of Arakan Muslims, to be taught in schools in Muslim areas of the state (Chan 2005: 411). Although the Mujahid had been defeated by the early 1960s, a series of Rohingya organizations continued to fight the government from the Bangladesh border zone. However, they were never able to launch a large-scale attack or benefit from extensive external support due to their internal divisions and inability to maneuver in politically restricted environments in both Myanmar and Bangladesh. Within each organization, divisions emerged between those who supported the jihad movement (armed struggle in the name of Islam), on the one hand, and those advocating citizenship and nationality rights, liberation from military oppression, and an autonomous territory for Muslims in Rakhine state, on the other (Singh 2007: 42–43).

ARSA was formed in 2012 as Harakah al-Yaqin, or the Faith Movement, in response to the violence that had erupted in Rakhine state in the period prior to its launch of a military campaign in 2016 (Johnston and Anagha 2016). While the organization's stated aim is the liberation of all persecuted Rohingya, the Myanmar government sees it as a jihadist movement advocating for the establishment of an Islamic state operating under sharia law. In September 2017, in an official press release, ARSA announced that it was requesting a ceasefire with the Myanmar government – which promptly rejected the request on the grounds that they 'do not negotiate with terrorists' (Chalmers and Siddiqui 2017).

While ARSA continues to operate using low-tech weapons with funds allegedly drawn from the Muslim diaspora from Myanmar, as well as private donors from Saudi Arabia and the Middle East, ARSA denies any involvement with transnational groups such as Al-Qaeda, although some transnational jihadist groups have publicly showed their support for the Rohingya in Myanmar (ICG 2018).

## Conclusion

Although the USDP government has made some progress in addressing Myanmar's decades-long conflicts, the prospects for national reconciliation under the NLD government continue to be limited by the sheer diversity and different goals of the armed groups, which have allowed the military to implement divide-and-rule tactics, as well as the lack of capacity, understanding and willingness of the Burman-dominated central government and military to relinquish and share power. This situation means that not only has the government failed to address the root causes of the conflict, but it has perpetuated and prolonged Myanmar's multi-faceted civil war by creating new grievances.

# References

Advisory Commission on Rakhine State (2017), *Towards a Peaceful, Fair and Prosperous Future for the People of Rakhine*, available at http://www.rakhinecommission.org/the-final-report/ accessed 29 May 2018.

Albert, Eleanor (2018), 'The Rohingya Crisis', Council on Foreign Relations, 20 April, available at https://www.cfr.org/backgrounder/rohingya-crisis accessed 29 May 2018.

Amnesty International (2018), 'Myanmar 2017/2018', available at https://www.amnesty.org/en/countries/asia-and-the-pacific/myanmar/report-myanmar/ accessed 29 May 2018.

Bertrand, Jacques, Alexandre Pelletier and Ardeth Thawnghmung (2018), 'First Movers, Democratization and Unilateral Concessions: Overcoming Commitment Problems and Negotiating a "National Cease-Fire" in Myanmar', *Asian Security*, 15 May, doi:10.1080/14799855.2018.1471466.

Buchanan, John (2017), *Militias in Myanmar*, San Francisco: The Asia Foundation.

Buchanan, John, Tom Kramer and Kevin Woods (2013), *Developing Disparity: Regional Investment in Burma's Borderlands*, Amsterdam: Transnational Institute.

BBC (2008), 'Burma Approves New Constitution', available at http://news.bbc.co.uk/2/hi/asia-pacific/7402105.stm accessed 29 May 2018.

Human Rights Watch (2000), 'Burma/Bangladesh-Burmese Refugees in Bangladesh: Still No Durable Solution', *Human Rights Watch* 12(3), available at https://www.hrw.org/reports/2000/burma/index.htm accessed 29 May 2018.

Chalmers, John and Danish Siddiqui (2017), 'After Insurgents' Truce, Myanmar Says "We Don't Negotiate with Terrorists"', *Reuters*, 10 September, available at https://www.Reuters.com/article/us-myanmar-rohingya/after-insurgents-truce-myanmar-says-we-dont-negotiate-with-terrorists-idUSKCN1BL0AG accessed 29 May 2018.

Chan, Aye (2005), 'The Development of a Muslim Enclave in Arakan (Rakhine) State of Burma (Myanmar)', *SOAS Bulletin of Burma Research*, 3(2), Autumn, 396–420.

Christie, Clive (2000), *A Modern History of Southeast Asia: Decolonization, Nationalism and Separatism*, New York: I.B. Tauris

Edroos, Faisal (2017), 'ARSA: Who Are the Arakan Rohingya Salvation Army?' *Al Jazeera*, 13 September, available at https://www.aljazeera.com/news/2017/09/myanmar-arakan-rohingya-salvation-army-170912060700394.html accessed 29 May 2018.

Johnston, Tim and Neelakantan Anagha (2016), 'The World's Newest Muslim Insurgency is Being Waged in Burma', *Time*, 14 December, available at http://time.com/4601203/burma-myanmar-muslim-insurgency-rohingya/ retrieved 29 May 2018.

Jolliffe, Kim (2016), *Ceasefires, Governance, and Development: The Karen National Union in Times of Change*, San Francisco, CA: The Asia Foundation.

Lintner, Bertil (1990), *The Rise and Fall of the Communist Party of Burma, CPB*, Ithaca, NY:Cornell University Press/Southeast Asian Program Publications.

ICG (International Crisis Group) (2016), 'Myanmar: A New Muslim Insurgency in Rakhine State', 15 December, available at https://www.crisisgroup.org/asia/south-east-asia/myanmar/283-myanmar-new-muslim-insurgency-rakhine-stat accessed 29 May 2018.

ICG (International Crisis Group) (2018), 'Myanmar's Rohingya Crisis Enters a Dangerous New Phase', 8 January, available at https://www.crisisgroup.org/asia/south-east-asia/myanmar/292-myanmars-rohingya-crisis-enters-dangerous-new-phase accessed 29 May 2018.

ISDP (Institute for Security and Development Policy) (2015), 'Myanmar Nationwide Ceasefire Agreement', October, available at http://isdp.eu/content/uploads/publications/2015-isdp-backgrounder-myanmar-nca.pdf accessed 29 May 2018.

Myoe, Maung Aung (2002), *Neither Friend Nor Foe: Myanmar's Relations With Thailand Since 1988: A View From Yangon*, Singapore: Institute of Defence and Strategic Studies, Nanyang Technological University.

Oo, Zaw (2014), *Understanding Myanmar's Peace Process: Ceasefire Agreements*, Bern: Swiss Peace Foundation.

Oo, Zaw, and Win Min (2007), *Assessing Burma's Ceasefire Accords*, Singapore: Institute of Southeast Asian Studies.

Rahman, Shameema, and Wendy Zeldin (2015), 'Burma: Four "Race and Religion Protection Laws" Adopted', *Global Legal Monitor*, 14 September, available at http://www.loc.gov/law/foreign-news/article/burma-fourrace-and-religion-protection-laws-adopted accessed 8 January 2019.

Silverstein, Josef (1997), *Burma: Military Rule and the Politics of Stagnation*, New York: Cornell University Press.

Singh, Bilveer (2007), *The Talibanization of South East Asia: Losing the War on Terror to Islamist Extremists*, Praeger Security International.

Smith, Martin (1991), *Burma: Insurgency and the Politics of Ethnicity*, Atlantic Highlands, NJ: Zed Books.

Smith, Martin (2006), 'Ethnic Participation and National Reconciliation in Myanmar: Challenges in a Transitional Landscape', in Trevor Wilson (ed.), *Myanmar's Long Road to National Reconciliation*, Singapore: Institute of Southeast Asian Studies.

Steinberg, David I., and Hongwei Fan (2012), *Modern China-Myanmar Relations: Dilemmas of Mutual Dependence*, Copenhagen: NIAS.

Thawnghmung, Ardeth Maung (2008), *The Karen Revolution in Burma: Diverse Voices, Uncertain Ends*, Washington, DC: East-West Center.

Thawnghmung, Ardeth Maung (2016), 'The Politics Of Indigeneity in Myanmar: Competing Narratives in Rakhine State', *Asian Ethnicity*, 17(4).

Thawnghmung, Ardeth Maung (2017), 'Signs Of Life in Myanmar's Nationwide Ceasefire Agreement? Finding A Way Forward', *Critical Asian Studies*, 49(3).

Thawnghmung, Ardeth, and Gwen Robinson (2017), 'Myanmar's New Era: A Break from the Past, or Too Much of the Same?' *Southeast Asian Affairs, 2017*.

The Nationwide Ceasefire Agreement between the Government of the Republic of the Union of Myanmar and the Ethnic Armed Organization, 15 October 2015, available at https://peacemaker.un.org/sites/peacemaker.un.org/files/MM_151510_NCAAgreement.pdf accessed 8 January 2019.

Woods, Kevin (2011), 'Ceasefire Capitalism: Military–Private Partnerships, Resource Concessions and Military–State Building in the Burma–China Borderlands', *Journal of Peasant Studies*, 38(4).

# 11 The chronic threat of insurgent groups in the Philippines

*Renato Cruz De Castro*

Since the Philippines became an independent state in 1946, the country has been bedeviled by the perennial insurgency problem. For more than seven decades, the Armed Forces of the Philippines (AFP) has long focused its attention, efforts, and resources on containing domestic rebel movements. During Gloria Macapagal Arroyo's nine-year presidency, the AFP waged a single-minded counter-insurgency campaign aimed at eventually neutralizing the various insurgent movements in the country by 2010. Her successor, former President Benigno Aquino III shifted the AFP's focus from internal to territorial defense during his six-year term. He spoke of "enhanced security" for national defense and put forward the country's claim for territories in the South China Sea through the modernization of its navy and the air force.

The Aquino Administration's defense goal was very modest—to develop a credible posture for territorial defense and maritime security through building a competent force capable of defending the country's interests and the land features it occupies in the South China Sea. These official pronouncements relative to modernizing the AFP were geared toward redirecting the Philippine military away from asymmetric/low intensity conflicts (LICs) to territorial defense/maritime security. This required providing the AFP with the necessary equipment, technical training, and expertise for external defense. In turn, the Philippine military must train its officers and personnel to broaden their skills, knowledge, and capability in territorial defense instead of merely discharging constabulary functions, and undertaking socio-civic activities—a role it has performed since the Philippines became independent in 1946.

Despite President Rodrigo Duterte's early statements indicating that he had no intention of pursuing the AFP's modernization program with as much vigor as his predecessor, he actually continued the program. In July 2016, President Duterte assured troops of the Sixth Infantry Division that he would continue the Aquino Administration's efforts to modernize the AFP. He declared that "there will even be no refocusing of the modernization thrust. We will only adjust our priorities (to internal defense)". His statement relative to the AFP modernization program was reflected in the 15% rise in the 2017 defense spending with the allocation for the modernization program being increased from Php15 billion (US$333million) to Php25 (US$555million). In mid-September 2016, the Department of National Defense announced that it and Hyundai Heavy Industries would sign a Php16 billion (US$355 million) deal for the PN's acquisition of two new frigates and their weapons systems. This project is part of the Aquino Administration modernization program that aimed to enhance the AFP's territorial defense and disaster response capabilities.

On 26 May 2017, however, hundreds of militants led by the Maute Group and Abu Sayyaf Group (ASG) and waving the black flag of Islamic State of Iraq and Syria (ISIS) occupied the shore-lake city of Marawi (Paddock and Villamor 2017). The militants took control of the city center, established, and controlled several checkpoints on several key bridges. They also deployed several well-armed and trained snipers in the city's several mosques (Paddock and Villamor 2017). Thousands of innocent civilians were trapped in the city center, rendering a full-scale AFP assault difficult and risky. The militants also positioned several snipers in the tall buildings which forced Philippine troops to maintain a safe distance from the center of the city (Paddock and Villamor 2017). It was also reported that several foreign militants from Malaysia, Indonesia, Chechnya, Yemen and Saudi Arabia fought alongside their Filipino counterparts. Consequently, the militants were able to occupy a fifth of the city. They skillfully defended their enclaves as the AFP—trained in and used to conducting counter-insurgency operations in the jungles—found it difficult to wage effective urban warfare against well-armed insurgents who were prepared to sacrifice their lives for their cause.

A new insurgent group called the Maute group and the notorious ASG led the siege of Marawi City. In the past, the two insurgent groups have been involved in several terrorist acts such as bombings, and criminal activities such as kidnapping, banditry, and piracy. However, by occupying Marawi, the International Alert1 regarded this joint operation as a new form of vertical conflict, i.e. a conflict between the national government and a non-state armed actor (Quilala 2018: 285). Consequently, Filipino authorities became alarmed that the alliance between the two insurgent groups might attract frustrated members of other armed insurgent groups involved in the decades-long Islamist insurgencies in the Southern Philippines (Peel 2017).

The five-month battle for Marawi City uncovered various security challenges confronting the AFP and the Philippine government. Despite efforts to develop its territorial defense capabilities since 2010, the AFP remains deficient in intelligence, surveillance, and reconnaissance capabilities. It also lacks basic infantry equipment such as bullet-proof vests, helmets, night-vision goggles, bullets, ordinance, modern ground-attack aircraft, and even tanks. The situation also exposed a major structural problem as the Philippine military modernizes its capabilities to confront a vast array of new challenges; the resilience of internal security threats has not only altered the country's security perceptions, but also imposed greater resource constraints as the Philippine military seeks to improve its overall capabilities. This chapter examines the major insurgent groups defying the Philippine government for control of territories and using political violence as a means to achieving their respective political goals.

## Complicating 21st century Philippines security: The armed insurgent groups

There are five major insurgent groups, along with diverse splinter groups and criminal gangs spread through the country's 7,000 islands, that challenge the Philippine state.

### *The New People's Army (NPA)*

The longest and most serious insurgent threat against the Philippine state is the military arm of the Communist Party of the Philippines (CPP), the New People's Army (NPA). Considered as a successor to the Communist-led *Hukbalahap* (*Hukbong Magpapalaya sa Bayan* or People's Liberation Army or Huks for short) guerillas against the Japanese and later against the newly independent Philippine republic, the NPA sought to violently overthrow the current government and establish a revolutionary regime. The NPA's origin could be traced during the split by 11 young student activists from the old *Partido Komunista ang Plipinas* (PKP) and their reestablishment of a new CPP "guided by Marxism-Leninism-Mao-Zedong thought" on 26 December 1968 (Lohr 1985). Following Mao's dictum that political power grows out of the barrel of a gun and the party controls the gun, the CPP's military wing, the NPA, was formed on 29 March 1969. The NPA first operated in the flat plains of Central Luzon in early 1969. Animated by the Chinese revolution, the NPA tried to cultivate the rugged mountains of Central and Northern Luzon as their equivalent of Mao Zedong's liberated guerrilla bases in Yan'an. These bases became the staging point for the Communist military offensive against the Nationalist forces during the latter part of the Chinese Civil War in the late 1940s. In the early 1970s, China sent the NPA two weapon shipments to equip the communist insurgents operating in the mountain ranges of Sierra Madre and the Central Cordillera. This was to accelerate the Maoist three-stage strategy to "encircle the city from the country-side" on the island of Luzon leading to a military offensive towards the seizure of the Philippine capital city of Manila (Linantud 2015: 1–18).

The AFP's successful counter-insurgency operation, the Philippine government's massive investments in infrastructure in Central Luzon, and the country's geographic isolation from mainland Asia prevented the CPP and NPA from effectively applying Mao's strategy of surrounding the city from the country-side. Despite its strategic setback in the early 1970s, the NPA was able to recover from a total collapse as it adapted the Maoist revolutionary theory to the Philippine condition. Strategically, the CPP developed an indigenous variant of the Maoist revolutionary model tailored to the Philippines' archipelagic condition. Instead of establishing large and concentrated guerilla bases in parts of the Philippines, the NPA created numerous decentralized guerilla fronts. Each front is comprised of several adjacent towns and villages controlled by a party organ, defended by an NPA unit operating within the area, and sustained by a clandestine network of civilian front organizations supporting the revolutionary movement (Lohr 1985). In the early 1980s, the NPA grew to 25,000 guerrillas who operated in 60 revolutionary fronts scattered in nearly all of the Philippines' 73 provinces and essentially controlled almost 20% of the country's barangays or villages (Lohr 1985).

In the mid-1980s, however, the CPP-NPA suffered from a major strategic setback from which it was not able to recover. The sudden fall of the Marcos dictatorship in 1986, the subsequent return of democracy under the late Corazon C. Aquino, and the factional infighting within the revolutionary movement greatly weakened the CPP and the NPA. The implosion of communist regimes in Central and Eastern Europe and China's adoption of market-oriented reforms have also rendered the communist movement in the Philippines politically isolated and ideologically discredited. The AFP under the Aquino and later the Ramos Administration launched a "total or comprehensive" approach to counter-insurgency that relied on long-term military deployments in communist guerrilla fronts, community-based civic action and economic development that was able to address some of the causes rather than the symptoms of the socio-economic discontent that has fueled the communist insurgency for decades. Both administrations also launched a policy of reconciliation by bringing to the negotiating table the key leaders of the CPP/NPA for peace talks to end the communist insurgency.

By the early 2000s, the number of NPA armed guerrillas decreased from a peak of 26,000 in 1986 to 6,875. Despite the drastic decrease in its armed regulars, the NPA remained faithful to its original goal of a regime change through a violent national democratic revolution. The communist insurgents' most tangible achievement after 50 years of protracted guerrilla war, however, is the de facto political and geographic separatism from the mainstream polity wherein guerillas levy revolutionary taxes and dispense their own brand of justice in isolated guerrilla fronts they control in the rural areas (Linantud 2015: 10). One observer notes: "When geography is taken into account, the NPA therefore appears to be the other separatist army in the Philippines along with the Muslim insurgents" (Linantud 2015: 10). Accordingly, in practice they cling on mainly by threatening violent reprisals against business (or wealthy individuals) that fail to pay what they call "revolutionary taxes" (*The Economist* 2017a: 45).

Way into the second decade of the 21st century, the NPA has decreased from 6,875 to roughly 5,000 guerrillas scattered all over the archipelago but mainly on the southern island of Mindanao. Although its revolutionary cause is hopeless, the NPA remains a deadly nuisance as it directs its attention, resources, and efforts on extorting money from businesses, setting fire to equipment owned by construction companies or blowing up base stations belonging to mobile networks that refuse to pay the insurgents' revolutionary taxes (*The*

*Economist* 2016: 2). It has been observed that the NPA has failed to mount a single major military operation in 2015 as its number had dwindled from 5,000 to fewer than 4,000 by 2016. As a result, NPA units tend to avoid combat with the military, so outbreaks of fighting between the communist guerrillas and the AFP have become rare and brief (*The Economist* 2016: 2).

Observing the state of the communist insurgency, *The Economist* notes:

> the minimum the NDF seems likely to accept in return for ending its rebellion is amnesty for its forces, whether detained or at large. It must press its demand before its revolution fizzles out completely and its leaders die of old age. The government, however, is disinclined to grant an amnesty. It not only wants the communists to agree to abandon the armed struggle permanently; it also wants convincing evidence that they will stick to such a pledge. The Philippine state, unlike the revolution and its leader, is not on its last legs, so has time on its side.
> 
> (*The Economist* 2017a: 45)

In 2016, President Duterte declared that he was willing to "walk an extra" mile to end the almost 50-year-old communist insurgency that has killed an estimated 35,000 soldiers, insurgents, and civilians. He appointed three left-leaning personalities into his cabinet upon the recommendation of the militant left, directly conversed with CPP-founder Jose Maria Sison by phone, and ordered the release of 19 communist leaders from detention as a gesture of goodwill before the commencement of peace talks between the CPP and the Government of the Republic of the Philippines (Cook 2018: 271). The Government of the Republic of the Philippines (GRP) and the CPP/NPA then implemented separate ceasefires in August 2016, paving the way for the resumption of the peace process in Oslo, which has been brokered by the Norwegian government since the early 1990s.

The start of 2017 suggested that GRP–CPP peace talks were bearing fruits as the two sides conducted the third-round of negotiations in Rome. In February 2017, the peace negotiations began to unravel as both sides accused each other of bad faith. The government criticized the NPA for continuously extorting revolutionary taxes from businesses and violating its own unilateral ceasefire when its guerrillas kidnapped and executed three soldiers who were in civilian clothes. The communists, in turn, blamed the government for treacherously taking advantage of the cease-fire to encroach on territory considered by the insurgents as their guerrilla fronts and reneging on its promise to release jailed communist leaders (Villamor 2017a). The communist leadership accused the GRP of treacherously taking advantage of the ceasefire given that the AFP had expanded into at least 500 villages in some 43 provinces and had deployed armed troops, police personnel, paramilitary units and death squads to engage in hostile actions, provocative movements, and other offensive operations against the CPP/NPA (Villamor 2017a). The Philippine Department of National Defense (DND) countered "that security forces will continue to maintain peace and order and run after lawless elements whoever and whatever they are and that it does not recognize the NPA's claims to areas which it believes are under its control" (*The Economist* 2017a: 45).

During the five-month siege of Marawi City as the AFP was preoccupied with fighting the Islamic militants, the government accused the NPA of using the occasion as an opportunity to violate the joint ceasefire agreement and intensify its armed attacks against government targets (Cook 2018: 271). Consequently, the Duterte Administration used the need to quell the communist insurgency in Mindanao as one of the justifications for the extension of martial law across the island until the end of 2017. In December 2017, President Duterte asked congress again for a one-year extension of martial law in Mindanao shortly after he suspended the peace talks with the CPP, whose armed unit, the NPA, had stepped up its attacks against government targets in remote communities in the said island (Villamor 2017b).

### *The Moro Islamic Liberation Front (MILF)*

The Moro Islamic Liberation Front (MILF) is considered the largest and most influential Muslim insurgent group in the Philippines. The MILF broke away from the Moro National Liberation Front (MNLF) in the late 1970s. The MNLF was formed in the late 1960s to fight for Muslim independence in the southern Philippines. In 1972, under the leadership of Nur Misuari, the MNLF fought the Philippines in a set-piece conventional war in Mindanao and in 1976, negotiated and signed the Tripoli Peace Agreement with the GRP. In 1978, MNLF members who were dissatisfied with Nur Misuari's leadership of the secessionist group broke away and formed the MILF. The formation of the MILF as breakaway faction from the MNLF led some analysts and commentators to assume that this would lead to a new and more Islamic thrust of the secessionist movement in Mindanao. However, although the MILF has emphasized the Islamic aspect of the secessionist movement, and has more Islamic clerics in leadership positions, the MNLF and the MILF have never differed in their goals. Their differences were primarily in terms of ethnicity and personalities but both are essentially ethno-nationalist movements focused on the control of territory (McKenna 2007: 7).

For the first 13 years of its existence, the Philippine government ignored the MILF as it negotiated with the MNLF. From 1989 to 1996, the Philippine government parleyed only with the Nur Misuari-led MNLF. Left out from the GRP–MNLF peace process, the MILF adopted a wait-and-see approach as it focused its efforts on expanding its armed strength from 5,000 in the 1980s to 15,000 armed insurgents by the end of 1999 (Buendia 2004: 2). The MILF also created 46 camps or community bases, also known as "MILF territories" in 13 out of the 15 provinces of Mindanao and Sulu archipelago (Buendia 2004: 2).

In 1996, the GRP and the MNLF signed a peace agreement that provided for the creation of the Autonomous Region of Muslim Mindanao (ARMM), the appointment of Nur Misuari as the first governor of the ARMM, and the integration of some members of the MNLF into the AFP. More significantly, the 1996 peace agreement also signaled the transformation of the MNLF from an armed insurgent group into a mainstream political organization. At the end of President Fidel Ramos's term in July 1997 and upon the assumption of Joseph Estrada as president of the Philippines, the GRP and the MILF began their formal peace negotiation. However, the talks failed to yield any substantial gains. Consequently, President Joseph Estrada took an intransigent position in the negotiations by demanding that the MILF lay down its arms, threatening this Muslim secessionist group with massive military retaliation as he imposed an absolute deadline for the conclusion of the peace talks (McKenna 2007: 2). In April 2000, full-scale armed hostilities between the AFP and the MILF broke out because of President Estrada's all-out-war policy against this secessionist movement (Buendia 2004: 2).

After President Estrada's peaceful removal as the president of the Philippines in 2001, the MILF and the GRP resumed their peace negotiations. Under a new president, Gloria Macapagal Arroyo, the GRP and the MILF continued their peace negotiation leading to the signing of the General Framework for the Resumption of Peace in Kuala Lumpur, Malaysia in 2001 (Buendia 2004: 2). In 2003, the two sides forged a ceasefire agreement that has held despite occasional armed clashes between the MILF and the AFP. The MILF is currently engaged in a long and protracted peace process with the GRP since it considered this as the only peaceful and civilized, and democratic way of solving the *Bangsamoro* problem in Mindanao (Buendia 2004: 5). A noted Filipino academic described this peace process as "highly volatile, tenuous, insubstantial, and limited to cease fire agreements and presently [has] run longer than the 1992–1996 GRP-MNLF peace talks" (Buendia 2004: 2).

While engaging the Philippine government in a protracted and tedious peace negotiation, the MILF was building a coalition of states sympathetic to its cause. In March 2003, acting upon the auspices of the Organization of Islamic Conference (OIC), Malaysia began brokering the peace negotiation between the GRP and the MILF. As a result, it played an important role in the formation and deployment of the International Monitoring Team (IMT) to Mindanao. Then showing panache and an unusual creativity, the MILF was able to compensate for some of its military setbacks and limited fighting space by harnessing an international coalition of states to support the peace negotiation (Abinales 2008: 301). Made up of Malaysia, Brunei Darussalam, the US, Japan, and Canada, this coalition of states applied subtle pressure on the Philippine government to extend more and substantive concessions to the MILF (Abinales 2008: 301). In November 2009, an International Contact Group (ICG) was formed to provide multi-faceted support to the GRP–MILF peace process. By engaging the GRP in a protracted peace negotiation, and harnessing international support to the peace process, the MILF became the de facto voice of Muslim separatism, whereas its older rival, the MNLF, by forging a peace deal with the GRP in 1996, was relegated to an ordinary political party weakened by serious disagreement within its leadership (Abinales 2008: 301).

In March 2014, the GRP and the MILF signed the Comprehensive Agreement on the *Bangsamoro* (CAB). The CAB was the final agreement that both sides signed after the two parties agreed on a framework deal in October 2012. For two years, the two sides conferred and settled on several annexes that contained detailed provisions on transition arrangements, wealth and revenue sharing, power-sharing, and normalization or decommissioning of the MILF's weapons and armed guerrillas (Landingin 2014). The CAB provides for the creation of the *Bangsamoro* political entity that will replace the 1996 ARM (MENA Report 2014). It promises that institutional designs of the proposed Bangsamoro government will be more representative and accountable than its predecessor (MENA Report 2014: 1). The CAB, however, must still be approved by the House of Representatives and the Senate through a passage of *Bangsamoro* Basic Law (BBL). Once Congress passes the BBL, the people within the core territory will ratify it through a plebiscite. After its ratification through a plebiscite, the BBL will formalize the establishment of the *Bangsamoro* Political Entity that will enjoy more enhanced political and fiscal autonomy than its predecessor, the ARMM (MENA Report 2014: 1).

In January 2015, however, a commando operation that killed a Malaysian terrorist in the marshland of Maguindanao triggered an unintended armed clash between the MILF and government forces resulting to the death of 44 Special Actions Forces (SAF) of the Philippine National Police (PNP). Public outcry at the killing and mutilation of the remains of the 44 police commandos scuttled the passage of the BBL in congress. Cognizant that it had already spent its political capital on pushing for the BBL's passage, the Aquino Administration accepted the stark reality that any meaningful effort to achieve a durable and lasting peace with the MILF would happen only after the 2016 presidential election.

President Duterte, for his part, decided to continue the Aquino Administration's peace process. His first step was to reinvigorate the stalled BBL in Congress by signing Executive Order 7 reconstituting the *Bangsamoro* Transition Commission (BTC) by increasing its members from 15 to 21. The reconstituted BTC was tasked to draft a revised BBL that would be agreed by the Philippine Congress. The five-month siege of Marawi City in 2017 convinced President Duterte to push congress for the BBL's immediate passage. He may have been convinced by the MILF's argument that "the slow progress and the very uncertainty of the BBL was dangerous and counterproductive as it undermined its legitimacy among the Muslims in Mindanao, while appealing to local terrorist groups like the Maute Group and ISIS that are becoming more attractive to frustrated Moro youth" (Cook 2018: 271). In April 2018, President Duterte persuaded key congressional leaders to push for the immediate passage of the BBL before the end of 2018 (Romero 2018).

## The Abu Sayyaf Group (ASG)

The Abu Sayyaf (Father of the Sword or ASG for short) was founded between 1990 and 1992 by Abdurajak Janjalani, a radical MNLF unit commander who had fought in Afghanistan in the late 1980s. The ASG has historical ties with Al Qaeda and has been strongly influenced by Wahhabism (Martin 2011: 7). Its goal was the "eradication of all Christian influence in the Southern Philippines and the creation of an Islamic State of Mindanao" (Martin 2011: 7). However, it was observed that the ASG had never issued a cohesive statement of its religious ideology, and much of its membership has been shown to be motivated purely by mercenary or criminal intentions (McKenna 2007: 2). In 1992, the ASG launched its first operation by conducting indiscriminate bombings in western Mindanao. In addition to bombing attacks, the ASG began its signature activity of kidnapping foreigners for ransom. In 1995, it launched a well-executed attack that devastated the Christian town of Ipil in the main island of Mindanao resulting in 50 civilian and military fatalities and 100 wounded (Briscoe and Downey 2004: 3).

Periodic attacks of the ASG continued until 1998 until members of the PNP killed Abdurajak Janjalani in an armed encounter. His death most likely caused the ASG's rapid transformation from a minimally ideologically motivated insurgent group into a primarily kidnap-for-ransom gang that used bombings to extort money from the local population in a terrorist version of the protection racket (Briscoe and Downey 2004: 3). Deprived of its leader and without any well-defined organizational structure, the ASG began to closely resemble a group of thugs rather that a terrorist or an insurgent organization (Martin 2011: 7). Nevertheless, the ASG gained notoriety in the early 21st century by conducting high visibility kidnappings of Western tourists. In 2000, the ASG kidnapped European hostages from Sabah, Malaysia and had them transferred to Sulu. In 2001, they abducted American hostages from Palawan and who were brought to Basilan.

In September 2001, the Joint Special Operations Task Force Philippines (JSTOF-Philippines) was formed by the US Pacific Command (PACOM) to help train and provide advice to the AFP on how to neutralize the ASG that had been involved in high-profile kidnappings, bombings, and beheadings of its kidnapped victims. Under this arrangement, American Special Forces (SOF) operating in the southern Philippines were not authorized for combat operation but played an advisory role on intelligence and surveillance, including the use of aerial drones for locating members of the small but violent ASG (Whaley 2014). In 2006, Khadafy Janjalani, who had replaced his brother as the head of ASG, was killed by AFP Special Forces. He was succeeded by Abu Sollaman, who was eventually killed by the Philippine military in January 2007. Subsequent military operations reduced the number of ASG insurgents from its high of 1,200 in 2001 to 100 dedicated militants and 200 to 300 active supporters in 2008 (Whaley 2014). Consequently, the ASG degenerated further from an insurgent group to a gang of thugs (Whaley 2014). However, it should be noted that the actual numbers of ASG militants fluctuates because support for this insurgent group is dependent on family and clan relationship and on ongoing AFP operations in Basilan and Sulu (Whaley 2014).

Sustained military operations in the Sulu and Basilan have also forced the ASG to disperse its command structure into two groups: a) the Sawadjaan faction in Sulu, which is notorious for kidnapping foreign hostages; and b) the Hapilon faction in Basilan, that was involved in low-key extortion activities to survive and has been recognized by the official Islamic State of Iraq and Syria (ISIS) as the Emir of ISIS Wilayah (province) in Southeast Asia (Franco 2017: 305). Hapilon was one of the ASG leaders that had been confirmed by ISIS as the Emir of Southeast Asia in 2016. Accordingly, his ASG faction was forced out of Basilan and transferred to the Maute territory in Maguindanao province in mainland Mindanao.

After Mayor Duterte became president in 2016, he ordered the military to destroy the ASG in Sulu and Basilan in reaction to a series of beheadings of its kidnapped victims. A military offensive against Hapilon faction of the ASG in mid-2016 forced the group to move its operational headquarters from the island of Basilan to the mountainous jungles of Lanao De Sur, a province in Central Mindanao. Hapilon then led the ASG Basilan faction to join the Maute Brothers in the siege of Marawi City in 2017. This was the first time that the Hapilon-led ASG joined forces with the Maute group in a major terrorist operation involving the seizure of a Philippine city (Paddock and Villamor 2017). During the five-month battle for the city, it was feared that the joint ASG–Maute Group would inevitably attract more foreign and local fighters, financial support, and media resulting in ISIS seeing Mindanao and the whole of Southeast Asia as a primary, extra-regional destination (for Islamist militants) as its fortunes continue to tumble in the Middle East and North Africa (Sanderson 2017: 5).

### *Bangsamore Islamic Freedom Fighters (BIFF)*

The Bangsamoro Islamic Freedom Fighters (BIFF) is a faction that separated from the MILF after it negotiated and signed a peace agreement with the GRP in 2014. Led by Ustadz Ameril Umbra Kato, a scholar and a former commander of the MILF's 105th Command, the group allegedly split from the main insurgent group to continue its struggle for independence. According to Umbra Kato, the MILF had strayed from the Bangsamoro nation's original goal and undermined the Islamic cause by settling only for autonomy not for independence. However, the AFP alleged that much of the BIFF's activities are simple banditry (Villamor 2017c). After Kato died from pneumonia in April 2015, the BIFF's leadership was passed to Ismael Abu Bakar. The BIFF is larger and better armed than the ASG, however, its influence is limited to two barangays (villages) in the province of Maguindanao.

Currently, the BIFF is divided between the pro-ISIS faction of Ismael Abu Bakar or Commander Bungos and the mainstream faction led by Imman Minimbang or Commander Karialan. Among the various Islamist insurgent groups that have pledged their allegiance to ISIS, the BIFF seems to be the least concerned with pan-Islamist narrative, and is more preoccupied with using its stature among other private, non-sectarian militias operated by Mindanao politicians as private armies (Franco 2017).

During the siege of Marawi City, 200 BIFF guerrillas attacked a government outpost and then retreated to a public school where they took 31 hostages in Pigcawayan, which is about 50 miles south of the besieged city. The AFP spokesperson called the attack opportunistic, suggesting that the insurgents attacked the town because the military was preoccupied with the battle for Marawi City. Nevertheless, the military down-played the attack as a case of simple "harassment" as the insurgents eventually withdrew into a marshland area after they released their hostages (Franco 2017). The Philippine government has included the BIFF on its list of 20 armed groups that are alleged to be aligned with ISIS, along with the ASG and the Maute group.

## *The Maute Group*

The Maute Group includes several members of a large clan in Lanao Del Sur and was led by the late brothers Abdullah and Omarkhayam Maute. The government and military initially dismissed the group as a small band of petty criminals. The government compared it with the ASG, a band of petty bandits involved in the bombings of cities and in criminal activities like kidnapping and extortion. Sidney Jones, the world's foremost expert on Southeast Asian militant groups, however, is more circumspect as she considered the Maute Group as "the smartest, best educated, and most sophisticated members" across the Philippines' numerous pro-ISIS groups (Sanderson 2017). Both the Maute brothers were educated in the Middle East and had links with jihadists in Indonesia (The Economist 2017b: 2). Accordingly, the Mautes were a new breed of extremists: young, charismatic, Arabic-speaking, educated in the Middle East, and social-savvy with extensive international connections. Their clan was part of Marawi City's political and business elite, as well as related to the MILF's highest echelons (Jones 2017).

The government was initially dismissive of the Maute Group erroneously thinking of it as simply a low-grade family mafia with links to Marawi City's former mayor, Solitario Ali, whom President Duterte denounced as a drug lord (*The Economist* 2017b: 2). The group started its operation as an extortion gang as it targeted sawmill operators and bombed electrical transmission towers belonging to the government-owned TRANSCO (Franco 2017). Then it started its terrorist operation in the 2 September 2016 bombing of a Davao night market that appeared to be an exception to its extortion-heavy modus operandi (Franco 2017). The Maute Brothers had planned, organized, and carried out the Davao bombing (Franco 2017). The government, however, ignored this as a wake-up call to the threat posed by this new insurgent group. In November 2016, the Maute Group occupied the vacant portion of Butig municipality in Lanao De Sur. The military conducted a five-day campaign and declared that they had recaptured the town and had the Maute Group on the run (Franco 2017). Earlier in June 2016, the military declared that the Maute Group stronghold, Camp Darul Iman, had been captured and the group had been dispersed after months of sporadic skirmishes in Lanao Del Sur beginning in February 2016. The government however, failed to appreciate the fact that the ISIS-friendly coalition had already extended beyond the ASG and that its leaders were driven by ideology rather than profit (Jones 2017). It also failed to grasp that the militants who were infiltrating into Marawi City were not just from the Lanao Sur group led by the Maute Brothers but also from the wider-pro-ISIS coalition including those coming from Basilan and even from Indonesia, Malaysia, and Saudi Arabia (Jones 2017).

In late May 2017, Hapilon-led ASG teamed up with the local Maute Group and several foreign militants to occupy and raise ISIS's black flag over Marawi City. The fighting erupted when a joint police-military task force tried to arrest Hapilon. Without any warning, about 700 militants emerged from their safe houses and in the name ISIS, seized the center of the city. The two militant groups were able to lay siege to the central portion of the city in an attempt to establish an ISIS enclave in Southeast Asia and have Mindanao designated as an ISIS province. Immediately, the Philippine military talked of a mopping up operation against the militants who were cornered into an area of a square kilometer, encompassing the commercial district. The AFP estimated that it would have control of Marawi City in 60 days. However, the military operations against the ASG/Maute Group dragged on for five months resulting in the deaths of hundreds of militants, 150 police and military personnel, the displacement of hundreds of thousands of civilians, and the destruction of a sizeable part of Marawi City, the largest city in the ARMM and the heart of Islam in the Philippines. The ability of the Maute Group-led ISIS network to quickly seize large parts of an urban center and hold it against the Philippine military for months underlined the government's serious intelligence short-comings, the AFP's limited capabilities, and the continuing severity of the terrorist (insurgency) threat in and emanating from Muslim Mindanao (Cook 2018: 271).

## Conclusion: Philippine security after the siege of Marawi City

In August 2017, during the height of the battle for Marawi City, President Duterte asked the Philippine Congress to provide funding for an additional 20,000 troops. With only about 130,000 personnel spread all over the country, there is now a concern about the AFP's ability to address a range of internal and external security threats following decades of strategic slack and underinvestment in the defense budget. This move stems from the most pressing problem facing the AFP, finding the delicate balance between internal and external security challenges that has long bedeviled any efforts to modernize the Philippine military since the mid-1990s. Well into the second decade of the 21st century, the Philippine state is still confronted by political violence waged by several armed insurgent groups. This is because, in the face of several armed insurgent groups that use political violence to pursue their material and ideational goals, the government still has to effectively and decisively exercise its monopoly on the use of legitimate violence to overcome the armed challenges posed by several non-state actors in Philippine society.

## References

Abinales, Patricio N. (2008), "The Philippines: Weak States, Resilient President", *Southeast Asian Affairs 2008*, Singapore: Institute of Southeast Asian Studies.

Briscoe, C.H., and Dennis Downey (2004), "Multiple Insurgents Groups Complicate Philippine Security", *Special Warfare*, 17(1).

Buendia, Rizal G. (2004), "The GRP-MILF Peace Talks: Quo Vadis?" *Southeast Asian Affairs 2004*, Singapore: Institute of Southeast Asian Studies.

Cook, Malcolm (2018), "The Philippines in 2017: Turbulent Consolidation", *Southeast Asian Affairs 2018*, Singapore: Institute of Southeast Asian Studies.

Franco, Joseph (2017), "Uncertainty in Duterte's Muslim Mindanao", *Southeast Asian Affairs 2017*, Singapore: Institute of Southeast Asian Studies.

Jones, Sidney (2017), "How ISIS Got a Foothold in the Philippines", *New York Times*, 4 June, available at https://www.nytimes.com/2017/06/04/opinion/isis-philippines-rodrigo-duterte.html accessed 20 June 2018.

Landingin, Roel (2014), "Philippines Signs Deal with Muslim Rebels", *Financial Times*, available at https://www.ft.com/content/c1961906-b5a2-11e3-81cb-00144feabdc0 accessed 20 June 2018.

Linantud, John (2015), "China, Rebalance, and the Silent War", *International Social Science Review*, 91(2), 1–18.

Lohr, Steve (1985), "Inside the Philippine Insurgency", *New York Times*, 3 November, available at https://www.nytimes.com/1985/11/03/magazine/inside-the-philippine-insurgency.html accessed 20 June 2018.

Martin, Jonathan (2011), "Comparing Strategies for Counter Terrorism and Insurgency in the Southeast Asia", *The White Head Journal of Diplomacy and International Relations*, 12(2).

McKenna, Thomas (2007), "Governing Muslims in the Philippines", *Harvard Asia-Pacific Review*, 9(1).

MENA Report (2014), "Philippines: Government Urges Unity for Success of Comprehensive Peace Deal with MILF", 25 March.

Paddock, Richard, and Felipe Villamor (2017), "Destroying a City to Save it from ISIS Allies", *New York Times*, 13 January, available at https://www.nytimes.com/2017/06/13/world/asia/marawi-philippines-islamic-state.html accessed 20 June 2018.

Peel, Michael (2017), "Militant Islamist Shift Focus to Southeast Asia", *Financial Times*, 18 June, available at https://www.ft.com/content/b830552a-5176-11e7-bfb8-997009366969 accessed 20 June 2018.

Quilala, Dennis (2018), "Narratives and Counter-Narratives: Responding to Political Violence in the Philippines", *Southeast Asian Affairs 2018*, Singapore: Institute of Southeast Asian Studies

Romero, Alexis (2018), "Duterte Racing against Time for Bangsamoro Basic Law Enactment", *Philippine Star*, 2 April.

Sanderson, Thomas (2017), "Testimony by Thomas Sanderson, Senior Fellow and Director, Transnational Threats Project, Center of Strategic and International Studies, Black Flag over Mindanao: Terrorism in Southeast Asia", 12 July, House Foreign Affairs Subcommittee on the Asia and the Pacific, Washington: Congressional Documents and Publications.

*The Economist* (2016), "Rebels in their Dotage; Communists in the Philippines", 27 August.

*The Economist* (2017a), "An Extra Mile; Communist Insurgency in the Philippines", 11 February.

*The Economist* (2017b), "Mosul in Mindanao: Banyan", 22 July.

Villamor, Felipe (2017a), "Communist Rebels in Philippines Say They'll End Cease-Fire", *New York Times*, 1 February, available at https://www.nytimes.com/2017/02/01/world/asia/philippines-cpp-npa-communist-ceasefire.html accessed 20 June 2018.

Villamor, Felipe (2017b), "Philippines Extends Martial Law in South for Another Year", *New York Times*, 13 December, available at https://www.nytimes.com/2017/12/13/world/asia/philippines-martial-law-duterte.html accessed 20 June 2018.

Villamor, Felipe (2017c), "Militants' Siege of Philippine Elementary School Ends after 12 Hours", *New York Times*, 21 June, available at https://www.nytimes.com/2017/06/21/world/asia/school-philippines-bangsamoro-islamic-freedom-fighters.html accessed 20 June 2018.

Whaley, Floyd (2014), "U.S. Phasing Out its Counter-Terrorism Unit in Philippines", *New York Times*, 27 June, available at https://www.nytimes.com/2014/06/27/world/asia/us-will-disband-terrorism-task-force-in-philippines.html accessed 20 June 2018.

# 12 Thailand's restive south
## Identity and neo-colonial resistance

*Zachary Abuza[1]*

## Introduction

Insurgency in the ethnic Malay majority region of southern Thailand is not new. Unrest has been a fact of life for the ethnic Malay community, who comprise over 80 percent of the population, in the three and a half provinces of Thailand's Deep South, since the border with Malaysia was codified in 1909. Unlike every other ethnic group along Thailand's borders who assimilated to Thai culture for the sake of citizenship, the ethnic Malay have steadfastly refused assimilation, and have fought to protect their ethnolinguistic and religious identity. The Thai government and military largely do not accept Malay national identity and have worked assiduously for over 100 years to inculcate Thai values and assimilate the Malays (Abuza 2007: chapter 1). Many view the Thai government, regardless of who is in power, as a neocolonial force. The Thai government declared victory over the insurgents in the early-2000s, after having been able to divide and conquer squabbling factions, offer generous amnesty terms, establish effective and innovative institutions, effectively cooperate with Malaysian security forces, and bring sufficient levels of economic development to the region. But there was never an attempt to seek a durable political settlement, or address core grievances. As such the insurgency rekindled. However, the current iteration is quantitatively and qualitatively different from early conflicts.

The ethnic Malay insurgency in southern Thailand is the single most lethal conflict in the heart of prosperous southeast Asia. Between January 2004 and December 2017, over 7,000 people were killed and over 10,000 wounded in more than 15,000 incidents of violence, including more than 4,200 attacks with guns, and over 3,400 bombings.

The violence disrupted the provision of social services in the south, led to the immigration of an estimated 20 percent of the Buddhist population, and sowed deep divisions between the government and the ethnic Malay majority, angered at the government's lack of political will to resolve the conflict and the impunity of its security forces. Though the majority of the casualties have been civilian, including women and children, security forces remain the militants' primary target (Bangkok Post 2018). And unlike previous iterations of the insurgency, the current movement has not only been willing to go after soft targets, they have engaged in beheadings and other acts of violence meant to terrorize the community. Also unlike previous insurgents, the Barisan Revolusi Nasional (BRN) has demonstrated a willingness to attack or threaten attacks beyond the Deep South into major tourist hubs, threatening the Thai economy.

Nonetheless, the insurgency remains a very low priority for the national government and the Royal Thai Army (RTA) leadership, which is far more concerned with elite political machinations, including staging two *coup d'états* since 2006 and consolidating political power and institutionalizing thorough checks on all forms of democratic governance.

Successive governments, including the military-installed government, have insisted that they were open to talks, but have shown absolutely no interest in making the necessary political concessions that would appease the BRN rebels and convince them to seek a political settlement (ICG 2016). At the end of the day, the conduct of war is about political will. And Thailand has displayed no political will to address core grievances of the Malay community and truly bring about an end to this conflict.

## Who are the insurgents?

The Malay insurgency is a horizontal movement that is comprised of a number of different militant groups and factions. When the insurgency recommenced in January 2004, the Thai government rounded up the previous generation of insurgents from the Patani United Liberation Organization (PULO), which had been bought out with amnesties and land packages. This was a disastrous policy that alienated the local community and had no bearing on the insurgency.

While various factions of PULO remain involved in the insurgency, there are also a number of other organizations, including the Barisan Islam Perberbasan Pattani (BIPP), the Gerakan Mujihideen Islami Pattani (GMIP), and most importantly the BRN. The BIPP commands no militants, but its leader remains an authoritative actor and ideologue. The GMIP is a group that has evolved from a criminal gang that was best known for running guns to Aceh's Gerakan Aceh Merdeka (GAM) rebels to a violent militant faction in the Deep South.

The group most responsible for the violence is the BRN, a movement that emerged out of a network of madrassas, centered on the Thamawittiyah Foundation School in Yala, and the Samphan Witthiyah School in Narathiwat, where Pattani culture, identity, and grievances are inculcated. The BRN's top leadership body is the Dewan Pimpinan Parti (DPP). In late 2016 to early 2017, the group's founding leaders died, and a second generation of leaders took over.

The different insurgent groups are all Sha'afi Muslims, not Wahhabis. Indeed, the growing Wahhabi community in the Deep South shares many of the prejudices against them that the Thai government and population do. That said, the spread of Wahhabism has made the Sha'afi community far more religiously conservative. Yet, their grievances remain ethnonational, not transnational.

The militants have been described as "shadowy", as they remain very guarded. They interact with the media, even the Malays' language media, very infrequently, and rarely expose their leaders. While PULO retains a small social media presence, the BRN intentionally does not. In the era of slick Islamic State social media, the BRN is decidedly old school, relying on personal contact, night letters, and other forms of messaging.

## What are their goals?

One of the reasons that the Thai security forces were able to quell the previous generation of insurgents is that they were riddled with factionalism, egos, and differences over goals and strategy. Some articulated the establishment of an independent homeland, some looked to (re)join Malaysia, others simply wanted autonomy within Thailand. The BRN and its partners very clearly are fighting for an independent homeland today. The real rift between them is the degree to which they would accept a measure of autonomy, if they could ever get the Thai government to accept that.

The BRN has more immediate short-term goals: 1) to make the region ungovernable; 2) to drive out the Buddhist community; 3) to eliminate political rivals within the Malay community; and, 4) force heavy handed government responses that would further sow seeds of mistrust from the Buddhist community.

With regards to the first, they have had mixed success. Thailand is a strong state that has tried to set up effective government institutions. Insurgents have routinely targeted village headmen and their deputies, in particular Muslim ones. Between 2009 and 2017, over 320 headmen, deputies or district-level officials were killed or wounded. The insurgents have focused their efforts on targeting the school system, the agents of assimilation. They have targeted teachers, nearly 200 have been killed or wounded since 2004. Insurgents have arsoned schools, and routinely set off bombs near schools targeting families. Most IED (improvised explosive device) attacks since 2007 have targeted security forces who are deployed on "teacher protection" detail, escorting teachers to and from rural schools. Although insurgents targeted district health clinics – another manifestation of the Thai state – in the early years of the insurgency, there was a public backlash. Because the insurgents offer no social services, they risk alienating their constituency if they destroy the government services upon which populations rely.

The second goal has largely been achieved: Thai officials expressed concern that over 20 percent of the Buddhist population has fled the region. Many fled to the Thai Buddhist-dominated city of Hat Yai in the upper south, others moved into the provincial capitals or town. Those that remained in the countryside, tended to consolidate themselves in small heavily guarded enclaves. There are few mixed villages in the countryside left. Key to stemming the flow of Buddhists in the region was stopping attacks on monks. Since 2009, eight have been killed and 11 wounded. A senior RTA officer told this author that Buddhists were down to 10 percent of the population at the end of 2014, a claim repeated by RTA officials who estimate that there are only 190,000 in the south today, although that seems extreme (Kerdphol 2014).

The third goal is to eliminate political rivals within the Muslim community. As mentioned above, insurgents have actively targeted Muslim headmen, their deputies, or members of village defense volunteers or Rangers, who they deem as collaborators. While the BRN has accepted more space for members of the BIPP, PULO, and GMIP at the peace talks (discussed on pp.00), they do employ violence against them, when they feel they are not respecting the BRN's leadership or are advocating positions inimical to their own.

The final short-term goal is to provoke heavy handed government responses. This was very effective in the early years when government missteps, such as the Krue Se Mosque raid and the Tak Bai massacre, fueled the insurgency. Thai security forces have improved after a very rocky few years, and there have been fewer over-reactions. Tactical restraint has helped quell some of the violence.

## What are their strategy and tactics?

The insurgency is very small and poorly resourced. Though insurgents frequently cross into Malaysia, it is by no means a safe haven or sanctuary for them where they can regroup, train, and safely build IEDs. The insurgents have no state sponsors, and very little external support, beyond the Pattani community within Thailand or working overseas. There are probably only a few thousand militants at most, and they are only part-time; they are farmers, rubber tappers, or workers. The insurgents claim to have cells in every village in the deep south, which is not an unreasonable estimate, but the majority of those cells do not engage in regular acts of violence. Indeed, five of the 37 districts in the deep south have very little violence.

This is an insurgency done on the cheap. Almost all weapons and ammunition are stolen or taken from victims. Indeed, this has been one of the key arguments against arming village defense volunteers. This can be seen in another way: insurgents use M79 grenades when they capture them; there is no steady supply. Insurgents use a mishmash of weapons, from old carbines, shotguns, to M-16s, AK47s, M16s, M4s and pistols; i.e. they use what the various Thai security forces use. Insurgents routinely deploy IEDs. Unlike the southern Philippines, where IEDs are frequently fashioned out of mortar or artillery shells, the IEDs in southern Thailand are made out of readily available materials, usually ammonium nitrate, a common fertilizer, packed into cooking gas tanks, fire extinguishers or other metal boxes. IEDs are either command detonated, or set off with a variety of remote radio devices, since the government has tried to better regulate and register cell phones. Insurgents routinely engage in arson, and target CCTVs, cell and electric towers.

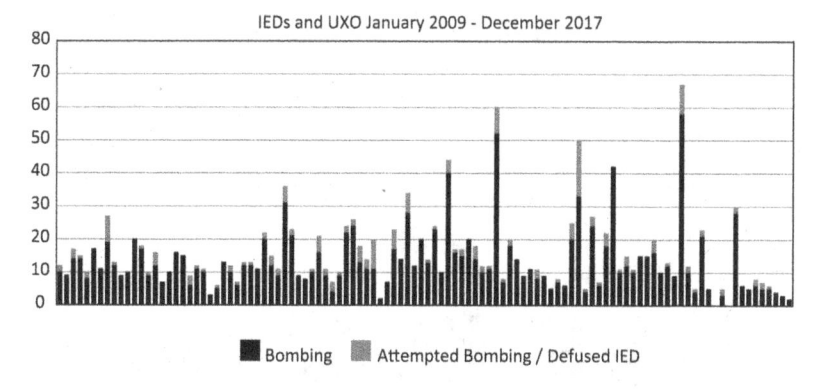

*Figure 12.1* IEDs and UXO (unexploded ordnance) January 2009 to December 2017
Source: Zachary Abuza.

The insurgents tend to be very conservative militarily. They do assault security force posts, but only when they have a high probability of success, or are running low on arms and ammunition. The average number of attacks on hardened positions has averaged around one per month since 2009. Likewise, insurgents engage in only one or two prolonged firefights with security forces a month, on average, though there are notable exceptions.

Most insurgent attacks are drive-by shootings, carried out by insurgents on motorcycles. These tend to be more targeted killings: going after rivals within the community, headmen, collaborators, or Thai security forces (especially when they are off duty). These types of attacks, which are in some ways the easiest, have declined steadily. In 2013, there were an average of 18 a month. By 2017, that had fallen to roughly 4 per month. In part it is because the government has put in place a very thorough network of checkpoints, and tried to blanket the region with CCTVs. But in large part it is because insurgents have driven away so many Buddhists or cowed political rivals.

There have been over 3,400 successful IED attacks since 2004, and countless more IEDs that either failed to go off or were defused. Since 2009 alone, there have been over 1,400, and nearly 200 more defused or IEDs that failed to detonate. While overall violence and casualty rates have gone down, since peaking in 2007, the average number of IEDs has remained relatively stable. Since January 2009, the average number of IEDs on a monthly basis has been just over 13. That figure dropped precipitously in 2017 to under six.

The real trend in IEDs, however, has not been in the number, but in who they have targeted. Insurgents have increasingly stopped attacks on soft targets in urban areas. Though they still happen, large attacks such as the truck bomb at the Big-C or a motorcycle bomb in a crowded Yala marketplace, are the exceptions, not the rule, and meant to pressure the regime. The vast majority of IEDs now target security forces on rural roads, with a smaller chance of collateral damage.

166  *Zachary Abuza*

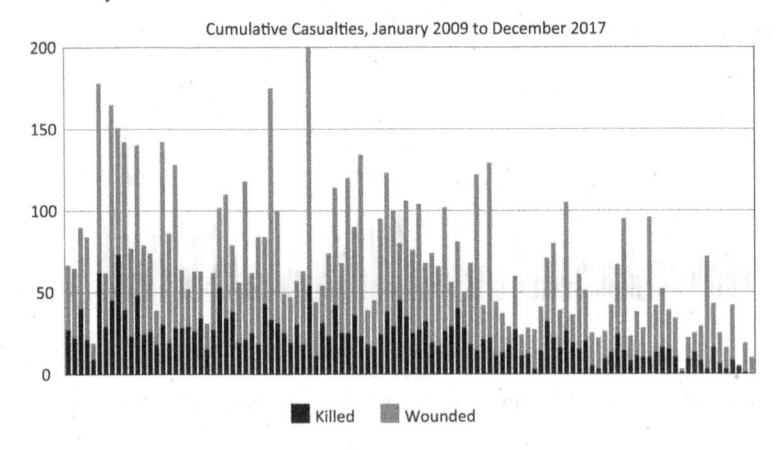

*Figure 12.2* Cumulative casualties, January 2009 to December 2017
Source: Zachary Abuza.

There has been a sharp decline in beheadings and gratuitous violence, such as the desecration of corpses, including setting them on fire. It is not that the insurgents view them as wrong. On the contrary, they see such tactics as very successful in sowing terror amongst the Buddhist community; but they have been under pressure from their own constituency who view it as culturally unacceptable. There have only been 12 beheadings and 63 desecrations since 2009; and the last beheading was in June 2014.

While over 7,000 people have been killed and over 10,000 wounded since January 2004, the number of casualties has declined steadily since its peak in 2007. The Royal Thai Army is buoyed by the decline in violence, which it states has fallen by 60 percent since the 22 May 2014 coup (Bangkok Post 2016). The local NGO and monitor, Deep South Watch, noted that in 2017, only 235 people were killed and 356 injured, in some 545 incidents, compared with a high of 892 people killed and 1,681 wounded in 2007 (Benar News 2017). There is no doubt violence has fallen. In 2009, 37 people a month were killed and 68 were wounded. By the end of 2017, that figure had fallen to six and 19, respectively. That trend carried on into 2018.

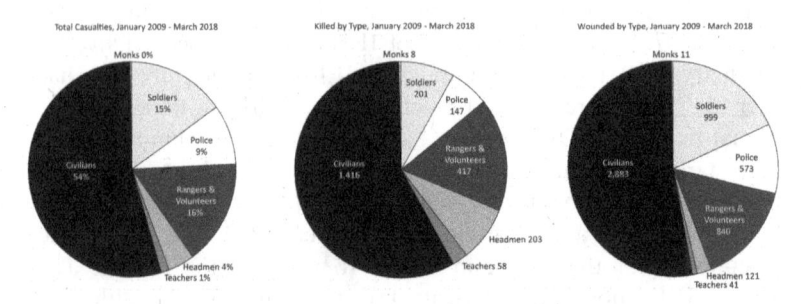

*Figure 12.3* Total casualties by type, January 2009 to March 2018
Source: Zachary Abuza.

By 2014, the violence was much more deliberate; a clear pattern of retaliatory actions, in response to government attacks, extra-judicial killings (EJKs) or successful raids and arrests of insurgents. That pattern of tit-for-tat violence has continued through 2018.

While civilians (54 percent) comprise the majority of the casualties, with teachers (1 percent) and headmen and deputies (4 percent), bringing the overall civilian total to 60 percent, still 40 percent of overall casualties are members of the various security forces, including soldiers, police, rangers, village defense volunteers and other units run by the ministry of the interior. Since January 2009 alone, 764 members of the security forces have been killed and 3,379 have been wounded.

And even amongst the security forces, there is a change, rangers and village defense volunteers now comprise the majority of casualties as the army continues to draw down its forces and implement the "Thung Yang Dang model" (Pathan 2016). Since October 2016, 8,700 troops seconded from the 1st, 2nd, and 3rd armies, have been withdrawn and replaced with 164 village defense volunteer units, and increased number of volunteer Ranger units. The RTA's goal is to withdrawal 3,000 more troops in 2018, leaving only 58,000 4th Army personnel in the Deep South (Bangkok Post 2018).

It is important to note that the violence does go through very distinct cycles. In part this is tied to the weather. In the rainy season, which causes mass flooding in the south in November to January, violence drops precipitously. Likewise, when there are spikes in violence, they are usually followed by lulls as insurgents regroup, resupply, and assess. Insurgents tend to be very responsive to the security environment. Thai forces step up deployments, patrols, and raids, following a series of attacks or spikes in the violence, and the insurgents go underground, waiting for the security forces to default back to complacency. While the government tends to take the credit for any decline in the violence, the reality is that the insurgents themselves usually determine the pace and scope of the violence. This is not to say that government measures do not work. There is no doubt that the network of checkpoints and CCTVs or increased patrols have made the security environment more difficult for insurgents. Several mid-level insurgents have acknowledged that operations require more logistical planning; they cannot attack with complete impunity as they did in 2007.

As long as the violence remains contained in the Deep South, the government is willing to accept this rate of casualties. The big question is will the insurgents ever go out of area and target Thailand's very lucrative tourism industry. Since 2004, only one group has detonated a bomb in Bangkok. PULO detonated a small IED in a non-tourist district of Bangkok in order to wrest a seat at the peace talks. No group has followed suit.

The BRN left a car bomb at the Phuket police station in December 2013. It did not detonate the device, simply leaving it there for security forces to find. The signal they sent was clear. On a few occasions the BRN has gone out of area: it has targeted Hat Yai, detonating a bomb in the Lee Gardens hotel, causing hundreds of casualties (mainly from smoke inhalation) in 2012. They detonated an IED at 11pm in the underground parking lot of a shopping center on the resort island of Koh Samui in April 2013, to send a signal, not cause casualties. More recently, In August 2015, they detonated a series of small IEDs in resort areas, or gateways to tourist destinations. Insurgents deployed 10 bombs and incendiary devices in tourist towns across the Upper South, killing and wounding 30; a sharp change in tactics (*The Nation* 2016a).

I have repeatedly asked insurgents why they do not go out of area more often, and the response that I have been consistently given, is that they consider it all the time, but ultimately have deemed such attacks as counter-productive. The Thai security forces would retaliate with the use of force, with broad public support. Moreover, the insurgents are fearful of losing what little international sympathy and support they do enjoy; they are cognizant that being labeled international terrorists would be highly counter-productive. So when they do go out of area, it is at a very low level, just enough to send a signal to the regime. What is seen instead is that the insurgents feel that they can go out of area, while staying in the region: i.e. they target tourist gateways, popular with Malaysians and important to the local economy: Betong, Sungai Golok, Sadao, and up to Hat Yai. While attacks there get Bangkok's attention, they elicit no response from the international community.

## What is the government's response?

Before addressing the government's response, it is important to briefly analyze its goals: In September 2014, the National Council for Peace and Order (NCPO) issued its policy document on the south (Kerdphol 2014). In it, the junta laid out four objectives:

1. To reduce the number of incidents in the area and resolve the problems through peaceful means.
2. To improve the well-being of the people.
3. To ensure that the southern border provinces become a strong and peaceful multicultural society.
4. To gain support and create correct understanding of government's efforts on the people both inside and outside the area as well as the international community [sic].

After many dozens of interviews over the past 14 years, I contend that the Thai government has four interrelated goals:

1. To prevent secessionism, but also maintain the unitary nature of the Thai state;
2. To reduce violence to tolerable levels that can be attributed to criminality;
3. To assimilate the Malay-dominated south into the Thai nationstate; and
4. To shore up the dwindling Buddhist community in the south.

First, the government's definition of "peace" is the absence of violence, not a durable and negotiated political settlement. I.e., the government seeks to return to pre-2004, when it had largely quelled the previous generation of insurgents, through buy-outs, amnesties, and development projects, though without a negotiated and legal political settlement. The Thai military-backed government believes that with successful enough counter-insurgency, it can "negotiate", i.e. dictate the terms of peace. In every round of negotiation with the insurgents, the Thai side has reiterated that autonomy is a non-starter. In April 2016, Prime Minister Prayuth Chan-ocha publicly stated that any form of autonomy for the Malay populations was unacceptable (*The Nation* 2016b). And there is no reason to believe that with the current charter in place, there ever could be any form of legal autonomy. Maintaining the unitary nature of the Thai state is a paramount objective.

Second, the government is elated with the decline of violence in the south. Violence is at acceptable rates, and is not forcing the government to make political concessions, or face popular backlashes from the beleaguered Buddhist community.

The third goal is to assimilate the south into the Thai nationstate. Thailand has long been frustrated that the Malay are the only minority group that has consistently resisted assimilation. The Malay do not see any space for them in the construct of the Thai state: the monarchy (a Hindu god king), religion (Buddhism) and the nation (Thai), whose southern border was codified in The Anglo-Siamese Treaty of 1909, and which Pattani nationalists believe to be occupied territory. Indeed, most Thais and Thai officials will not refer to the local population as Malay. The spokesman of Internal Security Operations Command (ISOC) Region 4 refused to identify them as Malay insisting that they were "Thai Muslims". Thai Muslims are ethnic Thai who profess the Islamic faith, and there are such communities in central and northern Thailand. The three southernmost provinces and parts of Songkhla are dominated by ethnic Malays. Yet, they are listed as "Thai" on their identity card, with no option for "Malay". The government has resisted using Melayu and its Arabic-based written script of Yawi from being employed in government or in schools.

Fourth, the government has not only tried to stem the flood of Thai Buddhists out of the region, made easier with the decline in violence, but has been offering subsidies and increased security measures to keep the Buddhists there. In several cases, they have actively resettled people from Issarn, in the northeast, to the region, in new development projects.

To achieve those four inter-related goals, the Thai government and military have focused on ten core means. Behind all of these has been a gradual improvement in capabilities and professionalism. Commanders in the Deep South are still rotated too quickly on an annual basis, and security forces still make terrible mistakes, but in general, there has been a significant improvement in their overall capacity, competency, and professionalism from what was in evidence in 2004–2007.

170  Zachary Abuza

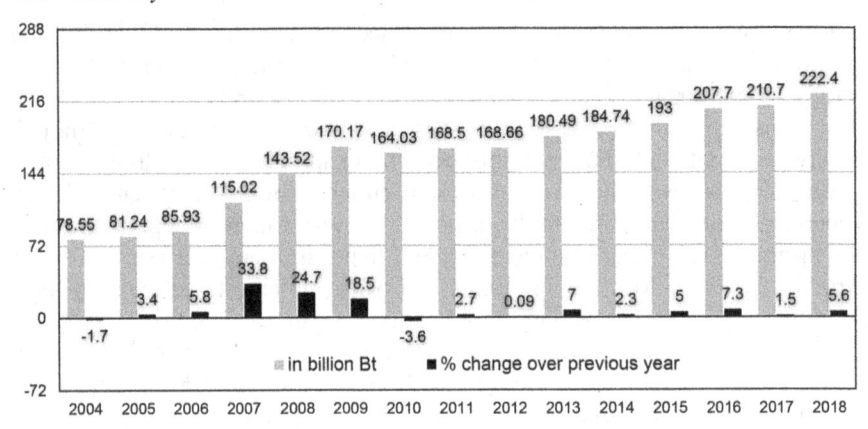

*Figure 12.4* Thai military expenditure, 2004–2018, in Thai Baht (billions)
Source: SIPRI.ORG, Bangkok Post & Janes, at http://www.janes.com/article/71418/thailand-announces-usd6-5-billion-defence-budget.

The military – unsurprisingly – rewarded itself with a 14.1 percent budget increase after the 2014 coup and 145.2 percent increase after the 2006 coup, from just under $3 billion to $6.1 billion. Sadly, few of those resources have been dedicated to the south. The military-backed government has funded a military backed solution to the problem, allocating $779 million for the Deep South for FY2015, approximately 8 percent of total government expenditure (Saiyasombut 2014; *Reuters* 2014). There was little transparency on how that money was spent or allocated across the 55 organizations and ministries that operate in the south, though the lions share, including development assistance, went through the ISOC and the RTA (Bangkok Post 2014a). The budget for FY2016 was Bt30.1 billion ($832 million), Bt4.4 billion higher than in FY2015, which was regarded as the highest ever (Charuvastra 2016). Between 2004 and 2015, the government claims to have spent Bt264 billion ($7.3 billion) in the south.

The budget has allowed the government to try to demonstrate the futility of violence through a robust security presence. At its peak, there were over 90,000 security personnel in the south. As already mentioned, the number continues to be reduced as violence declines. As the RTA transfers responsibilities to the Rangers and other paramilitaries, it has improved their capabilities and equipment, and hardened the network of checkpoints and CCTVs. The government has stepped up intelligence collection, and made very impressive investments in its forensic collection capabilities.

Unfortunately, the government continues to rely on tactics that undermine its support in the community, including extra-judicial killings, detention without trial, and torture. While the government deserves credit for trying to prosecute suspected insurgents through the court system, even pro-government courts in a military system have not been willing to do the junta's bidding. Over 80 percent of those who were detained were ultimately set free, acquitted

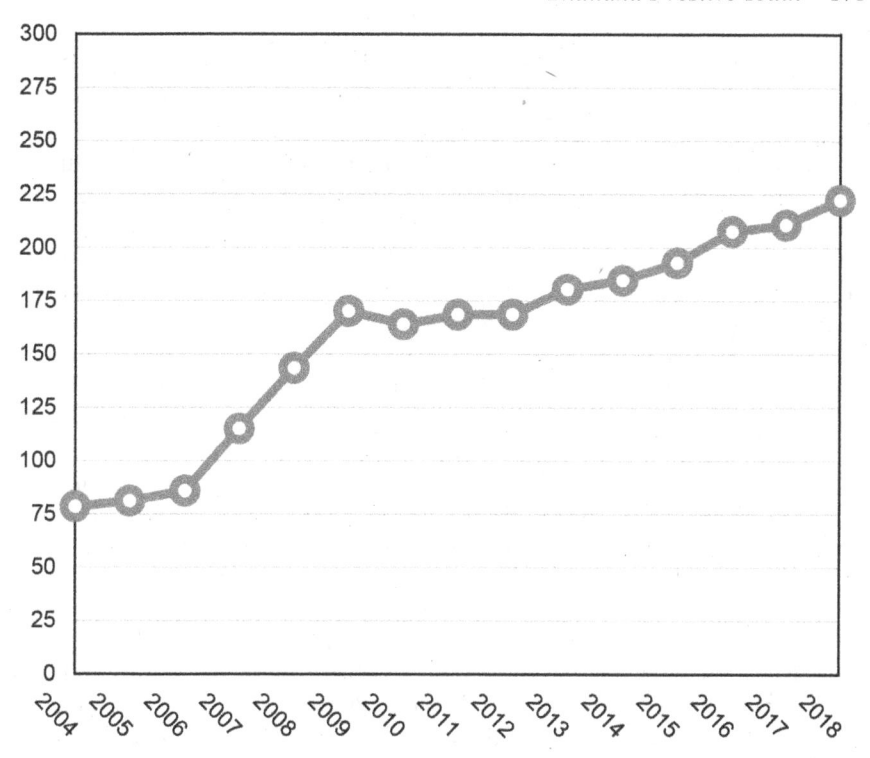

*Figure 12.5* What a few coups can do for you: Royal Thai Armed Forces budget 2004–2018 in Baht billions
Source: SIPRI.ORG, Bangkok Post & Janes, at http://www.janes.com/article/71418/thailand-announces-usd6-5-billion-defence-budget.

or saw their charges dropped due to lack of evidence. This resulted in both exasperation by the RTA towards the police, and a steady reliance on extra-judicial killings. Although a leading member of the National Human Rights commission told me that official complaints from the Deep South of torture and enforced disappearances are down since the coup, the number of extra judicial killings has increased (Interview with Angkhana Neelaphaijit 2015). Insurgents confirmed this. The National Human Rights Commission (NHRC) is concerned that there are more EJKs than are reported as families are often too scared to request post-mortems (Interview with Angkhana Neelaphaijit 2015).

In January 2016, three human rights organizations, the Thai Cross Cultural Foundation, the Patani Human Rights Network, and Duay Jai, issued a detailed report alleging that the rate of torture of suspects has doubled since the coup, 18 cases of alleged torture and ill-treatment. In 2015 alone, there were 15 recorded cases, whereas a total of 17 were recorded in 2014 (Prachatai 2016). This is a dramatic rise over previous years which saw only seven cases in 2013, two in 2011, and three in 2010 (no information was available for

2012). Complaints were filed against 48 military officers and 13 police officers for committing torture and ill-treatment, but no one has been indicted. Rather than take the allegations seriously and investigate any wrong doing, the military pressed charges against the authors of the report (Human Rights Watch 2017). In early 2018, the RTA sued a former detainee who alleged torture.

Finally the government continues to rely on the 2005 Emergency Decree to detain suspects without trial. This was most recently done in February 2018, when a Malay civil society activist was detained and held incommunicado. These human rights abuses continue to alienate the local Malay community.

As important as it is to study what the Thai government has done, it is as important to understand what they have not done, but which many have called for. Not all of these are difficult, and most simply require changes in existing policy, not law, and all would go a long way to addressing the grievances of the local community. That Thai security forces continue to operate with full legal immunity has created a culture that has completely alienated the local population and led to deep-seated mistrust of the Thai state. The most important of these are implementing a general amnesty and implementing educational reforms.

The military has been able to quash a general amnesty and to impose so many conditions and restrictions on partial amnesties as to render them useless. The RTA used general amnesties extremely effectively in the 1980s and 1990s in dealing with a host of insurgencies throughout the country, although they are extremely unwilling to do so at this time. The government was preparing for limited amnesties as part of the peace process with the BRN, which began in February 2013. In April 2013, a Deputy Prime Minister promised to revoke arrest warrants for those implicated in southern insurgency and charged under the Criminal Code. But the plan was shelved after army disapproval when the violence did not subside (Bangkok Post 2013a). The BRN made the release of all political prisoners a key condition for the peace talks in mid-2013. The organization raised the issue of amnesty in each of their three video-statements, two video interviews, and written demands presented to their Thai counterparts (*The Nation* 2013; Bangkok Post 2013a–f). These were rejected outright by the Thai side on each occasion. The RTA has been implementing a new program, "Bringing People Back Home", in which it claims to reintegrate former insurgents. This program is largely for show. In many cases the military simply goes into villages and compels people to publicly sign pledges they will not engage in violence. In other cases, the people that they reintegrate were from previous generations of the insurgency.

Regarding language reforms, the government has steadfastly refused to authorize the use of Bahasa Melayu as an official working language or medium of instruction in the schools. While Yawi, an Arabic script for Melayu, is often featured on the front of government buildings, it is neither a working language, nor do the vast majority of security forces or civil servants speak it. The Thai attitude is simple: the use of Melayu will impede assimilation and make people feel even less Thai. According to a 2010 survey by the Asia Foundation, 80 percent of the Malay population speaks a dialect of Bahasa as a first language (Asia Foundation 2010). Although previous governments made overtures and accepted proposals to implement language reform, the government installed following the May 2014 coup has been steadfast in its opposition both to language as well as the region's religious schools. Prime Minister General Prayuth Chan-ocha has reemphasized his belief that all education should be conducted in Thai, and has used several opportunities to emphasize that the country has only one official language. The junta's forced indoctrination of students across Thailand with the "12 core Thai values" identified by Prayuth and their curricular implementation will only draw additional ire in the south (Bangkok Post 2014b). The junta's hyperactive commitment to the King, Buddhism, and the overly centralized Thai state serve to create a greater sense of disenfranchisement.

## The peace process

Every Thai government has expressed a nominal willingness to engage in peace talks; though almost nothing has come of it (Abuza 2016). The government of Thaksin Shinawatra engaged in the "Langkawi process", sponsored by former Malaysian Prime Minister Mahathir Mohammed, however this did not include the BRN and quickly fell apart. The government of Yingluck Shinawatra made the most progress, in that it appeared willing to address some of the core grievances of the militants, but that quickly put it at odds with the military. The government and BRN began formal talks in February 2013, and held four rounds that year, before the military withdrew their support. To be fair, the BRN moved some of the goal posts, and made five additional demands as preconditions in the middle of those talks. The organization demonstrated a lack of professionalism and sincerity that did not help its efforts; but this also had to do with the demands and internal politics of the movement. The RTA had demanded that there be a total ceasefire as both a sign of goodwill and proof of command and control. Although violence against civilians dropped dramatically, the targeting of security forces actually increased, infuriating the Royal Thai Army leadership. The RTA publicly blamed the political stalemate between the government and opposition as the cause of the breakdown in negotiations, but the military had exercised its veto (Bangkok Post 2013g).

Following the May 2014 coup, the Junta has repeatedly expressed its willingness to reconvene peace talks, issued Order 230 on 26 November 2014 to establish a peace panel, and appointed a close confident of General Prayuth, Gen Aksara as its chairman. But the reality is that the Junta, which has worked to centralize power and quash civil society, is offering nothing to the insurgents. The Thai side is hoping to enter from such a position of strength, so that any concessions are completely unnecessary. The military government countenances no third party involvement. The Malaysian government is confined to facilitating the talks, not mediating.

In mid-2015, the Malaysian government brokered an agreement creating MARA-Patani, an umbrella organization to ensure representation at the talks. MARA-Patani is dominated by the BRN, which holds 50 percent of its seats and top leadership, but which includes the BIPP, PULO, and the GMIP.

There were three backchannel talks in mid-2015, to discuss the resumption of formal talks, with the government again demanding a ceasefire (Bangkok Post 2015). MARA laid down three reasonable demands: 1) to make the peace process a national priority; 2) provide legal immunity and protection for the MARA negotiators; and 3) formal legal recognition of MARA-Patani. The Junta was reluctant to accept any of these (Benar News 2015). By October 2015, the BRN publicly denounced the peace process with the government, which it called "insincere" (Prachatai 2015). In April 2016, Prayuth publicly stated that any form of autonomy was unacceptable (*The Nation* 2016a). The government has repeatedly rejected all calls for general amnesties, refused to implement language reforms, refused calls for autonomy, and steadfastly refused to prosecute members of their own security forces for crimes committed.

Though the BRN sent a representative to sit in on the few formal talks that were held in 2016–2017, the BRN made clear that it had quit the peace process. While the smaller groups have hoped to leverage their participation in MARA-Patani into some sort of political power, the BRN holds most of the cards, and continues to act as a spoiler. It is hard to blame the organization, in that the Thai government is unwilling to make any concessions. Its conception of peace is that the BRN surrenders, and there are no signs that the BRN has any need or will to do so. As such Thailand's Malay insurgency will continue its slow burn.

## Note

1 The views expressed here are the author's and do not reflect the opinions of the National War College or US Department of Defense.

## References

Abuza, Zachary (2007), *Conspiracy of Silence*, Washington, DC: USIP Press.
Abuza, Zachary (2016), *Forging Peace in Southeast Asia: Insurgencies, Peace Processes, and Reconciliation*, Maryland and London: Rowman Littlefield.
Asia Foundation (2010), "First In-Person Survey on Democracy and Conflict in Southern Thailand to Launch December 16", available at http://asiafoundation.org/in-asia/2010/12/08/first-in-person-survey-on-democracy-and-conflict-in-southern-thailand-to-launch-december-16/accessed 15 March 2018.
*Bangkok Post* (2013a), "Government Plans to Revoke Rebel Warrants", 10 May, available at http://www.bangkokpost.com/news/security/349265/government-dropping-arrest-warrants-against-some-militants-in-south accessed 15 March 2018.

*Bangkok Post* (2013b), "BRN Sets Peace Talk Conditions", 28 April, available at http://www.bangkokpost.com/news/local/347425/brn-vows-to-fight-and-talk-in-south accessed 15 March 2018.

*Bangkok Post* (2013c), "BRN's Latest Video Clip Provocative", 31 May, available at http://www.bangkokpost.com/opinion/opinion/352795/brn-latest-video-clip-provocative accessed 15 March 2018.

*Bangkok Post* (2013d), "BRN Negotiator Gives First Media Interview", 19 June, available at http://www.bangkokpost.com/news/local/355906/five-demands-remain-focus-of-peace-talks-says-brn-negotiator-hassan-taib accessed 15 March 2018.

*Bangkok Post* (2013e), "BRN Demands Troop Withdrawal as Condition for Ramadan Ceasefire", 25 June, available at http://www.bangkokpost.com/news/local/356831/troops-out-alcohol-ban-for-ramadan-among-new-conditions-set-for-peace-talks accessed 15 March 2018.

*Bangkok Post* (2013f), "BRN Submits Truce Demands", 26 June, available at http://www.bangkokpost.com/news/security/357059/brn-demands-officially-submitted-to-thai-malaysia accessed 15 March 2018.

*Bangkok Post* (2013g), "Prayuth Calls BRN Terms Unacceptable", 20 August, available at http://www.bangkokpost.com/archive/prayuth-calls-brn-terms-unacceptable/365425 accessed 15 March 2018.

*Bangkok Post* (2014a), "B20bn Tabbed for South Peace Effort", 24 November, available at http://www.bangkokpost.com/news/security/445162/b20bn-tabbed-for-south-peace-effort accessed 15 March 2018.

*Bangkok Post* (2014b), "Teaching our Children How to Kowtow", 23 July, available at http://www.bangkokpost.com/opinion/opinion/421872/teaching-our-children-how-to-kowtow accessed 15 March 2018.

*Bangkok Post* (2015), "Alliance of Insurgent Groups Joins Talks", available at http://www.bangkokpost.com/news/security/667584/alliance-of-insurgent-groups-joins-talks accessed 15 March 2018.

*Bangkok Post* (2016), "Govt Intensifies Election Security in South", 1 August, available at http://www.bangkokpost.com/news/general/1049285/govt-intensifies-election-security-in-south accessed 15 March 2018.

*Bangkok Post* (2018), "South Safest in 14 Years, Army Boasts", 5 January, available at https://www.bangkokpost.com/news/security/1390370/south-safest-in-14-years-army-boasts accessed 15 March 2018.

*Benar News* (2015), "Independence Still Primary Goal of Southern Thailand Rebels: Negotiator", 27 August, available at http://www.benarnews.org/english/news/thai/mara-pattani-08272015134159.html accessed 15 March 2018.

*Benar News* (2017), "Violence in Thai Deep South Reached Record Low in 2017", 26 December, available at http://www.benarnews.org/english/news/thai/thailand-bombings-12262017172216.html accessed 15 March 2018.

Charuvastra, Teeranai (2016), "Govt Approves Budget Hike to Quell Southern Insurgency", *Khaosod English*, 5 January, available at http://www.khaosodenglish.com/politics/2016/01/05/1451975374/ accessed 15 March 2018.

Human Rights Watch (2017), "Thailand: Drop Case Against Rights Defenders: Military Criminal Complaint in Retaliation for Torture Report", available at https://www.hrw.org/news/2016/06/08/thailand-drop-case-against-rights-defenders accessed 15 March 2018.

ICG (International Crisis Group) (2016), "Southern Thailand's Peace Dialogue: No Traction", Asia Briefing No. 148, 21 September, available at https://www.cri

sisgroup.org/asia/south-east-asia/thailand/southern-thailand-s-peace-dialogue-no-traction accessed 15 March 2018.

Interview with Angkhana Neelaphaijit, Pattani City, 20 February 2015.

Kerdphol, Aksara (2014), Chief of Staff and Secretary of the Internal Security Operations Command, National Council for Peace and Order, "Resolving the Problems in the Southernmost Provinces in Thailand: Policies of General Prayuth Chan-ocha Head of National Council of Peace and Order", September.

Pathan, Don (2016), "Thai Military and Insurgents Change Tack in Southern Provinces", *Nikkei Asian Review*, 15 August, available at https://asia.nikkei.com/Politics-Economy/Policy-Politics/Thai-military-and-insurgents-change-tack-in-southern-provinces?n_cid=NARAN012 accessed 15 March 2018.

*Prachatai* (2015), "Deep South's Most Active Insurgent Group Denounces Peace Talk", 12 October, available at http://prachatai.org/english/node/5535?utm_source=dlvr.it&utm_medium=twitter accessed 15 March 2018.

*Prachatai* (2016), "Allegations of Torture Against Malay Muslims in Deep South Double After Coup", 9 January, available at http://prachatai.com/english/node/5754 accessed 15 March 2018.

Reuters (2014), "Thai Junta Boosts Spending on Defense, Education in Draft Budget", 18 August, available at http://www.Reuters.com/article/2014/08/18/us-thailand-budget-idUSKBN0GI0MG20140818 accessed 15 March 2018.

Saiyasombut, Saksith (2014), "The Thai Junta's 2015 Draft Budget, Explained in 4 Graphs", Asian Correspondent, 22 April, available at http://asiancorrespondent.com/125880/thai-juntas-2015-draft-budget-infographics/ accessed 15 March 2018.

*The Nation* (2013), "BRN Wants Troops out of Far South", available at http://www.nationmultimedia.com/national/BRN-wants-troops-out-of-far-South-30202810.html accessed 15 March 2018.

*The Nation* (2016a), "Deep South Vote against Charter Showed Awareness, Observers Say", 9 August, available at http://www.nationmultimedia.com/politics/Deep-South-vote-against-charter-showed-awareness-o-30292491.html accessed 15 March 2018.

*The Nation* (2016b), "Prayut Dismisses Insurgent Demand of South Autonomy as Talks Falter", 22 April, available at www.nationmultimedia.com/national/Prayut-dismisses-insurgent-demand-of-South-autonom-30284452.html accessed on 15 March 2018.

# 13 Terrorism in Indonesia, Malaysia and Singapore
## Challenge and response

*Andrew T. H. Tan*

This chapter article focuses on the terrorist challenge in the key Malay Archipelago states of Indonesia and Malaysia, the two Muslim-majority countries in Southeast Asia. Singapore is also included due to its geographical location in the midst of these two larger states, and its strong economic and social ties with both, including significant kinship ties between its own population and ethnic kin in Malaysia. Indeed, these three countries form a sub-regional security complex in its own right (Tan 2004). The complex security situation in the southern Philippines and in southern Thailand is left to other writers in this volume.

This chapter begins by briefly examining the development and trends in the contemporary terrorist threat, followed by an analysis of what might explain these trends. It concludes by evaluating whether the countries concerned have met the evolving terrorist challenges effectively.

### Trends in the terrorist challenge

Despite the shock and surprise at the emergence of the Islamic State in the region in 2014, contemporary militant terrorism in the region does in fact have a local and historical context. In particular, the Darul Islam movement was present in the early days of the newly independent Republic of Indonesia soon after it was founded in 1945. Founded in 1947, the Darul Islam launched an armed rebellion from 1948 to 1962. It went underground after the demise of its rebellion, but revived in the 1980s after it sent volunteers to Afghanistan to participate in the anti-Soviet insurgency. Some 500 veterans of the Afghan conflict who subsequently returned then joined the Jemaah Islamiah (JI) network in 1993, whereupon they helped train thousands of regional militants in camps that they established in the southern Philippines and in Indonesia. The graduates of these training camps constitute the core of the Islamic State in the region today (Sholeh 2016: 95–96).

The JI established links with extremist elements and groups in the Middle East through the Afghan *mujahideen* network, and it was through this that it became linked to Al Qaeda. Suspicions of a possible link between militants in the Middle East and the region were proven by the arrest of JI operatives in

Singapore in late 2001, following the seminal terrorist attacks in the United States on 11 September 2001 (or 9–11). The operatives had planned, in coordination with Al Qaeda, a series of coordinated attacks in Singapore (MHA 2003).

The discovery of the JI and arrests of its operatives did not stop a string of deadly terrorist attacks carried out by the group in Indonesia. In 2002, the deadly Bali bombing resulted in the deaths of 202 people, including 88 Western tourists (*Straits Times* 2016a). Robust counter-terrorism efforts in Indonesia after the Bali attacks however, led to a steady deterioration of the capabilities of the JI. By 2012, an estimated 800 had been arrested and about 60 killed in counter-terrorism operations in Indonesia (*New York Times* 2012). The success of counterterrorism in Indonesia was such that by 2014, one study concluded that militant terrorists were now only able to carry out "low-tech, low-competence, low-casualty" attacks, given the significant decline in their operational capabilities (IPAC 2013: 1–2).

In Malaysia and Singapore, the heavy use of robust preventive detention laws, which are absent in Indonesia, resulted in the arrest and long-term incarceration of potential terrorists. This has proved to be an effective measure, as the security authorities have been able to swiftly neutralise any potential terrorist. Malaysia has had a long history of radical or "deviant" Muslim groups that have resorted to violence. From 1967 to 2015, Malaysia's Special Branch (famed for its role in countering communist insurgents in the 1950s), identified some 22 home-grown militant groups, including the Kampulan Mujahidin Malaysia (KMM) and the JI, both of which were dominated by ex-Afghan *mujahideen* fighters who had returned. However, the swift resort to preventive detention effectively dismantled these groups in Malaysia (El-Muhammady 2016: 106–107). Similarly, in Singapore, the discovery of the JI bomb plots in late 2001 led to the preventive detention and the dismantling of the JI's Singapore cell. Some 40 alleged JI operatives were subsequently detained at various points (*Straits Times* 2016b).

Since 9–11, the concerted global counterterrorism efforts led by the United States have considerably degraded Al Qaeda's operational capabilities. However, the rise of the Islamic State (IS) in the Middle East has had a profound impact on the terrorist threat in Indonesia, Malaysia and Singapore. The IS in 2014 succeeded where Al Qaeda had failed, that is, in capturing a vast territory in Syria and Iraq, including Mosul, Iraq's second largest city, and then declaring an Islamic caliphate, with IS leader Abu Bakr al-Baghdadi declaring himself as its caliph (*The Guardian* 2014a). This galvanised militants around the world, with volunteer *mujahideen* joining the IS in Syria and Iraq. By late 2015, at least 27,000 people from some 86 countries had travelled to the Middle East to join up with the IS (Soufan Group 2015).

In Southeast Asia, particularly in Indonesia and Malaysia, radical ideology from the IS spread very rapidly through extremist circles and social media. By early 2017, an estimated 1,000 had joined the IS in Syria and Iraq, the majority from Indonesia, followed by Malaysia, and a few individuals from the Philippines and Singapore (Liow 2017). In Indonesia, a number of local jihadists declared their support for the IS soon after it declared its caliphate in mid-2014, including Abu Bakar Bashir, the JI's spiritual leader. Sympathisers also organised fundraising and recruitment events throughout Indonesia (Emont 2014).

The Indonesian government was so concerned by the rapid development of the IS that it formally banned the group in August 2014 (*Washington Post* 2014). However, the IS itself has also taken an active interest in spreading its ideology as well as recruiting from the region. In July 2014, it produced a recruitment video entitled "Join the Ranks" featuring Indonesian members of the IS, in a direct appeal to militants in Indonesia. This indicated that it saw Indonesia as a fertile recruitment ground (ABC News 2014). In July 2016, it formed a Malay-speaking brigade in Syria, known as Katibah Nusantara, which has some 1,000 fighters from Southeast Asia, predominantly from Indonesia and Malaysia (Sholeh 2016: 101). This development raised serious concerns as it facilitates communication and further recruitment.

The IS inspired the first IS terrorist attack in Indonesia on 14 January 2016. Days before the attack, Aman Abdurrahman, who is the spiritual leader for the IS in the region, issued a much-shared *fatwa* or religious edict from his jail cell in Indonesia, calling for his followers to join the Islamic State in Syria, stating as well that "if you cannot emigrate then wage jihad with spirit wherever you are". Four operatives carried out a disorganised attack in Jakarta, aiming to kill police officers and tourists. In the end, they succeeded in killing four people before they were themselves killed. According to Sidney Jones, the competition amongst jihadist leaders (such as Bahrun Naim, who organised the Jakarta attack, Bahrumsyah, and Abu Jandal), the spread of extremism in Indonesian jails, and the prospect of trained fighters returning from Syria are factors that are likely to lead to further terrorist attacks in the future (*The Guardian* 2014b).

In Malaysia, the Syrian regime's brutality towards its own rebels, including the killing of civilians and children in counter-insurgency bombings, elicited strong sympathy amongst the worldwide Muslim community or *umma*. Together with effective IS propaganda, the IS was able to recruit a steady stream of Malaysians to its cause. Many of these are young and use social media to share information and recruit new members to the cause (El-Muhammady 2016). More seriously, the new local IS recruits have been involved in terrorist plots in Malaysia. In April 2015, for instance, 12 people were arrested by police in a remote area as they were testing improvised explosive devices (IEDs). The group had been planning to launch attacks on government facilities and night-clubs in the Klang Valley in Malaysia (*The Star* 2015).

In June 2016, Malaysia suffered the first IS terrorist attack at Puchong district, in Kuala Lumpur. A grenade attack on a bar where patrons were watching a live telecast of European soccer injured eight people. According to the authorities, the attack was ordered and coordinated by Muhammad

Wanndy Mohamed Jedi, a Malaysian IS fighter in Syria. Authorities later arrested 15 people, including two policemen (CNN 2016). Malaysia has been very proactive however in dealing with the IS threat, placing large numbers of alleged operatives and sympathisers under preventive detention. Of concern however, is the fact that a number of those arrested have been either police or military personnel. Indeed, Malaysia's Defence Minister informed parliament in April 2015 that at least 70 military personnel had joined the IS (*IB Times* 2015a). In May 2015, Malaysian police estimated that 11 Malaysians, including six suicide bombers, had been killed fighting for the IS in the Middle East, and that about 80 Malaysians had joined the group there. Malaysian authorities also reported that IS cells in the country were planning kidnapping for ransom as well as bank heists in order to fund their activities in the country (*Straits Times* 2015). By mid-2018, around 300 people had been arrested in Malaysia for their alleged links to the IS (IANS 2018).

Finally, the IS has also been able to penetrate Singapore, although the tight media control and the vigilance of its internal security apparatus has so far limited its impact. In January 2016, 27 Bangladeshi construction workers were arrested and repatriated to Bangladesh for planning terrorist attacks in their home country (Channel News Asia 2016a). In August 2016, the Singapore authorities announced that two local Singaporeans had been arrested under the Internal Security Act after they made plans to travel to Syria to fight for the IS, and another two had been issued restriction orders, under which they cannot change residence or employment or travel out of Singapore without prior approval from the authorities (Channel News Asia 2016b). At about the same time, Indonesian counter-terrorism police arrested six people in the island of Batam, which is close to Singapore, over an alleged plot to fire a rocket at Singapore's Marina Bay (Channel News Asia 2016c).

## Explaining terrorism trends

The rise in contemporary post 9–11 terrorism in the region can be explained by: the impact of external developments and trends in global terrorism as a result of events in the Middle East and Afghanistan; the persistent historical yearning for an Islamic state in the region amongst militants, and the enabling capacity of the modern information technology revolution in reaching out to millions of potential recruits.

The co-option of the JI by Al Qaeda demonstrated the essentially global and transnational nature of the new post 9–11 terrorism. In Southeast Asia, the JI operated as Al Qaeda's arm in the region, as it held similar ideological beliefs in rejecting secular governments and in the use of violence to establish a pan-Islamic caliphate ruled strictly according to the *sharia* or Islamic laws. Indeed, the founders of the JI built upon ex-*mujahideen* networks consisting of Southeast Asian volunteers who had fought against the Soviet invasion of Afghanistan in the 1980s (MHA 2003: 6). JI's spiritual leader, Abu Bakar Bashir, who established what became known as the Ngruki network of religious school alumnus in Indonesia and Malaysia, also built linkages with militants in Pakistan and Afghanistan (ICG 2002: 13).

Just as the Soviet invasion of Afghanistan led to the emergence of Al Qaeda and its *mujahideen* network in Southeast Asia, recent events in Syria and Iraq have had a significant impact in reviving the militant scene in the region. After 2010, the JI's operational capabilities were severely degraded through effective counter-terrorism action, particularly in Indonesia, but this also left a void for the Islamic State to fill. The surprising success of the IS in Syria and Iraq since 2014 galvanised militants all over the world, and has had a relatively strong impact in Southeast Asia, where it has been able to recruit local militants into its ranks.

Yet, despite the linkages with Al Qaeda and with global terrorism trends and developments, it is important to bear in mind that both the JI and the Islamic State have strong local roots. The JI was built upon a much earlier incarnation of militant terrorism, namely, that of the Darul Islam. Founded in 1947 by S. M. Kartosuwiryo, the Darul Islam (or House of Islam) advocated the establishment of an Islamic state in Indonesia ruled strictly according to the *sharia*. The Darul Islam itself however, was influenced by the Sarekat Islam that had been formed in 1911, and it was Kartosuwiryo's two-year sojourn with it from 1927–1929 that consolidated his views over what would be the best form of government for a newly independent Indonesia, namely, one that was ruled through the strict application of Muslim laws (Soebardi 1983: 110).

The appearance of the Darul Islam in 1947 coincided with deep rifts within the new Indonesian state over its identity as well as its constitutional direction. The three key forces in Indonesia, namely, the communists, the fundamental Muslims and the secular nationalists, fought a long and hard battle against each other in the years following independence. The communists were wiped out in a bloodbath after the Gestapu coup in 1965, after which the secular nationalists, in the form of military rule, dominated the political landscape until the Suharto regime was overthrown in 1997 and Indonesia became a democracy. The fundamentalists, however, have always been a significant presence within the Indonesian polity. While many fundamentalists and the vast majority of more moderate Muslims within mainstream Muslim organisations such as Nahdatul Ulama and the Mohammadiyah have been able to work within a secular state, a minority extremist, and violent, fringe has also always existed.

The Darul Islam rebellion that was launched in 1948 was suppressed in 1962, albeit with difficulty (ICG 2002: 7–10). However, Darul Islam was never fully extinguished, as it then went underground and its ideals continued to be passed on through religious schools and underground networks. The leaders of the JI, such as Abu Bakar Bashir, saw themselves as the Darul Islam's ideological heirs though the global contacts that they established led them to break away from Darul Islam with its Indonesia-centric goal of an Islamic state and to embrace the global salafi-jihadism of Al Qaeda and its objective of a pan-Islamic caliphate (Riviere 2016: 6).

After the Bali bombing in 2002, Indonesia set up a dedicated counter-terrorism police force, known as Densus 88. By 2010, its operations had drastically reduced the JI's operational capabilities, such that it could thereafter only conduct small-scale local attacks targeting in particular security forces (IPAC 2013: 1–2). The problem however, is that the militant problem has persisted. Degrading the JI's operational capabilities was never going to stamp out militancy, given the long historical yearning for an Islamic state which has existed in Indonesia since the formation of the Sarekat Islam in the 1911, operationalised on the battlefield by the Darul Islam in the 1950s and kept alive by developments within Indonesia as well as in the Middle East. Its persistence reflect enduring divisions within the Muslim polity as to the shape and character of post-independence Indonesia and indeed, the rest of the Malay archipelago where Muslims are a majority. More seriously, developments in militant movements in Indonesia have a direct bearing on the rest of the region, particularly in neighbouring Malaysia, and to a more limited degree, Singapore, given the transboundary linkages within the Malay archipelago.

The long years of political suppression, particularly of political Islam, under the Suharto regime, until its overthrow in 1998, merely meant that the militants had gone underground and focused on proselytising as well as spreading their radical ideology through religious schools such as in Ngruki. Abu Bakar Bashir had also sought refuge in Malaysia where he established a religious school and built his JI network. The democratisation that came to Indonesia after 1998 removed the shackles on political Islam, and inevitably, militant elements came out into the open. The Majelis Mujahideen Indonesia (MMI), an umbrella group of militant groups (including the old Darul Islam) was established by Abu Bakar Bashir in 1999 after the fall of the Suharto regime. The MMI's first congress was held in Yogjakarta in 2000 and was attended by 1,800 people, which elected Bashir as its spiritual leader, and issued a charter which stated that "it is obligatory to implement the Islamic Sharia for all Muslims in Indonesia and all over the world in general" (Hilmy 2010: 110). In a newly democratic Indonesia, the radicals were now out in the open, and could openly propagate their radical ideology. This has also meant that it could now reach potential militants in neighbouring Malaysia and Singapore.

The surprisingly rapid penetration by the Islamic State in the region after the declaration of its caliphate in Syria in mid-2014, demonstrated by the formation of the entirely Malay-speaking brigade, the Katibah Nusantara in July 2016, can be attributed to the efficacy of modern social media and social networking through the internet as well as the use of information technology to disseminate radical ideology. The Islamic State has produced online videos, and also disseminated its views through *Al-Fatihin*, its online newspaper, and *Dabiq*, its online magazine. It has its own official media outlet, Al-Hayat, which has content in non-Arabic languages. Together with associated websites and media outlets which produce pamphlets, e-books, articles and other publications, radical ideology has become freely available to millions of potential recruits in Southeast Asia (Kam 2016: 141). The effective use of social media and modern information technology has helped it reach out to tech-savvy younger Muslims who use social media to connect and access a variety of information. According to Malaysia's Home Ministry, around 75% of new IS supporters in Malaysia have in fact been recruited in this manner (*IB Times* 2015b). The free, democratic atmosphere in Indonesia has been a key enabler of this dissemination of radical ideology. Of the 3,000 pro-Islamic State social media sites in Southeast Asia, an estimated 70% originate from Indonesia (John 2016).

## Evaluating counter-terrorism responses

Given the trends in terrorism in these three countries and what explains them, the final question then is: How effective have counter-terrorism responses been? This section evaluates counter-terrorism legislation and police actions, as well as countering violent extremism (CVE) programs in these countries.

The security forces of all three countries have taken strong, proactive measures to deal with the terrorism threat since 9–11. Both Malaysia and Singapore have robust preventive detention laws which enable their governments to detain indefinitely anyone suspected of involvement in terrorist activities, and to compel them to undergo religious rehabilitation. Malaysia has used its Internal Security Act (1960) and its replacement, the Prevention of Terrorism Act (2015), to detain and thus disrupt terrorist plots by a number of militant organisations (El-Muhammady 2016: 117–118). By mid-2018, around 300 people had been arrested in Malaysia for their alleged links to the IS (IANS 2018). The proactive, preventive approach has undoubtedly disrupted many terrorist plots but the problem is that a disturbingly large number of those arrested have been security personnel, such as policemen and soldiers. This indicates that radical ideology has been able to penetrate the government and its security forces. An urgent task is to examine why this has happened and how the recruitment of the IS from within the security services themselves can be minimised.

Singapore too has used its own Internal Security Act to pro-actively disrupt terrorist activities. Under its Act, the government can detain a suspect for up to two years, although in less severe cases, a Restriction Order can be issued, under which an individual would be subjected to restrictions such as having to seek permission to travel abroad (National Library n.d.). Singapore's powerful Internal Security Department has been especially effective and vigilant in detecting any radical activity in the small island-state, and has been quick to detain any suspected terrorist. Regular counter-terrorism drills involving police and the army have been held as a deterrent and also to train the security services in responding to any terrorist attack (*Straits Times* 2016c). While Singapore's small size and its disciplined government are factors which help it take effective and robust measures against terrorism, other factors mitigate against optimism. Its very location, in the heart of the Malay archipelago, its open port status, and the presence of a large number of tempting targets in the form of Western multinational corporations and expatriate staff, make it vulnerable as a key terrorist target, especially for militants in neighbouring Indonesia and Malaysia.

Indonesia responded to the Bali bombing by setting up, with the assistance of the United States and Australia, Densus (or Detachment) 88 in 2003. The unit has chalked up a series of successes throughout the Indonesian archipelago as it has arrested or killed a large number of suspected terrorists. While this did not prevent several major terrorist incidents, such as the Jakarta terrorist attacks by the JI in 2009 and more recently by the Islamic State in 2016, the ability to detect and disrupt terrorist cells has undoubtedly prevented many other attacks. From 2010 to 2016, it was estimated that it had prevented 54 terrorist attacks (*Jakarta Post* 2016). In 2015, the Indonesian armed forces established a new elite rapid reaction force, known as the TNI Joint Special Operations Command or Koopsusgab, to supplement Densus 88 (Parameswaran 2015).

The involvement of the armed forces in dealing with terrorism threats in a vast country with a huge population and thousands of islands is also a logical development given the resources available to the armed forces. Indeed, the combined military-police operation (Operation Tinombala) against the IS-affiliated group, the Eastern Indonesia Mujahideen, in inhospitable terrain on Sulawesi island in 2016 demonstrated the efficacy and logic of such an arrangement, despite concerns over giving the military a domestic security role (Tempo 2016). Indeed, a whole-of-government approach involving other branches of government, not just Densus 88, would be the appropriate response to the rising threat posed by the IS.

Indonesia however, does not have the same robust preventive detention laws used in Malaysia and Singapore. Having suffered from the oppressive and arbitrary internal security environment during the Suharto era, there is little appetite in a democratic Indonesia for such laws. Indonesia's Anti-Terrorism Law in 2002, which defines acts that constitute terrorism, and provides substantial penalties, including death, for terrorism offences, provides the legal basis and supplements criminal law in dealing with terrorism. It was effectively used in convicting a number of terrorists since it was passed (Butt 2008: 3–4). In May 2018, after years of debate, and two weeks after terrorist attacks on Christian churches in Surabaya, Indonesia finally passed a revised law on terrorism. While still short of preventive detention, it strengthened the laws on terrorism. Under the new law, anyone suspected of planning a terrorist attack can be detained without charge for a maximum of 21 days, compared to seven days previously, and pre-trial-detention was now extended from 180 to 290 days. Furthermore, anyone who is a member of a "terrorist organisation" could also be jailed for up to seven years (Asianews.it 2018).

Aside from hard security measures, police operations and strengthening counter-terrorism laws, however, one distinguishing feature of regional counter-terrorism has been its use of "soft" approaches as well. This has included the religious rehabilitation of detained militants, followed by release and reintegration into society, as part of measures in countering violent extremism. Both Singapore and Malaysia understand, from historical experience with communist insurgency in the 1950s, that dealing with terrorism and insurgency requires a comprehensive approach. This refers to the use of security as well as non-military political, economic, social and psychological instruments in the context of a whole-of-government approach, with the objective of winning the hearts and minds of the population and isolating the extremists (Stubbs 1989). Thus, while Singapore and Malaysia have used tough preventive detention laws to detain alleged terrorists, the detainees have been generally well-treated and given religious counselling to de-radicalise them. Singapore, for instance, has a team of Muslim clerics in its Religious Rehabilitation Group, who counsel detainees, work with their families, and also assist those released in obtaining financial support from the government as well as employment (*Washington Post* 2009). In Malaysia, a similar rehabilitation program has been in place since 2001, consisting of ideological de-radicalisation, financial assistance and continuous monitoring after release. In January 2016, Malaysia's Home Affairs Ministry launched a new, structured rehabilitation program, led by a rehabilitation team, in order to counter the growing threat from the IS (El-Muhammady 2016: 118–120).

In addition to religious rehabilitation, Singapore and Malaysia have also established other counter-radicalisation programs. Singapore's approach has been to work closely with Muslim community groups, scholars and leaders. The Islamic Religious Council of Singapore (MUIS) has undertaken a number of initiatives to counter religious extremism, such as promoting interfaith dialogue, developing print and online material to counter the claims of the IS, and the registration of religious teachers (Kam 2016: 146–147).

Similarly, Malaysia has developed its own suite of CVE programs, in the context of a whole-of-government approach. Malaysia's Islamic Affairs Department (Jakim) has established a cross-agency committee, known as the Jihad Concept Explanation Action Committee, which has representations from government agencies, state religious leaders and private Islamic bodies to address misconceptions about *jihad*. The Committee carries out its work through programs and activities in universities and mosques. Another CVE program is operated in collaboration between public, private and religious bodies, and focuses on countering extremist narratives through public talks, videos and printed material. Malaysia's integrated, comprehensive approach, which involves the participation of various entities, is credited with having curtailed the growth of the IS. The rehabilitation program has also been reportedly very successful, with a low failure rate of 2.5% who revert to militancy after release (Today 2016).

CVE programs in Indonesia have been somewhat more problematic. As Gayan Vithanage observed, its de-radicalisation and rehabilitation programs contrast starkly with Singapore's, as it is not centrally administered and is not well-resourced (Vithanage 2015). The 2009 terrorist bombings in Jakarta led to the creation of a centralised agency, i.e. the BNPT or National Anti-Terrorism Agency (IPAC 2013: 3). The BNPT has organised the visits of psychologists, local Muslim clerics, and *ulamas* from Egypt and Jordan to prisons where they have preached moderation to convicted terrorists. Reformed militants have also been recruited to help convince convicted terrorists to reform (Hannah 2016). However, the BNPT's efforts have been plagued by the lack of research and information to effectively target its efforts in a large country that has 800,000 mosques, the lack of consensus amongst the broader Muslim community regarding what constitutes extremism, and the lack of cooperation from other government ministries for its National Terrorism Prevention Program (IPAC 2013). Its prisons' program has also floundered due partly to overcrowding in prisons, with the result that many convicted terrorists have left prison not only unreformed, but also more influential in local *jihadi* circles. Worse, prisons have become breeding grounds for the spread of extremism as convicted terrorists have been able to recruit within prisons (Hannah 2016).

Another pressing problem in Indonesia has been the lack of control over the spread of radical ideology through social and print media. This is partly due to the democratic nature of post-Suharto Indonesia, where there remain sensitivities regarding any state control of free speech. Militants have therefore been able to freely proselytise and propagate radical ideology, especially through the internet, as there is no law regulating such content (IPAC 2013: 19).

The need for better and more integrated CVE programs involving the whole-of-government and whole-of-society approaches similar to Malaysia and Singapore is obvious in the case of Indonesia. This requires more research to better target CVE efforts, more resources to be made available to the BNPT, and also stronger state support, for instance, in the crucial areas of prison reform and the passing of anti-hate legislation, both of which would help in limiting the spread of radical ideology.

## Conclusions

Terrorism in the region has not been a new development. The JI has strong local roots, and can trace its origins to the Darul Islam, which in turn can trace its roots to the Sarekat Islam that was founded in 1911. This demonstrates that there has been an enduring desire by some for an Islamic state in Indonesia, which in turn explains the persistence of terrorism. In the 1990s, the linkages that the JI established with militant organisations in the Middle East, particularly through ex-Afghanistan *mujahideen* from the region, and its subsequent co-option by Al Qaeda, however, transformed the extremist objective of establishing an Islamic state to one aspiring to a regional pan-Islamic caliphate encompassing the lands occupied by Muslims. Moreover, the transnational linkages with the Middle East and across borders in Southeast Asia also transformed the local terrorist threat to a regional, transnational one.

While the JI was progressively decimated by security forces after 9–11, the void it left was quickly filled by the Islamic State. Since its declaration of a caliphate in Syria in mid-2014, the IS has swiftly penetrated and grown rapidly in Indonesia and Malaysia. Deftly exploiting modern information technology and the media, the IS has been able to use the suffering of Muslims in Syria under the Assad regime, as well as tap into persistent local aspirations for an Islamic state, to find many new and willing recruits in the region. While all major Muslim organisations in Indonesia, Malaysia and Singapore have denounced the Islamic State, and the overwhelming majority of Muslims remain moderate and reject the violent *jihad* of the IS, the persistence of a militant minority since before even independence suggests an enduring alienation by some to the modern and independent post-colonial secular state. While this suggests the presence of fundamental political, economic and social grievances, it may well be that there will always be a small minority in the region that will not be satiated and will always continue to agitate for the destruction of the current socio-political arrangements and its replacement by an Islamic state.

This implies two things. Firstly, terrorism in the region will never really be defeated, and the realistic objective will therefore have to be containing it within acceptable boundaries. Secondly, this means that countering violent extremism, and countering terrorism more broadly, remain long-term endeavours. In sum, regional counter-terrorism remains a work in progress, with continued room and urgency for improvement, as the example of Indonesia in particular, demonstrates.

## References

ABC News (2014), "ISIS Recruitment Video Join the Ranks Urges Indonesian Muslims to Migrate to the Islamic State", 29 July, available at http://www.abc.net.au/news/2014-07-28/isis-releases-recruitment-video-target-indonesian-muslims/5629960 accessed 21 August 2018.

ABC Radio (2007), "Indonesian Anti-terror Raid Leaves 16 Dead", 24 January, available at http://www.abc.net.au/pm/content/2007/s1833134.htm accessed 28 August 2018.

Asianews.it (2018), "Jakarta Approves the New Anti-Terrorism Law in Wake of Surabaya Attacks", 26 May, available at http://www.asianews.it/news-en/Jakarta-approves-the-new-anti-terrorism-law-in-wake-of-Surabaya-attacks-43995.html accessed 21 August 2018.

Beech, Hannah (2016), "Indonesia's Overcrowded Prisons Are a Breeding Ground for Islamic Extremists", *Time*, 5 February, available at http://time.com/4208984/indonesia-extremism-deradicalization-prisons/ accessed 21 August 2018.

Butt, Simon (2008), "Anti-Terrorism Law and Criminal Process in Indonesia", ARC Federation Fellowship, Islam, Syari'ah and Governance Background Paper, University of Melbourne, Melbourne, available at http://law.unimelb.edu.au/__data/assets/pdf_file/0011/1547786/butt_final_forwebsite2.pdf accessed 21 August 2018.

Channel News Asia (2016a), "27 Bangladeshi Nationals Arrested in Singapore and Repatriated for Terror Links", 20 January, available at http://www.channelnewsasia.com/news/singapore/27-bangladeshi-nationals/2440886.html accessed 21 August 2018.

Channel News Asia (2016b), "4 Singaporeans Who Supported Islamic State Dealt With Under ISA", 19 August, available at http://www.channelnewsasia.com/news/singapore/4-singaporeans-who-supported-islamic-state-dealt-with-under-isa-7861620 accessed 21 August 2018.

Channel News Asia (2016c), "Plot to Hit Singapore's Marina Bay with Rocket from Batam Foiled", 5 August, available at http://www.channelnewsasia.com/news/singapore/plot-to-hit-singapore-s-marina-bay-with-rocket-from-batam-foiled-7869776 accessed 21 August 2018.

CNN (2016), "Islamic State Launches First Successful Attack in Malaysia", 4 July, available at http://edition.cnn.com/2016/07/04/homepage2/islamic-state-attack-malaysia/ accessed 21 August 2018.

El-Muhammady, Ahmad (2016), "Countering the Threats of Daesh in Malaysia", in *Countering Daesh Extremism: European and Asian Responses*, Singapore: Konrad-Adenauer-Stiftung.

Emont, Jon (2014), "The Islamic State Comes To Indonesia", *Foreign Policy*, 17 September. http://foreignpolicy.com/2014/09/17/the-islamic-state-comes-to-indonesia/ accessed 21 August 2018.

Hilmy, Masdar (2010), *Democracy in Indonesia: Piety and Pragmatism*, Singapore: Institute of Southeast Asia Studies, available at http://file.understandingconflict.org/file/2013/11/IPAC_Weak_Therefore_Violent.pdf accessed 21 August 2018.

IANS (Indo-Asian News Service) (2018), "7 Arrested in Malaysia for Suspected IS Links", 19 July, available at https://in.news.yahoo.com/7-arrested-malaysia-suspected-links-053403706.html accessed 21 August 2018.

IB Times (2015a), "Malaysia Army and ISIS: 70 Soldiers Have Joined Islamic State, Officials Say", 13 April, available at http://www.ibtimes.com/malaysia-army-isis-70-soldiers-have-joined-islamic-state-officials-say-1879299 accessed 21 August 2018.

IB Times (2015b), "ISIS Recruitment: 75% of New Islamic State Group Supporters in Malaysia are Recruited Online", 25 May, available at http://www.ibtimes.com/isis-recruitment-75-new-islamic-state-group-supporters-malaysia-are-recruited-online-1936440 accessed 21 August 2018.

ICG (International Crisis Group) (2002), *Al Qaeda in Southeast Asia: The Case of the Ngruki Network in Indonesia*, Asia Briefing No. 20, 8 August.

IPAC (Institute for Policy Analysis of Conflict) (2013), *Weak Therefore Violent: The Mujahidin of Western Indonesia*, Report No. 5, 2 December.

*Jakarta Post* (2016), "How Densus 88 Turned the Tide on Militants", 27 December, available at https://www.pressreader.com/indonesia/the-jakarta-post/20161227/281552290519509 accessed 21 August 2018.

John, Tara (2016), "Indonesia's Long Battle with Islamic Extremism Could Be About to Get Tougher", *Time*, 15 January, available at http://time.com/4181557/jakarta-terrorist-attacks-indonesia-isis/ accessed 21 August 2018.

Kam, Stefanie (2016), "Brunei", in Rohan Gunaratna, and Stefanie Kam (eds.), *Handbook of Terrorism in the Asia-Pacific*, London: Imperial College Press.

Liow, Joseph (2017), "The Counterterrorism Yearbook 2017: Southeast Asia", *The Strategist*, Australian Security Policy Institute, 28 March, available at https://www.aspistrategist.org.au/counterterrorism-yearbook-2017-southeast-asia/ accessed 21 August 2018.

MHA (Ministry of Home Affairs) (2003), *The Jemaah Islamiyah Arrests and the Threat of Terrorism*, Singapore: Ministry of Home Affairs.

National Library, "Internal Security Act", *Infopedia*, Singapore, available at http://eresources.nlb.gov.sg/infopedia/articles/SIP_2014-10-13_105937.html accessed 21 August 2018.

*New York Times* (2012), "Plot on U.S. Targets Cited in 11 Arrests by Indonesia", 28 October, available at http://www.nytimes.com/2012/10/29/world/asia/indonesia-police-make-arrests-in-suspected-terrorist-plo.html accessed 21 August 2018.

Parameswaran, Prashanth (2015), "The Trouble with Indonesia's New Counterterrorism Command", *The Diplomat*, 11 June, available at http://thediplomat.com/2015/06/the-trouble-with-indonesias-new-counterterrorism-command/ accessed 21 August 2018.

Riviere, Craig (2016), *The Evolution of Jihadist-Salafism in Indonesia, Malaysia and the Philippines, and its Impact on Security in Southeast Asia*, Canberra: Australian Defence College.

Sholeh, Badrus (2016), "Daesh in Europe and Southeast Asia: An Indonesian Perspective", in *Countering Daesh Extremism: European and Asian Responses*, Singapore: Konrad-Adenauer Stiftung.

Soebardi, S. (1983), "Kartosuwiryo and the Darul Islam Rebellion in Indonesia", *Journal of Southeast Asian Studies*, 14(1).

Soufan Group (2015), *Foreign Fighters: An Updated Assessment of the Flow of Foreign Fighters into Syria and Iraq*, available at http://soufangroup.com/wp-content/uploads/2015/12/TSG_ForeignFightersUpdate3.pdf accessed 21 August 2018.

*Straits Times* (2015), "ISIS in Malaysia Planning Heists, Abductions", 21 May, available at http://www.straitstimes.com/asia/se-asia/isis-in-malaysia-planning-heists-abductions accessed 21 August 2018.

*Straits Times* (2016a), "Timeline of Previous Bomb Attacks in Indonesia", 14 January, available at http://www.straitstimes.com/asia/se-asia/timeline-of-previous-bomb-attacks-in-indonesia accessed 21 August 2018.

*Straits Times* (2016b), "JI Arrests: 15 Years Later", 9 December, available at http://www.straitstimes.com/opinion/ji-arrests-15-years-later accessed 21 August 2018.

*Straits Times* (2016c), "Singapore Stages Biggest Islandwide counter-terrorism exercise", 18 October, http://www.straitstimes.com/singapore/singapore-stages-its-biggest-counter-terrorism-exercise accessed 21 August 2018.

Stubbs, Richard (1989), *Hearts and Minds in Guerilla Warfare: The Malayan Emergency 1948–1960*, Singapore: Oxford University Press.

Tan, Andrew T. H. (2004), *Security Perspectives of the Malay Archipelago: Security Linkages in the Second Front in the War on Terrorism*, Cheltenham: Edward Elgar.

*Tempo* (2016), "Tinombala Operation Deemed a Success", 20 July, available at https://en.tempo.co/read/news/2016/07/20/055788985/Tinombala-Operation-Deemed-a-Success accessed 21 August 2018.

*The Guardian* (2014a), "Isis Insurgents Seize Control of Iraqi City of Mosul", 11 June, available at https://www.theguardian.com/world/2014/jun/10/iraq-sunni-insurgents-islamic-militants-seize-control-mosul accessed 21 August 2018.

*The Guardian* (2014b), "A Bunch of Amateurs? Indonesia's Homegrown Jihadis Ridicule Isis After Jakarta Attack", 11 February, available at https://www.theguardian.com/world/2016/feb/11/indonesia-homegrown-jihadis-lethal-cocktail-terror-isis-jakarta accessed 21 August 2018.

*The Star* (2015), "Suspected Militants Nabbed While They Were Making Bombs", 27 April, available at http://www.thestar.com.my/news/nation/2015/04/27/cops-foil-ter

ror-attack-plans-suspected-militants-nabbed-while-they-were-making-bombs/ accessed 21 August 2018.

*Today* (2016), "Malaysia's Softer Approach to Radicals Reaping Rewards", 8 December, available at http://www.todayonline.com/world/asia/malaysias-softer-approach-radicals-reaping-rewards accessed 21 August 2018.

Vithanage, Gayan (2015), "Countering Violent Extremism: Lessons from our Region", Australian Institute of International Affairs, 18 June, available at http://www.internationalaffairs.org.au/australian_outlook/countering-violent-extremism-lessons-from-our-region/ accessed 21 August 2018.

*Washington Post* (2009), "The Best Guide for Gitmo? Look to Singapore", 17 May, available at http://www.washingtonpost.com/wp-dyn/content/article/2009/05/15/AR2009051502237.html accessed 21 August 2018.

*Washington Post* (2014), "The World's Largest Muslim Country Bans Support for the Islamic State", 7 August, available at https://www.washingtonpost.com/news/worldviews/wp/2014/08/07/the-worlds-largest-muslim-country-bans-support-for-the-islamic-state/?utm_term=.7d633f47475a accessed 21 August 2018.

# Part 4

# 14 Terrorist rehabilitation and community engagement in Southeast Asia

*Rohan Gunaratna*

## Introduction

An indispensable weapon in the fight against terrorism and extremism is rehabilitation and community engagement. Unless governments work with partners to rehabilitate terrorists and extremists, they will pose a threat to security, spread their ideology, and will be hailed as heroes. With terrorism and extremism emerging as the tier-one national security threat, it is vital for governments to maintain stability and security by developing rehabilitation programs for inmates and engagement programs for radicalized individuals in the community.

The Southeast Asian region has recognized the significance of rehabilitation but not all the countries challenged by terrorism have succeeded in developing rehabilitation capabilities. While Malaysia and Singapore developed comprehensive and structured programs, Indonesia and Philippines developed ad hoc and unstructured programs. Although the capabilities differed from country to country, ten modes of rehabilitation are practiced in the region. They are 1) religious, 2) social and family, 3) educational, 4) vocational, 5) entrepreneurial 6) cultural, 7) financial, 8) creative arts, 9) recreational and 10) psychological.

## Malaysia

The rehabilitation of terrorists and extremists in Malaysia was implemented after the 9/11 attacks in the US in 2001. The program was built in Kamunting Detention Centre in Taiping, where the communists were also rehabilitated. Laura Khor has written:

> The Malaysian concept of detainee rehabilitation can be traced to the Malayan Emergency, which was a colonial idea and program further developed and adapted to address both Islamic radicalization and provide pathways for terrorist disengagement. The intelligence philosophy and successful policies in the Malayan Emergency served as 'lessons

learned' for current Malaysian officials who have adapted them to achieve intelligence and counter-terrorism success.

(Khor 2013: 65)

The region including Malaysia witnessed the steadfast rise of Muslim threat groups in the 1990s after their nationals returned from Afghanistan. After fighting communism from 1948 to 1989, Malaysia witnessed the above mentioned two phases of threats – the al Qaeda centric and the ISIS/IS centric threat. In the first phase, 196 Jemaah Islamiyah (JI), Jemaah Anshorut Tauhid (JAT), al Qaeda (AQ), Darul Islam (DI) and Abu Sayyaf Group (ASG) members were arrested in Malaysia and most of these individuals were rehabilitated and reintegrated under the ISA. This enabled Malaysia to preventively detain its terrorists and extremists until it was abolished in 2011

## *Understanding Malaysia's deradicalization program: History and dynamics*

The foundation Malaysian Deradicalization program is a religious rehabilitation and re-education program to correct religious and political misconceptions. The rehabilitation programs conducted by the Department of Islamic Development (JAKIM) start after the Ministry of Home Affairs order to obtain an Order of Detention (OD) or a Restriction Order (RO). Internal Security Act (ISA) detainees were housed in the Kemunting Protective Detention Centre in Taiping under the purview of the Prisons Department. Malaysia's counter terrorism chief, Datuk Ayob Khan said: "From 2001 to 2012, we conducted rehab for 289 militant detainees with a 97% success rate. Only seven of those detainees returned to militancy" (Zolkepli 2017).

Influenced by its past experience of managing the communist threat, Malaysia's rehabilitation program has "focused on identifying and addressing the deep-seated causes of terrorism", rather than punishing them (Hamid 2007). The contemporary program in Malaysia was formulated and conducted in collaboration with the Police and Prisons Department and JAKIM (Padil 2009).

The religious programs aimed to rehabilitate the detainees by deepening and correcting their understanding about Islamic teachings. After identifying the detainees' levels of awareness based on an evaluation of their understanding and approach towards Islamic teachings, the program instilled awareness of the roles and responsibilities of a Malaysian citizen regardless of religion or race, and their responsibility to obey the King. The clerics explained to the detainees that their activities prior to their detention were a threat to the security of the country and against Islamic teaching.

The Malaysian program is based on the "Ahli Sunnah Wal Jamaah" approach, an Islamic jurisdiction to counter the extremist interpretations of Islam (Kamruddin et al. 2017). Approaches for rehabilitation programs were divided into four. The Tafaqquh Fiddin program was a monthly meeting on Islamic studies. The Special Rehabilitation program is a 4–7 day intensive program for ten detainees who have shown positive responses by renouncing their religious-militant struggle and ideology. In addition to the Evaluating and Monitoring program by the police, JAKIM conducted a bi-annual evaluation and monitoring of those who went through the programs. This procedure includes visits to their houses and the distribution of JAKIM publications. A program for the detainees' wives was created as a channel to discuss Islamic issues with regard to the detention of their husbands.

Shortly after the repealing of the Emergency Ordinance and ISA in July 2012, ISIS/IS and Jabhat al Nusra (JaN, and other interactions of al Qaeda in Syria) emerged presenting an unprecedented challenge to Malaysian security. ISA enabled police preventive detention – arrest of terrorist suspects before they mounted attacks. Like ISA, it allowed initial detention of 60 days with unlimited renewals based solely on the will of the Home Minister, the new law – Security Offence Act (Special Measures) 2012 (SOSMA) limited the detention period for up to 28 days after which the attorney-general can decide whether to prosecute. While those arrested under ISA were detained at two special facilities in Kuala Lumpur or Kemunting Protective Detention Centre in Taiping, those arrested under the newly gazetted SOSMA are detained at a normal prison. As long as ISA was intact, it deterred members of society from advocating, supporting and participating in violence. For inciting and facilitating Malaysians to fight in Syria, Yazid Sufaat was arrested on 21 February 2013. Unlike ISA, those arrested under SOSMA had to be tried in open court. Although SOSMA was used to disrupt terrorist networks, there was no rehabilitation and reintegration component. The flow of information was also impeded affecting the ability to disrupt activity and attacks. Under SOSMA, no bail was permitted, rehabilitation fell under the purview of the Prison Department.

The ISA was repealed by the then Prime Minister Najib Razak without consulting the counter terrorism leadership. The political leadership did not understand the global developments, the regional and national extremist and terrorist threat, the value of ISA in preventive detention and as a deterrence. After ISA was repealed, the police had no option but to release the detainees held in Kemunting.

The official residence for ISA, the Kemunting Protective Detention Centre in Taiping, was formally closed down for terrorist inmates in January 2014. However, due to the wide ranging agricultural and animal husbandry facilities in Kemunting, criminals were relocated and were rehabilitated. With the emergence of IS, a number of former detainees relapsed. With a dozen Malaysians relapsing, either traveling to other jihadi theatres or planning to mount attacks on Malaysian soil, the rehabilitation and reintegration program suffered a setback. With ISA repealed, many arrested had to be released. As the threat spiralled out of control, then Prime Minister Najib himself tabled a White Paper "Towards Combating the Threat of Islamic State" on November 26, 2014 in Parliament. The paper highlighted the renewed threat especially of Malaysians traveling to fight in Iraq and Syria and conducting attacks there. The Malaysian police have identified 39 Malaysians who have joined militant groups in Syria and Iraq. In addition, 40 individuals who have been influenced by militant ideologies including returnees from Syria have been arrested by the RMP.

Malaysia faces security risks following the return of militants from Syria and Iraq. They have the potential to carry out lone-wolf attacks. Moreover, those who did not have the opportunity to travel to conflict zones may also be inclined to carry out radical and terrorist activities (Prime Minister's Department 2014). Since February 2013, 92 IS leaders, members, and followers have been arrested on Malaysian soil, some of whom were planning to mount attacks. In response, Malaysia enacted the Prevention of Terrorism Act (POTA) on April 7, 2015. Similar to ISA, POTA enabled detaining suspected terrorists without a warrant up to a maximum of 60 days by the police, and up to two years and an extension of two years administered by the Terrorism Prevention Board. Those detained under POTA appear before the POTA board that decides if they will be released or continue for another two years. They reappear every two years and the POTA board makes a decision after reviewing the feedback from the prisons, police and their experts.

Rehabilitation is entrusted during the first six months to the prisons, the next six months to the police and the last six months together to the prisons and police when incarcerated at the Kemunting Protective Detention Centre in Taiping. Although rehabilitation is the objective of the facility, Kemunting Protective Detention Centre in Taiping operates under the Prisons Act. Both Malaysians and foreigners who were arrested belonged mostly to IS and imprisoned under POTA, POCA, Penal Code and SOSMA. Most of the foreigners were deported. The Ministry of Home Affairs of Malaysia constituted a panel of experts to deliver rehabilitation from 2016. On March 30, 2017, commissioned by the then DPM, Dato Seri ZAHID Hamidi at Prison Headquarters Kajang, the National Expert Rehabilitation Panel was launched. The Ministry of Home Affairs rehabilitation division set the policy for police and prison. A collaborative and holistic effort between the Royal Malaysia Police, Malaysian Prison Department, the Ministry of Home Affairs worked with Department of Islamic of Development Malaysia, Ministry of Education and others.

The Malaysian Prisons Department appointed a Deradicalization Panel of 46 expert members on May 30, 2017. This initiative was led by the then deputy prime minister Dato Seri Dr Ahmad Zahidi Hamidi who was very committed to rehabilitating terrorist offenders. The panel constituted clerics from Malaysian Islamic Development Department (JAKIM), psychologists, academics, social workers, entrepreneurial experts and security personnel. From the al Qaeda phase to the IS phase, the Malaysian rehabilitation program was institutionalized. The Prisons religious unit and Police Counter Terrorism Division E8 brought on a range of partners. The number of rehabilitation experts grew from 5–6 to 40–50. While religious rehabilitation remained the main focus, the approaches to rehabilitation grew in educational, vocational, social and family, recreational, creative arts, psychological and financial rehabilitation. Educational rehabilitation is a part of religious rehabilitation which not only imparts correct but also new knowledge. Vocational rehabilitation focused on entrepreneurship. In the social and family rehabilitation practices, a new dimension was added during Hari Raya where inmates were permitted hugs and to shake hands during Eid 2018. Hitherto personal contact – body to body – was permitted for well-behaved inmates.

Recreational rehabilitation focusing on sports for inmates is run by the prison department. The sports capability including sports officers engages inmates in a range of activity. Although there is no creative and performance arts component within Malaysian prisons, the Prison Department works along with other agencies – Cultural and Art Department and NGOs – in implementing it. By linking with both governmental and non-governmental entities, the Prison Department engages inmates with art, song, dance, music, puppetry, literature and other activities. Psychological rehabilitation was introduced in 2017 after a study showed that psychological counselling was essential for IS inmates – especially youth. The Ministry of Sports and Youth study on youth extremism in Malaysia where 39 individuals were interviewed by psychologists, clerics and profilers highlighted 12 commonalities. The majority are psychological – high narcissism to cognitive distortion – that required counselling and therapy. For financial rehabilitation, the police connect them to government and others who can provide seed funding. "Other government agencies such as Jabatan Kebajikan Masyarakat (the Social Welfare Department) and Pusat Zakat (the State Alms Centre) are helping these families gain financial support for their daily life" (Aslam et al. 2016).

Through the Police E8 rehabilitation team and the religious unit of the Prisons Department, Malaysia is developing a national rehabilitation capability to transform terrorist inmates. An Integrated Rehabilitation Module for Detainees was administered by prisons and police based on policy set by the Ministry of Home Affairs. The three phased rehabilitation program – orientation, reinforcing Sahsiah (good personality), and self-development courses – was delivered by a panel including clerics, psychologists and vocational instructors.

## Singapore

The impetus for Singapore's terrorist rehabilitation program was the enduring global, regional and local threat posed by al Qaeda and al Jemaah al Islamiyah (JI), two of the most active terrorist groups in Southeast Asia. Unknown to governments in Southeast Asia, both al Qaeda and its associate group, the JI, had been active in the region since 1993. Although the stated aim of JI is the establishment of an Islamic state (*Daulah Islamiyah*) in Indonesia, Malaysia, the southern Philippines, Singapore and Brunei, it opted to follow al Qaeda's trajectory of targeting Western and Christian targets. Influenced and supported by al Qaeda, JI spearheaded most of the significant terrorist attacks in the region from August 2000 onwards (Gunaratna and Ali 2014).

The existence of JI in Southeast Asia came to the attention of governments after 11 September 2001. In December 2001, Singapore's Internal Security Department (ISD) disrupted a plot to bomb US, British, Australian, and Israeli diplomatic as well as other targets. JI's operational leader Riduan Isamuddin, alias Hambali, a close associate of Khalid Sheikh Mohamed, the 9/11 mastermind, had financed and planned the operation. If the joint al Qaeda–JI operation, which involved four trucks carrying five tonnes of ammonium nitrate, had succeeded, it would have killed over 3,000 civilians, an attack comparable in scale to the destruction caused by the 9/11 attacks (Gunaratna and Ali 2014).

The then Indonesian government had stated the evidence was insufficient at the time to dismantle the fledging JI network on Indonesian soil. Al Qaeda provided the funds for JI to attack one of the region's best-known tourist hubs, Bali, in October 2002, killing 202 people including 88 Australians. Although the Indonesian authorities subsequently targeted JI, the group survived and was revived in Indonesia, conducting intermittent attacks. The threat of ideological extremism and operational terrorism persists. In this context, Singapore's global profile and its affiliation with Western countries such as the US has made it a legitimate target for extremists and terrorists in the region (Gunaratna and Ali 2014).

Singapore's leaders understood early on that although the country had the structures in place to fight the threat of terrorism, ideological extremism remained an ongoing concern. They perceived that a segment of the Muslim community could be swayed by violent extremist groups. As these threat groups were active outside Singapore and not within the jurisdiction of Singapore, the government had to create programs to reach out to vulnerable segments of the Muslim population.

Furthermore, a small number of Singaporean Muslims who had either joined terrorist groups or planned terrorist attacks were detained. They could not be held indefinitely, however, and Singapore had to develop strategies to meet the contemporary challenge of ideological extremism that was radicalizing and had radicalized a segment of its community. To reach out to the community, Singapore's Ministry of Home Affairs developed a robust Community Engagement Program (CEP). To rehabilitate terrorists in custody, the Religious Rehabilitation Group (RRG), a group of Muslim clerics in Singapore, developed a multifaceted rehabilitation program. These two programs are unique to Singapore's context of terrorist rehabilitation. Nonetheless, Singapore's deradicalization initiatives offer insights into existing and aspiring programs.

## *The origins of the rehabilitation program*

In December 2001, after mounting surveillance on the JI network for nearly three months, the Internal Security Department arrested 15 individuals, of whom 13 were members of JI. The 13 JI members were detained whilst the remaining two were released in January 2002 on a restriction order. In August

2002, the ISD arrested another 21 persons, all of whom, barring two, were members of the JI. These two were members of the Moro Islamic Liberation Front (MILF), a group with close training and operational links with the JI. Of the 18 detained, two JI members and one MILF member were released in September 2002 on restriction order. A team of psychologists interviewed the 31 detainees. All, with the exception of two of the JI detainees, were assessed to have average or above average intelligence (MHA 2003). A third had intelligence above the population norm, including two with superior levels of intelligence. All 31 individuals had received secular education and their knowledge of Islam was found to be either shallow or misguided. As a group, the psychologists concluded, most of the detainees regarded religion as their most important personal value. Many believed that they were fighting for Islam and the Muslim people. They underwent religious classes conducted for the masses. At these congregations, JI talent spotters recruited those eager to serve their faith and the community.

The potential JI recruit was usually recommended quite innocuously to Singapore JI leader and spiritual advisor Ibrahim Maidin's classes, usually by friends, relatives and colleagues. The majority of JI members were introduced to JI in this way. Many continued studying not only to enhance their religious knowledge, but also the sense of Muslim fraternity and companionship. The JI teachers would employ the tactic of inserting into lectures quotations from the Quran and Hadith, discussions on jihad and the plight of suffering Muslims worldwide (MHA 2003).

Gradually, the most committed individuals to the plight of Muslims in global and regional conflict zones were invited to join JI. "This recruitment process would usually take about 18 months. The few who were selected as members were further made to feel a strong sense of exclusivity and self-esteem" (MHA 2003). Furthermore, JI members were indoctrinated into believing that anyone who left the group was an infidel. On the other hand, those who remained enjoyed a sense of exclusivity and commitment of being in the in-group of a clandestine organisation. Secrecy, including secrecy over the true knowledge of jihad, helped create a sense of sharing and empowerment vis-à-vis outsiders. Esoteric JI language or "JI-speak" was used as part of the indoctrination process. Code names for instance, resulted in a strong sense of "in-group" superiority, especially since JI members were said to be closer to Allah as they believed in the "truth" (JI doctrine); even Muslims who did not subscribe to militant jihad were seen as infidels. This dogmatism convinced many within JI (Parker 2003; MHA 2003).

With the series of arrests, the Singapore government wanted to ensure that there was no backlash from the Muslim community. As such, the Internal Security Department together with the Ministry of Home Affairs, kept an open dialogue with Muslim community leaders. Over the years, Singapore has developed three modes of rehabilitation. The religious rehabilitation is spearheaded by RRG led by religious clerics well versed in Islam and the misinterpretation of Islamic concepts by terrorists and extremists (RRG 2018).

The social and family rehabilitation is led by the After Care Group (ACG) that ensures the stability of the family both during and after the detention of, in many cases, the bread winner of the household (Salleh 2015). The psychological rehabilitation is run by the Ministry of Home Affairs which is led by well qualified psychologists with expertise in counter terrorism and counter extremism (Beyley 2016).

## The IS scenario

Singapore witnessed two phases of threats from terrorism – the al Qaeda centric phase that was dominated by Singaporeans joining JI and the Islamic State centric phase which comprised Singaporeans as well as migrant workers mostly from Bangladesh and Indonesia. This latter phase saw the involvement of both men and women. After the spate of arrests during the JI period, the threat landscape in Singapore changed from physical to online space. With Singapore disrupting and dismantling JI, many opted to join al Qaeda or al Qaeda centric groups by linking up with either terrorist or extremist groups online.

The emergence of social media in 2004, especially Facebook, provided a more influential recruitment tool. As opposed to joining threat groups, individuals opted to self-radicalize themselves. By visiting extremist and terrorist sites, they ideologically indoctrinated themselves through the Internet. Some wanted to strike, others linked up with threat groups overseas to travel to conflict zones and fight.

With the emergence of the Islamic State (IS) in 2014, a few Singaporeans and their families left for Syria. Syaikhah Izzah Zahrah al Ansari, who wanted to travel to join IS in Syria in 2014, was the first Singaporean woman to be detained by the authorities in June 2017. The 22-year-old daughter of two Quranic teachers, planned to travel to Syria with her child. She had worked at a preschool for infants aged between two and 18 months, run by the People's Action Party (PAP) Community Foundation and claimed to have visions of being a martyr's widow (Cheong 2017).

Singapore has witnessed four trends during the IS phase that continue to have relevance. First, more youth and children were lured to join terrorist groups. Second, more women were radicalized. Third, foreigners employed in Singapore participated in terrorist support activity, and fourth, rather than recruit in the physical space, the Internet became the principal radicalizer.

After assessing the threat, Singapore strengthened the existing foundation built more than a decade earlier to fight JI. It is estimated that during this time, terrorism capabilities grew nearly 100%. In rehabilitation and community engagement, capabilities were enhanced. While the rehabilitation and reintegration initiatives were enhanced, the community engagement program evolved into the SGSecure initative. Yet, some challenges remained and the government, community and academic partners grappled to find solutions.

In rehabilitation, JI members had an ideological template and mainstream clerics counselled them. In the case of self-radicalised individuals, they made up their ideology and it was a challenge to counter their ideology. As the age of radicalized individuals became younger, the authorities picked up five teenagers, aged between 17 and 19 between 2015 and 2018. "We find a common thread when we pick them up. A heavy reliance on the Internet, social media, for information, including religious teachings", said Home Affairs Minister K. Shanmugam (Yi 2018). In response, RRG launched an awareness program for youths targeting those aged between 16 and 25. This program aimed to engage, educate and provide Muslim youth with a better understanding of Islam (Yi 2018). Similarly, International Center for Political Violence and Terrorism Research (ICPVTR) specialists working with RRG engaged both schools and youth organizations. However, engaging teenagers and others in cyber space remains a perennial challenge. Among research pioneered at ICPVTR to address the IS dominance of cyber space was a focus on digital rehabilitation.

Evidence has shown that the authorities have faced "more complex psychological and social issues" in rehabilitating self-radicalized personalities (Yi 2018). As such individuals appeared to be indoctrinated in "cut and paste Islam" picked up from the Internet, it was apparent that psychologists would be more effective than clerics in dealing with individuals who were self-radicalized (Yi 2018). "Singapore is still trying to develop the right tools to rehabilitate them", Minister Shanmugam added: "They hold on to their beliefs, they have a very limited understanding of Islam, they absorb whatever they see on the Internet, and they go with those views" (Yi 2018). Singapore's JI rehabilitation program was a success – Singapore suffered only two cases of recidivism. The unrepentant apex leadership and hardcore operatives remain in detention under ISA. In comparison to the 88% of JI members released, only 25% per cent of self-radicalized terrorists and extremists arrested since 2007 have been rehabilitated and released (Yi 2018). Although the scale of the problem was much less than in Europe, self-radicalization remains a key challenge for a nation with a zero-tolerance policy.

To counter divisiveness and foster cohesiveness, Singapore has developed a range of best practices. In September 2017, Singapore banned two foreign Christian preachers who described Allah as "a false god", and asked for prayers for those "held captive in the darkness of Islam". They had also insinuated that Buddhists were "lost" people who could be saved by being converted to Christianity. The preachers also variously referred to "the malevolent nature of Islam and Mohammed", stating that Islam was "not a religion of peace". In October 2017, Singapore denied entry to Ismail Menk and Haslin bin Bahari who sought to enter Singapore to preach on a religious-themed cruise. Menk had previously discouraged Muslims from wishing non-Muslims "Merry Christmas" or "Happy Deepavali", calling it the biggest sin a Muslim can commit.

With the rise of IS, Singapore enhanced its existing community engagement program with SGSecure, a national movement in Singapore. While the community engagement program focused on building resilience within the Muslim community, SGSecure was created to prepare the public in the event of a terrorist attack. Launching SGSecure on 24 September 2016, Prime Minister Lee Hsien Loong said that while the government has stepped up measures to combat terrorism, these efforts alone are not enough. "Terrorism threatens not just our physical safety, but also our social harmony and way of life", he said. "To protect ourselves, every Singaporean has to play his part" (Chia 2016). "SGSecure gives everybody a role in protecting ourselves, our families and our country," he added. "SGSecure will teach you the skills you need to do so."

## Philippines

The Philippines penitentiaries house a large terrorist population, made up of members of the Abu Sayyaf Group, Rajah Solaiman Movement (RSM) and various groups associated with IS. The number of inmates from IS centric threat groups has grown significantly since 2015 and is likely to grow in the coming years. International partners, community organizations and others have attempted to build rehabilitation capabilities to engage terrorists. The penitentiaries have no dedicated rehabilitation programs for terrorists.

Although the Philippines has not been successful in building effective rehabilitation capabilities against ASG, RSM and IS, the government was successful in mainstreaming two threat groups. This process involved creating job opportunities and resources to both serving and former fighters of these groups.

Rehabilitation works both at an individual and a group level; first, mainstreaming threat groups and their support bases by engaging and co-opting leaders; second, disengaging and deradicalizing surrendered and captured terrorists and extremists. The Philippines was able to mainstream both the Moro National Liberation Front (MNF) led by Nuri Misuari and the Moro Islamic Liberation Front (MILF) led by Haji Murad. Although the government has yet to address the grievances raised by these groups, they remain committed to the peace process.

The 1996 Peace Agreement between the Government of the Republic of the Philippines and the Moro National Liberation Front signalled the official end of more than two decades of the Moro struggle waged by the MNLF for self-rule in the Southern Philippines and later for autonomy. The final draft of the agreement was signed on September 2, 1996 in Manila between MNLF Chair Nur Misuari as Chairman of the MNLF negotiating panel and Manuel Tan for the Philippine Republic. The agreement officially put an end to the 24-year-old war that has claimed the lives of over 120,000 people, and the displacement of more than 300,000 families.

The agreement envisioned two phases of implementation. The first phase was the three-year transitional period which established the Special Zone of Peace and Development (ZOPAD), the Southern Philippines Council for Peace and Development (SPCPD), and the Consultative Assembly. During this period, the process commenced for the integration of former MNLF guerrillas into the Armed Forces of the Philippines (AFP) as well as into the Philippine National Police (PNP).

The second phase consisted, following the three-year transitional period, of a legislative action either amending or repealing the existing Republic Act 6734, otherwise known as the Organic Act of the Autonomous Region of Muslim Mindanao (ARMM).

## The Comprehensive Local Integration Program

On April 3, 2018, Administrative Order 10 was signed by President Rodrigo Duterte enhancing the Comprehensive Local Integration Program (CLIP), "centralizing all government efforts for the reintegration of the former rebels and creating for the purpose an inter-agency task force" by providing a complete package of assistance to former rebels (FR) who were members of the Communist Party of the Philippines (CPP), New People's Army (NPA), and National Democratic Front (NDF) as well as their immediate family members, who have surfaced beginning the date of the Effectivity of the Order and expressed their desire to abandon armed struggle and become productive members of the society.

For this purpose, an Inter-Agency Task Force for the reintegration of FRs, known as "Task Force Balik-Loob", was created and composed of representatives from the Department of National Defense (DND), Department of Interior and Local Government (DILG), Office of the Presidential Adviser on the Peace Process (OPAPP), Office of the President (OP), and the National Housing Authority (NHA). The Task Force is to be assisted by a Secretariat composed of technical staff from these agencies.

The Government of the Philippines also launched a program to rehabilitate members of the Abu Sayyaf Group (ASG). On March 28, 2018 the military confirmed the surrender of a notorious Basilan-based Abu Sayyaf leader Nurhassan Jamiri and 12 of his followers to soldiers of the 3rd Scout Ranger Battalion led by Lt. Col. Montano Almodovar and local government officials headed by Kaiser Hataman in Barangay Serongon, Hadji Muhammad Ajul, Basilan. They also turned over ten assorted firearms, 40 assorted magazines, 651 assorted ammunition, one MK52 Fragmentation Grenade and Bandoleers. Jamiri was earlier reported by Malaysian authorities to have been killed in a clash with security forces in Sabah on February 27 of that year, among the three alleged ASG militants who opened fire at policemen and were killed inside a plantation in Tawau town, about a kilometer from the main Kalabakan–Keningau Road. Malaysian authorities claimed that the killed militants were planning to carry out attacks in Sabah.

More than 100 Abu Sayyaf members in Basilan surrendered in batches to the Western Mindanao Command and the police through the intercession of provincial officials and the regional peace and order council led by ARMM Gov. Mujiv Hataman. As of May 2018, 173 former ASG members from the provinces of Basilan, Sulu and Tawi-Tawi had surrendered to the AFP or to local government units (LGUs).

Under the program, surrendered ASG members will be provided opportunities to reintegrate into society and will undergo interventions which include (1) psychosocial sessions, (2) medical check-ups, (3) introduction to farming systems, and (4) expository tours outside the island provinces, which are all designed to usher the complete reformation of the former combatants into decent and productive members of the society.

## Challenges and oppositions

The Philippines is yet to build a national rehabilitation program. After the IS Marawi Siege of 2017, if those incarcerated are not rehabilitated, IS ideology will spread through the prison system in the Philippines. With the support of various government agencies and non-governmental organisations, it is vital for the Manila government to conduct capacity building training programs and workshops with a focus on terrorist rehabilitation.

The Philippines' growing interest in terrorist rehabilitation programs is clearly reflected in its enthusiasm to develop its capacity to adopt strategic approaches to terrorist rehabilitation which has been practised by countries like Singapore, Sri Lanka and Saudi Arabia. The Philippine Government should appoint a leader dedicated to working with the AFP, PNP, National Intelligence Coordinating Agency (NICA), Anti-Terrorism Council (ATC), Bureau of Jail Management and Penology (BJMP), Directorate for Inmates Welfare & Development (DIWD), Salaam Police Centre, Salam Engagement Group Philippines Inc. (SEGP), Peoples Advocacy for Collaboration & Empowerment Inc., Ramos Peace & Development Foundation and others to spearhead a program on custodial and community rehabilitation.

ICPVTR has joined several national and international partners to successfully conduct three capacity building workshops in the Philippines between August 2013 and February 2014. The first workshop which lasted for a day was conducted on 14 August 2013, and funded by the Australian Embassy in the Philippines. It was organized by BJMP in partnership with ICPVTR. The objective of the workshop is to create awareness on the significance of rehabilitation programs among government agencies, the private sector and NGOs. The workshop brought together more than 50 participants made up of Muslim clerics and regional Imams, prison officers, wardens, policemen, teachers, vocational trainers, nurses, first aiders, psychologists, psychiatrists, counsellors, social workers, NGOs, academics and analysts.

## Indonesia

Indonesia witnessed the rise of violence in the name of religion after the end of President Suharto's 30-year reign in power. With many Indonesians returning from Afghanistan, Solo, in Central Java, emerged as a nerve center for

Jemmah Islamiyah (JI) under the leadership of Abdulah Sungkar and Abubakar Baasyir. After the US intervention in Afghanistan in response to the 9/11 attack, al Qaeda funded the JI bombing of Bali on October 12, 2002, where 202 people were killed. This attack, which killed 88 Australians in the tourist hotspot, catalyzed the creation of the Indonesian rehabilitation program. The Indonesian police chief General Da'i Bachtiar formed the "Tim Bomb" (team bomb) at the end of 2002. Created in 2003 to fight terrorism, D88 made use of more than just human intelligence such as technical intelligence as well.

The proponent of Indonesia's rehabilitation strategy was a former D88 chief, General Suryadarma Salim. "From the very beginning, I wanted to know why they become terrorists and consider the police, an enemy...." (General Suryadarma 2018). He added: "On that, I recalled Sun Tzu's advice: "If you want to know your enemy. Enter into the heart of the enemy's defence,' meaning, I have to disregard my police personality and develop the orientation to win over and carefully change the behaviour of my opponent" (General Suryadarma 2018). The guiding principle was "we are family". "Eventually, I was accepted, respected and loved by them", General Suryadarma said, adding: "even within the police team, I knew that there were those who were suspicious initially but eventually they too understood what I was doing. I became a good listener. I did not discuss what the terrorists did. After establishing family ties, many of them eventually changed" (General Suryadarma 2018). The passion and the commitment of General Suryadarma, a high risk taker, to rehabilitate and reintegrate extremists was not institutionalized, however. According to him: "I slept at the detention centre with them. I brought them to sleep at my house, and as such, until today, no-one dares to do such a thing again. I used to be alone in the vehicle with the 2 Marriott bomb prisoners" (General Suryadarma 2018).

To date, there is no comprehensive strategy or program to transform terrorists into peaceful and productive citizens, but Indonesia is creating the framework, institutions, and processes to deliver on rehabilitation. With the right leadership and political will, Indonesia will be able to transform the unstructured and ad hoc rehabilitation initiatives currently in place into a comprehensive and holistic program.

At a political level, the support to fight terrorism and to build a rehabilitation capability, was provided by Ansyaad Bai, head of counter terrorism (December 23, 2002 to October 2010) at the Coordinating Ministry of Law and Politics. The ministry coordinated all agencies (police, military and national security) to formulate a national policy on counter terrorism that evolved into a national body in July 2010. The National Agency for Combating Terrorism (Badan Nasional Penanggulangan Terorisme: BNPT) started to execute the policy. A former D88 intelligence chief, General Tito Karnavian became director of operations of BNPT, before becoming Jakarta police chief and National Police Chief.

In 2015, the Vice President of Indonesia Prof Boediono asked Ansyaad Bai to develop a blue print for the deradicalization of terrorists: "I recruited many academicians and researchers to BNPT. We used a soft approach – persuade the terrorists to leave their network and cooperate with BNPT and D88" (Bai 2018). The BNPT developed in 2013 an internal publication that spelt out a range of preventative and counter terrorism measures. These were encapsulated in four stages: "Identification, rehabilitation, re-education and re-socialisation" (Blueprint Deradikalisasi). The greatest challenges Indonesia faced was non mandatory rehabilitation, poor management of terrorist inmates as well as no reintegration control mechanism.

## The history of Indonesia's jihadists

Influenced by the ideology of al Qaeda, Indonesia produced just over 1,000 terrorists in the 2000–2015 period, a small number relative to the size of the country. After the rise of IS in 2014, Indonesia produced a comparable number of known terrorists, most of whom either travelled to Iraq and Syria or staged attacks in Indonesia.

Indonesia arrested 1,082 suspects for terrorism related activities from 2000–2015 (Dinansi 2018). As of March 2018, the prison population in Indonesia, which comprises convicts, detainees and prisoners on remand, stands at just over 240,000 in 464 facilities (Llewellyn 2018). This has meant that the prison system is overcrowded by 100,000, with just one guard for every 65 inmates (Cochrane 2017). The challenge in the Indonesian prison system is the threat of radicalization. As prison officers may not understand the extent of the crimes committed by such inmates, they may have developed sympathy towards them.

Terrorists well versed in their ideology typically assumed the status of imam in the prisons and detention centers. The non-terrorist inmates mix with terrorist inmates, except those in Nusakambangan's Batu and Pasir Putih where they are located in dedicated cells. As of June 2018, special prisons for terrorist convicts were also built in Nusakambangan, Central Java, and in Cikeas, Bogor Regency (*Tempo* 2018a). In addition to nearly 200 terrorist detainees in several facilities, Indonesia housed 289 terrorist convicts spread across 113 prisons (*Tempo* 2018b). According to BNPT, 325 individuals were subjected to rehabilitation programs and 128 beneficiaries became the source for the initiatives under BNPT. It is estimated there are 600 terrorists both in prisons and mostly in the community that have not been rehabilitated (*Jakarta Post* 2017).

Despite the intentions of the described initiatives, there is neither a structured rehabilitation or reintegration program. The Directorate General of Corrections and BNPT need a long term strategy to build a comprehensive program. To build a national rehabilitation capability, BNPT conducts unplanned and ad hoc interventions both in custodial rehabilitation and community reintegration. Indonesia's Department of Religious Affairs initially sent clerics to its prisons holding terrorists, but they did not understand the dynamics of extremist ideology. In addition, terrorist inmates viewed these clerics as apostates, hence rejecting the teachings delivered by them.

Subsequently, BNPT dispatched mainstream clerics, especially those from Nahdlatul Ulama who believe in Pancasila, as well as pro-al Qaeda clerics to visit the terrorist inmates. Cleric Sofyan Tsauri, a former inmate linked to JI, Abu Tholuth and Abdul Rahman Ayub visited prisons and held dialogue sessions and engaged the inmates. A handful of foreign clerics also engaged both the JI and IS leaders Abu Bakr Bashir and Aman Abdurrahman, but their efforts failed to yield any results. A similar dialogue with Egyptian and Jordanian clerics in December 2013 also proved fruitless.

## Modes of rehabilitation in Indonesia

With regards to education, there is no institutionalized framework to send teachers to prisons to engage and educate the terrorists and broaden their thinking. Nonetheless, individual leaders such as General Suryadarma, have taken the initiative. He said: "One matter I can put forth is that I schooled the terrorists in detention, sending them for classes. After being freed, I then placed them at the *mushola* (an area to conduct prayers), and then they completed an S2 (Masters). One of them became a lecturer and is taking an S3 (Doctorate)." He added: "Eye to eye contact is very much needed, to build relationships, create trust, and such." He goes on to cite the example of the son of an ex-terrorist who died after leaving prison, who will be completing an S1 in three months' time with the funding from Gories Mere (General Suryadarma 2018).

Contact with families and other socially orientated aspects are also not included in the rehabilitation process in Indonesia. Although prisons facilitate family access to terrorist inmates, there is no support given to the families to travel or stay. As over 70–80% of the terrorist population is poor, their families lack the resources to travel. In fact, there are only a handful of NGOs that provide support both for transport and the accommodation of family members visiting terrorist inmates.

BNPT has set up a cultural rehabilitation program called Klinik Pancasila, a program to replace terrorist ideology with the principles of the state philosophy to re-educate inmates in 2014–2015 (Sim 2016). Prof Irfan Idris of BNPT observed that "the substance of Clinic Pancasila is still running with another term *Pembinaan wawasan kebangsaan*" (Idris 2018). While the program attracted some support the most hardcore terrorist inmates refused to partake in it. The BNPT also encouraged the creative arts such as in Porong prison in East Java, where a puppet show was held in 2016. Again, there was a lack of interest amongst the inmates, who found puppetry to be un-Islamic. However, martial arts training was practiced including in Mako Brimob, the detention center housing terrorist inmates.

BNPT and a number of Indonesian NGOs have also trained both inmates and their families in entrepreneurship. Furthermore, they provided funds to start projects that would help them to sustain their lives including entrepreneurship. The inmates thus grew vegetables and raised ducks and sold them to the prison.

To support economic empowerment, the Mutual Aid Society in Lamongan also played a role. Starting in 2011, BNPT provided entrepreneurship training to wives and inmates. In Palu, next to Poso, BNPT encouraged terrorists to set up motor cycle repair shops. These automotive repair shops would help sustain them. Similarly, in Samarang, BNPT supported projects to grow cat fish and goats from 2016. Reflecting the thinking of BNPT, Prof. Irfan Idris of BNPT Saud said: "We try support them with more entrepreneurship training in order to make them busy and not to be jobless and hopeless" (Idris 2018).

BNPT also provides financial assistance to families of terrorists who cooperate with the authorities. From time to time, BNPT gave rupiah 5–10 million to reintegrated beneficiaries to set up new businesses. The only criticism was that the beneficiaries had to decide immediately what tools to shop for with the money. The beneficiaries were taken by BNPT to the markets in 2016–2017 and most of the money was spent on equipment. For instance, beneficiaries of Semarang prison Machmudi Hariono alias Yusuf Adirima of JI, former Kedung Pane and Nusa Kambangan prison inmate, bought a washing machine and dryer to start a business. Similarly, his colleague Sri Puji Mulyo Siswanto of JI bought love birds and his son bought watches to sell. BNPT provided assistance to former JI but not former IS inmates.

Like many other rehabilitation and reintegration programs worldwide, the Indonesian program is not without challenges. With nearly 1,000 terrorists released to the community by 2018, there is no Indonesian Government mechanism to monitor them. This has led to recidivism and in a few cases, a return to violence (BBC News Asia 2016).

To support reintegration, BNPT initiated plans to build a deradicalization center in Sentul, Bogor, West Java in 2014. Although rehabilitation requires multiple stakeholders providing support, the facility was far from Jakarta where both other government agencies and civil society organizations were located. The successive leaders of BNPT supported the idea but cautioned against establishing a facility in Sentul due to the distance to Jakarta.

It was apparent that BNPT had no capability to engage the most hardened terrorists. To compensate, BNPT tried to focus on the less ideologically committed inmates. Starting on February 22, 2017, seven disengaged terrorists were brought from Pasir Putih Prison on Nusa Kambangan Island to its deradicalization center in Sentul. BNPT released them on June 8, 2017 upon completing their three-month rehabilitation program.

In Sentul, 20–30 inmates were engaged by BNPT and other agencies. The programs included social and family rehabilitation where the inmate's family visit Sentul. In many of its programs, BNPT works in partnership with several organizations including Yayasan Lingkar Perdamaian [Foundation of Peace Circle] in Lamongan, which is founded by Ali Fauzi, a reformed Afghan and Moro fighter (Maharani 2018; Hadi 2018).

In response to the Indonesian government and partner efforts, the terrorists developed their own counter-radicalization program. "GASHIBU" (Gerakan

Sehari Seribu or "One Thousand Rupiah (US$0.1)-a-Day") was developed to challenge the Indonesian government's deradicalization program (Arianti and Arianti 2014). Due to the weak counter terrorism laws in Indonesia until May 2018, the terrorists and extremists produced publications and distributed them in prisons and detention centers (Yasin 2018).

In response to the circulation of extremist and terrorist content both in prison and in the community, both mainstream and repentant terrorists produced literature. In addition to Nasir Abbas and Ali Imron, Khairul Ghazali produced books and other publications to counter the extremist and terrorist message. This demonstrates that for rehabilitation to work inside prisons, several other CVE and PVE initiatives should work in tandem with custodial rehabilitation efforts. The greatest challenge Indonesia is now facing is the terrorist and extremist exploitation of the cyber space. To meet the challenge of terrorism, the Government of Indonesia discussed creating a comprehensive rehabilitation program by the Ministry of Law and Human Rights that is responsible for prison administration.

The lead national agency, BNPT attempted to develop an Indonesia wide approach by inviting 87 ministries/organizations to work together but it requires a dedicated wing within BNPT not only to coordinate but actually to do the work (BNPT 2017).

## Conclusion

With the enduring threat of the Islamic State and its global expansion, the field of rehabilitating terrorists and extremists is changing rapidly. Unlike al Qaeda centric groups that operated discretely, IS operates openly. As a large movement with mastery of social media, the scale, magnitude and intensity of radicalisation is appreciable.

With the global expansion of IS, those in custody for participating, supporting and advocating for IS are growing exponentially. Many governments and their community partners have been working to deter terrorist recruitment and radicalisation. Nonetheless, the appeal and seductive power of IS both in the physical and cyber space has made many vulnerable individuals susceptible to indoctrination and recruitment. To transform the lives of those affected, requires rehabilitation interventions both in custodial and community spaces. Without rehabilitation, prison will not prepare them to reject exclusivism and extremism and embrace coexistence and moderation.

Most countries have visions for the compressive rehabilitation of terrorists but have no real rehabilitation programs. There are a few countries that have developed ad-hoc and unstructured rehabilitation programs. There are fewer countries that offer comprehensive rehabilitation programs. Among them are Singapore, Saudi Arabia, and Sri Lanka. Under United Nations Interregional Crime and Justice Research Institute (UNICRI) leadership, the good practices from these programs have helped start new programs or improve existing programs. Although IS recruited from 120 countries, less than a fifth of the countries have programs for rehabilitation of terrorists and extremists. In Southeast Asia, Singapore and Malaysia have done well despite the repeal of the ISA in Malaysia. The Indonesian and Philippines ad hoc programs needs to be transformed into comprehensive programs. Thailand and Myanmar need leadership.

Building rehabilitation capabilities requires leadership, a legal framework, a dedicated organisation, infrastructure and expert resources. Increasingly the world has started to understand that no single agency can develop and implement a comprehensive criminal or terrorist rehabilitation. Rehabilitation is an enterprise where government, the private sector, community organisations and academia, work together in collaboration. There is recognition that the prison responsible for institutionalizing incarceration is the body responsible for holding the offender. Although prison is identified as the custodial setting, often prisons lack the knowledge and skills to transform those they hold. Only a few countries have the resources to build their prisons with the expertise to return those who abandoned family and society back to mainstream living. They rely on the private sector for resources, the community for support, and academics for assessment.

As part of Corporate Social Responsibility (CSR), the best private companies devote significant resources to equip inmates for employment, and after release recruit them as beneficiaries. Similarly, community leaders and institutions – social, religious, cultural, educational – pave the way and build bridges to bring deviants back into the mainstream. In community settings, the private sector and community organisations can support the beneficiary families too. Academia trains the specialists – religious scholars, social and family workers, teachers, vocational instructors, artists, bankers, sports instructors, counselors, and psychologists – to work in prison and community settings. In addition to training the security and intelligence practitioners, the institutions of higher learning and think tanks can develop and refine their assessments to measure the degrees of radicalisation and deradicalisation.

Under the different modes of rehabilitation, diverse partners come together to develop different approaches to intervention. To develop and sustain these multiple interventions, visionary leadership is central. At all levels, a goal-oriented rather than a rule-oriented leadership is essential to succeed. Creative and innovative leadership, and not classical and bureaucratic leadership, is at the heart of collaboration. If the three streams are to work together, the key is to understand and manage the risks and yet also invest and persist with the intervention. The process of rehabilitation is a risk but one worth taking as it provides for the common good of the individual, family, work place and community.

With the advent of Islamic State (IS) and its exploitation of cyber space, rehabilitation has become more complex. With the phenomenon of lone wolves, each pathway to transform such individuals is unique. To meet this challenge, leaders in the rehabilitation space should draw expertise and resources from different sectors, especially psychologists, to chart and sustain progress. Success depends on drawing from multiple sectors and relevant partners, and the ability to hold them together to achieve a common goal. The beneficiaries are best transformed in settings where they thrive. Some worked in the security forces and others in government jobs, at universities and institutions of learning. Some came from the private sector and a few were in detention and prison. The classic detention and prison environments are not the ideal settings for embracing change for the better. While punishment measures should be in place to deter reoffending, rehabilitation in preparation for release are also important and should be the twin goals of all prisons and detention facilities.

For rehabilitation to be successful, every government should build in parallel a reintegration program. To support reintegration, the community should be prepared through engagement. Without CVE (countering violent extremism) and PVE (preventing violent extremism) in the community, reintegration of beneficiaries is unlikely to work. In Southeast Asia, these programs are in different stages of development. For the security and stability of any nation, both rehabilitation and community engagement programs are vital. Community Engagement programs will enable governments and their partners to counter the ideological threat and treat the affected and influenced communities.

## Acknowledgement

I wish to thank Ambassador Ong Keng Yong, Executive Deputy Chairman of the S. Rajaratnam School of International Studies along with Prof. Benjamin Schreer, Dr Andrew Tan and Dr Julian Droogan for fostering research between Department of Security Studies and Criminology at Macquarie University, Australia and RSIS. For their invaluable guidance, my appreciation to Amresh Gunasingham, Mohammed Sinan Siyech and Vidia Arianti of the International Centre for Political Violence and Terrorism Research, Singapore.

## References

Arianti, Muh Taufiqurrohman and V. Arianti (2014), "The 'Anti-Deradicalization' Movement of Indonesian Terrorist Networks", *Counter Terrorist Trends and Analyses*, 11–17 April.

Aslam, Mohd Mizan bin Mohammad, Iffah Bazilah Binti Othman and Nur Aqilah Khadijah Binti Rosili (2016), "De-Radicalization Programs in South-East Asia: A Comparative Study of Rehabilitation Programs in Malaysia, Thailand, Indonesia and Singapore", *Journal of Education and Social Sciences*, Vol. 4, 154–160.

Bai, Ansyaad (2018), Interview by Rohan Gunaratna, *Creating the Deradicalization Programme in Indonesia*, 11 June.

BBC News Asia (2016), "Jakarta Attacks: Gunman from Widely Circulated Photo Identified", 17 January, available at https://www.bbc.com/news/world-asia-35320452 accessed 6 June 2018.

Beyley, David (2016), "The Prevention of Radicalisation to Violent Extremism", *Home Team Academy Journal*, 102–106.

BNPT (2017), "BNPT Working in Tandem with 87 Ministries/Organisations in a Coordination Meeting of Public Relations Synergy: Dissemination of Information to Eradicate Terrorism", BNPT, 17 December, available at https://www.bnpt.go.id/bnpt-gandeng-87-k-l-dalam-rakor-sinergitas-humas-diseminasi-informasi accessed 18 June 2018.

Cheong, Danson (2017), "First Woman Held under ISA for pro-ISIS Activities", *Straits Times*, 13 June, available at https://www.straitstimes.com/singapore/first-woman-held-under-isa-for-pro-isis-activities accessed 10 July 2018.

Chia, Lianne (2016), "SGSecure Launched to Prepare Public for Terror Attacks", *Channel News Asia*, 16 September, available at https://www.channelnewsasia.com/news/singapore/sgsecure-launched-to-prepare-public-for-terror-attacks-7785404 accessed 1 June 2018.

Cochrane, Joe (2017), "In Indonesia's Dysfunctional Prisons, Escapes Aren't the Half of It", *New York Times*, 19 August, available at https://mobile.nytimes.com/2017/08/19/world/asia/indonesia-prisons-bali-kerobokan.html accessed 29 May 2018.

Dinansi, Clarissa Ivana Kartika (2018), *Indonesia's Deradicalization Program*, Bachelor Thesis, Semarang: Universitas Deponegoro.

General Suryadarma (2018), Former Densus 88 Chief, Interview by Rohan Gunaratna, 12 June.

Gunaratna, Rohan (2018), "Counterterrorism: ASEAN Militaries' Growing Role – Analysis", RSIS Commentaries, 14 March, available at https://www.rsis.edu.sg/wp-content/uploads/2018/03/CO18042.pdf accessed 1 June 2018.

Gunaratna, Rohan and Mohammed Bin Ali (2014), *Terrorist Rehabilitation: A New Frontier in Counter-terrorism*, London: Imperial College Press.

Hadi, Nur (2018), "Ali Fauzi Demands Muhammadiyah Involved Handling Terrorism", *Tempo*, 26 May, available at https://en.tempo.co/read/news/2018/05/26/055918778/Ali-Fauzi-Demands-Muhammadiyah-Involved-Handling-Terrorism accessed 1 June 2018.

Hamid, Ahmad Fauzi Abdul (2007), *Islam and Violence in Malaysia*, Singapore: RSIS.

Hamidi, Ahmed Zahid (2016), "Malaysia's Policy on Counter Terrorism and Deradicalisation Strategy", *Journal of Public Security and Safety*, 1–19.

Idris, Irfan (2016), "Deradikalisasi: Pembinaan Wawasan Kebangsaan", *Damaila Indonesiaku*, 30 August available at https://damailahindonesiaku.com/deradikalisasi-pembinaan-wawasan-kebangsaan.html accessed 19 June 2018.

Idris, Irfan (2018), BNPT Interview by Rohan Gunaratna, 28 June.

*Jakarta Post* (2017), "BNPT Identifies 400 Ex-Terrorists 'Untouched' by Deradicalization Program", *Jakarta Post*, 2 March, available at https://www.google.com.sg/amp/www.thejakartapost.com/amp/news/2017/03/02/bnpt-identifies-400-ex-terrorists-untouched-by-deradicalization-program.html accessed 20 June 2018.

Kamruddin, Mohd Norzikri, Noor Nirwandy Mat Noordin and Abd Rashid Abd Rahman (2017), "Terrorist Deradicalziation Programme in Malaysia: A Case Study", *Journal of Media and Information Warfare*, Vol. 10, 25–49.

Khor, Laura (2013), *Malaysia and Singapore's Terrorist Rehabilitation Programs: Learning and Adapting to Terrorist Threats*, Thesis, St Andrews.

Khor, Laura (2013), "The Colonial Foundations of Malaysia's Terrorist Rehabilitation Program", *Malaysian Journal of International Relations*, Vol. 1, 65–79.

Llewellyn, Aisyah (2018), "Indonesia's Prison System Is Broken", *The Diplomat*, 23 May, available at https://thediplomat.com/2018/05/indonesias-prison-system-is-broken/ accessed 9 January 2019.

Maharani, Shinta (2018), "Ex-Terrorist Inmate: ISIS Loathe Me for Joining Deradicalization", *Tempo*, 18 May, available at https://en.tempo.co/read/news/2018/05/27/055918791/Ex-Terrorist-Inmate-ISIS-Loathe-Me-for-Joining-Deradicalization accessed 19 June 2018.

MHA (Ministry of Home Affairs, Singapore) (2003), *The Jemaah Islamiyah Arrests and the Threat of Terrorism*, Singapore.

Mohamed, Ustaz Ali H. (2009), Interview by Rohan Gunaratna, 1 September.

Padil, Iszam (2009), *Terrorist Rehabilitation: Malaysia's Experience, International Conference on Terrorist Rehabilitation*, Conference Report, Singapore: ICPVTR.

Parker, Randall (2003), "Jemaah Islamiyah in South East Asia", *Para Pundit*, 20 May, available at http://www.parapundit.com/archives/cat_terrorism_and_wmd.html accessed 1 July 2018.

Prime Minister's Department (2014), *Addressing the Threat of the Islamic State*, White Paper, Kuala Lumpur, Malaysia.

RRG (2018), "Countering Extremism", available at https://www.rrg.sg/ accessed 31 January 2018.

Salleh, Nur Asyiqin Muhammed (2015), "Efforts to Rehabilitate Detainees, Help Families", *Asia One*, 17 April, available at http://www.asiaone.com/singapore/efforts-rehabilitate-detainees-help-families accessed 1 July 2018.

Sim, Susan and Noor Huda (2016), "From Prison to Carnage in Jakarta: Predicting Terrorist Recidivism in Indonesia's Prisons (Part 2)", Brookings Institution, 28 January, available at https://www.brookings.edu/opinions/predicting-terrorist-recidivism-in-indonesias-prisons/ accessed 19 June 2018.

*Tempo* (2018a), "BNPT: Prison for Terrorist Convict to Focus on Deradicalization", 30 May, available at https://en.tempo.co/read/news/2018/05/30/055918859/BNPT-Prison-for-Terrorist-Convict-to-Focus-on-Deradicalization accessed 19 June 2018.

*Tempo* (2018b), "Jokowi: Special Terrorist Cell Construction Soon to be Completed", 24 May, available at https://en.tempo.co/read/news/2018/05/24/055918706/Jokowi-Special-Terrorist-Cell-Construction-Soon-to-be-Completed accessed 19 June 2018.

UN Women (2017), "Women's Role Vital in Countering Violent Extremism, UN Women, Asia and the Pacific", 24 October, available at http://asiapacific.unwomen.org/en/news-and-events/stories/2017/10/womens-role-vital-in-countering-violent-extremism accessed 18 June 2018.

Yasin, Muhammad Haniff Hassan and Nur Azlin Mohamed (2018), "Indonesian Prisons: A Think Tank for Terrorists", *Counter Terrorism Trends and Analysis*, August, 10–15.

Yi, Seow Bri (2018), "S'pore Still Trying to Develop Right Tools to Rehabilitate Self-Radicalised Individuals: Shanmugam", *Straits Times*, 13 March, available at https://www.straitstimes.com/singapore/spore-still-trying-to-develop-right-tools-to-rehabilitate-self-radicalise accessed 18 July 2018.

Zolkepli, Farik (2017), "Facing down Terror", *The Star* (Malaysia), 23 April, available at https://www.thestar.com.my/news/nation/2017/04/23/facing-down-terror-the-man-who-leads-a-bukit-aman-division-in-fighting-terrorism-has-many-tales-to-s/ accessed 19 June 2018.

# 15 Deradicalization of terrorist detainees and inmates

A soft approach to counter terrorism

*Malkanthi Hettiarachchi*

## Introduction

As terrorist networks expand their reach from local to global communities, the approach to combatting terrorism must shift from a unidimensional to a multidimensional platform. Counter terrorism strategies adopted today include the kinetic approach as well as the battle to 'win hearts and minds' on the ground, rehabilitation to deradicalize, and countering the social media's power to change perceptions, shift opinion, and shape thinking. The capacity to appeal and the glamour to attract vulnerable youth from a range of backgrounds have taken a leap with easy access to electronic devices, global connectivity and unrestricted social media platforms. The *Smart Approach* in combatting terrorism is a blend of hard and soft approaches. Nations impacted by terrorism and at risk of terrorism, now think in terms of regional security, across geographical boundaries, networking and collaborating to bring stability to the region, to ensure national security.

Few countries across the globe have well established formal terrorist rehabilitation programs, such as Singapore, Saudi Arabia, Sri Lanka, Pakistan and Malaysia. Other countries conduct ad hoc programs that include educational, vocational, religious, social programs and family counselling (Köhler 2017: 247–248).

This chapter will explore Sri Lanka's efforts to rehabilitate and reintegrate the Tamil Tiger terrorists of the Liberation Tigers of Tamil Eelam (LTTE). The LTTE was an insurgent and terrorist group that claimed the lives of two heads of state, conducted 1,188 terrorist attacks killing thousands of civilians, designed the suicide belt, and gripped civilians in a reign of terror for almost 27years (Ministry of Defense 2011: 8, 88–159; Silva 2013). After decades of unsuccessful attempts, the Sri Lankan government used a whole of nation approach, and its security forces militarily defeated the LTTE in May 2009 (Tozzi 2010: 10–11). Following the dismantling of the military capability of the LTTE, the state lost no time in engaging the captured and surrendered members of the LTTE within a comprehensive rehabilitation and reintegration program that followed a 'restorative justice' model (Dharmawardhane 2013: 33).

## The evolution of the Sri Lanka rehabilitation program

Sri Lanka initiated its first terrorist rehabilitation program following the defeat of the LTTE in 2009. Prior to the launch of this formal program, ad hoc rehabilitation initiatives had commenced in 2007. The presidential directive issued in July 2009 was explicit: 'it's time to launch "humanitarian mission 02", to get them back on track with their normal lives'. The state approach was that the detainees were 'misled by the terrorist leadership into engaging in terrorist activity' but were 'citizens' who would be given a second chance to re-engage in civilian life (DMHR 2009). The way forward was to rehabilitate the former Tamil Tigers with a view to reintegration into civil society.

The architects of the rehabilitation program studied how terrorists and their leaders manipulated followers to disengage from civil society, and legitimized violence.[1] The rehabilitation program was designed to address these distortions and gaps during rehabilitation and prepare the former LTTE beneficiaries of the program to re-engage in civilian life upon reintegration. The rehabilitees were referred to as 'beneficiaries' to reinforce their role in education within the center, and separate them from the identity of a terrorist, violent extremist, prisoner or inmate. The term 'beneficiary' was coined by Saudi Arabia's rehabilitation program, used in the Singapore program, and shared with the Sri Lanka program. Sri Lanka shared this term with Pakistan. The beneficiaries were supported in moving beyond disengagement from violence, into delegitimizing the need for violence. A key feature of the rehabilitation program was to understand the process of grooming a civilian into a terrorist and reversing the process of violent radicalization. Winning hearts and minds was the approach of each rehabilitation center. Independent assessors evaluated program effectiveness which helped the commissioner generals ensure standards of excellence (Kruglanski and Gelfand 2011; Kruglanski 2012). Sri Lanka has currently reintegrated 12,206 beneficiaries of this program into civil society.

## The approach

When a terrorist is captured or forced to surrender, the authorities are presented with a golden opportunity, perhaps the only opportunity, to commence the deradicalization process. How the detainee or inmate is handled every step of the way determines the progress made. The detainee in rehabilitation is resistant, resentful, angry, frightened and uncertain. Detainees watch and wait to see what will happen to them at the hands of their perceived enemy. This is a decisive time when the battle for 'hearts and minds' begins, within rehabilitation and in the community.

Winning the *hearts and minds* of the community is a significant battle that goes beyond the material into reconnecting and rebuilding damaged trust and relationships while providing goods and services. The 'charitable units' of Terrorist groups function as providers of goods, services, safety, security and healthcare, and project themselves as the saviors of the community, and the state as ineffective and uncaring. Therefore state authorities and the security sector must engage the affected communities and detainees in spite of the negative propaganda that attempts to polarize the community from the state and security sector. Civil engagement needs to reflect respect, care, stability, discipline and stand as an alternative to violence justifying and violence promoting groups. Interpersonal contact and engagement offered to and maintained with the community that is exposed to violent extremist groups that present themselves as self-appointed guardians of the community, stand as a counter point to the terrorist rhetoric on state authorities and security sector being disrespectful, uncaring, indisciplined, and discriminatory.

Many detainees and inmates expect harm and mistreatment in custody, the narrative projected by the terrorist leadership that filters down to its members, preventing its members from escaping or handing themselves over to the security forces. Custody provides the opportunity and space for inmates and detainees to reassess their thinking and critically assess the violence justifying narratives that kept them within the terrorist framework.

Rehabilitation Centers that are secure, safe and respectful, are the living example of the counter narrative that creates cognitive dissonance, and shifts the negative perceptions held by the beneficiaries. The determination and commitment of Rehabilitation Center staff to treat detainees with compassion during their period of rehabilitation has the greatest impact in transforming the detainee attitudes and opinions from within (Dharmawardhane 2013: 38). Cognitive transformation happens internally, when the detainee begins to reassess the justifications for violence and the need for violence, within an indoctrination free context.

## Understanding radicalization

To radicalize is to become extreme but what is of concern is radicalization into violence. Ideology is a 'set of beliefs' to which the individual subscribes based on political, religious, social or historical narratives (Kruglanski 2010: 2). Terrorist groups formulate an ideology through which the religio-political, ethno-nationalist or socio-political narratives are operationalized, facilitating terrorist groups to mobilize their membership.

The radicalization and deradicalization processes take place in the mind. Deradicalization is a skilled task that requires a psychological approach to dismantle the ideology that locks the mind into legitimizing violence (Hettiarachchi 2010). It is essential to engage with terrorists to identify violence justifying thoughts and beliefs, and facilitate critical thinking. Cognitive strategies utilized to build rapport, overcome resistance, access thoughts and beliefs in a non-threatening manner, help to identify errors and distortions in thinking. Using the Socratic method of questioning to explore alternative perspectives and responses to violence justifying narratives, questioning established beliefs and patterns of thinking, facilitates de-legitimizing the need for violence, and are methods to be used by the multidisciplinary staff team and not limited to psychologists.

## Groomed into terrorism

Individuals are groomed into terrorism and nurtured within a violent radical setting. This transformation of a civilian into a terrorist is multifactorial and requires a multifaceted response. Terrorist groups need *powerful emotive narratives that resonate with the community*. Depending on the dynamic nature of the message and the charisma of the messenger, the community generates potential recruits.[2] Some join the group as members, while a larger number remain as civilian supporters and sympathizers, who may graduate with time into members.

Recruits motivated sufficiently by *grievance narratives* are groomed into terrorism through *ideological indoctrination and training*. They develop an *identity* linked to the group and a sense of responsibility and loyalty to the group. The experience of power, dignity and significance in the eyes of the community, contribute to feeling like the defender of the cause. Indeed, LTTE recruitment of one member from each family entrenched families within the group and secured individual and family loyalty to the group. Tamil Tigers were bestowed with gifts, status, position and greater responsibilities for each successful operation. When members and fighters died in operations and suicide missions, they were martyred and martyr families held in high esteem. When training is provided, *self-efficacy*, a belief in one's ability to carry out duties required to redress grievances framed within the narrative, develops. The *ideology* provides the *moral justifications* to legitimize the use of violence to target the perceived enemy, to rescue the community and restore the *lost significance* (Hettiarachchi 2017: 219). The leaders of the organization or group present themselves as fair and just while the state is projected as unfair and unjust.

The recruit is then mentored into the group's subculture and *sustained* within the group. When *mobilised* to carry out violent activities, he or she gains significance within the group and becomes a valued member of the fighting cadres. This member gains the respect of the community, peers and leaders and becomes *self-motivated*. The fighter then goes on to develop *greater self-efficacy* with each attack and is celebrated, valued and further *entrenched within the terrorist group* (Hettiarachchi 2017: 219).

Practitioners engaged in deradicalization focus on reversing this process of radicalization into violence and terrorism. It is based on the premise that those groomed into violence can be guided back to a path of non-violence, and that what is learnt can be unlearnt.

## Process of radicalization

The Sri Lanka rehabilitation program identified basic rights and liberties manipulated and denied by the LTTE when grooming civilians into terrorists: denial of access to education and to engage in a vocation of choice; denial of access to family, and to engage in cultural and religious practises; denial of the freedom to engage in sport and extracurricular activities, that allows a sense of self to develop; denial of the freedom to think and act according to personal wishes and live within a free society.

The LTTE replaced education with indoctrination of the group, promoting anger and hatred towards the other, and legitimized the need for violence. Child orphanages were used to groom children into idolising and venerating suicide bombers and normalizing a culture of violence (Waldman 2003: 1–5). The LTTE recruited 'members' for training within the group and 'non-members' to engage in civil administrative duties guided by the LTTE. Vocational education and training provided was to facilitate LTTE acts of terror. This included weapons training, combat training, bomb making, suicide mission training, as well as businesses in money laundering, smuggling gold, arms and human smuggling, drug trafficking, that generated an income for the LTTE (O'Neil 2007).

Potential recruits absorbed into the pseudo family of the Tamil Tigers followed the LTTE culture of paying homage to the leader, socialized within the group, and married into the LTTE network. Members of the LTTE were ideologically indoctrinated to morally justify the need for violence to achieve the group's aim of a separate state. Creative arts such as music, drama, movies, street theatre, cartoons and billboards were used to project grievance narratives, the loss of significance, the need to go in quest of significance, gain significance and restore significance and pride, to secure a steady flow of recruits, supporters and funding from overseas.

## Reversing the process of radicalization

The very components that the LTTE manipulated in the direction of violence, polarization and rejection, were reversed within rehabilitation in the direction of personal growth, peace building, through exposure and engagement. Beneficiaries within the rehabilitation programs were empowered and supported to develop meaning and significance by reconnecting with their family, culture, society, and spirituality. They were also supported to expand their knowledge base through education, develop vocational skills through mainstream vocational training, build resilience and self-efficacy, develop critical thinking, emotional intelligence, delegitimize the need for violence, develop alternative meaning and significance in life and reduce their vulnerability to recruitment. Reversing the process of radicalization, countering radicalization, preventing radicalization were attempts to ensure safer communities.

## Rehabilitation

Rehabilitation is about facilitating the transformation of thinking and behaviour of terrorists, to move away from violent extremist thinking, prior to their reintegration into mainstream society.

While there is no common template for all rehabilitation programs, there are principles of rehabilitation and good practises applicable to global rehabilitation programs. Much can be learnt from countries that have established formal rehabilitation programs, from their challenges, successes and failures. The body of knowledge on rehabilitation is growing steadily as countries begin to engage in rehabilitation of terrorist inmates and detainees (Hedayah 2018).

Sri Lanka's 5R Model was a comprehensive post war strategy, that included *Reconstruction* and *Resettlement* as the regions held by the Tamil Tigers were almost 30 years behind the rest of the country, with more than 300,000 internally displaced persons (*Business Today* 2011). The Rehabilitation, Reintegration and Reconciliation phases were focused on achieving security and sustainable peace. A bureau dedicated to manage the rehabilitation and reintegration components of the 5R model was established.

## Dedicated bureau for rehabilitation in Sri Lanka

The Bureau for the Commissioner General for Rehabilitation (BCGR) was dedicated for the rehabilitation and reintegration of the former LTTE. It was resourced by the Ministry of Defence staff, under the Ministry of Prison Reforms and Rehabilitation. The BCGR worked in partnership with the security sector; and the Ministries of Defence, Justice, Prisons and Rehabilitation, National Reintegration and Reconciliation, Skills Development and Vocational Training, Women and Children, Health, Agriculture, Education, Sports, Cultural Affairs and Social Services. The BCGR also partnered NGOs and INGOs; the private and business sectors; community volunteers, professionals, and religious personnel to conduct over 48 programs to rehabilitate and reintegrate the former LTTE members (see BCGR website).

The BCGR initially managed 24 Protective Accommodation and Rehabilitation Centers (PARCs), to accommodate nearly 10,790 detainees in 2009 to one PARC by 2015, following reintegration (BCGR 2013). The rehabilitation program implemented within these centers included six modes of rehabilitation and a community engagement component referred to as the 6+1 Model (BCGR 2013: see Figure 15.1).

Post-reintegration *aftercare* in the community was also managed by the BCGR's Socioeconomic and Welfare Coordination Teams located in districts where beneficiaries were reintegrated. The Rehabilitation and Reintegration continues to be managed by the BCGR under the Ministry of Prisons and Rehabilitation.

## Assessment and categorization

Measurement is at the heart of any evidence based intervention program. The first step in rehabilitation was to assess and categorize the surrendered and apprehended detainees. Law enforcement agencies and intelligence services

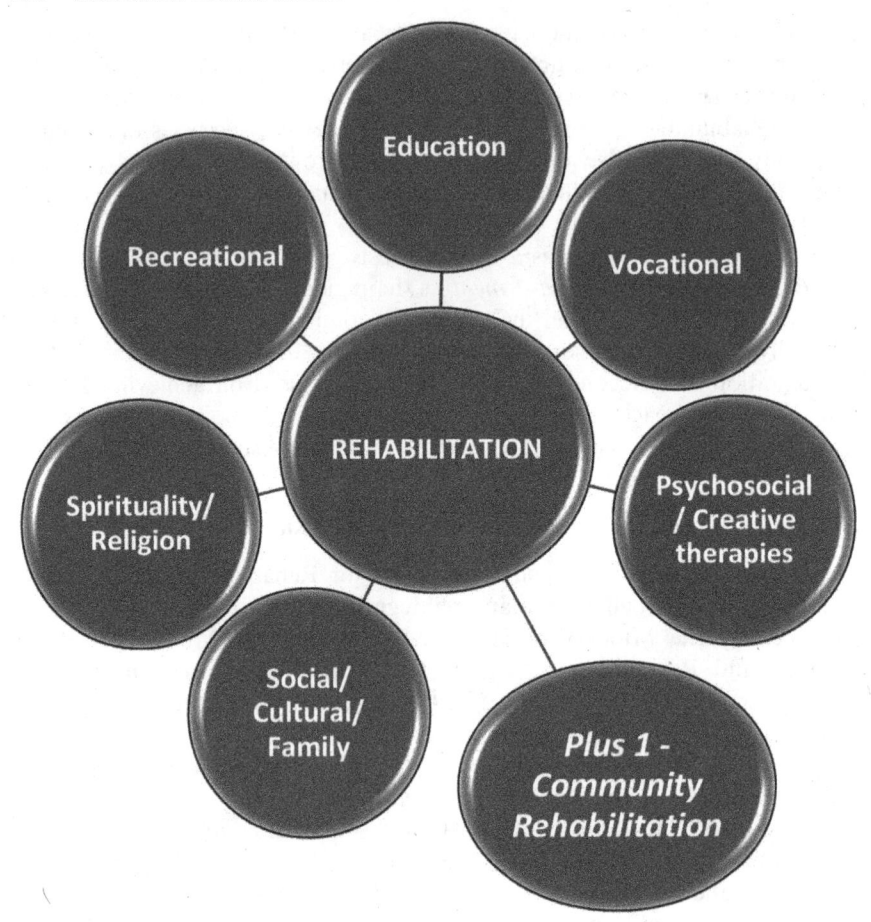

*Figure 15.1* 6+1 Model
Source: Malkanthi Hettiarachchi.

assessed the former terrorists and categorized them based on their depth of involvement, period of involvement, and activities conducted during involvement, into high, medium, and low risk. The detainees were then segregated to the different rehabilitation centers (BCGR 2010; DMHR 2009).

Categorization helped prevent the more radical detainees from sabotaging the program and preventing less radical individuals from participating in the programs and moving on. The more radical detainees were likely to label program participation as betrayal, support resistance, and encourage non-corporation. When detainees establish a sense of seniority, junior members become subservient and have difficulty making choices and resisting ideological pressure. Staff must be in control of the Rehabilitation Center at all times, and not allow senior or more authoritative members of the terrorist group to control other inmates at any time. Beneficiaries who engage must be empowered to make independent decisions, as they are now not within an environment controlled by the terrorist leadership.

Several types of assessments are required within rehabilitation: Detainee and inmate assessment, program assessment, center assessment and staff assessment. Assessments highlight potential risks, vulnerabilities and strengths of the individual, the program, the center and the staff team. These assessments inform program managers and funders on program effectiveness and where to target resources to improve the service. For example, assessments are used to identify levels of radicalization that helps tailor programs to meet individual and group needs, minimize risk and optimize learning (Hettiarachchi 2018).

Ongoing assessment to assess degree of radicalization and changing attitudes and opinions of the beneficiaries indicated a significant decline in the levels of radicalization attributed to the programs conducted, as well as quality of staff interaction with beneficiaries, where the beneficiaries felt respected and the center conditions were adequate (Kruglanski and Gelfand 2011). Independent assessment and evaluation of the rehabilitation program since its inception has led to a large body of evidence on effectiveness of rehabilitation. Hence, Sri Lanka's rehabilitation program is considered 'one of the few known terrorist rehabilitation programs' that has 'produced strong indicators of a positive impact on participants' ideological convictions through the program' (Köhler 2017: 248).

## The 6+1 Model

According to Daniel Köhler (2017: 248), 'the Sri Lankan rehabilitation and reintegration program can be counted among the most successful and best designed programs in the world'. The rehabilitation program was initiated using a common sense approach, the literature in the field, the models in Singapore and Columbia and the indigenous contextual requirements. Practise and theory gradually blended to form the 6+1 Model (Hettiarachchi 2013: 106).

Rehabilitation focused on reaching the 'Hearts and Minds' of beneficiaries by engaging them in several activities that were transformative. Livelihood concerns were addressed through educational and vocational programs. Beneficiaries were supported to reflect and get in touch with themselves through the spiritual programs. The psychosocial and creative therapies programs supported beneficiaries to address perceptions of self, others and the future; emotional, attitudinal and interpersonal relating issues; address personal issues through counselling, develop personal significance and meaning in life. Creative therapies such as art, music, dance, drama and comedy, helped beneficiaries give expression to their feelings and develop a sense of self. Beneficiaries were prepared to reconnect with civil society through, social, cultural and familial rehabilitation, to develop an appreciation for the country and strengthen family bonds. Social events provided the opportunity to engage with the different other, and cultural activities developed a respect for people of all cultural and religious backgrounds. Sports and extra-curricular programs supported beneficiaries to interact with each other in the spirit of competition and friendship, learn about winning and losing.

The various programs exposed beneficiaries to alternative ways of thinking about themselves, the world and the future. They were able to challenge their justification for the use of violence, and further delegitimize the need for violence. Through the several programs conducted within rehabilitation, beneficiaries were strengthened to develop personal resilience, think critically and engage with family and community instead of allegiance to a group.

## Preparation for community reintegration

The National Framework for the Reintegration of Ex-combatants into Civilian Life in Sri Lanka outlines several key aspects: rehabilitation, reinsertion, social reintegration, economic reintegration, as well as transitional justice, access to counselling, psychosocial wellbeing, gender, child protection, disability, health, access to education and access to vocations (DMHR 2009). These strategies and guiding principles were operationalized within rehabilitation centers and reintegration initiatives.

The reintegration process was geared to build community confidence and alleviate beneficiary anxiety related to acceptance and coping in the community. Through family visits, social, cultural and religious events celebrated within the center, beneficiaries were able to engage with members of the public and private sector that provided educational, vocational, counselling and social work services with kindness and compassion. Through these service providers of different ethnic and religious backgrounds, beneficiaries were exposed to the multicultural reality of the community, as opposed to the mono-ethnic ideology of the LTTE.

The close rapport between center staff and beneficiaries, exposed beneficiaries to the security forces who are responsible to protect its citizens and defend the nation when faced with terrorism, and in times of peace engaged in nation building. Beneficiaries learnt that the security forces have a dual role and are mobilized when there is a danger to national security irrespective of the nature of the threat group. The beneficiaries began to see the security forces as protectors and defenders of the nation.

The pro separatist *diaspora* invited to visit the rehabilitation centers provided an opportunity for beneficiaries to express their opinion to those who supported and funded terrorism from overseas. It was transformative for diaspora members to meet beneficiaries face to face and listen to the devastation caused by their funds to support terrorism and think of accountability. In turn the diaspora members were able to share the experiences of their family members incarcerated overseas, serving long sentences on terrorism charges with no access to rehabilitation.

## Reintegration and aftercare

The aim of rehabilitation is to reintegrate the beneficiary into the community. The reintegration phase requires the ideological transformation achieved during rehabilitation to be maintained during the aftercare phase in the community. Dharmawardhane highlights the effective cognitive transformation of the beneficiaries attributed to the programs and the interpersonal relationships with the BCGR staff (2013: 38). This ideological transformation from violence to non-violence is not an 'all or none' phenomenon. Ideological transformation that occurs in an artificial environment is tested when the individual returns to his or her own environment and is exposed to potential radicalizing elements yet again. A robust aftercare system was put in place to ensure that treatment gains were sustained, and to reduce recidivism.

The aftercare process enabled beneficiaries to draw from and be sustained by their cultural, religious and familial roots, consolidated within rehabilitation through a series of programs. Several factors come into play in the successful reintegration of a former terrorist: the reintegration into mainstream society and sustaining the individual within the mainstream frame work. The Socioeconomic and Welfare Coordination Teams conduct the aftercare phase of the rehabilitation program. These teams located within the civil administrative offices in each region where beneficiaries were reintegrated facilitated their smooth transition into civil society and prevented undue frustration with accessing services and facilities when re-entering civil society.

## Community reintegration

The reintegration ceremonies were graced by the President, Ministers, Commissioner Generals and dignitaries that supported the rehabilitation process (BCGR 2013). Each beneficiary was handed back to the family, with the community taking responsibility to maintain the peace. During this phase the beneficiary is supported towards a new beginning, a focus on the future and to consolidate the transformation (Ministry of Defense 2012). Strengthening ties to a supportive family and social network were to help the beneficiary remain engaged within a non-violent framework, as social pressures are likely to impact on the individual upon return to the community. Therefore a support network, livelihoods and access to the community aftercare team helped to anchor the person in the community.

## Community awareness programs

Community awareness programs were conducted by the BCGR with religious and community leaders to create awareness of the progress of the beneficiaries within the rehabilitation program and facilitate their acceptance into the community upon reintegration. Television, radio, newspapers, and magazines carried interviews and pictures of the rehabilitation and reintegration process across time. Exhibitions and billboards on 'bringing back the child' and on 'inter-religious harmony', throughout the country helped transform public opinion. These initiatives helped shift the perspective of the community on the state, the security sector and the beneficiaries. The community was able to witness the former terrorists that had gripped the nation with terror gradually transform into peaceful citizens, which helped the community accept the reintegrated beneficiary.

## Community engagement and reconciliation programs

Community Engagement Programs (CEP) are vital in preventing re-radicalization of the reintegrated beneficiaries (ICPVTR 2011). One such community initiative is the Civil Service Division (CSD) located in Kilinochchi, where beneficiaries and community members find employment and support wider livelihood and wellbeing projects in the community (Nathaniel 2018; Somarathna 2012). The Harmony Center in Killinochchi is yet another initiative that provides support to beneficiaries and community. Building resilient communities inoculates the community and prevents the reintegrated individual from relapsing into violence.

State efforts for reconciliation are led by the Ministry of National Integration and Reconciliation (NIR 2018). The Lakshman Kadirgamar Institute for International Relations and Strategic Studies (LKI), named after Mr Kadirgamar, a Lawyer and Statesman of Tamil heritage who was the Sri Lankan Foreign Minister assassinated by the LTTE in 2005, pioneered gathering community specialists in the field for a series of eight workshops from 2011 to 2013. These workshops were led by Asanga Abeygoonasekera, son of a member of parliament who was assassinated in 1994. The LKI conducted the Inaugural Conference on Reconciliation, Role of Business Community, Role of the Woman, Role of Education, Role of Information Technology (ICT), Role of Youth, Role of Arts and Culture and Role of Religion in Reconciliation, to discuss how each of these fields can support reconciliation within the country.[3]

Several community organizations conduct community and youth engagement programs. Research into engaging youth to counter youth radicalization is discussed by Anishka De Zylva (2017). Sri Lanka Unites, led by Prashan De Visser, is one of the leading youth reconciliation programs island-wide that bring together youth from all ethnic and religious backgrounds (SLU 2018). The Foundation of Goodness, is a values based initiative involving children, youth and adults, promoting reconciliation through sports in various parts of the country, founded by Kushil Gunasekera and Sri Lanka cricketers (FOG 2018). Youth leadership initiatives are conducted throughout the country by Unity Mission Trust, established by Bertyl Pinto Jayawardene (UMT 2018).

## Good practice guidelines

Experts in the field have come together to share good and ethical principles used within current terrorist rehabilitation and reintegration programs across the globe, commencing with the Rome Memorandum of Good Practices (ICCT and UNICRI 2011; GCTF 2015).

Organizations such as United Nations Interregional Crime and Justice Research Institute (UNICRI), International Center for Counter Terrorism (ICCT), International Institute for Justice and the Rule of Law (IIJ), Hedayah and the Global Counter Terrorism Forum (GCTF) have taken leadership in bringing experts together to draft several GPG documents that provide guidance for psychologists, religious scholars, educationalists and returning foreign fighters. According to General Douglas Stone, 'Sri Lanka practices all these aspects listed in the (Rome) memorandum, and it was before the memorandum was put together' in 2011 (Stone 2013). New and emerging programs are likely to benefit from these guidelines which are tested within established programs.

## Post-reintegration challenges

A criticism by some members of the Tamil community is that the rehabilitated former LTTE members have greater support and facilities than them. Though a legitimate resentment, it is about increasing the support to civilians, but not reducing the support offered to the reintegrated. The relationship between preventing recidivism by providing 'practical support' to the beneficiaries 'and their families' is well established (Rabasa et al. 2010: 44).

Dharmawardhane (2013: 38–39) identifies 'Sri Lanka's robust security platform which continued post-conflict' as being a 'strong factor for this post-conflict stability', five years into rehabilitation and reintegration of the rehabilitated former LTTE members. With a zero recidivism into terrorism and less than ten arrested for criminal activity (0.8%) in 2013, an unstable political environment in the latter part of 2014 into 2015, witnessed a rise in pro LTTE diaspora separatist activity, LTTE iconography, extremist exclusivist ideology, motor cycle gangs, violence and an unsuccessful assassination attempt, foiled by a former beneficiary of the deradicalization program who was keen to prevent a return to violence (Jeyaraj 2017; Balachandran 2017). These activities coincided with government dismantling the security and intelligence systems, creating the space for re-radicalization and re-igniting separatist ideology.[4]

The relatively low recidivism rates prior to 2015 are likely because the program 'carefully monitored and offered continued support to reduce the likelihood of recidivism', to maintain treatment gains (Rabasa et al. 2010: 44). Careful monitoring and continued support are two of the several 'key components identified in successful rehabilitation programs' as outlined by Rabasa and colleagues (2010: 42).

The challenges are many in sustaining the rehabilitated former terrorists within the mainstream when governments fail to maintain security and stability. A lesson to be learnt from Sri Lanka is that within a stable political and security context the reintegrated beneficiaries remained within the mainstream. However, when state policy undermines security and disregards potential risks, reintegrated beneficiaries (approximately 0.3%) were observed to become vulnerable to re-radicalization.

## Potential risks and cautions

De-radicalization is not an all-or-none phenomenon. Given that radicalization happens at a cognitive and emotive level over time, the rehabilitated individual could be vulnerable to re-radicalization by individuals or groups with a violent radical ideology. Therefore the longer the reintegrated former rehabilitees are supported to function independently and remain engaged with community, the more resilient the individual will become and more able to resist group pressure. The greater the distance in time and space to terrorism, the deeper the involvement in family and community, the more meaningful this new life becomes, the more resilient the former terrorist would be to re-radicalization. However, the de-radicalized and reintegrated former terrorist is likely to be vulnerable to re-radicalization, if the context is once again conducive to engaging in violence and terrorism.

Weak governance, undermining the potential reach and influence of terrorist funders and ideologues to reignite terrorist ideology, negotiating and re-engaging terrorist funders and proxy groups, discriminatory policies and practices, and undermined security, are factors likely to prepare the ground for terrorism to raise its head. These violent radical individuals and groups are likely to reach out with authority, to intimidate and re-engage the reintegrated beneficiaries, networks, links and resources. When a terrorist group is dismantled, the state, intelligence services and law enforcement need to be working harder to ensure that terrorism does not return at least within a ten year period.

## Conclusion

Sri Lanka succeeded in rehabilitating the leaders and members of one of the world's most dangerous terrorist and insurgent groups, the LTTE. The political will and belief that rehabilitation is the way forward, is one factor attributed to the success of the program. The Presidential Amnesty provided the hope and opportunity for beneficiaries to engage in the civilian process, with a presidential directive to 'treat them as your own children' (Rajapakse 2009). The leadership provided at every level within rehabilitation was vital to maintain the standards of care and security of each rehabilitation facility. The ethos of the rehabilitation centers were similar to residential training centers that conduct life skills training to develop spiritually, personally, professionally and promote peace and harmony.

Parallel to the process of rehabilitation, a clear message was issued that terrorism is a criminal offence and punishable by law. This was demonstrated through the indictments and prosecutions of terrorist criminals involved in assassinations and massacres. The understanding was that should any of the beneficiaries offend in future, they would be subject to the full extent of the law.

Rehabilitation, reintegration and community engagement is a counter terrorism strategy that is long lasting and sustained. Terrorists who are rehabilitated are vulnerable in the community to potential re-radicalization and recruitment. The community is the base from which individuals are recruited and groomed into terrorism. Therefore the rehabilitation and de-radicalization of former terrorists needs to be an ongoing process that requires continuous engagement and assessment.

Counter-terrorism initiatives that focus on shrinking the recruitment and funding bases would weaken the operational capability of terrorists. The kinetic response to terrorism is an essential aspect in diminishing the immediate threat, while intelligence gathering is invaluable in dismantling active and potential threats. Engaging in the 'battlefield of the mind' is an equally important counter terrorism strategy (Gunaratna 2011). This soft approach delegitimizes the justifications for the ideology used to recruit and polarize communities.

Leaders with the foresight to prevent radicalization by engaging in uphill prevention, downhill rehabilitation and reintegration, on a foundation based on community resilience-building are likely to be able to inoculate their communities against violent radicalization. Rehabilitation, reintegration and community engagement are robust and enduring soft approaches to counter terrorism.

Terrorist groups harness their resources to radicalize communities into violence, at multiple levels. A blend of both soft and hard approaches is the optimal strategy in managing and maintaining peace and stability within the country. To create an impact on this uphill battle against terrorism in the twenty-first century, counter terrorism approaches must be multifaceted, and interventions enduring, dynamic and creative.

## Notes

1 The first two Commissioner Generals of Rehabilitation, General Daya Rathnayake and General Sudantha Ranasingha together with Prof. Rohan Gunaratna and Ustaz Faizal Mohammed, ICPVTR, Singapore conceptualized and designed the program. The program continued to develop and grow over time with input from professionals and successive commissioner generals.
2 Emotion focused messages based on the perception of 'injustice' result in anger, hatred and revenge that push people to join militant groups. Attraction focused messages based on the perception of joining a militant group as being 'cool', 'strong', 'empowering', result in being pulled in to joining the group. Blended messages focus both on emotive push and attraction focused pull factors.

3 National Conferences on Reconciliation at the Lakshman Kadirgamar Institute: Inaugural Conference (24 November 2011), Role of Business Community (24 January 2012), Role of Education (13 March 2012), Role of the Woman (23 July 2012), Role of Information Technology (18 September 2012), Role of Youth (2 January 2013), Role of Arts and Culture (16 May 2013) and Role of Religion in Reconciliation (23 July 2013).
4 Community assessment, with beneficiaries, 31 March to 1 April 2018.

## References

Balachandran, P. K. (2017), 'Four Ex-LTTE Cadres Held for Plotting to Assassinate Tamil MP Sumanthiran', *The New Indian Express*, 29 January, available at http://www.newindianexpress.com/world/2017/jan/29/four-ex-ltte-cadres-held-for-plotting-to-assassinate-tamil-mp-sumanthiran-1564747.html accessed 18 June 2018.

BCGR (website), 'Bureau for the Commissioner General for Rehabilitation', available at http://bcgr.gov.lk/index.php accessed 26 August 2018.

BCGR (2010), *The BCGR Action Plan: Guidelines for Rehabilitation*, Colombo: BCGR.

BCGR (2013), *Rehabilitation of Ex Combatants*, compiled by D. Hettiarachchi, The Bureau of the Commissioner General of Rehabilitation (BCGR), Colombo: Department of Government Information.

Business Today (2011), 'IDPs, Resettlement, Rehabilitation and Reintegration of Ex-combatants in Sri Lanka', July, available at http://www.businesstoday.lk/article.php?article=3488 accessed 18 June 2018.

De Zylva, A. (2017), 'International Engagement in Countering Youth Radicalisation: Sri Lanka's Untapped Opportunities', in *Countering Youth Radicalization and Violent Extremism in Sri Lanka*, Consortium Of South Asian Think Tanks (COSATT), pp. 34–50, available at http://www.lki.lk/wp-content/uploads/2017/09/Countering-Youth-Radicalization.pdf accessed 18 June 2018.

Dharmawardhane, I. (2013), 'Sri Lanka's Post-Conflict Strategy: Restorative Justice for Rebels and Rebuilding of Conflict-Affected Communities', *Perspectives on Terrorism*, 7(6): 27–57.

DMHR (2009), *National Framework Proposal for Reintegration of Ex-Combatants into Civilian Life in Sri Lanka*, Ministry of Disaster Management and Human Rights, Colombo: DMHR.

FOG (2018), *Foundation of Goodness: Unconditional Compassion*, available at http://www.unconditionalcompassion.org/indexc.php accessed 18 June 2018.

GCTF (2015), *Addendum to the Rome Memorandum of Good Practises for the Rehabilitation and Reintegration of Violent Extremists*, Global Terrorism Forum (GCTF), September, available at https://www.thegctf.org/Portals/1/Documents/Toolkit-documents/English-Addendum-tothe-Rome-Memorandum-on-Legal-Frameworks.pdf accessed 18 June 2018.

Gunaratna, R. (2011), 'Terrorist Rehabilitation: A Global Imperative', *Journal of Policing, Intelligence and Counter Terrorism*, 6(1): 65–82.

Hedayah (2016), *Malta Principles for Reintegrating Returning Foreign Terrorist Fighters (FTFs)*, available at http://www.hedayahcenter.org/Admin/Content/File-26102016223519.pdf accessed 18 June 2018.

Hedayah (2018), *Experts' Workshop on Curriculum Development: Prevention, Rehabilitation and Reintegration Practices for Vulnerable and Radicalized Youth and Children*, January 15–17, Rome: Hedayah.

Hettiarachchi, M. (2010), *Psychological Aspects of Radicalization*, available at http://www.rsis.edu.sg/publications/conference_reports/RSIS_PakistanReport_2010.pdf accessed 18 June 2018.

Hettiarachchi, M. (2013), 'Sri Lanka's Rehabilitation Program: A New Frontier in Counter Terrorism and Counter Insurgency', *PRISM Journal for Complex Operations*, 4(2): 105–121.

Hettiarachchi, M. (2017), *Radicalization and Deradicalization: The Tamil Tiger Case Study* (PhD thesis, Macquarie University, Australia).

Hettiarachchi, M. (2018), 'Assessment and Evaluation of Terrorist Rehabilitation Programs', in R. Gunaratna and S. Hussin (eds.), *Deradicalisation and Terrorist Rehabilitation: A Framework for Policy Making and Implementation*, London: Routledge.

ICCT and UNICRI (2011), *Rome Memorandum of Good Practices*, International Center for Counter Terrorism (ICCT) and United Nations Interregional Crime and Justice Research Institute (UNICRI), available at https://www.thegctf.org/Portals/1/Documents/Framework%20Documents/A/GCTF-Rome-Memorandum-ENG.pdf accessed 18 June 2018.

ICPVTR (2011), *International Conference on Community Engagement (ICCE)*, International Center for Political Violence and Terrorism Research, 21 September, Singapore.

Jeyaraj, DBS (2017), 'Overseas LTTE Backed Plot to Assassinate TNA MP Sumanthiran in Jaffna Revealed', *Daily Mirror*, 28 January, available at http://www.dailymirror.lk/article/Overseas-LTTE-backed-plot-to-assassinate-TNA-MP-Sumanthiran-in-Jaffna-revealed-122886.html accessed 18 June 2018.

Köhler, D. (2017), *Understanding Deradicalization: Methods, Tools and Programs for Countering Violence*, New York: Routledge.

Kruglanski, A. W. (2010), 'The Mind of a Terrorist: Interview with Tom Jacobs', *Pacific Standard*, 24 February.

Kruglanski, A. W. (2012), 'Rehabilitation of Tamil Tigers', Sri Lanka Defence Seminar, available at https://www.youtube.com/watch?v=lXw4_HOOF3A accessed 18 June 2018.

Kruglanski, A. W. and M. J. Gelfand (2011), *Rehabilitation of Former LTTE Cadres in Sri Lanka: A Preliminary Report*, College Park, MD: University of Maryland.

Ministry of Defense (2011), *Humanitarian Operation: Factual Analysis*, Ministry of Defence, Democratic Socialist Republic of Sri Lanka, Rajagiriya: Central Bank Printing Press.

Nathaniel, C. (2018), 'Ex-LTTE Cadres Contribute to Economy', *The Sunday Leader*, 2 April, available at http://www.thesundayleader.lk/2013/02/17/ex-ltte-cadres-contribute-toeconomy/ accessed 18 June 2018.

NIR (2018), Ministry of National Integration and Reconciliation, available at http://nirmin.gov.lk/web/index.php?option=com_content&view=article&id=102:columbian-delegation-visitssri-lanka-to-study-reconciliation-initiatives&catid=8:news-events&lang=en&Itemid=101 accessed 18 June 2018.

O'Neil, S. (2007), *Terrorist Precursor Crimes: Issues and Options for Congress*, CRS Report for Congress, Congressional Research Service, 24 May available at http://www.fas.org/sgp/crs/terror/RL34014.pdf accessed 18 June 2018.

Rabasa, A., S. L. Pettyjohn, J. J. Ghez and C. Boucek (2010), *Deradicalising Islamist Extremists*, RAND Corporation Monograph Series, RAND Corporation, Santa Monica, CA.

Rajapakse, M. (2009), Briefing on How to Conduct Rehabilitation to the Commissioner General of Rehabilitation at the Launch of the National Framework on Rehabilitation, Colombo, June.

Silva, de S. (2013), *Change and Continuity in Terrorism: An Examination of the Lifecycle of the Liberation Tigers of Tamil Eelam* (PhD Thesis), Wollongong University, Wollongong, Australia.

SLU (2018), *Sri Lanka Unites: Youth Movement for Hope and Reconciliation*, Sri Lanka Unites: Youth Movement for Hope and Reconciliation, available at http://srilankaunites.org accessed 18 June 2018.

Somarathna, R. (2012), 'CSD Job Boon for Ex-LTTEERS – Over 1800 Apply', *Sri Lanka Brief*, 26 June, available at http://srilankabrief.org/2012/06/csd-job-boon-for-ex-ltteers-over-1800-apply/ accessed 18 June 2018.

Sri Lanka Rehabilitation and Reintegration Ceremonies of the Former Tamil Tigers, available at http://www.bcgr.gov.lk/docs/Rehabilitation%20of%20Ex-Combatants%20(Compiler%20-%20Brigadier%20Dharshana%20Hettiarrachchi).pdf accessed 18 June 2018.

Stone, D. (2013), '*Rome Principles in Action*', Hedayah Conference, Abu Dhabi, 3 June.

Tozzi, F. L. (2010), *How to Kill a Tiger: Measuring Manwaring's Paradigm Against Sri Lanka's Counterinsurgency Strategy (Master's Thesis)*, George Town University, Washington DC.

UMT, (2018), *Unity Mission Trust: Unite, Heal, Integrate*, available at http://www.unitymission.lk accessed 18 June 2018.

Waldman, A. (2003), 'Masters of Suicide Bombing: Tamil Guerrillas of Sri Lanka', *New York Times*, 14 January, available at http://www.nytimes.com/2003/01/14/world/masters-of-suicidebombing-tamil-guerrillas-of-sri-lanka.html?pagewanted=all accessed 18 June 2018.

# 16 Counter-terrorism and counter-insurgency in Asia

*Andrew T. H. Tan*

## Introduction

Asia faces a diverse and complex set of terrorism and insurgency threats, as the preceding chapters have made clear. The question then is how Asia has responded to the challenges. This concluding chapter to the book evaluates counter-terrorism and counter-insurgency efforts in the region. It consists of a brief discussion of the conceptual issues and counter-terrorism methodology, followed by an assessment of the counter-terrorism responses adopted by affected states in South Asia, Southeast Asia and East Asia. The chapter concludes with the argument that political violence, in the form of terrorism and insurgencies, has been a persistent and enduring security challenge in Asia and from the evidence thus far, will remain the case for the foreseeable future.

## Terrorism challenges in Asia

The terrorism/insurgent challenge in Asia is broad and diverse, affecting South, Southeast and East Asia. The conceptual difficulty is differentiating between terrorism and insurgency. According to Dennis Pluchinsky, the key factor determining whether a group is an insurgent group is "whether or not it directly controls or has significant influence over a particular piece of territory", compared to terrorist groups, which do not control territory (Pluchinsky 2006: 42). Insurgent groups therefore aim to set up what is in effect a counter-government in territory that they are able to wrest from the control of the central government.

State responses to terrorism and insurgency have varied according to the nature of the threat. Crelinsten has developed a matrix which encapsulates the continuum in terrorism violence in which more individual acts of violence are traditionally treated as crimes, and those which involve larger numbers of people and weaponry, are treated more as war. Thus, there are usually two models of counter-terrorism: the criminal justice model of counter-terrorism and the war model of counter-terrorism. In the former, which treats terrorism as a crime, the rule of law is paramount, while in a war model, terrorism is treated as war (Crelinsten 2002: 84–87). Treating terrorism as crime suggests a strategy that is designed to limit the frequency of actions and to reduce their destructiveness. Treating terrorism as war militarizes it, creates stresses on civil liberties, and can lead to the expansion of the terrorist challenge (Lutz and Lutz 2013: 295). Treating terrorism as war often includes the use of paramilitary forces and extrajudicial measures, such as extrajudicial killings.

In a full-blown insurgency involving fairly large numbers of combatants intent on seizing territory and forming some kind of counter-government, however, counterinsurgency is usually waged by the state against the insurgents. This normally involves the military and the use of conventional weapons systems including armour, artillery, the air force and military special forces. Today, it is considered best practice, following the lessons of the Malayan Emergency in the 1950s and more recent counterinsurgency campaigns in Iraq and Afghanistan by Western forces, to adopt a comprehensive approach to counterinsurgency. This consists of political, economic, security and information measures designed to win over the population and reinforce the legitimacy of the affected government. Crucially, non-military means are regarded as the most effective elements, with military forces playing an enabling role (*Counterinsurgency Guide* 2009: 2).

The following section evaluates the effectiveness of counterterrorism and counterinsurgency responses by the affected states in all three sub-regions in Asia, namely, South, Southeast and East Asia.

## South Asia: Threat and response

It is clear that of the three key sub-regions of Asia, the terrorist/insurgent challenges are most severe in South Asia, compared to East or Southeast Asia. In South Asia, the situation in Afghanistan is particularly serious. There, an intense insurgency has been waged against the US-imposed regime in Kabul by the Taliban since 2001. Afghanistan is a multi-ethnic state which has never had the attributes of a Weberian state. Instead, it is a patchwork of often warring ethnic groups such as the Pastun, Tajik, Hazara, Uzbek and others. After the terrorist attacks in the United States on 9–11, the Taliban regime's alliance with Al Qaeda led to the US attack and occupation of the country in late 2001. This resulted in a US-imposed regime led by Hamid Karzai in 2002, and the establishment of the NATO-led International Security Assistance Force or ISAF, which then waged the subsequent counterinsurgency against the Taliban (BBC News 2016).

The end of the ISAF mission at the end of 2014 placed the onus of counterinsurgency on the Afghan National Army (ANA), which proved to be unequal to the task given the ease with which Taliban insurgents were able to overrun Kunduz in September 2015 (*Al Jazeera* 2015). The emergence of the Islamic State in mid-2014 in Afghanistan, where it now has an estimated 3,000 fighters, has added to the insurgent threat (VOA News 2017). The severity of the violence can be seen from the huge number of casualties as a result of what is in effect an Afghan civil war. According to the Costs of War project, some 111,000 people have been killed and more than 116,000 injured in Afghanistan from 2001 to mid-2016 (Costs of War 2016). The severity of the violence and continuing weaknesses in the ANA have meant that the United States still retained 15,000 troops in the country in March 2018, as the situation on the ground continued to deteriorate (Foxnews.com 2018).

Afghanistan has been a classic counterinsurgency theatre. The lessons of Western counterinsurgency (or "classic counterinsurgency") have been well-summarised by the likes of Frank Kitson, David Galula, Robert Thompson and others (Kitson 1971; Galula 1964; Thompson 1966). In particular, Sir Robert Thompson's five principles of counterinsurgency, distilled through British success in defeating insurgency during the Malayan Emergency in the 1950s, have been especially influential. These five principles are: the government must have a clear political aim; the government must function within the law; the government must have an overall plan; the government must give priority to defeating the political subversion, not the guerrillas; and finally, in the guerrilla phase of an insurgency, a government must secure its base areas first (Mumford 2010: 180–190).

The problem is that counterinsurgency in Afghanistan has been problematic for a number of reasons. The US and Western objective of a functioning unitary Weberian state in Afghanistan after the US-led attack in late 2001 was always going to be challenging given the patchwork nature of the country's complex tribal and ethnic alliances. Rising insurgent attacks since ISAF troops began their withdrawal in 2014 demonstrated that the insurgents have been able to continue to attract support by shifting their propaganda from resisting foreign occupation to confronting the "puppet" government in Kabul, a line that resonates in many tribal areas since the regime in Kabul was indeed initially put into place by a foreign Western invasion force in 2001 (ICG 2014). According to the International Crisis Group (ICG), historical feuds and unresolved local grievances have worsened after being temporarily contained by the presence of ISAF forces, while mistreatment of Afghans at the hands of government forces has fed the insurgency. Pakistan has also not reduced safe havens for the Afghan Taliban (ICG 2014).

The government has thus not functioned within the law nor has it managed to secure its own base areas. The government has also failed to adopt a more comprehensive approach to counterinsurgency, instead emphasising a "kill and capture" approach that has led to the alienation of sections of the local population (Schmeidl 2016). Worse, the infighting within the government has not led to a coherent strategy towards the insurgents. The bitterly contested national election in 2014 led to months of intense politicking before Ashraf Ghani was appointed as president as part of a power-sharing deal (*New York Times* 2014). The result has been a country that remains fragile and unstable, in spite of over US$110 billion in US non-military aid since 2001, more than the cost of the Marshall Plan that rebuilt a devastated Europe after World War Two. More seriously, nearly 70 percent of Afghanistan's annual income is dependent upon international donors, with around 42 percent of this going to defence (*Al Jazeera* 2016). Indeed, the severity of the violence and continuing weaknesses in the ANA have meant that the United States still retained 15,000 troops in the country as in March 2018 (Foxnews.com 2018).

The other major theatre in South Asia is Pakistan. After the terrorist attacks in the United States on 9–11, Pakistan made available its military facilities for the US attack on Afghanistan, and also undertook domestic counter-terrorism operations against Al Qaeda, arresting over 1,000 of its operatives and leaders (Gunaratna and Iqbal 2011: 267). However, the subsequent rise of militancy in the country has plunged it into a near-state of civil war. From 2003 to 2016, an estimated 60,000 terrorists/insurgents, security personnel and civilians have been killed (Zahid 2016). There has been a string of major terrorist attacks, including the deadly attack on an army school in the Peshawar in 2014, leading to the deaths of 141 people, the majority children, and attacks in Quetta that killed 60 lawyers and 61 police cadets in 2016 (BBC News 2014; Jamal 2016).

The government's response to the terrorist threat has been mixed. Pakistan has banned a number of terrorist groups and military counterinsurgency operations have been carried out in the northwestern provinces (namely, the Federally Administered Tribal Areas or FATA) bordering Afghanistan, where Pakistan Taliban militants have found sanctuary. After the deadly army school attack in 2014, the government responded to the public outcry by promulgating a new counter-terrorism policy known as the National Action Plan (NAP). Under the Plan, convicted terrorists would be executed, special courts created to try terrorism suspects and measures would be taken to counter hate speech and extremist material, among other measures (Zahid 2016).

The use of the war model of counter-terrorism as well as counterinsurgency, not surprising as the military has dominated counter-terrorism policies and responses, has been problematic for a number of reasons. The first is the lack of any coherent policy on counter-terrorism. This reflects the lack of a national political consensus on strategy, which in turn has been the result of constant politicking amongst the political parties as well as by the military, a very powerful institution in Pakistan. Pakistan's political leadership, including its government, has continued to woo various sectarian and militant groups, which continue to operate openly even though they are supposed to be banned under the NAP (Jamal 2016). As the ICG reported, the military has continued to distinguish between "bad" jihadi groups, such as those targeting the security forces, and "good" jihadi groups, such as those that could promote Pakistan's strategic objectives in India and Afghanistan. Thus, the Jumaat-ud-Dawa (formerly known as Lashkar-e-Tayyaba or LeT, which is banned), has expanded its activities in the country through charity fronts, while militant Afghan insurgents such as the Haqqani network, have not been targeted in counterinsurgency operations in the FATA region (ICG 2015: i).

Another problem has been the constant denial over the strategic nature of the terrorist challenge, despite the many terrorist attacks and the high number of casualties, a result of the inconsistent approach to dealing with militant elements in the country. Thus, the Quetta terrorist attacks were attributed to support from Afghanistan (Jamal 2016), and the military insists that the Islamic State has not made any inroads into Pakistan, despite the fact that leaders of the banned Tehrik-e-Taliban (TTP) and the Lashkar-e-Jhangvi have pledged allegiance to it (Jamal 2016; Rana 2015). The lack of conviction in dealing with the terrorism problem as an existential threat to the Pakistan state is reflected in the weakness of the judicial system which has had very low conviction rates for terrorism offences (Zaidi 2016). Although the death penalty has been reinstituted, the vast majority of executions have been for crimes unrelated to terrorism, and military courts which have been set up to speed up the process of dealing with terrorism cases, have undermined constitutional protections and due process (ICG 2015: i).

Shahjehan has also observed that the government has not pursued some of the promised objectives of the NAP, such as reforms to religious boarding schools or *madrassas*, no differentiation among the terrorist groups, reform of the judicial system and rehabilitation programs (Shahjehan 2016). Similarly, the ICG adjudged that "efforts to regulate the *madrasa* sector, curb hate speech and block terrorist financing have been haphazard at best" (ICG 2015: ii). Moreover, emblematic of the military's influential role in the country, including in counter-terrorism, coordination between the military and police has remained poor (Lieven 2017: 174).

On the other hand, Pakistan has learnt from its earlier counterinsurgency failures in the FATA region. Offensives prior to 2009 were characterised by the blunt application of military force, including the use of scorched earth policies, with little systematic development aid provided to conflict-afflicted areas nor effective efforts to secure the support of locals. These alienated local people and led to the rise of militancy in those areas (Jones 2010: xiv–xv).

After 2009, improved counterinsurgency strategies accompanied by a considerable amount of construction and development work, especially on communications and schools led by the military's Frontier Works Organisation, have led to success in quelling the insurgency in the FATA areas (Lieven 2017: 174). In Baluchistan, where there remains insurgent violence, the containment of the violence has been successful enough for China to develop road, rail and energy links from western China through Pakistan to the Baluchistan port of Gwadar on the Arabian Sea in a multi-billion dollar investment (Lieven 2017: 167).

Thus, the picture in Pakistan is mixed. Counterinsurgency operations appear to have succeeded in containing the terrorist problem in the FATA regions and in Baluchistan, but militant and sectarian groups continue to operate in the Pakistan heartland, including in the major cities, posing a growing threat to the country's security, given recent deadly terrorist attacks. This is the historical legacy of the government having promoted such movements in the past, and failing today to recognise the strategic challenge that militant and sectarian groups pose to the Pakistan state. The lack of a coherent counter-terrorism strategy remains a stumbling block, but this reflects the lack of a national consensus on how to deal with the militants. As Ahmad Rashid noted, "Pakistan blames its neighbours for terrorism instead of co-operating with them in fighting it, and uses militants as an appendage to foreign policy", observing as well that the army and the civilian government "have different agendas towards the militant groups which makes establishing a united front difficult ... the failure of the state to adopt a common strategy and a believable narrative is emboldening the terrorists, weakening the state and making solutions harder to find" (Rashid 2017).

Finally, India, too has had to deal with terrorist and insurgent challenges. However, compared to Pakistan, India has far more resources and much better governance, enabling it to contain these problems within acceptable boundaries. Like Pakistan, India has in fact suffered rather large casualties, totalling around 66,000 from 1994 to mid-2017. These consisted of 31,000 terrorists/insurgents, 25,000 civilians and almost 10,000 security personnel (South Asia Terrorism Portal). A senior Indian military officer has categorised the terrorist threat to India as falling into four main categories. According to Vice-Air Marshal Arjun Subramaniam, these are: transnational terror networks, organised crime syndicates, proxy groups, and indigenous outfits. Transnational terrorist networks refer to those formed by Al Qaeda and Taliban, while organised crime syndicates have obtained sanctuary in Pakistan and financed attacks in India. Proxy groups refer to militant groups such as the Lashkar-e-Taiba (LeT), Jaish-e-Mohammad (JeM) and the Harkat-ul-Jihad-Islami (HUJI) which have received funding from Pakistan's intelligence agencies. Finally, there are local terrorist/insurgent groups including left-wing extremists who have been involved in insurgencies but have now resorted to terror attacks after failing to attract mass support (Subramaniam 2012: 400–402).

Left-wing extremist violence can be traced to the Naxalite rebellion in 1967 in West Bengal. The current threat stems from the Communist Party of India (Maoist), which numbers around 8,500 in 2017 and has a presence in the "Red Corridor" states of Chhattisgarh, Odisha, Jharkhand, Bihar and Andhra Pradesh. The massive deployment of army, police and paramilitary forces has resulted in the dwindling strength of the Maoists (*Al Jazeera* 2017). Apart from Maoist rebels, there are also separatist movements in the northeast Indian states of Assam, Manipur, Nagaland and Tripura, where there remain strong sentiments favouring either autonomy or independence in these states, as they are only tenuously linked to the Indian state by a narrow strip of land known as the Siliguri Corridor (Bhaumik 2007).

Of particular concern today are terrorist groups operating in Jammu and Kashmir, which are disputed territory with Pakistan. The Kashmir problem arose when India intervened in 1947 at the request of the prince of Kashmir, Hari Singh, who faced attacks from tribesmen backed by Pakistan. Since then, Pakistan has contested India's control over the territory. Growing dissatisfaction by young Kashmiris in the 1980s to Indian rule led to the outbreak of a separatist insurgency in the 1990s led by militant groups such as the Hizb-ul-Mujahideen which Pakistan has supported (Murphy 2012: 123). In its initial phase in the mid-1990s, the insurgency was fairly widespread in Kashmir, with a large number of attacks taking place. However, counter-insurgency operations by the military have gradually reduced the threat (BBC News 2012).

Today, the main threat comes from two groups in particular. The first is the LeT, which was responsible for the spectacular attack on the Indian parliament in Delhi in 2001, and the Mumbai attacks in 2008 which killed 165 people. Pakistan banned the group in 2002. The group has continued its attempts to infiltrate into Indian-administered Kashmir (BBC News 2012). The second is the Hizb-ul-Mujahideen, which continues to attract adherents. The death of one of its leaders, Burhan Wani, at the hands of the security forces in 2016 led to mass protests, with over 50,000 people turning up for his funeral procession (Dasgupta 2016).

The combination of counter-terrorism by war and the use of counter-insurgency to deal with the problem of terrorism and insurgency has seen mixed progress. While it has reduced the threat of insurgency in Jammu, Kashmir, the "Red Corridor" states and northeast India, it has paradoxically led to an increase in small-scale terrorist attacks on soft targets in urban areas, bypassing the Indian Army altogether. The police and paramilitary forces have thus struggled to cope as they lack the training, equipment and "public-centric" focus to cope with the changed threat environment (Subramaniam 2012: 405, 407).

Another problem has been the failure to go beyond blaming Pakistan for terrorist attacks. This has resulted in the failure to articulate a counter-terrorism strategy that can take into account the changing threat landscape, such as the emergence of the Islamic State in Tamil Nadu, Karnataka and Maharashtra, and the fact that a number of terrorist groups are no longer under the control of Pakistan (Narain and Rajakumar 2016). As well, even counterinsurgency operations have been mostly kinetic and military in focus, with a more comprehensive people-centric strategy adopted only in 2006. Even then, it has not been applied effectively in Kashmir, leading to a generation of disaffected youth ready to join anti-India terrorist/insurgent groups (Ray 2016).

## The rest of Asia: Threat and response

Compared to South Asia, both Southeast and East Asia face less serious terrorism/insurgency challenges, though they have also involved relatively large numbers of casualties. In Burma (Myanmar), ethnic minorities living along its periphery rebelled against the central government upon independence in 1948. These rebellions involved the Kachin, Karen, Mon, Shan, Chin and other ethnic minorities fighting against majority Burman rule, and have continued to the present-day (Smith 2007: 293–296). The Burmese army carried out counterinsurgency operations under its kinetically oriented "Four Cuts" strategy which was marked by severe human rights abuses, such as summary executions, rape and forced labour, leading to large numbers of internally displaced persons (Human Rights Watch 2007).

The political reforms from 2011 carried out by President Thein Sein led to the end of military rule when Aung San Suu Kyi's National League for Democracy (NLD) overwhelmingly won the national elections in 2015, though the military remains a powerful institution. This has helped in the reconciliation process, as the NLD has appointed ethnic Karen, Kachin and Chin to important positions in the newly elected parliament (Paode 2017). However, despite efforts at resolving ethnic minority issues through the "21st Century Panglong Union Peace Conference" process, the new democratic government has continued to face armed resistance from the Northern Alliance, which includes the powerful Kachin Independence Army as well as a renewed insurgency by Muslim Rohingyas rebelling against decades of persecution, with the powerful armed forces continuing to carry out counter-insurgency operations against such groups (Frontier Myanmar 2017). The government's very tough approach to dealing with the Rohingyas, in particular, has sparked worldwide condemnation over alleged "ethnic cleansing" that has also led to a huge refugee crisis, with some 700,000 fleeing to neighbouring Bangladesh (BBC News 2018).

The Philippines has also faced insurgencies from both the Maoist New People's Army (NPA), the armed wing of the Communist Party of the Philippines (CPP), as well as Muslim Moro separatists in the south. The Maoist insurgency, which broke out in 1968, has claimed over 30,000 lives, with enduring socio-economic disparities ensuring its continuation to the present-day. Despite waging counterinsurgency for decades, the armed forces have not been able to defeat the NPA. The presidential electoral victory of Rodrigo Duterte in 2016, however, changed the dynamics on the ground, as Duterte has purported communist sympathies. In August 2016, the CPP and the government agreed, under Norway's mediation, to an indefinite ceasefire to facilitate final peace negotiations. However, this proved short-lived, as a number of violent incidents led to its breakdown in early 2017 (Rappler.com 2017).

The other long-running insurgency has been the Moro Muslim separatist insurgency which began in 1972. In March 2014, however, a final peace agreement was signed between the government and the Moro Islamic Liberation Front (MILF), after the conflict had claimed over 100,000 lives (Rappler.com 2015). The end of the MILF's insurgency appears to vindicate the new comprehensive counterinsurgency strategy adopted by the Philippine Armed Forces in 2011. Unlike the previous kinetic approach which included extra-judicial killings, the new strategy has been designed for "winning the peace", to be achieved through greater transparency, an end to human rights violations, the promotion of good governance, less use of large-scale military operations, and greater emphasis on non-military tactics, including development and other measures designed to address the underlying fundamental causes of conflict (Zenn 2010).

However, the problem is the presence of militant Islamist groups such as the Abu Sayyaf as well as the presence of private militias in the south. In May 2017, militants who have sworn allegiance to the Islamic State also took over parts of the southern city of Marawi, leading to fierce clashes with the armed forces (*Guardian* 2017). The Islamic State, which has attracted adherents in the south, has an estimated 1,200 fighters and is clearly a growing terrorist threat to the country (Channel News Asia 2017).

In Thailand, bouts of low-level insurgency have occasionally broken out since the Malay Muslim provinces in the south were annexed by Thailand in 1909. In the 1980s, a more comprehensive approach emphasising accommodation and development was adopted which led to a sharp reduction in violence. However, the strongman tactics adopted by the Thaksin administration from 2001 led to a renewed insurgency which has claimed 6,500 lives since 2004 (Pongsudhirak 2007: 267–269; Reuters 2017). Thailand's counter-insurgency strategy in the 1980s had been innovative in its adoption of the comprehensive approach, involving an emphasis on socio-economic programs in combination with traditional security measures, which had previously led to the defeat of the country's communist insurgency. However, the problem in southern Thailand today is that the military's counterinsurgency has suffered due to the lack of political direction and cohesion as a result of the political infighting in Bangkok between pro and anti-Thaksin forces (Kassam 2014). The insurgency has thus continued, albeit at a low-level.

The terrorist challenge and response in Indonesia, Malaysia and Singapore has been dealt with in some detail in an earlier chapter, suffice to note here that Malaysia and Singapore have gone beyond a criminal justice approach to dealing with it, by adopting indefinite preventive detention as well as compulsory religious rehabilitation. This very proactive approach, which has led to the detention without trial of all suspected militants, has undoubtedly pre-empted an undetermined number of terrorist attacks. As a democracy, Indonesia has largely practiced a criminal justice approach to counter-terrorism, but the robust operations of its counter-terrorism police force, Densus 88, which has resulted in the deaths of a large number of militant suspects in shoot-outs, suggests the use of extra-judicial measures.

Unlike the robust and proactive judicial and preventive detention laws that exist in Malaysia and Singapore, Indonesia has generally been reactive in its response to terrorist threats. However, in May 2018, after years of debate, and two weeks after terrorist attacks on Christian churches in Surabaya, Indonesia finally passed a revised law on terrorism. While still short of preventive detention, it strengthened the laws on terrorism. Under the new law, anyone suspected of planning a terrorist attack can be detained without charge for a maximum of 21 days, compared to seven days previously, and pre-trial-detention was now extended from 180 to 290 days. Furthermore, anyone who is a member of a "terrorist organisation" could also be jailed for up to seven years (Asianews.it 2018).

Following the first Islamic State attack in Jakarta in January 2016, Indonesia has been deliberating on strengthening its counter-terrorism laws to include giving the military a greater role in counter-terrorism, revoking the citizenship of terrorists, strengthening anti-hate legislation and preventive detention for up to six months without trial. However, no final decision has been made due to criticisms over the erosion of human rights and concern over giving the military a greater role (*Jakarta Post* 2017).

Finally, China has faced a series of terrorist attacks from disaffected Muslim Uighurs in Xinjiang, after it forcibly crushed the short-lived state of East Turkistan and re-established control in 1949. Thereafter, the large-scale influx of Han Chinese and fears over the erosion of their language and culture have led to periodic outbursts of violence. In recent years, both Al Qaeda and the Islamic State have openly targeted China over its treatment of its Muslim Uighurs (BBC News 2015). China's government has pursued a comprehensive approach towards the Uighur problem, through enhanced regional economic growth, stronger internal security capabilities and more robust control over ethnic and religious activities (Tanner and Bellacua 2016: iii). However, a number of recent deadly terrorist attacks, such as the March 2014 mass knifing attack in Kunming that killed 29 people and wounded 130, has galvanised China to take tough counterterrorism measures (CNN 2014). This has included a crackdown on religious practices, increased surveillance, and a strong police presence in Xinjiang (BBC News 2015). China's approach thus goes well beyond the criminal justice approach but is short of full-blown counterinsurgency. In other words, China has practiced counterterrorism by war, using a full range of extra-judicial measures and paramilitary forces to counter the terrorist violence. This has kept violence within limits, but has not resolved the underlying grievances of the Uighurs.

## Conclusions

Counter-terrorism responses in Asia have thus varied according to the scale of the terrorist/insurgent challenge. The diverse and complex nature of the terrorist challenge in Asia has meant that a variety of responses have been adopted by states in the region. They include the criminal justice approach to counter-terrorism, the war model of counter-terrorism, and the waging of counterinsurgency operations. However, in some cases, the effectiveness of counter-terrorism and counterinsurgency have been affected by the lack of legitimacy, governance issues, national politics, and the failure to adopt a comprehensive approach that could win over the population as well as address underlying grievances.

It is clear that the threat is most serious in South Asia, where Afghanistan has had to rely on Western military and economic aid to counter the Taliban insurgency. While Pakistan has managed to impose state control over the restive FATA provinces, it is also awash with militant groups. Indeed, the terrorist threat in the urban heartland has grown over time, to the extent that Pakistan appears to be struggling to contain the terrorist challenge. India has also suffered greatly from a variety of terrorist and insurgent groups but it does possess much more resources to deal with the threats and to contain them through a mixture of strategies, including the use of counterinsurgency. Yet, problems of state legitimacy continue to exist long after independence in 1947, namely, in Kashmir, the north-eastern states and in the eastern states affected by Maoist insurgencies. It is thus not surprising, given the severity of the terrorist challenges, that states in South Asia, namely Afghanistan, Pakistan and India, have adopted a combination of terrorism by war and/or counterinsurgency in dealing with the threat.

Southeast Asia has also suffered from terrorism and insurgent threats. The problems in southern Thailand, the southern Philippines and Burma (Myanmar), while somewhat contained today, are historical and deep-seated, involving various minorities that have never wanted to be part of the central state. Terrorist challenges in Indonesia are clearly present but despite terrorist attacks by militants linked to Al Qaeda and the Islamic State, they are of much smaller scale and intensity than in Pakistan or India. This indicates that Indonesia, the world's largest Muslim country as well as a functioning democracy, has done relatively well to contain, though not eradicate militant violence. Malaysia and Singapore have been proactive and have demonstrated the efficacy of preventive detention in disrupting terrorist plots and preventing attacks. While all three have essentially adopted counterterrorism through the judicial system, they have in fact moved away from it, through the use of preventive detention in the cases of Malaysia and Singapore, and evidence of extra-judicial killings in the case of Indonesia. In the case of China, the enormous resources available to what is today the world's second largest economy has meant that it has been able to impose authoritarian control over Xinjiang and contain though not solve the terrorist problem.

What the above analysis demonstrates is that terrorism and insurgency in Asia have been persistent, enduring and in some cases, severe. Sustained counterterrorism and counterinsurgency have generally led to the problem being contained, in some cases, with difficulty. However, its very persistence, for various reasons that is not within the scope of this article, suggests that political violence in the form of terrorism and insurgencies in Asia is an enduring, long-term challenge. This means that countering terrorism will always be a security challenge for a number of states in the region.

## References

*Al Jazeera* (2015), "Poor Leadership Blamed for Kunduz Fall: Report", 22 November, available at http://www.aljazeera.com/news/2015/11/poor-leadership-blamed-kunduz-fall-report-151121153803402.html accessed 21 August 2018.

*Al Jazeera* (2016), "World Donors Pledge $15 billion for Afghanistan", 6 October, available at http://www.aljazeera.com/news/2016/10/afghanistan-aid-donors-pledge-billions-brussels-161005130723718.html accessed 21 August 2018.

*Al Jazeera* (2017), "India's Maoist Rebels: An Explainer", 27 April, available at http://www.aljazeera.com/indepth/features/2017/04/india-maoist-rebels-explainer-170426132812114.html accessed 21 August 2018.

Asianews.it (2018), "Jakarta Approves the New Anti-Terrorism Law in Wake of Surabaya Attacks", 26 May, available at http://www.asianews.it/news-en/Jakarta-approves-the-new-anti-terrorism-law-in-wake-of-Surabaya-attacks-43995.html accessed 21 August 2018.

BBC (2016), Afghanistan Profile, 11 February, available at http://www.bbc.com/news/world-south-asia-12011352 accessed 21 August 2018.

BBC News (2012), "Who Are the Kashmir Militants?" 1 August, available at http://www.bbc.com/news/world-asia-18738906 accessed 21 August 2018.

BBC News (2014), "Pakistan Taliban: Peshawar School Attack Leaves 141 Dead", 16 December, available at http://www.bbc.com/news/world-asia-30491435 accessed 21 August 2018.

BBC News (2015), "Xinjiang: Has China's Crackdown on Terrorism Worked?" 2 January, available at http://www.bbc.com/news/world-asia-30373877 accessed 21 August 2018.

BBC News (2018), "Myanmar Rohingya: What You Need to Know about the Crisis", 24 April, available at https://www.bbc.com/news/world-asia-41566561 accessed 21 August 2018.

Bhaumik, Subir (2007), "Insurgencies in India's Northeast: Conflict, Co-option and Change", July, No. 10, Washington Working Papers, Washington, DC: East-West Center.

Channel News Asia (2017), "Indonesia Says 1,200 Islamic State Operatives in Philippines", 4 June, available at http://www.channelnewsasia.com/news/asiapacific/indonesia-says-1-200-islamic-state-operatives-in-philippines-8910832 accessed 21 August 2018.

CNN (2014), "Knife-Wielding Attackers Kill 29, Injure 130 at China Train Station", 3 March, available at http://edition.cnn.com/2014/03/01/world/asia/china-railway-attack/index.html accessed 21 August 2018.

Costs of War (2016), *Update on the Human Costs of War for Afghanistan and Pakistan, 2001 to Mid-2016*, available at http://watson.brown.edu/costsofwar/files/cow/imce/papers/2016/War%20in%20Afghanistan%20and%20Pakistan%20UPDATE_FINAL_corrected%20date.pdf accessed 21 August 2018.

Kitson, Frank (1971), *Low Intensity Operations: Subversion, Insurgency, Peacekeeping*, Harrisburg, PA: Stackpole Books.

Counterinsurgency Guide, United States (2009), available at https://www.state.gov/documents/organization/119629.pdf accessed 21 August 2018.

Crelinsten, R. D. (2002), "Analysing Terrorism and Counter-Terrorism: A Communication Model", *Terrorism and Political Violence*, 14(2).

Dasgupta, Piyasree (2016), "Who Was Burhan Wani and Why is Kashmir Mourning Him?" *Huffington Post*, 7 November, available at http://www.huffingtonpost.in/burhan-wani/who-was-burhan-wani-and-why-is-kashmir-mourning-him_a_21429499/ accessed 21 August 2018.

Frontier Myanmar (2017), "Mixed Results at Latest Panglong Peace Conference", 30 May, available at http://frontiermyanmar.net/en/mixed-results-at-latest-panglong-peace-conference accessed 21 August 2018.

Foxnews.com (2018), "16 Years On, US Military Presence in Afghanistan Growing", 12 March, available at http://www.foxnews.com/us/2018/03/12/16-years-on-us-military-presence-in-afghanistan-growing.html accessed 21 August 2018.
Galula, David (1964), *Counterinsurgency Warfare: Theory and Practice*, New York: Praeger.
*Guardian* (2017), "Explainer: How and Why Islamic State-linked Rebels Took over Part of a Philippine City", 29 May, available at https://www.theGuardian.com/world/2017/may/29/explainer-how-and-why-islamic-state-took-over-part-of-a-philippine-city accessed 21 August 2018.
Gunaratna, Rohan, and Khuram Iqbal (2011), *Terrorism in Pakistan*, London: Reaktion Books.
Human Rights Watch (2007), "Burma: Army Attacks Displace Hundreds of Thousands", 25 October, available at https://www.hrw.org/news/2007/10/25/burma-army-attacks-displace-hundreds-thousands accessed 21 August 2018.
ICG (International Crisis Group) (2014), *Afghanistan's Insurgency after the Transition*, Asia Report No. 256, 12 May, available at https://d2071andvip0wj.cloudfront.net/afghanistan-s-insurgency-after-the-transition.pdf accessed 21 August 2018.
ICG (International Crisis Group) (2015), "Revisiting Counter-Terrorism Strategies in Pakistan: Opportunities and Pitfalls", Asia Report No. 271, 22 July, available at https://d2071andvip0wj.cloudfront.net/271-revisiting-counter-terrorism-strategies-in-pakistan-opportunities-and-pitfalls.pdf accessed 21 August 2018.
*Jakarta Post* (2017), "Antiterrorism Bill Threatens Law Enforcement System", 6 January, available at http://www.thejakartapost.com/academia/2017/01/06/antiterrorism-bill-threatens-law-enforcement-system.html accessed 21 August 2018.
Jamal, Umair (2016), "Quetta Police College Attack Highlights Pakistan's Internal Divisions", 31 October, available at http://thediplomat.com/2016/10/quetta-police-college-attack-highlights-pakistans-internal-divisions/ accessed 21 August 2018.
Jones, Seth G. and C. Christine Fair (2010), *Counterinsurgency in Pakistan*, RAND: Santa Monica, CA.
Kassam, Sabrin (2014), "The Thai Way of Counter-Insurgency", *IISS Voices*, 3 November, available at https://www.iiss.org/en/iiss%20voices/blogsections/iiss-voices-2014-b4d9/november-4b85/the-thai-way-of-counter-insurgency-35d3 accessed 21 August 2018.
Lieven, Anatol (2017), "Counter-Insurgency in Pakistan: The Role of Legitimacy", *Small Wars and Insurgencies*, 28(1).
Lutz, James, and Brenda Lutz (2013), *Global Terrorism*, Abingdon, Oxford: Routledge.
Mumford, Andrew (2010), "Sir Robert Thompson's Lessons for Iraq: Bringing the 'Basic Principles of Counter-Insurgency' Into the 21st Century", *Defence Studies*, 10 (1–2).
Murphy, Eamon (2012), *The Making of Terrorism in Pakistan: Historical and Social Roots of Extremism*, London: Routledge.
Narain, Akanksha, and Vikram Rajakumar (2016), "Revamping India's Counter-Terrorism Approach", RSIS Commentary, No. 71, 4 April available at https://www.rsis.edu.sg/wp-content/uploads/2016/04/CO16071.pdf accessed 21 August 2018.
*New York Times* (2014), "Afghan Presidential Rivals Finally Agree on Power-Sharing Deal", 20 September, available at https://www.nytimes.com/2014/09/21/world/asia/afghan-presidential-election.html?_r=0 accessed 21 August 2018.

Paode A. (2017), "Why Myanmar's New Peace Process Is Failing", *The Diplomat*, 4 March, available at http://thediplomat.com/2017/03/why-myanmars-new-peace-process-is-failing/ accessed 21 August 2018.

Pluchinsky, Dennis (2006), "Ethnic Terrorism: Themes and Variations", in Andrew T. H. Tan, ed., *The Politics of Terrorism*, London: Routledge.

Pongsudhirak, Thitinan (2007), "The Malay-Muslim Insurgency in Southern Thailand", in Andrew T. H. Tan, ed., *Handbook of Terrorism and Insurgency in Southeast Asia*, Cheltenham, UK: Edward Elgar.

Rana, Muhammad Amir (2015), "The Impact of the Islamic State on Pakistan", Norwegian Peacebuilding Resource Centre, January, available at http://www.peacebuilding.no/var/ezflow_site/storage/original/application/049ee274000481e510fd0414ba61d63b.pdf accessed 21 August 2018.

Rappler.com (2015), "Infographic: From Marcos to Aquino: The Cost of War in Mindanao", 8 October, available at http://www.rappler.com/move-ph/issues/mindanao/107585-marcos-aquino-cost-war-mindanao accessed 21 August 2018.

Rappler.com (2017), "NPA Ends Ceasefire but Says Talks Should Continue", 1 February, available at http://www.rappler.com/nation/160132-communist-rebels-end-ceasefire-peace-talks accessed 21 August 2018.

Rashid, Ahmed (2017), "Militant Groups Forge Ties as Pakistan Havens Remain", *FT.com*, 24 February, available at http://blogs.ft.com/the-exchange/2017/02/24/militant-groups-forge-ties-as-pakistan-fails-to-tackle-their-havens/ accessed 21 August 2018.

Ray, Ayesha (2016), "The Case for Revising India's Counterinsurgency Strategy in Kashmir", *War on the Rocks*, 14 September, available at https://warontherocks.com/2016/09/the-case-for-revising-indias-counterinsurgency-strategy-in-kashmir/ accessed 21 August 2018.

*Reuters* (2017), "Biggest Insurgent Attack in Years in Thai South Wounds 12 Police", 3 April, available at http://www.*Reuters*.com/article/us-thailand-south-idUSKBN1750TO accessed 21 August 2018.

Schmeidl, Susanne (2016), "ISIS is the Least of Afghanistan's Problems", *The Interpreter*, Lowy Institute, 26 February.

Shahjehan, Hassan (2016), "Pakistan's Counter-Terrorism Policy", *Pakistan Today*, 29 August, available at https://www.pakistantoday.com.pk/2016/08/29/pakistans-counter-terrorism-policy/ accessed 21 August 2018.

Smith, Martin (2007), "Ethnic Conflicts in Burma: From Separatism to Federalism", in Andrew T. H. Tan, ed., *Handbook of Terrorism and Insurgency in Southeast Asia*, Cheltenham, UK: Edward Elgar.

South Asia Terrorism Portal, *India Fatalities: 1994–2017*, available at http://www.satp.org/satporgtp/countries/india/database/indiafatalities.htm accessed 21 August 2018.

Subramaniam, Arjun (2012), "Challenges of Protecting India From Terrorism", *Terrorism and Political Violence*, 24(3).

Tanner, Murray Scot, and James Bellacua (2016), *China's Response to Terrorism*, CNA Analysis and Solutions, available at https://www.uscc.gov/sites/default/files/Research/Chinas%20Response%20to%20Terrorism_CNA061616.pdf accessed 21 August 2018.

Thompson, Robert (1966), *Defeating Communist Insurgency: Experiences in Malaya and Vietnam*, London: Chatto and Windus.

VOA News (2017), "US Forces Vow to Defeat Islamic State in Afghanistan This Year", 22 March, available at http://www.voanews.com/a/us-forces-vow-defeat-islamic-state-afghanistan-this-year/3777755.html accessed 21 August 2018.

Zahid, Farhan (2016), "Counter Terrorism Policy Measures: A Critical Analysis of Pakistan's National Action Plan", *The Mackenzie Institute*, 19 July, available at http://mackenzieinstitute.com/counter-terrorism-policy-measures-a-critical-analysis-of-pakistans-national-action-plan/ accessed 21 August 2018.

Zaidi, Syed Manzar Abbas (2016), *Terrorism Prosecution in Pakistan*, United States Institute of Peace, Washington.

Zenn, Jacob (2010), "Philippine Armed Forces Adopts New Counter-Insurgency Strategy", *Terrorism Monitor*, 8(44), Jamestown Foundation, available at https://jamestown.org/program/philippine-armed-forces-adopts-new-counter-insurgency-strategy/ accessed 21 August 2018.

# Index

Note: Page numbers in *italics* denote references to Figures.

Abdurrahman, Aman 179
Abeygoonasekera, Asanga 224
Abu Bakar, Ismael 156–157
Abu Sayyaf Group (ASG) 36–37, 148, 155–156, 202, 203–204
Abu Sollaman 155
Adime, Wetti 109
*Adivasi* insurgency 8–9
*adivasis* (people living in the forests): displacement of 106; on-going grievances of 103; marginalising 102, 104
Afghanistan: Al-Qaeda sanctuary in 45; building security forces in 62–63; Chinese investment in 53; corruption 50–51; Costs of War project 233; drone strikes in 65–66; foreign intervention in 20; fractured insurgencies 51–53; geographical position of 53–54; identity-based power relationships 48–50; instability, sources of 7–8; insurgencies 232; IS emerging in 4, 232; Islamic State presence in 52–53; kill and capture approach 233; kinetic campaign 65–66; long-term solution in 66; maternal mortality rates 60; militia groups 63–65; negotiated political settlement 66–68; Operation Enduring Freedom 45; parallel governance structures 60; power dynamic in 47–48; Russian concerns on 53; sources of instability in 46–47; Soviet invasion of 77–78, 181; Taliban insurgency 59–60; unemployment rates 60; US counterterrorism mission in 92; US-led invasion of 77–78; US strategy in 46, 54, 66–68; war economy in 22; Western strategy in 8, 58, 233
Afghan Local Police (ALP) 49–50, 64
Afghan National Army (ANA) 4, 232
Afghan National Defence and Security Force (ANDSF) 60, 62–63
Afghan Security Forces (ASF) 46
Ahmadinejad, Mahmoud 81
Ajul, Hadji Muhammad 203
Akilov, Rakhmat 89–90, 97
al-Adnani, Abu Mohammad 94
al-Baghdadi, Abu Bakr 178
al Jamaah al Islamiyah (JI) 197–200
al-Julani, Abu Mohammad 95
All Burman Students' Democratic Front (ABSDF) 133
Almodovar, Montano 203
al Nusra Front 89, 93, 94, 95
Al Qaeda: al Nusra Front 89, 93; declarations of allegiance to 36; approach to international attacks 93–96; Jemaah Islamiah network and 177–178, 180; in Singapore 197; taking refuge in Waziristan region 78; use of e-magazines 33
al Zawahiri, Ayman 90, 95
Anglo-Siamese Treaty of 1909 169
Ansarulah Bangla Team (ABT) 34
Aquino, Benigno, III 147
Aquino Administration, defense goal 147–148
Arakan Army (AA) 140
Arakan Rohingya Salvation Army (ARSA) 142–144
Armed Forces of the Philippines (AFP) 10; counter-insurgency operations 149–150, 203; focus of 147; Marawi

## Index 247

assault 148; modernization program 147–148
armed rebellions *see* rebellions
Arroyo, Gloria Macapagal 147, 153
Ataturk International Airport 86
attraction focused messages 227n2
Aung San Suu Kyi 139, 142
Autonomous Region of Muslim Mindanao (ARMM) 152–153, 203
Azimov, Abror 90
Azimov, Akram 90

Bai, Ansyaad 205
Balcells, Laia 16
Baloch, Jeander 81
Baluchistan Liberation Front (BLF) 80
Baluchistan Liberation United Front (BULF) 80
Baluchistan tribal region 79–81
Baluch Liberation Army (BLA) 80
Baluch Republican Army (BRA) 80
Bangladeshi Supreme Court 37
Bangladesh Jamaat-e-Islami ('Islamic Assembly - JEI) 37–38
*Bangsamoro* Basic Law (BBL) 154
Bangsamoro Islamic Freedom Fighters (BIFF) 156–157
*Bangsamoro* Transition Commission (BTC) 154
Barisan Islam Perberbasan Pattani (BIPP) 162
Barisan Revolusi Nasional (BRN) 162–163, 173–174
Bashir, Abu Bakar 180, 182
*Beidou* GPS system 126
Bertyl Pinto Jayawardene 224
Bharatiya Janata Party (BJP) 9
bin Bahari, Haslin 201
Bishkek, Kyrgyzstan 88–89, 95
blended messages 227n2
BNPT (National Anti-Terrorism Agency) 185–186
Boediono, Prof 205–206
Bonn Agreement 54–55
Brahimi, Lakhar 54
"Bringing People Back Home" program 172
Bureau for the Commissioner General for Rehabilitation (BCGR) 219
Burma *see* Myanmar
Burmese separatism 9

Cambodia, foreign intervention in 20
Camp Darul Iman 158

Central Asian terrorism: categories of 91; decline in 91–92; economic migration and 87; factors for 87; in Germany 91–92; internal factors 86; international expansion of 86–87, 93; misconceptions of 90; split between IS and Al Qaeda 93; terrorist attacks 88–90; *see also* terrorism, terrorist attacks
Central Intelligence Agency (US) 65
Central Reserve Police Force (CRPF) 105
Chandra, Pravir 105
Chan-ocha, Prayuth 169, 173
Chataev, Akhmed 88
Chen Quanguo 120, 122
China: Afghanistan investment 53; banned websites 39–40; Counter-terrorism Law 121; counterterrorism measures 240; cross-border trade 135; face recognition system 125; family planning rules 124; First Xinjian Work Forum 119; implementing people's war strategy 121; national assistance pairing program 124; One Belt, One Road development initiative 120; People's Armed Police (PAP) 121–122; preventing copycat acts 121; Second Xinjiang Work Forum 120; social media state control and censorship 39–40; social revolution of 16; supporting Communist Party of Burma 134; surveillance system 125; Uighur separatists 6; Uyghur community 38–41, 119–120, 240; *see also* Xingjiang, China
China-Pakistan Economic Corridor (CPEC) 53, 80, 81
Chinese Embassy bombing in Bishkek 88–89
civil peace model 16
civil wars: annexations and 19–20; clustering of 17–18; foreign intervention in 18–20; greed argument for 21; human and economic impacts of 14–15; international borders 19; political instability 16; poverty and 20–21; risk factors for 20–21; underlying causes of 15–16; *see also* internal wars
Collier, Paul 21
Communist Party of Burma (CPB) 134–135

# 248  Index

Communist Party of India (Maoist, CPIM) 104; capitalist economy 106; legitimacy of 111; New Democratic Revolution 111; steering insurgency in India 102
Communist Party of India (Marxist Leninist, CPIML) 9, 103
Communist Party of the Philippines (CPP) 149–150, 203, 238
community awareness programs 223–224
community engagement program 200–202, 211 see also reintegration
community reintegration 222–223
Comprehensive Agreement on the Bangsamoro (CAB) 154
Comprehensive Local Integration Program (CLIP) 203
Corporate Social Responsibility (CSR) 210
countering violent extremism (CVE) programs 35, 185–186
counter-insurgencies: abstruse approach 105; dominant approach to 23; enemy-centric approach 107–109; hearts and minds approach to 23; integrated and holistic approach 109–110; kill and capture approach 233; non-kinetic approach 105–106; in Pakistan 235; people-centric approach 106–107; in Thailand 239
counter terrorism: in China 240; criminal justice model of 231–232; evaluating responses 183–186; initiatives 227; intelligence-sharing 99; by Pakistani state 74–75, 78–79, 84, 234–235, 236; rehabilitation program 11–12; religious rehabilitation programs 185; smart approach to 11; social media and 35; soft approaches to 184–185; strategies 214, 227; war model of 231–232
creative arts rehabilitation 197, 221–222
criminal justice model of counter terrorism 231–232, 239
Cuomo, Andrew 98

Darul Islam movement 177, 181–182
data mining 34
decolonisation 5
Deep South Watch 166
Densus 88 182, 184
Deobandism 82
deradicalization 216, 226 see also rehabilitation programs, reintegration
De Visser, Prashan 224

Dewan Pimpinan Parti (DPP) 162
diaspora communities 97
digital media technologies: *Beidou* GPS system 126; enabling terrorism 87; encrypted networking tools 96–97, 98; face recognition system 125; Skynet surveillance system 125; surveillance system 125; Telegram messenger platform 97; virtual dimension of extremist activities 92; WhatsApp 97; *see also* Internet
Duay Jai 171
Duterte, Rodrigo 147, 151–152, 154, 158, 203, 238

East Turkestan Islamic Movement (ETIM) 39, 126, 127
*Economist, The* 151
educational rehabilitation 197
emotion focused messages 227n2
Erawan Shrine, Bangkok 127
Estrada, Joseph 153
ethnic Malay *see* Malay insurgency, Thailand
external wars 18–20

Facebook *see* social media
Federally Administrated Tribal Areas (FATA) 54, 72–73, 84
Filkins, Dexter 50
financial rehabilitation 197
First Xinjian Work Forum (IXWF) 119

GASHIBU (Gerakan Sehari Seribu) program 208–209
Gerakan Mujihideen Islami Pattani (GMIP) 162
Germany 91–92
Ghani, Ashraf 233
Giddens, Anthony 19
greed/grievance debate 20–22, 23
grievance *see* greed/grievance debate
GRP-CPP peace talks 151
GRP-MILF peace process 153–154
GRP-MNLF peace process 152–153
Gunasekera, Kushil 224
Gurr, Ted 21

Haibtullah Akhundzada, Maulawi 52
Han-Uyghur marriages 123–124
Hapilon faction of ASG 156, 158
Haqqani, Jalauddin 52
Haqqani, Siraj 52
Harakah al-Yaqin (Faith Movement) 144

Hariono, Machmudi 208
Harkatul Mujahideen 76
Hataman, Kaiser 203
Hataman, Mujiv 203
hearts and minds program 23, 215–216, 221
Hekmatayr, Gulbuddin 52
Heupel, Monika 22
Hironaka, Ann 19
Hizb-ul-Mujahideen 237
Hizb ut-Tahrir (HT) 34
Hoeffler, Anke 21

ideology, definition of 216
Idris, Irfan 208
Ilham Tohti 129
India: Central Armed Police Forces 109; Central Reserve Police Force (CRPF) 105; communist movement in 103; conflict over Kashmir 72–73, 75–77, 236–237; countering insurgency 105–110; Indian Forest Act of 1878 102; IS operating in 4; local terrorist/insurgent groups 236; Maoist insurgency 5, 8–9; marginalising *adivasis* (people living in the forests) 102, 104; National Investigations Agency (NIA) 109; National Policy and Action Plan 109; Operation Anaconda 108; Operation Green Hunt 108; Operation Monsoon 108; Operation Steeplechase 105; recognising rights of forest dwelling communities 107; regional autonomy 105; Surrender-cum-Rehabilitation Scheme 109; terrorist/insurgent challenges 236; transferring proprietary rights over forests 102; transitioning from colonial to independent status 102–103; *see also adivasis* (people living in the forests), Communist Party of India (Marxist Leninist, CPIML), Maoist insurgencies
Indonesia: Anti-Terrorism Law of 2002 184; arresting suspected terrorists 206; Bali bombing 178; countering violent extremism (CVE) programs 185–186; counter terrorism 182; counter-terrorism efforts in 178; counter terrorism laws 240; criminal justice model of counter terrorism 239; cultural rehabilitation programs 207; Darul Islam movement 177, 181–182; Densus 88 182, 184; education process 207; IS recruitment in 179, 187; National Agency for Combating Terrorism 205–209; prison system 206–207; rehabilitation modes 207–209; rehabilitation program 204–209; suppressing political Islam 182; terrorism laws 239–240; TNI Joint Special Operations Command 184

insurgencies: on-going 4–6; terrorism vs. 231
intelligence-sharing 99
Internal Security Act (ISA) 183, 195
internal wars 14, 17–20 *see also* civil wars
international borders 19
International Center for Political Violence and Terrorism Research (ICPVTR) 201, 204
International Contact Group (ICG) 153
International Crisis Group (ICG) 233
International Monitoring Team (IMT) 153
International Security Assistance Force (ISAF) 4, 46, 61–62
Internet: Counter-terrorism Law and 121; jihadist ideologies on 96–97; terrorists use of 31; *see also* digital media technologies, social media
Inter-services Intelligence Service (ISI) 67, 74
Iran: Baluchistan tribal region and 79–81; Taliban support 67
Islamic Jihad Union (IJU) 91
Islamic Movement of Uzbekistan (IMU) 53, 78, 89
Islamic State (IS): in Afghanistan 232; attacks inspired by 94; BIFF allegiance to 157; global expansion of 209; ideology, spread of 4; in Indonesia 178–179, 187; approach to international attacks 93–96; jihadists declaring support for 179; Kazakh fighters 93; in Malaysia 178–179, 187; in Philippines 239; presence in Afghanistan 52–53; recruitment process 34–35, 179–180; rise of 3–4; in Singapore 178, 180; social media, use of 183, 187; Tajik Jamaat 93; transforming followers 11; use of e-magazines 33; use of social media 34–35, 200; Uyghurs joining 127

Istanbul: Ataturk International Airport 86, 88; Reina nightclub massacre 89, 98

Jaish al-Adl (Army of Justice) 81
Jaish-e-Muhammad (Muhammad's Army) 76
Jamaat Ansarullah (JA) 94
Jamaat-e-Islami ('Islamic Assembly - JEI) 37–38
Jamaat-ud-Dawah 77
Jamiri, Nurhassan 203
Janjalani, Abdurajak 155
Janos, Andrew 16
Jedi, Muhammad Wanndy Mohamed 179–180
Jemaah Islamiah (JI) network 10, 177–178, 181, 186, 204–205
Jihad Concept Explanation Action Committee 185
jihadists: declaring support for IS 179; Middle East insurgency 92–93
Joint Special Operations Task Force Philippines (JSTOF-Philippines) 155
Jones, Sidney 157, 179
Jumaat-ud-Dawa 234
Jundallah (Soldiers of God) 81

Kabul Process 54–55
Kachin Independence Organization (KIO) 137
Kalyvas, Stathis 16
Kamilov, Abdulaziz 97
Kaplan, Robert 22
Karen National Union (KNU) 135, 137, 138
Karnavian, Tito 205
Kartosuwiryo, S.M. 181
Karzai, Ahmed Wali 51
Kateeb al-Imam Shamil (The Imam Shamil Battalion) 90, 95
Kateebat at Tawhid wal Jihad (KTJ) 93
Kateeba Tawhid wal Jihad (KTJ) 88–89
Kateebat Imam Al-Bukhari (KIB) 93
Katibah Nusantara 4
Kato, Ustadz Ameril Umbra 156
Kazakh Jamaat 93
Kemunting Protective Detention Centre 195
Khadafy Janjalani 155
Khadem, Rauf 53
Khan, Datuk Ayob 194
Khor, Laura 193–194
kinetic campaign in Afghanistan 65–66

Kofi Annan 143
Köhler, Daniel 221
Komra, Jageshwar 108
Kyrgyzstan 88–89

Lakhvi, Zakiur Rehman 76–77
Lakshman Kadirgamar Institute for International Relations and Strategic Studies (LKI) 224
Langkawi process 173
Lashkar-e-Baluchistan (LeB) 79
Lashkar-e-Jhangvi (The Army of Jhangvi) 3, 81, 235
Lashkar-e-Taiba (LeT) 73–77, 82, 234, 236–237
Liberation Tigers of Tamil Eelam (LTTE): recruitment process 217; Sri Lanka defeating 214–215; vocational education and training 218
Loas, foreign intervention in 20

Majelis Mujahideen Indonesia (MMI) 182
Malayan Emergency 193–194, 232–233
Malay insurgency: casualty rates 166–167, *166*; death totals 161; description of 162–163; driving out Buddhist community 163–164; eliminating political rivals 164; goals of 163–164; IEDs, use of 164–165, *165*; strategy/tactics of 164–168; Thai government's response to 168–173; threatening Thai economy 162; types of attacks 165; violence decline 166
Malay Muslim separatism 5
Malaysia: brokering GRP-MNLF peace negotiations 153; brokering MARA-Patani agreement 174; Department of Islamic Development (JAKIM) 194–195; deradicalization program 194–197; Internal Security Act 183, 195; IS recruitment in 179–180, 182–183, 187; Jihad Concept Explanation Action Committee 185; Malay insurgency and 164; Police E8 rehabilitation team 196, 197; Prevention of Terrorism Act 183, 196; preventive detention laws 178, 183, 239; rehabilitation program 185; religious rehabilitation 185; Security Offence Act (Special Measures) 2012 195; security risks 196
Malaysian Prisons Department 196
Maoist Communist Centre of India 104

Maoist insurgencies: countering 105–110; decline in 111–112; genesis of 103–105, 238; leaders surrender 108–109; revenue generation for 104–105; strengthening legitimacy 104; *see also* Communist Party of India (Maoist, CPIM)
Marawi City: security after siege 158–159; siege of 4, 157
Markaz Dawa al Irshad 76
Masharipov, Abdulqodir 89, 98
Masood Azhar, Maulana 76
Mattis, James 60
Maute, Abdullah and Omarkhayam 157–158
Maute Group 148, 157–158
Mazumdar, Charu 103
McChrystal, Stanley 61
McMaster, H.R. 60
Mehsud, Baitullah 78
Mehsud, Hakimullah 78–79
Menk, Ismail 201
micro-mobilisation contexts: corruption and governance 50–51; definition of 47; formation of power 47–48; fractured insurgencies 51–53; geopolitical agendas 53–54; identity politics 48–50
migrant vulnerabilities 96–98
militarisation of RSM strategy 65–66, 68
militia groups 63–65
Minimbang, Imman 157
Misuari, Nur 152, 153, 202
mobile phones 33
Mohammed, Mahathir 173
Moro Islamic Liberation Front (MILF) 5, 152–154, 199, 202, 238
Moro Muslim separatist rebellion 5, 238
Moro National Liberation Front (MNLF) 152, 202
Mother of All Bombs (MOAB) 66
Mujahid party 143–144
Murad, Haji 202
Musharraf, Pervez 76
Mutual Aid Society 208
Myanmar: animosity between Buddhists and Muslims 142–143; anti-Islamic sentiment 133; anti-state alliances 138; constitution 136; cross-border trade 135; divide and rule policies 134; Four Cuts strategy 238; influencing anti-state armed resistance 134; minority ethnicities in 133; National Convention 136; National League for Democracy 136, 238; National League for Democracy (NLD) 139–140, 144; Nationwide Ceasefire Agreement 136–138; rebellions 237–238; Robingya issue 142–144; secessionist insurgencies 5; *see also* Myanmar anti-state armed groups
Myanmar anti-state armed groups: agreeing to NCA process 141–142; ceasefire arrangements 135–136; financial activities 134; Kachin Independence Organization 137; Karen National Union 135, 137, 138; National Democratic Front 138; New Mon State Party 137; origins of 133; Restoration Council of Shan State 138; Shan State Army-Restoration Council of Shan State 137; United Nationalities Federal Council 138; United Wa State Army 137
Myanmar National Democratic Alliance Army (MNDAA) 140
MySpace *see* social media

narrowcasting 34, 37
National Coalition Government of the Union of Burma (NCGUB) 133
National Council for Peace and Order (NCPO) 168
National Democratic Front (NDF) 138, 203
National League for Democracy (NLD) 136, 139–140, 144, 238
National Unity Government (NUG) 49, 50–51
nation-state building 5
Nationwide Ceasefire Agreement (NCA) 136–139
Naxalite rebellion 236
negotiated political settlement 66–68
Nehru, Jawaharlal 111
New Mon State Party (MNSP) 137
New People's Army (NPA) 149–152, 203, 238
new wars thesis 21–22
New York truck attack 90, 97–98
Ngruki network of religion school alumnus 180–181
Nicholson, John 60
North Atlantic Treaty Organization (NATO) 58, 62, 68
Northern Distribution Network 53
Nusantara, Katibah 179, 182

Obama administration 61–62
Omar, Mullah 52
online terrorist activities 31
Operation Anaconda 108
Operation Enduring Freedom 45, 75–76
Operation Freedom's Sentinel 58
Operation Green Hunt 108
Operation Monsoon 108
Operation Steeplechase 105
Oram, Jual 110
Organization of Islamic Conference (OIC) 153

Pakistan: Baluchistan tribal region 73, 79–81; banning terrorist groups 234; conflict over Kashmir 72–73, 75–77, 236–237; counter-terrorism and 74–75, 78–79, 84, 234–235, 236; geographic sphere of 72–73; as "Ground Zero" in global terrorism 3–4; improved counterinsurgency strategies 235; as key interlocutor with Taliban 54; National Action Plan 234; Operation Enduring Freedom and 75–76; population of 72; sheltering insurgent groups 45; social transformation of 73–74; state sponsored jihadism 77; supporting jihadi organisations 75, 79; supporting non-state groups 75; terrorism trends in 8; US policy toward 67; vulnerable to terrorist violence 74; worsening violent extremism 74
Pancasila, Klinik 207
Patani Human Rights Network 171
Patani United Liberation Organization (PULO) 162–163
Patek, Umar 31
Paul, Rand 54
People's Republic of China *see* China
People's War Group 104
Philippines: Abu Sayyaf Group (ASG) 36–37, 148, 155–156; Bangsamoro Islamic Freedom Fighters 156–157; Communist Party of the Philippines (CPP) 149–150, 203, 238; Davao night market bombing 157–158; GRP-CPP peace talks 151; GRP-MILF peace process 153–154, 238; GRP-MNLF peace process 152–153, 202; independence of 147; insurgent groups defying government 10, 238; IS recruitment in 239; local integration program 203–204; Marawi siege 4, 152; Maute Group 148, 157–158; Moro Islamic Liberation Front (MILF) 152–154; Moro Muslim separatist rebellion 5; National Defense Department (DND) 151–152; New People's Army 149–152; rehabilitation program 202–204; reintegration of former rebels 203; Southern Philippines Council for Peace and Development (SPCPD) 202–203; Special Zone of Peace and Development (ZOPAD) 202–203
Pillai, G.K. 107, 111
Pluchinsky, Dennis 231
Police Cloud System 125
political settlement 66–68
Popular Uprising militias 64
Porta, Della 47
post-colonial states 19
poverty, relative deprivation and 21
power: absolute corruption of 47–48; social phenomenon of 47–48
Power Transition Theory 23–24n3
Prabhu, Ade 108
Prasad Rao, G.V.K. 108
preventing violent extremism (PVE) programs 35
Prevention of Terrorism Act 2002 (POTA) 108, 196
psychological rehabilitation 197, 221

Quader Molla, Abdul 38
Quetta terrorist attacks 235

radicalization 96–98; community reintegration 222–223; ongoing assessments 221; process of 217–218; reversing process of 218; understanding 216–217; *see also* rehabilitation programs
Rajah Solaiman Movement (RSM) 202
Rakhine Muslims 143
Ramos, Fidel 153
Rao, Koteswara 108
Rashid, Ahmad 236
Ravinder, Chambala 108–109
Razak, Najib 195
Razzik, Abdul 50
rebellions: causes of 20–22; civil peace model and 16; clustering of 17; military power and 16; poverty and 20; *see also* civil wars
recidivism 208, 225
recreational rehabilitation 197

recruitment process, terrorist: attraction focused messages 227n2; blended messages 227n2; emotion focused messages 227n2; in Indonesia 179, 187; Islamic State (IS) 34–35, 179–180; Liberation Tigers of Tamil Eelam (LTTE) 217; in Malaysia 179–180, 187; in Singapore 180; social media and 200
refugee camps 18
refugee flows 18
Regan, Patrick 20
rehabilitation 11–12, 218–219
rehabilitation programs: 5R Model 219; for Abu Sayyaf Group 203–204; ad-hoc and unstructured 209–210; Ahli sunnah Wal Jamaah approach 194; building capabilities 210; community reintegration 222–223; complexities of 210–211; creative arts rehabilitation 197; cultural rehabilitation 207; economic empowerment 208; educational rehabilitation 197; financial rehabilitation 197; hearts and minds approach to 221; in Indonesia 204–209; in Malaysia 193–197; in Philippines 202–204; psychological rehabilitation 197; recidivism in 208; recreational rehabilitation 197; self-radicalised individuals 201; in Singapore 198–200; social and family rehabilitation 197, 200; Special Rehabilitation 194–195; Tafaqquh Fiddin program 194–195; types of 196–197; vocational rehabilitation 197; as weapon against terrorism 193; youth awareness programs 201; *see also* radicalization, reintegration, religious rehabilitation, Sri Lanka rehabilitation program
Reina nightclub attack 89, 98
reintegration: aftercare phase 223; ceremonies 223; of former rebels 203; post-reintegration challenges 225–226; programs 211; recidivism rates 225; support for 208; *see also* community engagement program, rehabilitation programs
relative deprivation 21
religiosity, as motivation for terrorism 122
religious rehabilitation 185, 194, 198, 239

Resolute Support Mission (RSM): Afghan militias and 63–65; commencement of 59; dependent on Pakistan 67; hub and spoke arrangement 59; kinetic operations and 65–66; militarisation of 65–66, 68; NATO strategy vs. 62; negotiated political settlement 66–68; structural flaws of 61; train, advise and assist mission 58; transitioning from ISAF to 61–62
Restoration Council of Shan State (RCSS) 138, 141
Roddwell, Warren 37
Rohingya Muslims 5
Rome Memorandum of Good Practices 225
Royal Thai Army 166, 170–171, *171*, 172, 173
Rubio, Marco 123
Russia: Central Asians living in 97; concerns on Afghanistan 53; Saint Petersburg metro bombing 87, 90, 95, 97; Taliban support 67

Saeed, Hafez Mohammad 77
Saint Petersburg metro bombing 87, 90, 95, 97
Saipov, Sayfullo 90, 98
Saloh, Abu 95
Salwa Judum (People's Resistance Movement) 106–107
SAMADHAN doctrine 110
Saudi Arabia 83
Sauerland cell 91–92
Sawadjaan faction of ASG 156
Scheduled Tribes and Other Traditional Forest Dwellers (Recognition of Forest Rights) Act 2006 107, 109–110
Second Xinjiang Work Forum (2XWF) 120, 124–125
sectarianism 82–83
Security Offence Act (Special Measures) 2012 (SOSMA) 195
self-radicalised individuals 200–201
separatist rebellions 5
Sha'afi Muslims 162
Shanmugam, K. 201
Shan State Army-Restoration Council of Shan State (SSA-RCSS) 137
Sharif, Nawaz 77
Sharif, Raheel 83
Sharion, Radulan 36
Shinawatra, Thaksin 173

Shinawatra, Yingluck 173
Sierra Leone 22
Singapore: community engagement program 200–202; Community Engagement Program (CEP) 198; counter-terrorism drills 183; Internal Security Act 183; Internal Security Department 198–199; IS recruitment in 180; preventive detention laws 178, 183, 239; rehabilitation program 198–200; religious rehabilitation 185; Religious Rehabilitation Group 185, 198–201
Singh, Manmohan 5, 106
Singh, Rajnath 110
Sipah-i-Sahaba Pakistan (SeS - Guardians of the Prophet's Companions) 81
Sison, Jose Maria 151
Siswanto, Sri Puji Mulyo 208
Skocpol, Theda 15–16
Skynet surveillance system 125
Smith, Chris 123
Sobels 22
social and family rehabilitation program 197, 200
social media: Abu Sayyaf Group (ASG) 36–37; case studies 35–41; censorship 39–40; characteristics of 31; counter terrorism and 35; cultivating social solidarity 39; data mining 34; definition of 41n1; dynamics of 41; encrypted networking tools 98; influence on terrorist organisations 32–34; IS use of 183; Jamaat-e-Islami ('Islamic Assembly - JEI) 37–38; limiting use of 35; narrowcasting 34, 37; peer-to-peer content transmission 32; preventing violent extremism programs 35; as recruitment tool 200; self-radicalization by 200; social aspect of terrorism on 34–35; spreading terror and engineering panic 33–34; strategic branding and 36; Uyghur community 38–41; vulnerabilities and risks 41; *see also* digital media technologies
social media platforms: secure communications and 33; terrorists use of 31–32; virtual privacy networks 40
social revolutions 15–16
Soufan Group 3, 4
South Asia 232–237 *see also* Afghanistan, Pakistan

Southern Philippines Council for Peace and Development (SPCPD) 202–203
Special Inspector General for Afghanistan Reconstruction (SIGAR) 60
Special Rehabilitation program 194–195
Special Zone of Peace and Development (ZOPAD) 202–203
Sri Lanka: Bureau for the Commissioner General for Rehabilitation (BCGR) 219; Civil Service Division 224; community engagement 223–224; defeating LTTE 214–215; Harmony Center 224; rehabilitation program 11–12; youth engagement programs 224
Sri Lanka rehabilitation program: 5R Model 219; 6+1 Model *220*, 221–222; aftercare phase 223; approach to 215–216; assessment and categorization 219–221; civil engagement 216; community awareness programs 223–224; dedicated bureau for 219; evolution of 215; reintegration ceremonies 223; reintegration process 222–223; winning hearts and minds approach 215–216
Sri Lanka Unites 224
Stockholm truck attack 89–90
Stone, Douglas 225
strategic branding 36
*Strategy and Tactics of the Indian Revolution* (STIR) 104, 110–111
Subramaniam, Arjun 236
suicide attacks 86, 88–89
Suu Kyi, Aung San 5
Syaikhah Izzah Zahrah al Ansari 200
Syria 92–93

Ta'ang National Liberation Army (TNLA) 140
Tafaqquh Fiddin program 194–195
Tajik fighters 94
Tajik Jamaat 93
Taliban: emergence of 4; Iranian support for 67; Kunduz city take-over 59; mediating in tribal disputes 51; negotiating with 55; Russia's support for 67; tribal alliances 52
Tan, Manuel 202
Tehrik-e-Taliban Pakistan (TTP) 3, 52–53, 78–79, 84, 235

Telegram messenger platform 97
terrorism: definition of 121; digital media technologies and 87, 98; individuals groomed into 217; insurgency vs. 231; as international threat 8; kinetic response to 227; religiosity as motivation for 122; sectarianism and 82–83; social aspect of 34–35; state responses to 231; transnational terrorist networks 236; *see also* Central Asian terrorism
terrorist act, definition of 108
terrorist attacks: Bishkek bombing 88–89, 95; Chinese Embassy bombing in Bishkek 88–89; Davao night market bombing 157–158; involving Uyghurs 126–127; IS-inspired 3; Istanbul airport 88; by nationalised citizens 86–87; New York truck attack 90, 97–98; Quetta attacks 235; Reina nightclub 89, 98; Saint Petersburg metro bombing 87, 90, 95, 97; Stockholm truck attack 89–90; by truck 3
terrorist groups: developing counter-radicalization programs 208–209; online migration of 31–32; use of social media 33–35
Thai Cross Cultural Foundation 171
Thailand: alleged torture of suspects 171–172; Anglo-Siamese Treaty of 1909 169; counter-insurgency strategy 239; cross-border trade 135; Emergency Decree to detain suspects 172; ethnic Malay refusing assimilation 161; government's definition of peace 169; insurgencies 239; language reforms 172–173; Malay Muslim separatism 5; military expenditures *170, 171*; National Council for Peace and Order (NCPO) 168; National Human Rights Commission (NHRC) 171; peace process 173–174; response to Malay insurgency 168–173; Royal Thai Army 166, 170–171, *171*, 172; Sha'afi Muslims 162; Thung Yang Dang model 167; Wahhabi community 162–163; *see also* Malay insurgency
Thein Sein 143, 238
Tiananmen Square attack 126
Tillerson, Rex 46
Tilly, Charles 18
TNI Joint Special Operations Command 184

train, advise and assist (TAA) mission 58
transnational terrorist networks 236
Tripoli Peace Agreement 152
truck attacks *see* terrorist attacks
Trump administration: Afghanistan approach 60–61; ending Pakistan security aid 79; new Afghan strategy 46
Tsauri, Sofyan 207
Turkish Islamic Party (TIP) 39
Turkistan Islamic Party (TIP) 88–89, 126

Umariyon, Abu 94
Union Solidarity and Development Party (USDP) 136, 138–139, 140, 143, 144
United Nationalities Federal Council (UNFC) 138
United States: Afghanistan counterterrorism mission 92; Afghanistan state building as priority for 50; air strikes 65–66; Mother of All Bombs (MOAB), use of 66; New York truck attack 90, 97–98; Obama administration's Afghan strategy 61–62; Operation Enduring Freedom 45; Operation Freedom's Sentinel 58; Pakistan, policy toward 67; Trump administration's Afghan strategy 46, 54, 66–68
United Wa State Army (UWSA) 137, 141–142
Unity Mission Trust 224
Unlawful Activities (Prevention) Act 1967 108
US Pacific Command (PACOM) 155
Uyghur community 38–41, 119–120, 123–124, 127–129 *see also* Xingjiang, China

Vietnam, foreign intervention in 20
virtual networks 32
virtual privacy networks (VPNs) 40
vocational rehabilitation 197

Wahhabi community 162–163
Wahhabism 83, 163
Wang Lequan 119
war model of counter terrorism 231–232, 234
war on terror 45
Weiner, Myron 17
WhatsApp platform 97

Xi Jinping 120, 124–125, 127
Xingjiang, China: banning baby names 123; birth control compensation 124; coercive strategy 121–123; convenience police stations 126; education rules 122; ethnic intermingling policy 120; ethnic mingling 124; intermarriage payments 123–124; job creation and work placement 124; leapfrog development strategy 120; marginalising Uyghur cultural identities 128; political education centers 123; population of 119; preventing terrorist activities 119; religious extremism 122–123; reward-based strategy 123–125; surveillance/monitoring strategy 125–126; terror tip-offs rewards 123; winning hearts and minds 124; Work Forums 119–120, 124–125; *see also* China

youth engagement programs 224
Yu Zhengsheng 124

Zangl, Bernhard 22
Zhang Chunxian 119, 120